EARLY AMERICAN MUSIC

MUSIC RESEARCH
AND INFORMATION GUIDES
(VOL. 13)

GARLAND REFERENCE LIBRARY
OF THE HUMANITIES
(VOL. 1007)

MUSIC RESEARCH AND INFORMATION GUIDES

1. *Opera: A Research and Information Guide*, by Guy Marco
2. *Latin American Music: A Reference Guide*, by Malena Kuss
3. *Dance: An Annotated Bibliography*, by Fred Forbes
4. *Popular Music: A Reference Guide*, by Roman Iwaschkin
5. *Folk Music in America: A Reference Guide*, by Terry Miller
6. *The Art Song: A Research and Information Guide*, by Douglass Seaton
7. *The Blues: A Bibliographic Guide*, by Mary L. Hart, Lisa N. Howorth, and Brenda M. Eagles
8. *Chamber Music: A Research and Information Guide*, by John H. Baron
9. *Performance Practice, Medieval to Contemporary: A Bibliographic Guide*, by Roland Jackson
10. *Piano Information Guide: An Aid to Research*, by Robert Palmieri
11. *The Traditional Music of Britain and Ireland: A Research and Information Guide*, by James Porter
12. *Polish Music: A Research and Information Guide*, by William Smialek
13. *Early American Music: A Research and Information Guide*, by James R. Heintze

EARLY AMERICAN MUSIC
A Research and Information Guide

James R. Heintze

GARLAND PUBLISHING, INC. • NEW YORK & LONDON
1990

Library of Congress Cataloging-in-Publication Data

Heintze, James R.
    Early American music : a research and information guide / James R.
Heintze.
        p. cm. — (Music research and information guides ; vol. 13)
(Garland reference library of the humanities ; vol. 1007)
    Includes indexes.
    ISBN 0–8240–4119–4 (alk. paper)
    1. Music—United States—History and criticism—Bibliography.
I. Title. II. Series. III. Series: Garland reference library of
the humanities ; vol. 1007.
ML120.U5H46   1990
016.78'0973'09033—dc20   89–16904
                                                                CIP
                                                                MN

Printed on acid-free, 250-year-life paper
Manufactured in the United States of America

CONTENTS

INTRODUCTION   ix

**PART ONE
GENERAL REFERENCE WORKS**

I.   ENCYCLOPEDIAS AND DICTIONARIES

American Music in General Works   3
Specialized Works on American Music   11

II. BIBLIOGRAPHIES AND INDEXES OF
       PUBLISHED LITERATURE AND MUSIC

General Works   13
Specialized Works on American Music   28
     Music and Literature   28
     Songsters   40
Periodical Indexes
     General Indexes   41
     Music Indexes   45
Newspaper Guides and Indexes   48

III.   LIBRARY, MUSEUM, AND HISTORICAL
          SOCIETY RESOURCES

    General Guides   53
    Guides to Regional Libraries and Collections   54
    Guides to Individual Libraries and Collections   57
    Exhibition Catalogs and Literature   68

IV.   SPECIAL REFERENCE WORKS

    Broadsides   81
    City and Trade Directories   82
    Copyright Records   85
    Diaries and Letters   86
    Travel Accounts   88
    Discographies   90
    Obituaries   91
    Parish and Other Church Records   92
    Probate Records   92
    Theses and Dissertations   93
    Atlases   96

**PART TWO
HISTORICAL STUDIES**

V.   HISTORIES, CHRONOLOGIES, AND AREA
         STUDIES

    *General Histories of Music and American
        History*   99
    Histories of American Music   102
    Chronologies   121
    Area Studies   122

VI.   TOPICAL STUDIES

    Sacred Music   165
    Secular Music   171

Vocal Music 193
Psalmody and Singing Schools 207
Hymnody 241
Music of Ethnic and Religious Groups 252
    Afro-American 252
    Baptists 258
    Brethren Church 260
    Catholics 261
    Dutch 263
    Ephrata Cloister 264
    Episcopalians 268
    French 269
    Harmonists 270
    Italians 271
    Jews 271
    Lutherans 272
    Mennonites 274
    Methodists 278
    Moravians 279
    Presbyterians 299
    Quakers 300
    Schwenkfelders 301
    Shakers 301
    Spanish Mission Music 305
    Unitarian 310
    Wissahickon Mystics 310
Printing and Publishing 311
Dance 317
Theater 321
Organology 336

VII. BIOGRAPHIES 361

Indexes 361
Collective Biographies 362
Individual Biographies 366

VIII. CRITICAL AND FACSIMILE EDITIONS OF MUSIC — 419

AUTHOR-TITLE INDEX — 427

SUBJECT INDEX — 479

INTRODUCTION

This guide is intended to serve as an introduction to the materials available for research and information on early American music. Included are books, articles, dissertations, papers, published sermons and discourses, catalogs, lists, directories, and other materials that deal with America's musical history from its beginning to 1820. This cut-off date was chosen because it represents approximately the end of America's colonial cultural period. Although comprehensive, this study does not include every work that pertains to American music, nor does it cover exhaustively every subject, but rather it is intended to bring together a core collection of bibliographical and informative materials with references to other relevant works.

There are a number of excellent reference works that deserve attention and should be used in combination with the present study. Donald Krummel's *Bibliographical Handbook of American Music* (see entry 107), published in 1987, is the first comprehensive bibliographical study of American music covering all periods. The annotations are excellent and readers will find the narrative commentary especially helpful. David Horn's *Literature of American Music in Books and Folk Music Collections: A Fully Annotated Bibliography* (see entry 100), published in 1977, with an extensive 1988 supplement, covers in detail a broad range of books pertaining to music in America before 1820. Another work deserving particular attention is Thomas Warner's *Periodical Literature on American Music, 1620-1920: A Classified Bibliography with Annotations* (see entry 123), completed in 1988, and the first and only work that systematically brings together articles on all aspects of American music in both music and non-music journals. Readers should rely on Warner's work for articles published through 1980 that are not found in the present study. Added to this group of works is *Resources of American Music History: A Directory of Source Materials from Colonial Times to World War II* (see entry 175), a joint collaboration by Donald Krummel, Jean Geil, Doris J. Dyen and Deane L. Root. This is the principal tool for accessing significant, but also lesser-known collections of manuscripts and printed primary sources. Other similarly useful works are described in the entries that follow.

The present study is divided into two parts. Part 1 examines general reference works, including encyclopedias and dictionaries, bibliographies of literature and music, songsters, periodical and newspaper guides, collections, and indexes, and library, museum, and historical society resources. In addition, I have included a section on exhibition catalogs and literature that has information on music and instruments not described in other sources. Chapter 4 in this part covers special reference works, including broadsides, city and trade directories, copyright records, diaries and letters, travel accounts, discographies, obituaries, parish and other church records, probate records, theses and dissertations, and atlases. A few additional reference works are listed in various other sections in this book.

Part 2 focuses on historical studies, including general histories and area studies, topical histories, studies of ethnic and religious groups, and biographical studies. Chapter 8 in this part consists of critical and facsimile editions of music, including tunebooks, collections of instrumental and vocal works, and operatic works.

Brief introductions provide additional information about each section, as well as supplemental reference tools. Citations are arranged alphabetically under appropriate classifications. Due to their subject matter, some entries could have been listed under more than one section. It is recommended, therefore, that topics being examined be cross-checked using the Subject Index. Titles that are not annotated are either self-explanatory or were not available for examination. In addition, a number of publications that were printed during the 18th and 19th centuries have been included to reflect, to a degree, the development of American musical thought. A few cross-references are provided in the main body of this guide, with citations given in short form followed by entry number. Readers should note that master's theses are not included in this study, but are thoroughly covered to 1983 in my *American Music Studies: A Classified Bibliography of Master's Theses* (see entry 293). Doctoral dissertations are included, however, and are based on *Dissertation Abstracts International* (see entry 292) through January 1989.

A few of the topics included below need explanation. I have cited only a few items that pertain to folk music. That subject is covered extensively in Terry Miller's *Folk Music in America: A Reference Guide* (see entry 112). Likewise, readers will not find comprehensive coverage of the Afro-American tradition, but should refer to Dominique René de Lerma's monumental *Bibliography of Black Music* (see entry 89). In addition, the music of native Americans has been included only to the extent that it relates to the missionary efforts of the Moravians, and music and instruments of the Spanish missions in the West.

The value of utilizing a broad range of historical materials for a thorough study of early American music cannot be overemphasized. Researchers should be well-acquainted with church records, court records, probate records, genealogical records, town records (including city directories), trade directories, local histories, copyright records, vital records, newspapers, diaries, letters, travel accounts, and other categories of documents that are likely to reveal information concerning musicians, instruments, musical events, and so forth. For that reason, I have included below a few examples of sources that represent some of these categories (see chapter 4, for example). However, there are general reference tools recently published that describe these types of documents in greater detail. An excellent introductory work that is well-organized is Francis Prucha's *Handbook for Research in American History* (Lincoln: University of Nebraska Press, 1987). Prucha (cited in several sections below) provides excellent bibliographical coverage, with extensive narrative commentary, of principal reference works and categories of materials.

An excellent series of guides that describe state historical documents for the colonial period and thereafter and offer a wealth of information is titled "Research Outlines" and is published by the Family History Library (Salt Lake City, Utah, 1988). Each outline focuses on an individual state and provides detailed information on historical documents, such as church records, probate records, vital records, newspapers, and numerous other local documents that are associated with that state. A separate general "Research Outline" titled "United States" introduces readers to the major types of records used for conducting research, regional differences in record-keeping, and search strategies.

The preparation and publication of this guide were made possible by a grant from the University Library and the Senate Research Committee of The American University. A number of persons deserve special thanks for their suggestions and interest in this book. To Gillian Anderson (Library of Congress) for examining the first draft and her helpful advice; Thomas Warner (Bucknell University), my sincerest gratitude for reading the entire manuscript and offering a number of corrections and excellent suggestions; Kate Van Winkle Keller (Sonneck Society) who graciously reviewed the section on dance and pointed out a number of significant publications; to J. Bunker Clark (University of Kansas) for providing a bibliography of early American music based on the holdings at his university library; J. Terry Gates (University of New York at Buffalo) for information pertaining to his articles; to John Fesperman and Cynthia Adams Hoover (Smithsonian Institution) for providing information on exhibition catalogs and other literature; to Laurence Libin (Metropolitan Museum of Art) for use of his typewritten bibliography on American instruments and makers. This book is dedicated especially to my sister Anna May.

Early American Music

PART ONE
GENERAL REFERENCE WORKS

I. ENCYCLOPEDIAS AND DICTIONARIES

American Music in General Works

Well-known general encyclopedias such as *Encyclopedia Americana* and
Collier's Encyclopedia and the foreign *Dizionario Enciclopedico
Italiano* do allot some space to early American music. However, the
biographies and articles included are few in number and are, in
part, based on standard histories of American music such as those
cited below. Further, such works may not reflect the true extent of
musical activity in colonial America. Whether or not one chooses to
use these sources depends on the type of information desired. For
an excellent essay on the history of music dictionaries published in
the United States, see Diane O. Ota's article, "Dictionaries," in
The New Grove Dictionary of American Music, vol. 1, 617-22 (see
entry 30). Note also Robert Stevenson's article, "The Americas in
European Music Encyclopedias," in *Inter-American Music Review* 3/2
(Spring-Summer 1981), pp. 159-207 and 5/1 (Fall 1982), pp. 109-16
that documents articles and other sources not listed below.
Included below are works covering the areas of American history and
music in general, as well as noteworthy specialized encylopedias of
religious groups.

1. *Academic American Encyclopedia.* Danbury, Conn.: Grolier Inc.,
   1987. 21 vols.

   Includes 32,000 entries, many signed, covering a broad
spectrum of subjects. This encyclopedia, "first published in 1980,
is an entirely new reference work, the only completely new general
encyclopedia in more than a decade." Includes brief articles by
Elwyn A. Wienandt titled "American Music," "Fuging Tune," and
"Hymn," and an unsigned article on William Billings. Topics include
the New England tradition, musical immigrants, and the Moravians.
Begin a search under the heading "American Music" in the index
(volume 21).

2. *The Brethren Encyclopedia.*   Philadelphia: The Brethren Encyclo-
      pedia, 1983.   3 vols.

      Focuses on Brethren life, belief, practice, and heritage.
Often overlooked by musicologists, this handy work includes several
excellent but brief articles on musical practices.   Begin a search
referring to the article "Music" where numerous references to other
relevant articles are cited with asterisks.   There is an excellent
article on the "Ephrata Community," including a selection of old
photographs.   See also "Ephrata Press" where the bibliography lists
other useful articles.   See also biographical articles such as that
on Johann Conrad Beissel, the article on "Hymnals," which includes
citations with descriptions, and the article "Moravian Church."   An
excellent "Chronology of Brethren History" in volume 3 includes
musical and social events.

3. *Complete Encyclopedia of Music.*   Comp. by John W. Moore.
      Boston: Oliver Ditson, 1854.   1,004p.; 1880 ed. has appendix
      to 1876 with the copyright date 1875; 45p.   Reprint of 1880
      ed., New York: AMS Press, 1973.

      Mostly European-oriented but does include some American
entries, such as that on William Billings.   The article on psalmody
is based, in part, on Hood's *A History of Music in New England* (see
entry 495).   An article on Andrew Law can be found in the appendix.

4. *Dictionary of American History.*   Revised edition.   New York:
      Charles Scribner's Sons, 1976.   8 vols.

      Includes 7,200 entries covering all aspects of American
history.   Gilbert Chase has contributed the article on music in
America; discussed briefly are the New England tradition and music
in the middle colonies.   However, ethnic groups such as the
Moravians are not mentioned.   An article by Cecelia Hodges Drewry on
Afro-American music is brief.   No biographies.   Index is volume 8.

5. *Dictionary of Hymnology: Origin and History of Christian Hymns
      and Hymnwriters of All Ages and Nations.*   Ed. by John Julian.
      London: J. Murray, 1907.   Reprint, Grand Rapids, Mich.: Kregel
      Publications, 1985.   2 vols.

      Despite its early date of publication. this work remains a
standard reference tool, comprising an extensive index of first

lines of hymns. Of note is a section on "American Hymnody" that includes a list of hymnists by denominations, and a chronological list under "Psalters, English" that includes those English psalters in use during the 17th and 18th centuries in the American colonies.

6. *A Dictionary of Protestant Church Music.* Ed. by James Robert Davidson. Metuchen, N.J.: Scarecrow Press, 1975. 349p.

A general dictionary that includes some early American terms, including, for example, "Anthem," "Camp Meeting," "Fuging Tune," "Hymn Meter," and "Hymnody."

7. *Dizionario Enciclopedico Universale Della Musica e dei Musicisti.* Ed. by Alberto Basso. Torino: UTET, 1984. 2 vols.

Victor Yellin has contributed the article "Stati Uniti" (volume 2). Equal emphasis is placed on folk and art music. Mentions such early musicians as John Antes, Johannes Herbst, Justin Morgan, Daniel Read, et al. Includes one of the better facsimiles of the frontispiece from William Billings' *New-England Psalm-Singer* (1770).

8. *Enciclopedia della Musica.* Milano: G. Ricordi, 1964. 4 vols.

Includes a fairly long article on American music for a foreign publication of this sort. See "Stati Uniti D'America e Canada," volume 4, pp. 276-80, by recognized authority Donald M. McCorkle. Divided by period; see especially "Il Periodo coloniale e quello della prima America (1620-30—1830-40 c.)" where the New England school, Moravian and Ephrata settlements, and middle colonies are discussed with equal emphasis. Names and dates are cited for over 30 musicians and musical organizations.

9. *Encyclopedia of American History.* 6th ed. by Richard B. Morris. New York: Harper and Row, 1982. xiv, 1,285p.

A comprehensive work divided into three primary parts: "Basic Chronology," "Topical Chronology," and "Five Hundred Notable Americans." Part 2 includes a section titled "Music" subdivided into a "Pioneer Period, 1640-1800" and "Early National and Antebellum Years, 1800-60."   Valuable for a comparison of musical and general historical events.   Index.   No bibliography.

10.   *The Encyclopedia of American Music.*   Comp. by Edward Jablonski. New York: Doubleday, 1981.   xvi, 629p.

Chronologically arranged.   Chapters 1-3 are titled "In the Beginning (ca. 1620-1750)"; "A Time of Revolution (1750-1800)"; and "From the Second Awakening to the Second New England School (1800-1865)."   Each includes an essay followed by an annotated alphabetical list of representative composers; includes entries on composers not found in *The New Grove Dictionary of American Music* (see entry 30).   Discography and general index.

11.   *Encyclopedia of Black America.*   Ed. by W. Augustus Low.   New York: McGraw-Hill, 1981.   xx, 921p.

Includes 1,400 biographies and some 325 unsigned articles contributed by specialists (see list of contributors).   Includes names and topics.   An excellent survey of the history and development of black music in America.   Index.

12.   *Encyclopédie de la Musique et Dictionnaire du Conservatoire.* Paris: Librairie Delagrave, 1922.   3,403p.

A general work arranged principally by countries and geographic areas.   Includes an extensive article on American music titled "États-Unis D'Amérique" (pp. 3,245-3,336) by Esther Singleton that includes information on the African influence on music in America, patriotic songs of the Revolutionary War, music in the colonies, including the New England tradition, concerts, ballad opera, and instruments.   Surprisingly, the article includes the names of a number of lesser-known American musicians.

13.   *Encyclopédie des Musiques Sacrées.*   Published under the direction of Jacques Porte.   Paris: Éditions Labergerie, 1968-70. 4 vols.

International in scope, with signed essays.   In volume 3 (pp. 328-34) under the heading "États-Unis" is an article "L'Église protestante aux XVIIIe et XIXe siècles" by Robert Stevenson.   He discusses early New England psalters and that tradition, represen-

tative 18th-century American musicians, with sections on Andrew Law
and Martin Madan. Other topics are also briefly mentioned. Volume
4 consists of recordings to accompany the essays; American music
examples are not included, however.

14. *Das grosse Lexikon der Musik.* Ed. by Marc Honegger and Günther
      Massenkeil. Freiburg, Germany: Verlag Herder, 1978-82. 8
      vols.

        A revised translated edition of *Dictionnaire de la Musique*
(Paris: Bordas, 1970-76). See "Vereinigte Staaten von Amerika,"
volume 8, by Nicholas Slonimsky. Two columns are devoted to early
American music; mentions principal composers and gentlemen amateurs
such as Benjamin Franklin and Thomas Jefferson. Extensive
bibliography (in English) for a work of this sort.

15. *The Harper Dictionary of Music.* Comp. by Christine Ammer. 2nd
      ed. New York: Harper and Row, 1987. vi, 493p.

        A general dictionary of terms, styles, and persons. Includes
very brief entries on a few early American musical terms. Includes
a short entry on William Billings.

16. *Harper's Encyclopaedia of United States History.* New York:
      Harper and Brothers, 1912. 10 vols.

        In volume 6 under "Music and Musicians of the United States,"
a brief chronology (not reliable), including 12 dates to 1820.

17. *The International Cyclopedia of Music and Musicians.* 11th ed.
      by Bruce Bohle. New York: Dodd, Mead and Company, 1985.
      2,609p.

        First published in 1939, this 11th ed. is essentially a
reprinting of the 10th ed. (2,511p.), with an addendum (pp. 2,513-
2,609) which includes revisions of some articles and various new
entries. Currently largest and most comprehensive English work in
one volume; topical articles written by various leading international scholars. Relevant articles are arranged alphabetically and
include: "African Music and the New World," by Darius L. Thieme;
"American Music," by Robert Sabin; "Folk Music in America," by Alan
Jabbour. Includes a few cross-references. Biographies include John

Antes, William Billings, Anthony P. Heinrich, Benjamin Franklin, James Hewitt, Oliver Holden, Samuel Holyoke, Francis Hopkinson, and others.   No bibliographies.

18. *Larousse Encyclopedia of Music.*   Ed. by Geoffrey Hindley.   New York: World Publishing Company, 1971.   576p.

A brief survey (pp. 433-34); principal composers mentioned include William Billings, Francis Hopkinson, and Johann Friedrich Peter.

19. *The Mennonite Encyclopedia.*   Hillsboro, Kan.: Mennonite Brethren Publishing House, 1955-59.   4 vols.

Considered "the most accessible and authoritative reference work available on a host of Anabaptist and Mennonite topics." See especially "Music, Church" in volume 3, pp. 791-94 which includes information on the Mennonite Church in Europe and the Old Order Amish in North America. For additional information on this work, see Rachel Waltner, "From Anabaptism to Mennonitism: The Mennonite Encyclopedia as a Historical Document," in *Mennonite Life* 37/4 (December 1982), pp. 13-19.

20. *La Musica.*   Ed. by Guido M. Gatti.   Torino: Unione Tipografico-Editrice Torinese, 1966-71.   6 vols.

International in scope. Includes biographies and articles on topical subjects. Two principal parts: an encyclopedia (volumes 1-4) and a dictionary (volumes 5-6); the latter includes numerous short articles on individuals and terms not in part 1. See especially "America: Stati Uniti" in volume 1, pp. 46-63, and written by Diego Carpitella, Gilbert Chase, and Victor Yellin. Discussed are Afro-American music, with excerpts of Negro spirituals, the New England tradition from its beginning to 1790, including facsimiles from Billings' *New-England Psalm-Singer* (Boston, 1770) and the *Bay Psalm Book* (1640), and the period 1790-1865 with emphasis on secular music of the English middle colonies.

21. *Die Musik in Geschichte und Gegenwart; allgemeine Enzyklopädie der Musik.*   Ed. by Friedrich Blume.   Kassel: Bärenreiter, 1949-79.   14 vols. with a two-volume supplement through 1983.

Signed articles written by specialists. The standard indispensable multivolume encyclopedia for scholars of European musicology, but not so for American music; includes brief coverage by Karl H. Wörner in volume 1, columns 417-19. See also article titled "Vereinigte Staaten," volume 13, where the section on music before 1820 (columns 1,467-71) by Irving Lowens and translated by Ursula Klein focuses on the New England tradition, Moravian music, and music of the English middle colonies. Also includes a biography by Hans Nathan of William Billings in volume 1 (columns 798-99) of the Supplement. Bibliography (to 1947 only). Index to be published.

22. *The New Grove Dictionary of Music and Musicians.* Ed. by Stanley Sadie. London: Macmillan; dist. in U.S. by Grove's Dictionaries of Music, New York City, 1980. 20 vols.

Practically a rewriting of the previous *A Dictionary of Music and Musicians.* Includes some 22,500 articles by 2,300 contributors. In 1980, was considered a significant reference work for American music, even though the work is far from being comprehensive in that area; musicians of the pre-1820 period are not given separate entries. Of note, there is no general index and cross-references provided do not represent all of the instances in which various topics are treated in two or more entries. A good article to start with is "United States of America: Art Music, 1620-1820." Others include "Folk Music"; "Hymn: The American Hymn"; "Libraries: North America—USA"; "Psalmody"; and "Shape-Note Hymnody." Considered the most comprehensive source in this group. A useful companion aid for identifying relevant reviews is James R. Heintze's *The New Grove: A Bibliography of Reviews and Other Writings* (Washington, D.C.: The American University, 1985). By 1986, all of the articles on American music in this work had been collected, many of them revised, with new entries added, and published as a separate work titled *The New Grove Dictionary of American Music* (see entry 30). Of note is volume 6, the American *Supplement* (vii, 438p.), to *Grove's Dictionary of Music and Musicians* (1935) which contains information on early American music presented in a format different than later editions of the *Dictionary.* Included for example, are lists of early concerts and operas performed 1785-93 and organizations 1744-1800, and a "Chronological Register" of American musicians, including information not necessarily found in other sources.

23. *The New Grove Dictionary of Musical Instruments.*   Ed. by
      Stanley Sadie.   New York: Macmillan, 1984.   3 vols.

     The principal reference work of its kind by contributing
authors, with entries in alphabetical order.   For American musical
instruments, therefore, readers will have to browse to identify
relevant headings.   See, for example, "Musical Glasses" and
"Armonica."   In addition, under "Collections—United States of
America," readers will find most major musical instrument collections in museums and other institutions cited.

24. *The New Harvard Dictionary of Music.*   Ed. by Don Michael
      Randel.   Cambridge: Belknap Press of Harvard University
      Press, 1986.   xxi, 942p.

     Previous edition: *Harvard Dictionary of Music* (1969; ed. by
Willi Apel).   This is the standard English dictionary of musical
definitions and brief topical articles; no biographical entries.
Readers should begin with the article on "United States"; cross-
references to other topics, such as "Psalmody," "Hymns," "Anthems,"
and "Fuging Tunes" are included.   Very brief bibliographies.

25. *The New Oxford Companion to Music.*   Ed. by Denis Arnold.
      Oxford: Oxford University Press, 1983.   2 vols.

     First published in 1938 under the title *The Oxford Companion
to Music*, with subsequent editions (ed. by Percy Scholes), this is
virtually a new work and one of the best dictionaries "oriented
toward the general reader."   Articles are signed and include cross-
references.   International in scope.   Principal relevant article is
titled "United States of America" written by recognized scholar
Richard Crawford.   He provides a concise and very interesting thesis
regarding American colonial versus European development of music
under the sub-headings "Introduction" and "Musical Life in Early
America," pp. 1878-80.   Brief bibliography.

26. *Sohlmans Musiklexikon.*   Stockholm: Sohlmans Förlag, 1975-79.   5
      vols.

     First edition 1948-52.   The principal Scandinavian music
encyclopedia.   Signed articles.   The article "USA," reviewed for
publication by J. Vinton in volume 5, has several columns devoted to
American music.   Discussed are the New England school, 1600-1750,

the Revolutionary War period, and music of the middle colonies.
Includes facsimiles of the frontispiece of William Billings' *New-England Psalm-Singer* (1770) and the 1640 edition of the *Bay Psalm Book*.

27. *University Musical Encyclopedia.*   Ed. by Louis C. Elson.   New
       York: University Society, 1910.   12 vols.

        A topical encyclopedia with over 40 contributors, with each
volume devoted to a particular aspect of music, including, for
example, history of music, great composers, vocal music, opera, and
theory.   Volume 2 (378p.) consists of a history of music in America,
with chapters on the New England tradition and psalmody, opera,
hymnody, and American songs.   Includes brief biographies of early
American musicians, including William Billings, John Cole, Lewis
Edson, Jeremiah Ingalls, Stephen Jenks, Jacob Kimball, Jr., Daniel
Read, and others.   Yet other early American composers are also
included in volumes 9-10, "University Dictionary of Music and
Musicians."   A refreshing account for its time in that the author is
concerned with the study of early American music: "The value of our
American hymn-tune composers has never been justly estimated."

Specialized Works on American Music

28. *The American History and Encyclopedia of Music.*   Ed. by W.L.
       Hubbard.   New York: Irving Squire, 1908.   10 vols.

        Not an encyclopedia in the usual sense, each volume is
devoted to a particular musical subject, such as opera, theory,
dictionary of terms, etc. Volumes 2 and 3 are "Musical Biographies"
and contain a few entries on early American composers such as
William Billings and Daniel Read. Volume 4 (reprint, New York; AMS
Press, 1976 (356p.)) deals with American music; the chapters on
"Psalmody and Church Music," "Musical Education," and "Instrumental
Music," for example, are relevant topics, but must be read with
caution due to a lack of sources.   Bibliography.

29. *A Handbook of American Music and Musicians, Containing*
       Biographies of American Musicians and Histories of the
       Principal Musical Institutions, Firms and Societies.   Ed. by
       F.O. Jones.   Canaseraga, New York: F.O. Jones, 1886.   182p.

Reprint, New York: Da Capo Press, 1971.   2nd ed.   Buffalo: C.W. Moulton, 1887.

One of the few sources of its type published during the latter part of the 19th century.   Jones presents his material in brief encyclopedic form; entries include composers and performers and topics such as tunebook collections, opera, organ, and music publishers.   Readers will find an entry on Thomas Walter, but not on John Tufts.   Under the entry on William Billings, Jones states that "previous to his [Billings] time the Colonies had no music, except a few old tunes imported from England."   Although the information in this work should not be considered necessarily reliable, it does identify a number of musicians, including Gottlieb Graupner, Thomas Hastings, Oliver Holden, Samuel Holyoke, Jeremiah Ingalls, Stephen Jenks, Jacob Kimball, Andrew Law, Elias Mann, and others.

30.   *The New Grove Dictionary of American Music*.   Ed. by H. Wiley Hitchcock and Stanley Sadie.   New York: Macmillan Press, 1986.   4 vols.

The principal encyclopedia (topics and individuals) in English.   Often compared to *The New Grove Dictionary of Music and Musicians* (see entry 22).   The present work has three times as many articles and represents a substantial revision.   Signed articles by recognized scholars cover the history of American music from its beginnings to 1985.   Includes popular, classical, country music, and jazz.   "It is a critically organized repository of historically significant information, not a directory; that is a role served by other kinds of reference work" (H. Wiley Hitchcock and Stanley Sadie, "Preface," vol. 1, p. ix).   Bibliographies at the end of articles are current.   "List of Contributors" in volume 4.   No general index necessitates some searching through topical articles for various individuals and other subjects not treated separately. Some of the noteworthy articles are cited below in various sections.

II. BIBLIOGRAPHIES AND INDEXES OF PUBLISHED LITERATURE AND MUSIC

General Works

Included below are general bibliographies of the arts, folklore, local and state histories, American history, and religion.

31. *American Culture Series.* [1493-1875.] Ann Arbor, Mich.: University Microfilms, 1956-76. 643 microfilm reels; 35 mm. Printed guide.

   Has 5,600 titles, including 45 music titles. This collection of books and pamphlets includes sermons, religious treatises, descriptions and histories of the early colonies. For example, reel 50 is Increase Mather's *An Arrow Against Profane and Promiscuous Dancing* (Boston: Samuel Green, 1694). Refer to the printed guide, *American Culture Series, 1493-1875*, which includes author, title, and subject indexes.

32. *Arts in America: A Bibliography.* Ed. by Bernard Karpel. Washington, D.C.: Smithsonian Institution Press, 1979. 4 vols.

   A compilation of 21 annotated bibliographies each representing a separate discipline by a separate compiler. Focuses primarily on the visual arts, but volume 3 contains a bibliography on music by Bertrun Delli. Although there are many sources relevant to music before 1820 in America, one must search under broad headings such as "Regional Studies" and "Church and Religious Music." Delli states, "All the material cited here concerns writing about American music and musical practice in America from the early days to now."

33.   *A Basic Music Library: Essential Scores and Books.*   2nd ed.
      Ed. by Robert Michael Fling.   Chicago: American Library
      Association, 1983.   xii, 357p.

      Includes 2,262 entries.   "It is designed to serve as a buying
guide or selection tool for those who have responsibility for
collecting music materials in small and medium-sized libraries,
whether public or academic."   Divided principally into scores and
music literature.   In the latter section, see especially "Music of
the United States," which includes "General Works" (entries 2158-
77), and works focusing specifically on the 18th and 19th centuries
(entries 2178-84 and 2185-91).   Not annotated.   Index.

34.   Bassett, T.D. Seymour.   *Vermont: A Bibliography of Its History.*
      Bibliographies of New England History, 4.   Boston: G.K. Hall,
      1981.   xxxiv, 391p.

      An extensive bibliography on all aspects of Vermont history.
Includes entries on music and musicians such as the composer Justin
Morgan.   Begin a search under the heading "Music and Musicians" in
the index.

35.   Beers, Henry Putney.   *Bibliographies in American History, 1942-*
      1978: Guide to Materials for Research.   Woodbridge, Conn.:
      Research Publications, 1982.   2 vols.

      ". . . a comprehensive guide to bibliographic listings,
including articles, compilations in progress and manuscript
bibliographies."   Covers a broad spectrum of arts, humanities, and
sciences.   In addition to a section on music in volume 1, pp. 397-
400, the index at the back of volume 2 cites additional entries
under the heading "Music."

36.   *Books in Print: An Author—Title—Series Index to the*
      "Publishers' Trade List Annual."   New York: R.R. Bowker,
      1948- ; annual with mid-year supplement.   From April 1982,
      available on microfiche.

      Subtitle omitted after 1972.   The principal reference work
for books currently in print.   "The available books new and old,
indexed by author and by title with full ordering information."
Includes author, title, publisher, and subject indexes.   Begin a
search under the heading "Music, American" in the subject index.   A

separately published *Forthcoming Books* (bi-monthly) and *Paperbound Books in Print* (semi-annual) are also available.

37.   Brockman, William S.   *Music: A Guide to the Reference Literature.*   Littleton, Col.: Libraries Unlimited, 1987.   xv, 254p.

Has 841 entries, including general reference sources, bibliographies, discographies, and other aids.   Although there are only a few entries pertaining to early American music, there are annotations for periodicals, such as *American Music*, and professional societies, such as the Sonneck Society, that emphasize American music.   Author-title and subject indexes.

38.   Brunkow, Robert deV., ed.   *Religion and Society in North America: An Annotated Bibliography.*   Clio Bibliography Series, 12.   Santa Barbara, Calif.: ABC-Clio Press, 1983.   xi, 515p.

Includes 4,364 entries taken from volumes 11-18 of *America: History and Life* (see entry 129).   Billed as a guide to periodical literature on the United States and Canada since the seventeenth century, this work includes numerous articles on pre-1820 American music.   See the section under "Music," and also other relevant headings under "Religious Groups."

39.   Burr, Nelson R.   "A Critical Bibliography of Religion in America: Religion in the Arts and Literature; Music," in *Religion in American Life.*   Princeton, N.J.: Princeton University Press, 1961, vol. 4, pp. 808-46.

An excellent bibliographic essay describing general reference works and histories, Anglo-American colonial music, denominational sources, psalmody, hymnody, and revival and gospel songs and spirituals.   Included are books, dissertations, and articles of both general and local interest.   Readers can expect to find information on Spanish and French mission music, the New England tradition, Jewish religious music, and Germans in Pennsylvania, including the Moravians and the Ephrata Cloister.

40.   *Cumulative Book Index: A World List of Books in the English
        Language*, 1898- . New York: H.W. Wilson, 1898- . Monthly
        except August with annual and multiyear cumulations.

An annual bibliography which lists books published in
English.   Lists entries in one index for author, title, and subject
entries.   Includes full imprint data.   Look under "Music—United
States—History and Criticism."

41.   Duckles, Vincent H. and Michael A. Keller.   *Music Reference and
        Research Materials: An Annotated Bibliography*.   4th ed.   New
        York: Schirmer, 1988.   XV, 714p.

This is one of the best general bibliographies of music
literature covering a broad range of materials and subjects.
However, coverage of American music is not extensive.   Begin a
search under the heading "American Music" in the index.   Readers
should be aware that a number of entries that pertain to American
music are cited under other subject headings.

42.   Duffy, John.   *Early Vermont Broadsides*.   Hanover, N.H.:
        University Press of New England for the University of
        Vermont, 1975.   xx, 51p.

Each broadside includes a facsimile and description.
Included in the section on "Verses, Psalms & Hymns" is "A Christmas
Hymn Composed for the Hon. Royall Tyler, Chief Justice of the State
of Vermont, and Sung at Clarement, N.H. 1793," published ca. 1810.

43.   *Early American Imprints, 1639-1800*.   New York: Readex
        Microprints Corp., 1984.   Microfiche; 11 x 15 cm.

Based on Charles Evans' *American Bibliography* (see entry 45).
Has 40,000 titles, including books, pamphlets, and broadsides
printed in the United States from 1639 through 1800.   Not only are
numerous errors in Evans corrected, but also the publishers have
added several thousand titles.   Arranged chronologically by Evans
number.   For an index to this collection, refer to the *National
Index of American Imprints through 1800: The Short-Title Evans* (see
entry 74).   Another index, *American Bibliography: A Chronological
Dictionary* (see entry 45), provides somewhat better bibliographic
descriptions, however.   Continued by *Early American Imprints, Second
Series* (see entry 44).

44.   *Early American Imprints, Second Series: Shaw-Shoemaker
        Bibliography, 1801-1819.*   New York: Readex Microprint Co.,
        1964-1982.   50,000 microopaques; 16 x 23 cm.

        Based on Shaw and Shoemaker's *American Bibliography* (see
entry 73), this is a continuation of *Early American Imprints* (see
entry 43).   For an index to this collection, refer to *American
Bibliography* mentioned above.

45.   Evans, Charles.   *American Bibliography: A Chronological
        Dictionary of All Books, Pamphlets, and Periodical
        Publications Printed in the United States of America from
        the Genesis of Printing in 1639 Down to and Including the
        Year 1820.*   Chicago: printed for the author, 1903-59.   14
        vols.   Reprint, New York: Peter Smith, 1941-67.

        The first important compilation of early American
publications, including books, pamphlets, and serials.   Includes
full imprint data, and items are arranged chronologically by dates
of publication.   Indexes include author, subject, and printers and
publishers.   A *Supplement* (Charlottesville: University Press of
Virginia, 1970) compiled by Roger P. Bristol adds some 11,200
entries to the Evans list.

46.   Gephart, Ronald M.   *Revolutionary America, 1763-1789: A
        Bibliography.*   Washington, D.C.: Library of Congress, 1984.
        2 vols.   xi, 1,671p.

        Includes 14,810 entries.   A comprehensive, fully annotated
"guide to the more important printed primary and secondary works in
the Library's collection," including books, dissertations, and
articles.   Readers should ignore the publication date, for this work
is current only as of December 31, 1972, and therefore does not
include the many books that were published during the Bicentennial.
Nonetheless, this is a major reference work for the colonial period.
Of note is that works are not only listed under a vast array of
topics, but also principal bibliographies for 20 states are arranged
conveniently by state.   In the index are relevant headings under
"Music," "Moravians," and other topics.

47.   Gregory, Julia.   *Catalogue of Early Books on Music (before
        1800).*   Prepared under the direction of O.G. Sonneck.
        Washington, D.C.: Library of Congress, 1913.   312p.

Includes 1,500 entries for publications in western Europe and America between 1518 and 1799. A *Supplement* (Washington, D.C., 1944) compiled by Hazel Bartlett adds some 500 books acquired by the Library from 1913 to 1942. Gregory and Bartlett list some 15 titles by William Billings, John Cotton, Thomas Symmes, John Todd, Thomas Walter, and others.

48. *Guide to Reference Books*. 10th ed. Ed. by Eugene P. Sheehy. Chicago: American Library Association, 1986. xiv, 1,560p.

More than 16,000 items, including 353 music titles; 1984 cutoff date. The principal general reference tool for the arts, humanities, and sciences. Classified arrangement. Most of the headings used are general so a certain amount of scanning is necessary to identify items relevant to early American music. See the section "Theater and Performing Arts." The annotations are excellent. Some entries have references to reviews. No subject index although there is a general index of authors, editors, and compilers.

49. *Guide to Reference Materials*. 4th ed. Ed. by A.J. Walford. London: The Library Association, 1980-87. 3 vols.

This is the British counterpart of Sheehy's *Guide* (see entry 48). In volume 3, "Generalities, Languages, the Arts and Literature," a substantial section on music is found. The entries are arranged by types of reference materials. Although the individual entries relevant to early American music are neither as numerous nor as current as Sheehy, there are a few items cited here that are not in Sheehy. Moreover, the annotations include additional useful information. Includes some references to reviews. Cumulated subject and author-title indexes.

50. *A Guide to the Study of the United States of America; Representative Books Reflecting the Development of American Life and Thought*. Prepared under the direction of Roy P. Basler by Donald H. Mugridge and Blanche P. McCrum, 1960. Washington, D.C.: Library of Congress, 1960. Reprint, St. Clair Shores, Mich.: Pub. Center, 1977. xv, 1,193p.

Includes 6,487 items. Although dated, is still extremely useful due to its excellent and lengthy annotations, some of which compare similar topical studies. Books on music are arranged under

general headings, including "Localities," "Religious Music," and
"Choirs." Includes an introduction to the bibliography of earlier
American music. The index reveals some relevant items not found in
the general section on music. A *Supplement* for 1956-65 was
published in 1976.

51. *Harvard Guide to American History.* Revised edition by Frank
    Freidel. Cambridge, Mass.: Belknap Press of Harvard
    University Press, 1974. 2 vols.

    Cites books and articles published to 1970. This principal
aid for students of American history lists reference works and
topical histories, including a section on music. Items are not
annotated and are listed under broad headings such as "Religious
Music," "Composers," etc. There is also much relevant useful
background material to be found under general historical headings
such as "Rise of Anglo-America," "Histories of Special Subjects,
1607-1789," etc. Index of names.

52. Haskell, John D., Jr. *Maine: A Bibliography of Its History.*
    Bibliographies of New England History, 2. Boston: G.K. Hall,
    1977. xlix, 279p.

    Includes 5,355 entries. This principal guide to materials
related to the history of Maine has a number of music items worthy
of note. The index's subject headings include "Music," "Musical
Instruments," and "Musical Societies."

53. Haskell, John D., Jr. and T.D. Seymour Bassett. *New Hampshire:
    A Bibliography of Its History.* Bibliographies of New England
    History, 3. Boston: G.K. Hall, 1979. xxx, 330p.

    Includes 6,542 entries. A major guide to materials on New
Hampshire history. Includes music histories and works pertaining to
the Shakers. Begin a search under the headings "Music" and
"Shakers" in the index.

54. Haywood, Charles. *A Bibliography of North American Folklore
    and Folksong.* 2nd ed. New York: Dover Publications, 1961.
    2 vols. xxx, 1,301p.

A significant bibliography. The title should not mislead readers for this work contains numerous sources that pertain to early American music, but which are considered by some to fall under a folk tradition. For example, Haywood includes a considerable number of tunebooks and lists them under the heading "White Spirituals." Highlights of this work include its bibliography of Shakers, Pennsylvania-Germans, and songsters. General index and index of composers, arrangers, and performers.

55.   Hildeburn, Charles R. *Issues of the Press in Pennsylvania, 1685-1784*. Philadelphia, 1836. Reprint, New York: Burt Franklin, 1968. 2 vols.

An alphabetical list of publications in Pennsylvania during the years studied. Entries include full imprint data. Readers can expect to find many music publications cited here. Begin a search using titles and authors (there are no music subject headings) in the index. See, for example, *Tunes in Three Parts* (Philadelphia: Anthony Armbruster, 1763; 1764), nos. 1930 and 1079.

56.   Jenkins, John H. *Early American Imprints: A Collection of Works Printed in America between 1669 and 1800*. Austin, Tex.: The Jenkins Company, 1977. No pagination.

Includes 597 entries. A bookseller's catalog based on items in Evans (see entry 45). Each entry provides full imprint data with a description. Arranged chronologically. Item 120 is "Words for a Funeral Anthem. . .To be Performed at the Funeral of the Reverend Dr. Samuel Cooper, on Friday, Jan. 2, 1784" (Boston, 1784). This broadside is not in Evans. See also item 238, "Sweet Lillies of the Valley. . .Composed by Mr. Hook" (Philadelphia: Printed for Carr & Co., 1793). See also Jenkins' entries 191, 240, and 425. No index.

57.   Johnson, Hazel A. *A Checklist of New London, Connecticut, Imprints, 1709-1800*. Charlottesville: University Press of Virginia, 1978. xliii, 492p.

A chronological list containing full imprint data for each entry.

58.   Kepple, Robert J. *Reference Works for Theological Research: An
      Annotated Selective Bibliographical Guide.* 2nd ed. Lanham,
      Md.: University Press of America, 1981.   xiv, 283p.

      A selective work, containing several hundred annotated
entries arranged topically.   Although there is a section on "Church
Music," readers might find other more general headings just as
useful.   See, for example, "Denominational Bibliographies" and
"Theological Bibliographies."   Author-title index.

59.   Lewis, Thomas P. *The Pro/Am Guide to U.S. Books about Music:
      Annotated Subject Guide to Current and Backlist Titles.*
      White Plains, N.Y.: Pro-Am Music Resources, 1987.   viii,
      203p.

      This guide to current books is arranged by categories and is
based on "favorable reviews from a list of about 30 significant
review publications."   Although early American music is covered, one
must search through an array of general headings.   Further, the lack
of an author-title index lengthens a search for any one item.   A
1987 supplement (90p.), which includes books not found in the parent
volume, is available.   Includes 18,000-entry cumulative index.

60.   Lippy, Charles H. *Bibliography of Religion in the South.*
      Macon, Ga.: Mercer University Press, 1985.   xvi, 498p.

      A comprehensive topical bibliography that includes
denominational studies, religion and society, education, local
studies, and other subjects relating to the American South.   There
is also a section on art, architecture, and music.   The author
presents his bibliography first in a narrative format, and includes
a discussion of Black spirituals, camp meeting hymnody, and the
sacred harp tradition, followed by a list of 74 relevant works.
This work is recommended for its bibliography of Indian mission
studies.   The only drawback to Lippy's study is its lack of a
general index.

61.   Marcell, David W. *American Studies: A Guide to Information
      Sources.* American Studies Information Guide Series, 10.
      Detroit: Gale Research Company, 1982.   xx, 207p.

      Includes 1,109 entries.   Although a broad perspective of
American studies is covered, works relating to music are far too

few to properly represent the discipline. Perhaps the best feature of this book is its 133 entries dealing with the history, theory, curriculum, and programs of American studies. Annotations are brief. Author, title, and subject indexes.

62.   Marco, Guy A., Ann M. Garfield and Sharon Paugh Ferris. *Information on Music: A Handbook of Reference Sources in European Languages.* Littleton, Col.: Libraries Unlimited, 1975- .

The principal work for non-English languages sources. However, in volume 2 (1977), "The Americas (296p.)," the section on the United States includes a number of general and topical histories, biographies, and discographies written in English and devoted specifically to American music before 1820. All entries are fully annotated and are useful for their comparisons of relevant titles. Author-title and subject indexes. The series is in progress.

63.   *The Microbook Library of American Civilization.* Chicago: Library Resources, 1971-72. 12,474 microfiches; 8 x 13 cm., plus catalog (4 vols.).

". . . a collection of materials on microfiche relating to all aspects of American life and literature from their beginnings to the outbreak of World War I." Includes pamphlets, periodicals, documents, biographies, and more. The four volumes are, respectively, Author, Title, Subject, and Biblioguide Indexes. Included are references to standard and later nineteenth-century books on various topics of early American music. See volumes 3 and 4 of the printed catalog under the headings "Music-American" and "Musicians," and relevant non-music headings such as "Shakers," "Moravians," and "Hymns."

64.   *National Union Catalog: Music, Books on Music, and Sound Recordings,* 1973- . Washington, D.C.: Library of Congress, 1973- .

Supercedes the previous *National Union Catalog: Music and Phonorecords* (1953-1972). Expands its coverage to include not only LC cataloged works, but also works cataloged by other libraries. Includes scores, sheet music, and books and libretti on all areas of music. (Note, however, that most of the Library of Congress early

American sheet music collections are not cataloged.) Cumulations for 1963-67 (3 vols.), 1968-72 (5 vols.), 1973-77 (8 vols.) and 1978-80 (7 vols.) are published. For publications printed prior to 1953, consult the *Catalog of Copyright Entries* (3rd series, Part 5, *Music*, 1947- . See also Part 3, *Musical Compositions*, 1906-1946.

65.   Parks, Roger, ed. *Connecticut: A Bibliography of Its History.*
        Bibliographies of New England History, 6. Hanover:
        University Press of New England, 1986. xlii, 591p.

        Includes 9,778 entries. A comprehensive bibliography of publications related solely to Connecticut. Entries are arranged by state, county, and cities and towns. Begin a search in the index under the headings "Music and Musicians" and "Music and Religion." There are entries for Andrew Law, organs, and aspects of early psalmody.

66.   Parks, Roger, ed. *Rhode Island: A Bibliography of Its History.*
        Bibliographies of New England History, 5. Hanover:
        University Press of New England, 1983. xxxiv, 229p.

        Includes 4,125 entries. A significant guide that includes both published and unpublished items pertaining to early church music, histories of music of Rhode Island, and composers, including Charles T. Pachelbel and Oliver Shaw. Begin a search under the headings "Music and Musicians" and "Music and Religion" in the index.

67.   *Performing Arts, 1876-1981: Books.* Foreword by Peter J. Fay.
        New York: R.R. Bowker, 1981. xviii, 1,656p.

        Includes 50,000 entries classified under 12,000 Library of Congress subject headings. An excellent bibliography and means of identifying in one volume Library of Congress cataloged entries for the performing arts back to 1876. Subject access to early American music is found under a number of headings. See, for example, "Music, American History and Criticism" and "Hymns, English."

68.   Pochmann, Henry A. *Bibliography of German Culture in America
        to 1940.* Revised by Arthur R. Schultz. Millwood, N.Y.:
        Kraus International Publications, 1982. cclxxxvi, 489p.

Over 18,000 entries with substantial entries for music, including religious music, songs, music history, musical culture and musicians. Lists psalm books and tunebooks printed by German presses in America before 1820. In the index are other relevant headings, such as "Moravian Church" and "Ephrata." Continued by Arthur R. Schultz, *German-American Relations and German Culture in America: A Subject Bibliography, 1941-1980.* 2 vols. (Millwood, N.Y.: Kraus International Publications, 1984).

69.   Powell, Martha C. *A Selected Bibliography of Church Music and Music Reference Materials.* Louisville, Ky.: Southern Baptist Theological Seminary, 1977. Typescript. v, 95p., with *Supplement* (10p.).

Covers a broad spectrum of sources. Several sections, such as "Church Music—History" and "Hymns—History and Criticism," include citations for a number of useful works relating to the study of hymns in early America. Annotated.

70.   Rogers, A. Robert. *The Humanities: A Selective Guide to Information Sources.* 2nd ed. Littleton, Col.: Libraries Unlimited, 1979. xviii, 355p.

Has 1,200 entries, including 180 annotated music entries. Includes principal music reference sources under general headings such as "Bibliographies of Music," "Dictionaries," "Histories," and "Special Topics and Countries." The indexes are author-title and subject; the latter is organized by type of material, so the reader needs to browse through the various headings in order to identify items which pertain to American music before 1820.

71.   Sabin, Joseph. *Bibliotheca Americana: Dictionary of Books Relating to America from Its Discovery to the Present Time.* Begun by Joseph Sabin, and continued by Wilberforce Eames for the Bibliographical Society of America. New York: Sabin, 1868-92; Bibliographical Society of America, 1928-36. 29 vols.

More than 106,000 numbered entries. A significant bibliography of books, pamphlets, and periodicals on America printed in the Western hemisphere. Arranged principally by author with some entries under title (for anonymous works) and geographical locations. Provides full imprint data. Some library holdings are

noted.   For browsing, look under keyword in titles such as "Music,"
"Moravians," and individual states.   For an author-title index, see
John Edgar Molnar, *Author-Title Index to Joseph Sabin's Dictionary
of Books Relating to America.*   (Metuchen, N.J.: Scarecrow Press,
1974.   3 vols.)   A reexamination of books in Sabin as well as others
not identified by Sabin is in progress; see Lawrence Sidney
Thompson, *The New Sabin: Books Described Again on the Basis of
Examination of Originals, and Fully Indexed by Title, Subject, Joint
Authors, and Institutions and Agencies.*   (Troy, N.Y.: Whitston,
1974-83.)   9 vols. to date.

72.   Sayre, John L. and Roberta Hamburger.   *Tools for Theological
Research.*   6th ed.   Enid, Okla.: Seminary Press, 1981.   v,
104p.

An excellent aid for identifying major reference works for
conducting theological research; some titles are useful for
research in early American music.   Included are bibliographies,
dictionaries, indexes and abstracts, directories, handbooks,
periodicals, and other works.   For example, included are hymn tune
indexes and concordances, the latter helpful for identifying first
line texts.   Entries are unnumbered.   Lacking are principal
reference works for individual denominations.   Author-title index.

73.   Shaw, Ralph R. and Richard H. Shoemaker.   *American
Bibliography: A Preliminary Checklist, 1801 to 1819.*   New
York: Scarecrow Press, 1958-66.   23 vols.

Extends Evans' *American Bibliography* (see entry 45) to 1819.
Includes imprint data for music book and cites some library
holdings.   Volumes 1-19 arranged alphabetically: A/T entries (1
volume per year).   Volume 20 contains addenda, list of sources and
library symbols.   Volume 21 lists titles cited in volumes 1-20.
Volume 22 includes a list of corrections and an author index.
Volume 23 includes printer, publisher and bookseller, geographical
indexes, and a list of omissions.   Some locations are provided.   For
a tool that identifies books about music in this work, see Donald W.
Krummel's "American Music, 1801-1830" (see entry 106).

74.   Shipton, Clifford K. and James E. Mooney.   *National Index of
American Imprints through 1800: The Short-Title Evans.*
Boston: American Antiquarian Society, 1969.   2 vols.

The best index to use for identifying the titles and
sequence numbers in *Early American Imprints, 1639-1800* (see
entry 43). Arranged alphabetically by main entry. An additional
10,035 items identified since the publication of Evans'
bibliography (see entry 45) are included, as well as corrections to
Evans.

75.   Stillwell, Margaret Bingham. *Incunabula and Americana, 1450-
        1800: A Key to Bibliographic Study.* New York: Cooper Square
        Publishers, 1961. xviii, 483p.

A principal work for the identification of bibliographies of
books printed in early America. Bibliographies include Metcalf,
American Psalmody or Titles (see entry 111) and *American Writers and
Compilers of Sacred Music* (see entry 1682), Sachse, *The Music of the
Ephrata Cloister* (see entry 1142), and Sonneck, *Bibliography of
Early Secular American Music* (see entry 119). Also includes a
number of books, arranged by state, on printing and engraving in
early America.

76.   Tanselle, George Thomas. *Guide to the Study of United States
        Imprints.* Cambridge: Belknap Press of Harvard University
        Press, 1971. 2 vols.

A compilation of some 10,000 works consisting of published
research on publications in the United States from colonial times.
Titles are arranged under 9 categories (regional lists, author
lists, catalogues, etc.). One section is on "Music Books"; however,
relevant works can also be found in other categories. Begin a
search under the heading "Music" in the index. For additional
information concerning music found in this work, see Donald W.
Krummel, "American Music Bibliography: Four Titles in Three Acts"
(see entry 105).

77.   Tolzmann, Don Heinrich, comp. *German-Americana: A Biblio-
        graphy.* Metuchen, N.J.: Scarecrow Press, 1975. xi, 384p.

Consists of 5,307 entries. Covers a wide range of topics
from the colonial period to the present. Includes a section on
music with some 127 items of mostly periodical articles, a number of
which are not included in *Music Index* (see entry 147). See also
various sections devoted to individual German sects, including the
Ephrata Cloister, Mennonites, Amish, etc. Although there is an

author index, the work lacks a subject index, making searching
somewhat tedious.

78.   *United States Local Histories in the Library of Congress: A
         Bibliography.*   Ed. by Marion J. Kaminkow.   Baltimore: Magna
         Carta Book Company, 1975.   5 vols.

         Arranged by state, this comprehensive work is essential for
the identification of relevant local histories that include
information on music in early America.   Includes imprint data with
Library of Congress call numbers.   There is no subject index.
Therefore, a certain amount of browsing is required to identify
relevant works.   Volume 5 is a supplement and personal name index.

79.   Warner, Thomas E.   *An Annotated Bibliography of Woodwind
         Instruction Books, 1600-1830.*   Detroit Studies in Music
         Bibliography, 11.   Detroit: Information Coordinators, 1967.
         xvi, 138p.

         An excellent work that includes full imprint data and library
locations for a number of instruction books printed in America.
Included are works by Benjamin Carr, Gottlieb Graupner, F.C.
Schaffer, Oliver Shaw, Robert Shaw, and others.   Cities represented
include Albany, N.Y., Baltimore, Boston, New York, Philadelphia, and
others.

80.   *Western Americana, 1550-1900: Frontier History of the Trans-
         Mississippi West.*   New Haven, Conn.: Research Publications,
         1975.   617 microfilm reels; 35mm. with guide, *Western
         Americana: Guide and Index to the Microfilm Edition* (2
         vols.).

         Collection of printed sources representing the trans-
Mississippi West for the history of its discovery, exploration,
settlement, and development.   Consists of personal narratives,
memoirs, travel accounts, federal and state documents, guidebooks,
state and regional histories, directories, broadsides, and
pamphlets.   Includes both primary and secondary histories.

81.   Winesanker, Michael.   *Books on Music: A Classified List.*   N.p.:
         Texas Association of Music Schools, 1979.   166p.

Includes 1,877 items. A general bibliography arranged by Library of Congress classification format, which includes a wide range of disciplines within the field of music. For books on American music, refer to the subject index under "Music, United States" where the following sub-headings are listed: "Bibliography"; "Composers"; "Dictionaries"; "History and Criticism"; "Instruction and Study." See also the heading "America," pp. 27-29. Author, title, and subject indexes. No annotations.

Specialized Works on American Music

This section includes bibliographies and other lists that focus specifically on music by Americans and literature on American music. For a definition, narrative account, and selective list of bibliographies on American music, see Donald W. Krummel's article, "Bibliographies," in *The New Grove Dictionary of American Music*, vol. 1, pp. 205-13 (see entry 30).

Music and Literature

82.   *American Music before 1865 in Print and on Records: A Biblio-Discography*. I.S.A.M. Monographs, 6. New York: Brooklyn College, Institute for Studies in American Music, 1976. ix, 113p.

A classified annotated bibliography of music in print composed before 1865 and a discography of 33 1/3 rpm disc recordings. Includes a list of early American tunebooks in facsimile reprint editions. For supplements to the discography, refer to Heintze (see entries 281-82). A new and greatly expanded edition is forthcoming.

83.   Britton, Allen. "Theoretical Introductions in American Tune-Books to 1800." Ph.D. dissertation, University of Michigan, 1949. 2 vols., 686p. UM 1505. *DAI* 10/1 (1950): 97-98.

Despite its date, this dissertation continues to be one of the significant works to consult for a study of early American tunebooks. Part 1 includes a comprehensive discussion of tunebook instructions, including "materials and methods" or theory, performance practice, notation, harmony and composition, and philosophies. Part 2 includes an extensive and significant bibliography of tunebooks published in the United States before 1800 (some also after 1800) and for that reason is listed here. Entries are cited alphabetically by compiler and include complete imprint data with added annotations. Library holdings are noted. Continued by Lindsley (see entry 108) for the period 1800-1810. Refer also to Perrin (see entry 949).

84.   Britton, Allen and Irving Lowens. "Unlocated Titles in Early
          Sacred American Music." *Notes* 11/1 (December 1953): 33-48.

          Lists 82 unlocated tunebooks and works from the 18th and 19th centuries. Includes imprint data (if known) and Evans (see entry 45) numbers.

85.   Carman, Judith E., William K. Gaeddart, and Rita M. Resh. *Art-
          Song in the United States, 1801-1976.* New York: National
          Association of Teachers of Singing, 1976. 308p.

          This annotated bibliography contains a section by Gordon Myers for the period 1759-1810.

86.   Clark, J. Bunker. "The Renaissance of Early American Keyboard
          Music: A Bibliographic Review." *Current Musicology* 18
          (1974): 127-32.

87.   Condit, Lester. "Editions of Little & Smith's *Easy Instructor,*
          1807-1817." *Papers of the Bibliographical Society of America*
          40/3 (1946): 233-36.

          Cites titles and imprint data for the 1807, 1808, 1811, 1812,
1813, 1814, 1815, and 1817 editions.

88.   Crawford, Richard A. "Connecticut Sacred Music Imprints, 1778-
          1810." *Notes* 27/3 (March 1971): 445-52; 27/4 (June 1971):
          661-79.

          Some 30 tunebooks were published in Connecticut during the period studied. In part 1, the author includes a list of these with

full imprint data and library locations. Part 2 consists of an
essay on the composers and music represented by them.

89.   De Lerma, Dominique René. *Bibliography of Black Music.* The
       Greenwood Encyclopedia of Black Music. Westport, Conn.:
       Greenwood Press, 1981-84. 4 vols.

       This work is well on its way to becoming a landmark
publication. It is comprehensive and well organized. The four
volumes focus on the following areas: "Reference Materials," "Afro-
American Idioms," "Geographic Studies," and "Theory, Education, and
Related Studies." Included are many citations for African
influences, spirituals, songsters, general histories, dissertations
and theses. Readers should refer to this work for books and
articles not included in the "<u>Afro-American</u>" section below.

90.   De Venney, David P. *Early American Choral Music: An Annotated
       Guide.* Berkeley, Calif.: Fallen Leaf Press, 1988. xx, 150p.

       A list of choral works arranged alphabetically by composer.
Includes psalm tunes, anthems, and hymns for the period 1670 to
1825. A total of 32 composers are cited representing the New
England and Moravian traditions, and music of the English middle
colonies. Also contains an annotated bibliography of books and
articles pertaining to the works and composers included in the
catalog. General index and index of titles, and list of tunebooks
and other collections searched.

91.   Dichter, Harry and Elliott Shapiro. *Early American Sheet
       Music: Its Lure and Its Lore, 1768-1889.* New York: R.R.
       Bowker, 1941. 287p.

       An essential reference work that lists sheet music by
classifications and includes full bibliographical descriptions and
commentary. Of note is a "Directory of Early American Music
Publishers" arranged alphabetically and including publishers'
addresses. A number of illustrations of title pages are included.
Index.

92.   Dichter, Harry. *Handbook of American Sheet Music.*
       Philadelphia: Harry Dichter, 1947. Intro. by John Tasker
       Howard. 100p.

Includes 2,013 entries.   Primarily a dealers catalog.   The author states, "This catalog is the first attempt at a handbook to standardize a field of Americana neglected for many years." Arranged by subject.   Includes photos of title pages.   No composer-title index necessitates tedious browsing through various categories to find desired items.   Fastest method is to search using the section "Imprints" where the music is arranged by publisher.

93.   Dox, Thurston J.   *American Oratorios and Cantatas: A Catalog of Works Written in the United States from Colonial Times to 1985.*   Metuchen, N.J.: Scarecrow Press, 1986.   2 vols., 1,306p.

Includes 3,455 numbered entries.   The earliest oratorio cited in this book dates from 1775.   However, without knowing either a composer or title, it is difficult to identify where these early works are cited in this book.   Author, title, and topic indexes.

94.   Floyd, Samuel A., Jr. and Marsha J. Reisser.   *Black Music in the United States: An Annotated Bibliography of Selected Reference and Research Materials.*   Millwood, N.Y.: Kraus International Publications, 1983.   xv, 234p.

A standard source for all aspects of black music.   The annotations are thorough and lengthy.   Subjects include African music and its survivals in the United States and spirituals. Especially useful for its list of repositories and archives, arranged by state.   Indexes include titles, authors, editors, and compilers, and subjects.

95.   Gillespie, John and Anna Gillespie.   *A Bibliography of Nineteenth-Century American Piano Music.*   Music Reference Collection, 2.   Westport, Conn.: Greenwood Press, 1984.   xii, 358p.

An excellent source for identifying the piano music of early American composers such as James Bremner, William Brown, Benjamin Carr, Anthony Philip Heinrich, John Christopher Moller, Peter K. Moran, and others.   A second section consists of biographies of the composers listed.

96.   Harris, Ernest E.   *Music Education: A Guide to Information
       Sources.*   Detroit: Gale Research Co., 1978.   xvii, 566p.

       A comprehensive work that includes a wide array of reference
sources.   A section on "American Music" includes 37 annotated
entries consisting of principally dictionaries and histories.   See
also books on music in America before 1820 under the heading
"Religious Music."   Author, title, and subject indexes.

97.   Heard, Priscilla S.   *American Music, 1698-1800: An Annotated
       Bibliography.*   Waco, Tex.: Baylor University Press and
       Markham Press Fund, 1975.   246p.

       An index to all entries pertaining to music recorded in Evans
and Shipton, *American Bibliography* (see entries 45 and 74).   Divided
into three principal sections: entries purported to include music;
entries related to music but which do not contain musical notation;
and unlocated items.   Heard's study is often compared to a similar
work by Donald Hixon (see entry 99).   However, each has notable
differences and therefore should be used in tandem.   Heard lists the
titles chronologically and by Evans numbers; Hixon alphabetically by
composer-compiler and title.   Hixon provides full titles of entries,
whereas the titles in Heard are often given in shortened form.
Hixon's work includes biographies, while Heard provides references
to publications in which certain entries are discussed.   Index.

98.   Hitchcock, H. Wiley.   "Sources for a Study of American Music."
       American Studies International 14/2 (1975): 3-9.

99.   Hixon, Donald L.   *Music in Early America: A Bibliography of
       Music in Evans.*   Metuchen, N.J.: Scarecrow Press, 1970.   xvi,
       607p.

       An index to items having printed musical notation recorded in
Evans' *American Bibliography* (see entry 45) and in *Early American
Imprints, 1639-1800* (see entry 43).   Hixon includes an alphabetical,
composer-compiler, title, and numerical index to works included in
EAI.   Also included is a list of works that have not yet been issued
in *EAI.*   Another section contains brief biographical sketches of the
composers, musicians, editors, and compilers cited in the book.
(See entry 97 for additional comments.)

100.   Horn, David. *The Literature of American Music in Books and*
       Folk Music Collections: A Fully Annotated Bibliography.
       Metuchen, N.J.: Scarecrow Press, 1977.   xiv, 556p.

       Includes 1,388 annotated entries.   Compiled in England, this
compilation is a good starting place for identifying principal books
representing most areas of American music.   Included are popular,
folk, and cultivated traditions.   Relevant books for music in
America before 1820 are found under several headings, including
"Histories," "Church Music," "Musical Life," "Hymnody," "Moravians
and German Pietists," and "The Musical Tradition to 1800."   The
annotations are excellent; see especially those on psalters used in
early New England.   An appendix lists additional books.   Index.   A
substantial supplement (570p.) was published in 1988.

101.   Jackson, Irene V. *Afro-American Religious Music: A*
       Bibliography and a Catalogue of Gospel Music. Westport,
       Conn.: Greenwood Press, 1979.   xiv, 210p.

       Includes 873 entries.   A good source for identifying books
and articles on Afro-American religious music and culture, folk
songs, slave songs, and spirituals.   Index.

102.   Jackson, Richard. *U.S. Bicentennial Music I.*   New York:
       Brooklyn College, Institute for Studies in American Music,
       1977.   iv, 20p.

       ". . . a selective list of musical Americana published at
the time of the Bicentennial of the American Revolution.   The list
includes music that specifically celebrated or exploited the
Bicentennial (such as pieces on American subjects patriotic music,
and folk-music settings that appeared mostly between 1973 and 1976)
and reprints and new editions of older American music published
between 1970 and 1976."   Arranged by medium, choral music, band
music, et al.   No index necessitates searching through various
categories for specific composers or titles.   Includes a list of
publishers' names and addresses.

103.   Jackson, Richard. *United States Music: Sources of*
       Bibliography and Collective Biography. I.S.A.M. Monographs,
       1. New York: Brooklyn College, Institute for Studies in
       American Music, 1973.   vii, 80p.

Includes 90 annotated items. The first book-length
reference work to sources specifically in American music.
Classified arrangement, including "Reference Works," "Historical
Studies," "Regional Studies," and "Topical Studies." Recommended as
a general tool and for its critical commentary.

104.   Krohn, Ernst C. "The Bibliography of Music." *Musical
            Quarterly* 5 (1919): 231-54.

A brief survey of music bibliography spanning the 15th
century to the 20th century. The collections of the Boston Public
Library, the Lenox Library (New York City), and the Newberry Library
(Chicago) are also described. Of note is a list of publications on
American music between 1860 and 1917.

105.   Krummel, Donald W. "American Music Bibliography: Four Titles
            in Three Acts." *Yearbook for Inter-American Musical
            Research* 8 (1972): 137-46.

Reviews publications concerning early American imprints as
cited by Hixon (see entry 99) and Tanselle (see entry 76).

106.   Krummel, Donald W. "American Music, 1801-1830, in Shaw-
            Shoemaker (American Music Bibliography, V)." *Yearbook for
            Inter-American Musical Research* 11 (1975): 168-89.

An important tool for identifying books about music in Ralph
R. Shaw and Richard H. Shoemaker, *American Bibliography* (see entry
73). The entries are arranged by classifications. Notably there
are a few sheet music entries cited herein which are in Shaw (see
entry 73), but not in Wolfe (see entry 126).

107.   Krummel, Donald W. *Bibliographical Handbook of American
            Music.* Urbana: University of Illinois Press, 1987. 269p.

Includes 750 books, periodicals, and other literature from
1698 to the present. An excellent thorough guide to principal
sources for all periods of America's musical history in both a
narrative and bibliographical format. See especially the section
"Music before 1825" and sections on regional studies and ethnic
groups. Name and subject index.

108.   Lindsley, Charles Edward.   "Early Nineteenth-Century American
       Collections of Sacred Choral Music, 1800-1810: Part 1, A
       Historical Survey of Tune-Book Production to 1810.   Part II,
       An Annotated Bibliography of Tune-Books, 1800-1810."   Ph.D.
       dissertation, University of Iowa, 1968.   283p.   UM 69-8766.
       DAI 29/11 (May 1969): 4041-42-A.

       The survey is divided into two chronological periods: 1775-
1810 and 1800-10.   The bibliography is thorough and includes full
imprint data, physical description and content, and library
holdings.   Facsimiles.   Index of composers, compilers and their
works.   Continues Britton's similar study for the years prior to
1800 (see entry 83).   Refer also to Perrin (see entry   ).

109.   Lowens, Irving.   *American Composers and American Music.*
       Boston: W. Schwann, 1975.

       A list of 648 American composers and a list of 115 books on
American music and American composers.

110.   McCutcheon, Meredith Alice.   *Guitar and Vihuela: An Annotated
       Bibliography.*   New York: Pendragon Press, 1985.   xlv, 353p.

       Organized chronologically according to historical periods
and includes a section on general histories, national histories,
iconographies, and design and construction.   Includes a
comprehensive list of books, dissertations, book reviews, and
articles.   See especially the section on the "United States" where
articles on Benjamin Carr, guitarists and guitar concerts in America
during the 18th and 19th centuries are cited.   Index.

111.   Metcalf, Frank J.   *American Psalmody or Titles of Books
       Containing Tunes Printed in America from 1721 to 1820.*   New
       York: Charles F. Heartman, 1917.   Reprint with new introd.
       by Harry Eskew, New York: Da Capo Press, 1968.   x, 54p.

       Extends Warrington's similar work (see entry 125) to include
additional items discovered after 1898.   Arranged alphabetically by
compiler and title and identifies subsequent editions.   Although
full imprint data are not given, library holdings are provided.
Includes some facsimile illustrations.   Of note, this work is far
from complete in identifying American tunebooks.

112.   Miller, Terry E. *Folk Music in America: A Reference Guide.*
New York: Garland Publishing, 1986.   xx, 424p.

A comprehensive source containing 1,927 entries. Its recent
publication makes this work the principal source for American folk
music. Readers should consult it for works not cited in the present
guide. Of note are chapters on native Americans, Anglo-American
folk music, psalmody and hymnody, singing schools, the shape-note
tradition, and Afro-American music. Author and subject indexes.
See a review by Jennifer C. Post in *Ethnomusicology* 32/3 (Fall
1988), pp. 452-53.

113.   Mott, Margaret M.   "A Bibliography of Song Sheets: Sports and
Recreations in American Popular Songs." *Notes* 6/3 (June
1949): 379-418; 7/4 (September 1950): 522-61; 9/1 (December
1951): 33-22.

A somewhat extensive bibliography of songs arranged by
categories from the late 1700s on. Only partial imprint data are
provided. Of note are the reproductions of title pages.

114.   *The National Tune Index: Early American Wind and Ceremonial
Music, 1636-1836.* Comp. by Raoul F. Camus. New York:
University Music Editions, 1988. Microfiche. With *User's
Guide.*

A computer-generated seven-part index of 20,733 citations
taken from 1,077 pieces of sheet music and 298 collections found in
the United States and other countries. Included are tutors for
various instruments, collections of social and ceremonial music,
wind band arrangements, field music manuals, and military
regulations pertaining to various military instruments. Source,
text, music, author/performer, and theater works indexes.

115.   *The National Tune Index: 18th-Century Secular Music.* Comp. by
Kate Van Winkle Keller and Carolyn Rabson. New York:
University Music Editions, 1980. 78 microfiche. With *User's
Guide* (xiv, 92p.).

A major reference work. This index to 38,500 Anglo-American
secular tunes, songs, and dances is based on some 520 printed and
manuscript sources in the United States, Great Britain, and Canada.
Five principal parts include: index of titles and first lines, music

indexes of incipits in scale degrees, in stressed note order, and in
interval sequence, and a source index of bibliographic information.
Source material is arranged under 6 broad headings: "American
Imprints"; "Musical Theatre"; "Country Dances"; "Airs without
Words"; "Manuscripts"; "Songs."   General bibliography.

116.   Phelps, Roger P.   *A Guide to Research in Music Education.*
       3rd ed.   Metuchen, N.J.: Scarecrow Press, 1986.   xiii,
       368p.

       The principal guide to theory and historical research
methodology in music education.   In the chapter on "Historical
Research," the author discusses his discovery of a complete set of
the Three Trios, op. 3 by John Antes and a "Parthia IX" by David
Moritz Michael in the Moravian Archives in Winston-Salem, N.C.   (See
Phelps, pp. 164-67.)   Index.

117.   Pruett, James W. and Thomas P. Slavens.   *Research Guide to
       Musicology.*   Sources of Information in the Humanities, 4.
       Chicago: American Library Association, 1985.   ix, 175p.

       A recently published guide to historical methodology for
musicology that includes topical bibliographies under general
headings, such as dictionaries, encyclopedias, histories and
chronologies, etc.   Includes annotations.   There is a short section
on American music with an essay discussing principal histories, and
a brief bibliography.   Author-title and subject indexes.

118.   Sonneck, Oscar George.   "The Bibliography of American Music."
       Bibliographical Society of America, Proceedings and Papers 1
       (1904-05): 50-64.

       Reprinted in *Oscar Sonneck and American Music.*   Ed. by
William Lichtenwanger.   Urbana: University of Illinois Press, 1983,
pp. 17-30.   Discusses some early attempts at compiling
bibliographies of early American music.   Sonneck's work represents
the first call for a general bibliography on the history of American
music.

119.   Sonneck, Oscar George.   *A Bibliography of Early Secular
       American Music: Eighteenth Century.*   Revised and enlarged by
       William Treat Upton.   Washington, D.C.: Library of Congress

Music Division, 1945.   Reprint, New York: Da Capo, 1964.
xvi, 616p.

The first reference work on music printed in America before
1800.   A meticulous and major work despite its date of publication.
Entries (unnumbered) are arranged alphabetically by title.   Full
imprint data cited along with library holdings.   Includes lists of
articles and essays relating to music, composers, songsters, first
lines, American patriotic music, opera librettos, publishers,
printers and engravers.   Also includes a section of biographical
sketches of composers, musicians, and others.   General index.
Continued for 1801-25 by Wolfe (see entry 126).

120.   Stanislaw, Richard J.   *A Checklist of Four-Shape Shape-Note
        Tunebooks.*   I.S.A.M. Monographs, 10.   New York: Brooklyn
        College, Institute for Studies in American Music, 1978.   ix,
        61p.

The standard list for this medium.   Includes 305 entries
based on both primary and secondary sources, and a title index.   The
annotations include imprint data and library locations.

121.   Von Ende, Richard Chaffey.   *Church Music: An International
       Bibliography.*   Metuchen, N.J.: Scarecrow Press, 1980.   xx,
       453p.

Has 5,445 entries arranged by topic.   Includes a number of
works on early American music.   See headings under "Denominations,
Faiths and Orders," "Psalmody," and "National—United States."   No
annotations.   Author, editor and compiler index.

122.   Wagner, John W.   "The Music of James Hewitt: A Supplement to
       the Sonneck-Upton and Wolfe Bibliographies."   *Notes* 29/2
       (December 1972): 224-27.

Includes vocal and instrumental compositions with full
imprint data and library locations.

123.   Warner, Thomas.   *Periodical Literature on American Music,
       1620-1920: A Classified Bibliography with Annotations.*
       Bibliographies in American Music, 12.   Warren, Mich.:

Harmonie Park Press for the College Music Society, 1988. xli, 644p.

A significant reference work citing 5,348 articles published through 1980, a large portion of which are not found in other sources, such as the *Music Index* (see entry 147) or *RILM* (see entry 148). The range of categories is broad, and includes research and reference materials, historical studies, theory and composition, ethnomusicology, organology, and special topics. Specific subjects include ethnic groups, psalmody, hymnody, singing schools, mission music, music collections, composers, musicians and much more. Author and subject indexes.

124. Warrington, James. "A Bibliography of Church Music Books Issued in Pennsylvania, with Annotations." *Penn Germania* 13 (1912): 170-77, 262-68, 371-74, 460-65, 627-31, 755-59.

Serves as a supplement to Warrington's *Short Titles of Books* (see entry 125).

125. Warrington, James. *Short Titles of Books Relating to or Illustrating the History and Practice of Psalmody in the United States, 1620-1820.* Philadelphia: privately printed, 1898. 96p.

Actually items cited span 1538-1898. A chronological listing of short titles, including place and date of publication, with subsequent editions noted. A useful concise work in its day. More than half the listings are pre-1820. Unfortunately library holdings are not included. (See also entry 124.)

126. Wolfe, Richard J. *Secular Music in America, 1801-1825: A Bibliography.* Intro. by Carleton Sprague Smith. New York: New York Public Library and Astor, Lenox & Tilden Foundations, 1964. 3 vols.

Includes 10,168 entries. The principal reference work for the identification and description of secular music published in America between 1801-25. Continues Sonneck-Upton (see entry 119). Information includes verbatim transcription of title page with complete imprint data, including pagination and size of the item. Includes library holdings as well as short biographies of "lesser known composers and arrangers listed here." An appendix of items

not recorded in the Sonneck-Upton bibliography is useful. Indexes
include title, first lines, publishers, engravers and printers,
publishers' plate and publication numbering systems, and general
index. Readers should be aware that the first line and title
indexes are not fully comprehensive in that contents of collections
are not always included.

Songsters

Irving Lowens (see entry 128) defines a songster as a collection of
three or more secular poems intended to be sung, but not including
music. See also Arthur Schrader's definition in his article
"Songster," in *The New Grove Dictionary of American Music*, vol. 4,
pp. 260-61 (see entry 30). For a comprehensive article that
includes facsimiles of title pages of songsters, refer to Lowens,
"Eighteenth-Century Massachusetts Songsters," in *Music in Colonial
Massachusetts* (see entry 533). In addition, in the colonial period,
individual songs with text only were frequently printed in
newspapers and as broadsides. Refer below to the sections on
"Newspaper Guides and Indexes" and *"Broadsides."* (See also entry
801.)

127.   Lowens, Irving. "The American Songster before 1821: A List of
        Incomplete and Unlocated Titles." *Papers of the
        Bibliographical Society of America* 54/1 (1960): 61-69.

        Includes a list of 75 items dated 1750-1820.

128.   Lowens, Irving. *A Bibliography of Songsters Printed in
        America before 1821.* Worcester, Mass.: American Antiquarian
        Society, 1976. xxxviii, 229p.

        Includes 649 entries. The principal work for the
identification and location of songsters. Includes a "Geographical
Directory of Printers, Publishers, Booksellers, Engravers, etc.," a
"Compilers, Authors, Proprietors, and Editors" index, and title
index. Includes a list of bibliographies cited.

Periodical Indexes

General Indexes

In addition to music journals, articles on early American music can
be found in a number of journals that focus primarily on American
history and society.   Principal indexes to these periodicals are
described below.   Readers should refer to Thomas Warner's *Periodical
Literature on American Music, 1620-1920: A Classified Bibliography
with Annotations* (see entry 123) for articles not found in the
indexes cited below or in the body of this volume.   For a guide to
periodicals which focus on specific geographical areas, see
Directory of State and Local History Periodicals (comp. by Milton
Crouch and Hans Raum.   Chicago: American Library Association, 1977).
For a list of music periodicals published in the United States from
1820 on, see the article, "Periodicals," in *The New Grove Dictionary
of American Music*, vol. 3, pp. 505-35 (see entry 30).   Irving Lowens
includes "A Check-List of Writings about Music in the Periodicals of
American Transcendentalism (1835-50)," in *Music and Musicians in
Early America* (see entry 371).   Other lists of early American music
periodicals are described below.

129.   *America: History and Life*, July 1964- .   Vol. 1- .   Santa
       Barbara, Calif.: ABC-Clio, 1964- .   Quarterly.

       A major guide to periodical articles on American history
with over 2,000 journals indexed.   Covers a number of journals that
are likely to include articles on early American music but which are
not in *Music Index* (see entry 147).   Begin a search under the
heading "Music" in the subject index and also under relevant
headings "Moravians," "Shakers," "Hymns," "Songs," "Folk Song,"
"Opera," etc.

130.   *American Periodical Series, 18th Century*.   Ann Arbor, Mich.:
       University Microfilms, 1942-46.   33 microfilm reels; 35 mm.

       More than 1,100 early American periodicals.   For an index to
this series and its continuation, see Jean Hoornstra and Trudy
Heath, *American Periodicals, 1741-1900: An Index to the Microfilm
Collections* (Ann Arbor, Mich.: University Microfilms International,
1979).   Its index includes a number of magazines that include music,
such as *American Musical Magazine* (1786-87.   Reprint also,

Scarsdale, N.Y.: Annemarie Schnase, 1961), Andrew Law's *Musical Magazine* (1792-1801?), and *The Boston Magazine* (1802-06). Each periodical has its own annotation, and library locations for print copies are cited. Title and subject indexes. Continued by entry 131.

131. *American Periodicals, 1800-1850.* Ann Arbor, Mich.: University Microfilms International, 1946-1978. 1,966 microfilm reels; 35 mm.

Continued by *American Periodical Series, 1850-1900, Civil War and Reconstruction.* 771 reels; 35 mm. These three series (see entry 130) represent holdings in some 300 libraries.

132. *American Popular Culture: A Historical Bibliography.* Santa Barbara, Calif.: ABC-CLIO, 1984. vii, 246p.

Includes 2,719 annotated entries. Index to periodical literature in some 2,000 journals based on ABC-Clio Information Service's American history data base. Included is a section on music where a few articles on popular songs of the 18th-19th centuries are cited with annotations.

133. *Articles in American Studies, 1954-1968: A Cumulation of the Annual Bibliographies from American Quarterly.* Ed. by Cohen Hennig. Ann Arbor, Mich.: Pierian Press, 1972. 2 vols.; 898p.

Includes a broad range of American studies topics based on some 200 journals. Non-cumulative, annotated entries in classified arrangement. The absence of a general subject index requires readers to search the "Music" category each year for relevant articles. Useful for articles not readily identified elsewhere. Author/main entry and subject: personal names index.

134. *Arts and Humanities Citation Index*, 1976- . Vol. 1- . Philadelphia: Institute for Scientific Information, 1978- . Three issues per year with annual cumulations.

Indexes more than 1,000 journals in the arts and sciences. Its principal feature is its comprehensiveness covering every item

of substance in each journal.   Includes a number of journals indexed
in *Music Index* (see entry 147).

135.   *Bibliographic Index: A Cumulative Bibliography of
         Bibliographies*, 1937- .   Vol. 1- .   New York: H.W. Wilson,
         1938- .   Semiannual with annual and additional cumulations.

         An excellent source for identifying bibliographies on early
American music published separately or published in books,
pamphlets, and journals.   Begin a search under "Music—United
States."

136.   *Early American Periodicals Index to 1850*.   New York: Readex
         Microprint Co., 195- .   1,074 microopaques; 23 x 16 cm.

         Approximately 650,000 entries.   Originally a Works Progress
Administration project which is revised, in part.   Includes a broad
range of some 350 periodicals published 1730-1850.   Separate indexes
for poetry and songs.

137.   *Humanities Index*, April 1974- .   New York: H.W. Wilson, 1974-.
         Quarterly with annual cumulation.

         The level of sophistication is somewhat higher in this index
to English language periodicals than in *Readers Guide* (see entry
142) and serves as a worthy adjunct to *Music Index* (see entry 147).
Includes a number of general and local American history journals
that are likely to include occasionally articles on American music.
The subject headings used for musical topics are extensive.   See
especially "Music-United States" and "Music, American."   Includes
some music journals indexed in *Music Index*.

138.   *Library Literature*, 1921/32- .   Vol. 1- .   New York: H.W.
         Wilson, 1934- .   Bimonthly with annual cumulation.

         "An author and subject index to materials on library and
information sources."   An excellent source for identifying recent
articles on library collections of early American music as well as
exhibits.

139. *Magazine Index*, 1976- . Los Altos, Calif.: Information Access
        Corp., 1976- . Monthly. Microfilm.

Similar to *Readers Guide* (see entry 142) in its type of
magazines indexed. Readers will find this index to be somewhat more
current than *Readers Guide* and the notable difference being its
citations include only the most recent 5-year period; after that
entries are discarded. However, over 400 periodicals are indexed
here. Entries are found under subjects and personal names. Begin a
search under the heading "Music, American."

140. *Nineteenth Century Readers' Guide to Periodical Literature*,
        1890-99. Edited by Helen Grant Cushing and Adah V. Morris.
        New York: H.W. Wilson, 1944. 4 vols.

Includes only a few references to American music.

141. *Poole's Index to Periodical Literature*, 1802-81. Rev. ed.,
        Boston: Houghton, 1891.   Reprint, New York: P. Smith,
        1938; Gloucester, Mass.: P. Smith, 1963. 2 vols.

One of the earliest and longest running indexes. Provides
only subject (no author) access. Includes a surprisingly extensive
number of entries on music. Supplements for the period 1882-1907 (5
vols.) were issued. Begin a search under the heading "Music." See
Marion V. Bell and Jean C. Bacon, *Poole's Index: Date and Volume Key*
(Chicago: Association of College and Reference Libraries, 1957) for
a list of journals indexed in the parent work.

142. *Readers' Guide to Periodical Literature*, 1900- . Vol. 1- .
        New York: H.W. Wilson, 1905- . Vol. 1- . Semimonthly
        with annual cumulation.

The best-known index to periodical articles and book
reviews. Currently 189 periodicals are indexed. Of general
interest, this work indexes articles in magazines not covered by
specialized indexes such as the *Music Index* (see entry 147), and is
especially useful as a tool before 1948, the year the *Music Index*
was begun. Begin a search under the headings "Music" and "Music,
American." Cross-references are provided for additional relevant
headings.

143.   *Religion Index One: Periodicals*, 1949- .   Vol. 1- .   Chicago:
         American Theological Library Association, 1953- .
         Semiannual and annual cumulation.

         Previously titled *Index to Religious Periodical Literature*,
this work indexes some 230 scholarly religious journals.   There are
a subject index, author index, and an index to book reviews.   After
1975, the author index includes abstracts for articles written by
the authors.   There is a surprisingly extensive section on music.
Begin a search under "Music and Religion," "Musicians," and other
relevant headings.

144.   *Religious and Theological Abstracts*, 1958- .   Vol. 1- .
         Myerstown, Pa.: Religions and Theological Abstracts, Inc.,
         1958- .   Quarterly (index in no. 4 of each volume).

         Classifies significant articles under categories of
"Biblical, Theological, Historical," and "Practical."   Useful for
denominational history.   For music, not nearly as comprehensive as
Religion Index One (see entry 143).

145.   *Writings on American History: A Subject Bibliography of
         Articles*, 1902- .   Ed. by James J. Dougherty and others.
         Millwood, N.Y.: Kraus-Thomson [for] American Historical
         Association, 1904- .   Annual.

         Based on the section "Recently Published Articles" of
American Historical Review.   Includes a section on "Music," which
includes articles from periodicals not indexed by *Music Index* (see
entry 147) or *RILM* (see entry 148).   This series is a must for
anyone needing to identify articles on early American music that are
not necessarily cited elsewhere.   Arranged by subject with author
index.

<u>Music Indexes</u>

146.   *Music Article Guide*, 1966- .   Vol. 1- .   Philadelphia:
         Information Services, 1966- .

         "Geared exclusively to the special needs of school and
college music educators," readers are not likely to find

comprehensive coverage for articles on early American music but, nonetheless, deserves notice for its extensive periodicals list.

147. *Music Index: A Subject-Author Guide to Current Music Periodical Literature*, December 1949- . Vol. 1- . Detroit: Information Coordinators, 1950- . Monthly with annual cumulation.

The principal author and subject index which cites articles on classical, popular, jazz, folk and ethnic music, performance, pedagogy, and musicology in some 350 journals. Relevant subject headings for early American music include specific authors and titles, and Afro-American music. Begin a search under the heading "United States." Includes an annual subject headings list.

148. *RILM Abstracts: Répertoire International de la Littérature Musicale/International Repertory of Music Literature*, 1967- . Vol. 1- . New York: International RILM Center, 1967- . Quarterly.

An international classified list of abstracts of books, articles, reviews, theses and dissertations, guides and catalogs, reviews, and other publications that is accessible online as well. Contains references to publications not included in other indexes such as *Music Index* (see entry 147), but should be used in tandem with that index to insure thorough coverage. Readers should bear in mind that compared to other indexes, *RILM* is a relatively recent publication and the appearance of the printed version lags behind online access by some five years. Begin a search using the author-subject index under the heading "USA."

Other works are also important for providing information on early American music periodicals:

149. Davison, Sister Mary Veronica. "American Music Periodicals, 1853-1899." Ph.D. dissertation, University of Minnesota, 1973. 2 vols., 635p. UM 74-10498. *DAI* 34/11 (May 1974): 7265-A.

This study pertains to some 300 journals. A reference for identifying "publishers, editors, runs, title changes, contents, and locations of copies."

150.   Johnson, H. Earle.   "Early New England Periodicals Devoted to
         Music."   *Musical Quarterly* 26 (1940): 153-61.

         Includes information on *The Euterpeiad* (1820), *Massachusetts
Magazine (1791), *Monthly Anthologie* (1803-1811), and *Polyanthus*
(1812), as well as the Handel and Haydn Society in Boston, and a
notice regarding a musical event in Boston in 1818 as published in
the *Columbian Centinel.*

151.   *19th Century American Music Periodicals on Microfilm.*
         Guilford, Conn.: Opus Publications, 1986.   4 microfilm
         reels; 35 mm.   With printed guide (165p.).

         Includes 21 American music periodicals, each having a
different run, for the period 1849-1905.   The series is scheduled to
include 309 periodicals.   The printed guide lists all of the titles,
including library locations, and has a handy "Chronological Register
of American Music Periodicals, 1850-1900."   Refer also to William
Weichlein's *A Checklist of American Music Periodicals, 1850-1900*
(see entry 152).

152.   Weichlein, William J.   *A Checklist of American Music
         Periodicals, 1850-1900.*   Detroit Studies in Music
         Bibliography, 16.   Detroit: Information Coordinators, 1970.
         103p.

         Knowledge of nineteenth-century music periodicals is
important for identification of sources that might have articles
referring to early American music.   Weichlein has cited 309 such
sources and lists them alphabetically.   Includes years of issuance
and library holdings.   Other lists include a chronological and
geographical arrangement and an index of editors and publishers.
Includes library holdings.   Refer also to *19th Century American
Music Periodicals on Microfilm* (see entry 151).

153.   Wunderlich, Charles Edward.   "A History and Bibliography of
         Early American Musical Periodicals, 1782-1852."   Ph.D.
         dissertation, University of Michigan, 1962.   796p.   UM 62-
         2810.   *DAI* 23/2 (August 1962): 651.

         Based on holdings in 30 libraries.   The bibliography
includes 66 entries with full descriptive data.   Appendixes include
alphabetical and geographical indexes and "a register-index

containing names, addresses, and biographical information for more than 800 publishers, printers, engravers, editors, composers, and authors who had connections with musical periodicals before 1852."

Newspaper Guides and Indexes

One of the most important primary sources for the study of American music of the eighteenth and nineteenth centuries are newspapers. In a sense, they represent a living, chronological record of musical events and musicians that is not found in other sources. Oscar Sonneck, writing some fifty years ago, was the first to recognize the value of newspapers for the study of early American music. His was a pioneering effort in examining early newspapers for their musical content. Today, however, there are many early newspapers Sonneck did not read that have yet to be thoroughly examined. Below is a brief list of the principal reference aids for the identification of newspapers and repositories and where they are held. Refer to Francis Prucha's *Handbook for Research in American History* (Lincoln: University of Nebraska Press, 1987), pp. 58-60 for a list of state directories. Of note is Gillian B. Anderson's *Freedom's Voice in Poetry and Song* (see entry 753), which is an excellent model for future similar topical studies of early newspapers. Song texts printed in early newspapers can be accessed through J.A. Leo Lemay's *A Calendar of American Poetry in the Colonial Newspapers and Magazines* (see entry 159). In addition, readers should refer below to the section on "Obituaries" which describes guides to notices taken from early newspapers.

154.   Anderson, Gillian B. *Music in New York during the American Revolution: An Inventory of Musical References in Rivington's New York Gazette.* MLA Index and Bibliography Series, 24. Philadelphia: Music Library Association, 1987. xxix, 135p.

Indexes references to music and instruments, balls, concerts and other assemblies, and music instruction in the *Gazette* which was published weekly in New York, 1773-83.

155.   Brigham, Clarence S. *History and Bibliography of American Newspapers, 1690-1820.* Worcester, Mass.: American

Antiquarian Society, 1947. Reprint, Hamden, Conn.: Archon
Books, 1962. 2 vols.

The principal tool for the identification of early American
newspapers. Arranged alphabetically by state. Provides background
information on the newspapers, citing extant copies, including
library holdings. There is a "List of Libraries," "List of Private
Owners," "Index of Titles," and "Index of Printers." A supplement,
*Additions and Corrections to History and Bibliography of American
Newspapers, 1690-1820* (50p.), was printed in 1961.

156. *A Check List of American Eighteenth Century Newspapers in the
      Library of Congress.* Originally compiled by John Van Ness
      Ingram. 2nd ed. revised and enlarged by Henry S. Parsons.
      Washington, D.C.: 1936. Reprint, New York: Greenwood Press,
      1968. vi, 401p.

Many extant copies of early American newspapers are held by
the Library of Congress. Therefore, this guide is handy for
identifying specific newspapers. Titles are cited alphabetically
under state, then city.

157. *Guide to Newspaper Indexes in New England.* Holden, Mass.: New
      England Library Association, 1978. 91p.

Useful for its identification of unpublished typescript
indexes. Arranged alphabetically by state, then by city and name of
newspaper.

158. Lathem, Edward Connery. *Chronological Tables of American
      Newspapers, 1690-1820.* Barre, Mass.: American Antiquarian
      Society and Barre Publishers, 1972. 131p.

A handy tool for identifying what newspapers were published
in any given year. Arranged by state, then city. Indicates if
copies are extant. Serves as a companion to Brigham (see entry 155)
which, however, supplies more information about newspapers than
Lathem.

159. Lemay, J.A. Leo. *A Calendar of American Poetry in the
      Colonial Newspapers and Magazines through 1765.* Worcester,
      Mass.: American Antiquarian Society, 1972. xxxi, 353p.

A means for accessing song texts in early newspapers and magazines.

160.   *Microprint Edition of Early American Newspapers, 1704-1820.*
       New York: Readex Microprint Corp., 1966.   Micro-opaques and
       catalog (55p.).   Ed. by Nathan Cohen.

       Includes 30 newspapers, each with a different run.

161.   Milner, Anita Cheek.   *Newspaper Indexes: A Location and
       Subject Guide for Researchers.*   Metuchen, N.J.: Scarecrow
       Press, 1977-1979.   2 vols.

       In the past, indexes to newspapers have been difficult to
locate in that most of them are unpublished in the form of clipping
files, typed lists, or index cards.   This is a useful tool for the
identification of those indexes.   The author provides a general
overview of subjects that have been indexed for newspapers cited in
the book and name of repository.   Although Milner identifies some
extant copies, Brigham (see entry 155) is a better tool for
identifying all known copies.   Considering the date of Milner's
work, the information provided on fees and procedures for obtaining
copies should be confirmed by contacting the repository.

162.   Moore, John Hammond.   *South Carolina Newspapers.*   Columbia:
       University of South Carolina, 1988.   352p.

       Listed here as an example of a regional list of newspapers.
Includes title, place of publication, history of each newspaper, and
location of existing runs, for the years 1732-1987.

163.   *Newspapers in Microform: United States, 1948-1983.*
       Washington, D.C.: Library of Congress, 1984.   2 vols.

       A cumulative listing of all newspapers now known to be on
microform.   Newspapers are cited in alphabetical order by state,
then city.   Volume 2 includes a title index.

164.   *United States Newspaper Program National Union List.*   Dublin,
       Ohio: Online Computer Library Center [OCLC], 1985.   44

microfiches; 11 x 15 cm., with 1 pamphlet (42p.). Also available in print format.

This project was begun with an objective of identifying all American newspapers to be bibliographically described in a single database. Currently includes some 25,000 titles with location information.

General Guides

Identifying the repositories and collections that hold primary
source material on early American music is a first step in a
thorough search for information on a specific topic.   The general
guides described below are useful tools.

165.   *Directory of Archives and Manuscript Repositories in the
        United States.*   2nd ed.   Phoenix, Ariz.: Oryx Press, 1988.
        872p.

        Includes information on over 4,500 collections.   Each entry
includes information on repository holdings, including diaries,
letters, papers, photographs, and more.

166.   *Directory of Historical Societies and Agencies in the United
        States and Canada.*   12th ed.   Comp. and ed. by Tracey
        Linton Craig.   Nashville, Tenn.: American Association for
        State and Local History, 1982.   vi, 416p.

        The principal reference work of its kind that includes brief
descriptions of major programs.   A "Special Interest Index" includes
some culturally relevant headings under "Ethnic Heritage, Race,
Religion."

167.   *National Union Catalog of Manuscript Collections,* 1959/61- .
        Hamden, Conn.: Shoestring Press, 1962- .   Annual with
        cumulations every five years.

        The principal guide to manuscript collections in
repositories throughout the United States.   Collections are arranged
alphabetically and given item numbers.   Lists letters, diaries,

personal papers, and accounts, with a typical entry including the
number, description, and location of the items.   There are numerous
references to music and readers should be aware that there are
likely to be descriptions of collections not included in *Resources
of American Music History* (see entry 175).   Begin a search using the
index under "Music and Musical Affairs," "Hymns," "Songs," and under
personal names.   A forthcoming *Index to Personal Names in the
National Union Catalog of Manuscript Collections, 1959-1984*
(Alexandria, Va., Chadwyck-Healey) will include some 200,000 names
arranged alphabetically.

Guides to Regional Libraries and Collections

168.   Bradley, Carol June.   *Music Collections in American Libraries:
         A Chronology.*   Detroit Studies in Music Bibliography, 46.
         Detroit: Information Coordinators, 1981.   xiii, 249p.

         Not as comprehensive as *Resources of American Music History*
(see entry 175), Bradley's guide to major music collections in
American libraries overlooks many early American music collections.
The collections are not described in detail.   However, citations to
literature about the collections are abundant.   Entries are arranged
chronologically by date of establishment of repository.   General
index.

169.   Coover, James.   *Musical Instrument Collections: Catalogues and
         Cognate Literature.*   Detroit Studies in Music Bibliography,
         47.   Detroit: Information Coordinators, 1981.   464p.

         Includes pamphlets, brochures, catalogs of collections and
exhibits, books, and articles as well as library holdings.
International in scope, this work includes a number of titles that
include references to early American instruments.   The bibliography
is arranged by city so a certain amount of browsing is required to
identify relevant items.   General index.

170.   *Directory of Music Collections in the Greater New York Area.*
         Comp. by Nina Davis-Millis.   Ed. by Lakshmi Kapoor.   N.p.:
         Music Library Association, Greater New York Chapter, 1982.
         44p.

Collections are described differently albeit briefly here
than in *Resources of American Music History* (see entry 175).   Cites
hours, addresses, and telephone numbers.

171.   *Directory of Music Libraries and Collections in New England.*
         6th ed.   Comp. and ed. by the Publications Committee of the
         Music Library Association, New England Chapter.   New London,
         Conn.: Greer Music Library, Connecticut College, 1981.   93p.

         Descriptions of collections are scanty.   Not the first
source to consult.

172.   Fuld, James J. and Mary Wallace Davidson.   *18th-Century
         American Secular Music Manuscripts: An Inventory.*   MLA Index
         and Bibliography Series, 20.   Philadelphia: Music Library
         Association, 1980.   xiii, 225p.

         Includes 85 collections.   The principal bibliographic
reference work for the identification of 18th-century music
manuscripts.   This guide is arranged by collections with individual
manuscripts listed and described.   Manuscripts in the Moravian Music
Foundation at Winston-Salem, N.C. and Bethlehem, Pa. are excluded
due to previously published inventories which cover those
collections.   Refer to the Preface for yet other categories of
manuscripts excluded.   Included is an index of titles, first lines,
subjects, musical forms, and geographical and personal names.

173.   Keller, Kate Van Winkle.   *Popular Secular Music in America
         through 1800: A Preliminary Checklist of Manuscripts in
         North American Collections.*   MLA Index and Bibliography
         Series, 21.   Philadelphia: Music Library Association, 1981.
         xviii, 140p.

         Arranged by state, this work, along with Fuld, *18th-Century
American Secular Music Manuscripts* (see entry 172), *Resources of
American Music History* (see entry 175), and *The National Tune Index*
(see entry 115) are the major sources for the identification of
music manuscripts in early America.   The index is comprehensive.   Of
note, psalm tunes for secular use are also listed.

174.   Lichtenwanger, William. *A Survey of Musical Instrument
       Collections in the United States and Canada.* Ann Arbor,
       Mich.: Music Library Association, 1974. xi, 137p.

Provides brief descriptions of collections arranged by
state. Includes references to early American musical instruments,
but they are not described conveniently in one place in the indexes.
For example, Benjamin Franklin's armonica is listed under
"Idiophones" in the index of instruments. There is, however, an
index of "Instruments of Western Civilization," organized by period.

175.   *Resources of American Music History: A Directory of Source
       Materials from Colonial Times to World War II.* Comp. by
       D.W. Krummel, Jean Geil, Doris J. Dyen, and Deane L. Root.
       Urbana: University of Illinois Press, 1981. 463p.

The principal guide to collections of music Americana in
1,689 libraries, historical societies, museums, and other
repositories in the United States and foreign countries. This work
has received glowing reviews and rightly so for it identifies
hundreds of historically valuable, but little-known collections of
music (both printed and manuscript), scrapbooks, programs,
playbills, personal papers, photographs, recordings, catalogs,
newspaper and other clippings, and much more. Each entry includes
the title of repository, address, descriptions of the holdings, and
number of items. Most entries are signed. Additional relevant
sources and literature for individual entries are included.
General index. For additional information on this work, see Donald
W. Krummel's article, "Little RAMH, Who Made Thee? Observations on
an American Music Census," in *Notes* 37/2 (December 1980), pp. 227-
38.

176.   Spencer, Jon Michael. *As the Black School Sings: Black Music
       Collections at Black Universities and Colleges, with a Union
       List of Book Holdings.* Music Reference Collection, 13. New
       York: Greenwood Press, 1987. xvi, 185p.

Includes inventories, compositions, hymnals, broadsides,
articles, books, and more. See a review by Dena J. Epstein in *Notes*
45/1 (September 1988), pp. 67-68 which compares this work with
Resources of American Music History (see entry 175).

177. Young, William C. *American Theatrical Arts: A Guide to Manuscripts and Special Collections in the United States and Canada.* Chicago: American Library Association, 1971. ix, 166p.

Of lesser value. Some 138 repositories are surveyed. Although this guide identifies primarily items related to theater, it does include a number of music entries, as well as serving as an excellent guide to early opera houses where music was likely performed. Collections cited here may not necessarily be cited in *Resources of American Music History* (see entry 175). See, for example, entry no. 75 where the records of the New Brunswick Band (1813-17) and other early musical organizations held at Rutgers University are cited. Name and subject indexes.

Guides to Individual Libraries and Collections

There are numerous guides to individual libraries and collections. A number of guides to significant collections, including, for example, the American Antiquarian Society and the Massachusetts Historical Society, are not described below. Readers should refer to *Resources of American Music History* (see entry 175) for information on them. For another noteworthy list of significant collections throughout the United States, see Mary Wallace Davidson and D.W. Krummel, "Libraries and Collections" in *The New Grove Dictionary of American Music*, vol. 3, pp. 46-84 (see entry 30). For a list of the important public and private collections of musical instruments in the United States, see Laurence Libin, "Instruments, Collections of," vol. 2, pp. 492-94 in the same work. Of note also is the *National Inventory of Documentary Sources in the United States* (Teaneck, N.J.: Chadwyck-Healey, 1983-), a recent project which when completed will include a series of reprints of printed guides òn microfiche. Its four series include: *Federal Records*; *Manuscript Division, Library of Congress*; *State Archives, Libraries and Historical Societies*; and *Academic Libraries and Other Repositories*. This series is likely to be more detailed in its descriptions than the *National Union Catalog of Manuscript Collections* (see entry 167). Another list worth referring to is Francis P. Prucha's "Guides to Individual Collections and Repositories," in *Handbook for Research in American History* (Lincoln: University of Nebraska Press, 1987), pp. 48-51. Another informative list is *A Guide to Special Collections in the OCLC Database*, compiled and edited by Philip Schieber, Virginia G.

Voedisch, and Becky A. Wright (Dublin, Ohio: Online Computer Library
Center, 1988). In addition, there are library catalogs from the
18th and 19th century that are not included in modern reference
books, but do include references to music books and provide much
evidence as to the musical interests of that period. For example,
see Stephen Clark's *Catalogue* (1783), which includes a number of
music books (see entry 184). Readers should also make note of
Donald Krummel's excellent article on the history of music
collections in the United States in *Bibliographical Handbook of
American Music*, pp. 161-65 (see entry 107).

178.   Alden, John.   "Some Recent Additions to the Rare Book
            Collection: The Musical Library of Francis Hopkinson."
            Library Chronicle 15 (1949): 65-67.

        Discusses Francis Hopkinson's music library housed in the
University of Pennsylvania Library.

179.   Boeringer, James.   "Musical Instruments: Lititz Congregation
            Musical Instruments, a Catalogue." *Moravian Music Journal*
            26/4 (Winter 1981): 88-89.

        The museum is in Lititz, Pa.   Includes string and brass
instruments.

180.   Boeringer, James.   "Musical Instruments: The Lititz Instrument
            Collection." *Moravian Music Foundation Bulletin* 25/2 (Fall-
            Winter 1980): 11-12.

        A list and description of instruments in the Lititz Museum.
The instruments date from the 1700s on.

181.   Breton, Arthur J.   *A Guide to the Manuscript Collections of
            the New-York Historical Society*.   Westport, Conn.: Greenwood
            Press, 1972.   2 vols.

        Includes 3,691 entries.   A major source that includes
entries for early fife music, songs, music of the Shakers, and
musicians such as John Anderson. Although the contents are listed
in *Resources of American Music History* (see entry 175), the
annotations here are more lengthy. Contents are also cited in *18th-
Century American Secular Music Manuscripts* (see entry 172).

182.   Butterfield, Lee S.   "Music in the Moravian Museum." *Moravian Music Journal* 30/1 (Spring 1985): 20-22.

Discusses musical instruments in the Moravian Museum in Bethlehem, Pa.   Photos.

183.   *A Checklist of Keyboard Instruments at the Smithsonian Institution.*   Comp. by Cynthia Adams Hoover.   2nd ed. Washington, D.C.: Smithsonian Institution, 1975.   87p.

The catalog includes a number of instruments made in the United States before 1820, including those of Charles Albrecht (Philadelphia), William Bent (Boston), John Geib (New York), Eben Goodrich (Boston), John Harper (Philadelphia), and others.

184.   Clark, Stephen.   *A Catalogue of the Annapolis Circulating Library* (Annapolis, 1783).

Included here as an example of an early library catalog of some 1,500 books, including John Hawkins' "General history of the science and practice of music," Charles Burney's "tour through Germany" and "France and Italy," and a number of collections of songs.   Reprinted in *Early American Imprints*, no. 17872 (see entry 43).

185.   Claypool, Richard D.   "Archival Collections of the Moravian Music Foundation and Some Notes on the Philharmonic Society of Bethlehem." *Fontes Artis Musicae* 23/4 (October-December 1976): 177-90.

Includes historical background of the Moravians, but principally the musical contents of the Archive.   Included is a handy list of major collections, manuscripts copied by Immanuel Nitschmann, items with Johann Friedrich Peter's signature on them, and a list of "payments for music listed in Collegium Musicum account books."

186.   Claypool, Richard D. and Robert F. Steelman.   "The Music Collections in the Moravian Archives." *Transactions of the Moravian Historical Society* 23/2 (1979): 13-49.

Discusses the Moravians and their music collections.

187.   Claypool, Richard D.   "Rare Music in the Philharmonic Society
        Collection." *Moravian Music Foundation Bulletin* 22/1
        (Spring-Summer 1977): 2-5.

Discusses rare compositions in the Moravian Archives by non-
Moravian musicians, including a Symphony in E-flat Major by the
Philadelphia composer, Charles Hommann.

188.   *Computer Catalog of Nineteenth-Century American-Imprint Sheet
        Music for the University of Virginia.* Charlottesville:
        University of Virginia, 1977.   2 vols., with typescript
        index compiled by Lynn T. McRae (12p.); available also, 8
        microfiche; 11 x 15 cm.

An example of a computer-generated list that provides a rich
source of data which can be used to complement the Wolfe
bibliography (see entry 126).   Includes 7,700 titles for the
collection held in the Rare Book Room of the Alderman Library.   Some
32 different categories are available for various retrieval
strategies.   Lists title, composer, arranger, editor, lyricist,
publisher, city, address, date, plate number, and other imprint
data.   A copy is available in the Performing Arts Reading Room of
the Library of Congress.

189.   Crawford, Richard and H. Wiley Hitchcock.   *The Papers of
        Andrew Law in the William L. Clements Library.*   Bulletin [of
        the William L. Clements Library], 68.   Ann Arbor: University
        of Michigan, 1961.   13p.

The collection comprises some 1,900 items, including
letters, accounts, manuscript music, memoranda, and other items.
This guide describes principal facets of the collection as well as
providing biographical information on Andrew Law.

190.   Cumnock, Frances, ed.   *Catalog of the Salem Congregation
        Music.*   Chapel Hill: University of North Carolina Press,
        1980.   ix, 682p.

A catalog of extant music of the Moravian Congregation
Collection and Sisters Collection in the Moravian Music Foundation
Archives in Winston-Salem, North Carolina.   The author provides
composers' names, titles, musical incipits, and other pertinent
information.   Indexes of composers and titles.

191.   Cumnock, Frances.   "The Salem Congregation Collection: 1790-
         1808." *Moravian Music Foundation Bulletin* 17/1 (Spring-
         Summer 1972): 1-4.

       Information on the formation of the collection, composers
represented in it, and its principal compiler, Johannes Reuz (1752-
1810).

192.   Dinneen, William.   "Early American Manuscript Music-Books."
         Musical Quarterly 30/1 (January 1944): 50-62.

       Discusses a manuscript book compiled by Eunice Carew in
Norwich, Conn. in 1790; a manuscript owned by Ellen Maria Byrne in
Philadelphia in 1797; and a manuscript owned by Sussana Mueller in
Lititz, Pa. in 1800.   These manuscripts are held in the Harris
Collection of American Poetry at Brown University, Providence, R.I.

193.   Filby, P. William.   "Music in the Maryland Historical
         Society." *Notes* 32/3 (March 1976): 503-17.

       Discusses key printed and manuscript collections
representing the 18th and 19th centuries.   Mentions imprints of
Joseph Carr (1794-1819), Thomas Carr (1819-23), and John Cole (1799-
1855).   Facsimiles.

194.   Finney, Theodore M.   "The Psalmody Controversy: A Catalogue."
         *Perspective: A Journal of the Pittsburgh Theological
         Seminary* 9/3 (Fall 1968): 286-96.

       A bibliography of books on psalmody from 1780-1924 in the
Warrington Collection in Hymnology in the Clifford E. Barbour
Library of the Pittsburgh Theological Seminary.

195.   Ford, Worthington C.   "The Isaiah Thomas Collection of
         Ballads." *Proceedings of the American Antiquarian Society*
         33/1 (1923): 34-112.

       Consists of over 300 broadsides presented to the American
Antiquarian Society by Isaiah Thomas.

196. Fuld, James J. "Surrounded by One's Friends." *Notes* 32/3
      (March 1976): 479-90.

      Fuld, an authority and collector of 18th-19th-century
American music, describes and lists the contents of his personal
collection, including manuscripts from the 18th century, tunebooks,
and other printed sheet music from the period. (See also entry 172.)

197. Geil, Jean. "American Sheet Music in the Walter N.H. Harding
      Collection at the Bodleian Library, Oxford University."
      Notes 34/4 (June 1978): 805-13.

      The collection consists of over 60,000 pieces of sheet music
representing the period ca. 1790-1924. Geil describes the
collection and includes a list of subject categories.

198. Gombosi, Marilyn, ed. *Catalog of the Johannes Herbst
      Collection.* Chapel Hill: University of North Carolina,
      1970. xix, 225p.

      The Johannes Herbst (1735-1812) Collection is held in the
Moravian Archives in Winston-Salem, N.C. The collection consists of
close to 500 manuscripts of some 1,000 anthems and arias that were
apparently used in Moravian church services. Each entry includes
thematic incipit, instrumentation, and other information. Refer to
the corrections noted in a review in *Notes* 29/2 (December 1972), pp.
258-59. Should be used in conjunction with Joan O. Falconer's
dissertation on Johannes Herbst (see entry 1796). Refer also to *The
Johannes Herbst Collection* (see entry 201).

199. *Guide to the Lester S. Levy Collection of Sheet Music.*
      Introd. by Lester S. Levy. Baltimore: Milton S. Eisenhower
      Library, Johns Hopkins University, 1984. viii, 40p.

      The collection is housed in the Special Collections
Division, Eisenhower Library, and includes 190 boxes of some 30,000
sheets of music as well as 55 bound volumes of music. The guide
lists 38 topics from "Baltimore Publishers" to "World War I";
facsimiles of sheet music covers representing most topics. (See
also entry 205.)

200. Heintze, James R. "Music of the Washington Family: A Little-
Known Collection." *Musical Quarterly* 56/2 (April 1970):
288-93.

Discusses the collection of late 18th- and early 19th-
century sheet music in the George Washington Masonic Museum,
Alexandria, Va. Individuals discussed include George, Anne, and
Bushrod Washington, John J. Frobel, and others.

201. *The Johannes Herbst Collection.* New York: University Music
Editions, 1976. Microfiche with index (29p.). Also
available in rollfilm edition.

The complete collection of manuscripts held in the Archives
of the Moravian Music Foundation, Winston-Salem, N.C. Period spans
ca. 1752-1812. Includes over 1,000 musical works (11,676p.). Four
principal sections: "Congregation Music"; "Larger Vocal-Instrumental
Works"; "Miscellaneous Scores"; and "Texts to Congregation Music."
See also *Catalog of the Johannes Herbst Collection* (see entry 198)
and Cumnock (see entry 191).

202. John, Robert W. "The Irving Lowens Collection of American
Tunebooks." *Moravian Music Foundation Bulletin* 16/2 (Fall-
Winter 1971): 1-2.

The collection is located in the Moravian Music Foundation
Archives in Winston-Salem, N.C. Includes a general description.

203. Keck, George Russell. "Pre-1875 American Imprint Sheet Music
in the Ernst C. Krohn Special Collections, Gaylord Music
Library, Washington University, St. Louis, Missouri: A
Catalog and Descriptive Study." Ph.D. dissertation,
University of Iowa, 1982. 973p. UM 82-222245. *DAI* 43/4
(October 1982): 967-A.

Includes a history of sheet music published before 1875, a
discussion of illustrated covers, a catalog of the collection (5,120
items) arranged alphabetically by composer, with full imprint data.
Represented are 325 different publishers. Some of the citations
represent the pre-1820 period. There are indexes for publishers,
music engravers and printers, and lithographers and artists.

204. Kramer, Marilyn M. and Elaine K. Pease. "Harrisburg Imprints
      from the German American Imprint Collection in the Franklin
      and Marshall College Library." *Journal of the Lancaster
      County Historical Society* 85/2 (Easter 1981): 63-80.

A total of 181 books from 1797 to 1897. Includes Joseph
Doll's *Leichter Unterricht in der vocal Musik* (John Wyeth, 1814);
Lieder die bey der Evangelisch Lutherischen Synodal-Versammlung
(Johann S. Wiestling, 1818); and Isaac Gerhart's *Choral-Harmonie*
(John Wyeth, 1818).

205. Levy, Lester S. "Recollections of a Sheet Music Collector."
      Notes 32/3 (March 1976): 491-502.

The Lester S. Levy Collection of sheet music is located in
the Eisenhower Library, Johns Hopkins University, Baltimore, Md.
Levy describes how he collected the music, much of which constitutes
18th-century imprints, and how it is arranged. Facsimiles. (See
also entry 199.)

206. Lindsley, Charles Edward. "An Important Tunebook Collection
      in California." *Notes* 29/4 (June 1973): 671-74.

An introduction to the 650 tunebooks in the Robert G.
McCutchan Collection of Hymns and Hymnology in the Honnold Library
for the Claremont Colleges.

207. Lowens, Irving. "The Warrington Collection: A Research
      Adventure at Case Memorial Library." *Hartford Seminary
      Foundation Bulletin* 12 (January 1952): 29-38.

The James Warrington Collection is a significant early
American tunebook collection which, according to Thomas Warner (see
entry 123), is now held in Emory University in Atlanta, Georgia.
Reprinted in Lowens, *Music and Musicians in Early America* (see entry
371).

208. *Manuscript Sources in the Library of Congress for Research on
      the American Revolution.* Comp. by John R. Sellers,
      Gerald W. Gawalt, Paul H. Smith, and Patricia Molen van Ee.
      Washington, D.C.: Library of Congress, 1975. 372p.

Includes 1,617 entries consisting of original manuscripts, microfilms, and other reproductions. Two principal sections: "Domestic Collections" and "Foreign Reproductions." Includes 7 entries under the heading "Music" in the subject index. Subjects include "Revolutionary War Songs and Ballads," "Hymnbooks," "Account Books," "Journals," "Diaries," and other manuscript papers.

209.   "Music Archives' Rarities: Bach Family Works Found." *Moravian Music Foundation Bulletin* 2/2 (Spring-Summer 1958): 1, 4.

Describes and lists briefly works by members of the Bach family discovered by Donald M. McCorkle in the Moravian Archives in America in 1955.

210.   "Music Archives' Rarities: Manuscripts Discovered in Nazareth Moravian Church." *Moravian Music Foundation Bulletin* 4/3 (Fall 1960): 1, 4.

The first announcement of the discovery of musical works found in the Moravian Church in Nazareth, Pa. in 1960. Describes contents, including works by John Antes, Johannes Herbst, Johann Friedrich Peter, and others.

211.   Pedley, Avril J.M. *The Manuscript Collections of the Maryland Historical Society*. Baltimore: Maryland Historical Society, 1968. xii, 390p.

A standard reference work for the study of music in colonial and federal Maryland. Includes references to music manuscripts, instruments, musical societies and clubs beginning with the Annapolis Tuesday Club musicians around 1750. See entries under "Music," and "Songs and Ballads." Contents are cited in *Resources of American Music History* (see entry 175).

212.   Pike, Kermit J. *A Guide to the Manuscripts and Archives of the Western Reserve Historical Society*. Cleveland: Western Reserve Historical Society, 1972. xviii, 425p.

Includes references to a number of early 19th-century music items. Refer to the index under "Music and music societies." Contents also cited in *Resources of American Music History* (see entry 175). See also Pike's supplement, *A Guide to Major*

Manuscript Collections Accessioned and Processed by the Library of the Western Reserve Historical Society since 1970 (Cleveland: The Society, 1987).   See also entry 1329.

213.   Rau, Albert F. and Hans T. David.   *A Catalogue of Music by American Moravians, 1742-1842.*   Bethlehem, Pa.: 1938. Reprint, New York: AMS Press, 1970.   118p.

Based on the holdings at the Archives of the Moravian Church at Bethlehem, Pa.   Anthems for the following composers are listed: John Frederick Peter, Jacob van Vleck, John Christian Till, George Godfrey Müller, Johannes Herbst, David Moritz Michael, Johann Christian Bechler, Peter Ricksecker, Peter Wolle, Francis Florentine Hagen, and others.   Each entry includes imprint data and is annotated with commentary.   Musical examples.

214.   "Recent Discoveries in the Foundation Archives."   *Moravian Music Foundation Bulletin* 19/1 (Spring-Summer 1974): 3.

Describes discoveries in the Moravian Archives in Winston-Salem, N.C., including a first edition of "The Star-Spangled Banner" (Baltimore, 1814) and works by Jeremiah Dencke.

215.   Rice, Albert R.   "Instrumental Tutors and Treatises at Winston-Salem."   *Moravian Music Journal* 30/2 (Fall 1985): 34-35.

Discusses the Moravian Music Foundation collection of 41 instruction books "for no less than thirty-three instruments," published 1800-1910.   Includes mention of a rare copy of George E. Blake's *New Instructions for the Piano Forte* (Philadelphia: E. Blake, ca. 1818).

216.   Rose, Kenneth.   "The Story of a Music Collection."   *Tennessee Historical Quarterly* 15 (1956): 356-63.

Rose discusses his collection of sheet music representing the 1790s on.

217. Schrader, Arthur F. "Broadside Ballads of Boston, 1813: The Isaiah Thomas Collection." *Proceedings of the American Antiquarian Society* 98/1 (1988): 69-111.

Discusses a gift of a few hundred broadsides (no music, but 19 tunes named) by Isaiah Thomas to the American Antiquarian Society in 1814. The author names Thomas as "the first known broadside ballad 'collector' in the United States." An excellent article that details the problems involved in matching a tune with a broadside text.

218. Skemer, Don C. and Robert C. Morris. *Guide to the Manuscript Collections of the New Jersey Historical Society.* Newark: New Jersey Historical Society, 1979. 245p.

Includes 1,057 entries. A useful guide with a number of items pertaining to early American music, including: poems set to music by Richard Davis, ca. 1790-97; lyrics for a song titled "A Song of the Times," ca. 1776-78; a collection of New Jersey music from 1811-30. Begin a search in the index under the heading "Music."

219. Steelman, Robert, ed. *Catalog of the Lititz Congregation Collection.* Chapel Hill: University of North Carolina Press, 1981. 488p.

Includes 530 entries. Although Lititz, Pa. was a small colonial Moravian town, the musical activities that took place there were extensive. This catalog serves as a testament to those activities. It is based in part on catalogs that date back to Johannes Herbst's own catalog dated 1794. Each item cites composer, musical incipit, and annotation. Included are both European and American composers, the latter including John Antes, Johann Christian Bechler, Jeremiah Dencke, Johannes Herbst, and others. Facsimiles. Composer and title indexes.

220. Stokes, Allen H., Jr. *A Guide to the Manuscript Collection of the South Carolinian Library.* Columbia: University of South Carolina, 1982. xvi, 493p.

Describes a number of music items, including an Eliza Smith music book (ms., 1805). Begin a search under the heading "Music and Musicians" in the index.

221.   Upton, William Treat.   "Eighteenth Century American Imprints
       in the Society's Dielman Collection of Music."   *Maryland
       Historical Magazine* 35/4 (December 1940): 374-81.

       Describes 18th-century American sheet music in the Louis H.
Dielman Collection in the Maryland Historical Society, Baltimore,
Md.   Consists of both vocal and instrumental music, including works
by Benjamin Carr, John B. Gauline, James Hewitt, W. Langdon,
Alexander Reinagle, and Rayner Taylor.

222.   Wood, David A.   *Music in Harvard Libraries: A Catalogue
       of Early Printed Music and Books on Music in the
       Houghton Library and the Eda Kuhn Loeb Music Library.*
       Cambridge: Harvard University Press, 1980.   xiv,
       306p.

       Includes 1,628 entries.   Mostly European music but does
contain a few entries on early American music.   Bibliography and
index (names only).

Exhibition Catalogs and Literature

Exhibition catalogs are excellent sources for obtaining information
and illustrations on early American music and instruments not
described elsewhere.   Unfortunately, such catalogs are not always
easy to identify or locate.   Copies of catalogs are often discarded
or misplaced after an exhibit is dismantled.   Fortunately, a number
of indexes, such as *RILM* (see entry 148), have made an effort in
recent years to include citations for exhibit catalogs.   Check the
index under the heading "Exhibitions."   *Library Literature* (see
entry 138) is another source for similar citations.   Check entries
under the heading "Music—Exhibits and Displays."   See also *America:
History and Life* (see entry 129) under the heading "Exhibits and
Expositions" in the subject index.   Refer also to James Coover's
Musical Instrument Collections: Catalogues and Cognate Literature
(see entry 169) for additional exhibit catalogs.

223.   Albrecht, Otto E.   *Francis Hopkinson, Musician, Poet and
       Patriot: 1737-1937.*   Reprinted from the Library Chronicle of
       the University of Pennsylvania, vol. 6, no. 1, March 1938.
       15p. (Copy in Library of Congress: ML 410.H81A7.)

An exhibition guide and essay accompanying an exhibit "to celebrate the bicentennial of the birth of Francis Hopkinson, the first graduate of the University of Pennsylvania. . ." held at the library December 1937. The exhibit included manuscripts, books, music, and other documents. No illustrations.

224. *American Patriotic Songs: Yankee Doodle to The Conquered Banner with Emphasis on The Star-Spangled Banner. An Exhibition Held at The Lilly Library, Indiana University, Bloomington, July-September 1968.* Foreword by David A. Randall. [45p.] (Copy in Library of Congress: ML 141.B55L5.)

Consists of descriptions and facsimiles of sheet music from the Federal period through the Civil War, including War of 1812 songsheets. Examples of facsimiles prior to 1820 include: "New Yankee Doodle" (Boston: P.A. von Hagen, 1799-1800); "Adams & Washington A New Patriotic Song" by P.A. von Hagen, Jr. (Boston, 1797-98); "Washington's March" (Boston: G. Graupner, ca. 1803); "Hail Columbia. A Patriotic Song, Sung by Mr. Williamson. . ." (New York: G. Gilfert, ca. 1798); "Song of Liberty," broadside, ca. 1800; "The Siege of Tripoli" by Benjamin Carr (Philadelphia: Carr & Schetky, 1804-05; "Our Rights on the Ocean, or Hull, Jones, Decatur & Bainbridge" by John Bray (Philadelphia: G.E. Blake, 1813); "Death of Commodore O.H. Perry. Deplored as a National Misfortune" by Oliver Shaw (Providence: O. Shaw, 1820?); "Elegiac Verse to the Memory of James Lawrence" by Francis Arden (New York: E. Riley, 1814); "Wreaths to the Chieftain" by L.M. Sargent (Boston: G.K. Jackson, 1815).

225. "Anacreon Revisited." New-York Historical Society, Fall 1981. Prepared by Jean Bowen. No formal catalog exists.

Discussed in *Institute for Studies in American Music Newsletter* 11/1 (November 1981), p. 5.

226. *The Art of Music: American Paintings and Musical Instruments, 1770-1910.* Clinton, N.Y.: Fred L. Emerson Gallery, Hamilton College, 1984. Essays by Michael Edward Shapiro, Frederick R. Selch, H. Nichols, G. Clark, and Celia Betsky. (Copy in Library of Congress: ND 1460.M87A77.)

227.   *Billings to Joplin: Popular Music in 19th Century America: An
       Exhibition March-May 1980.*   Arranged and described by
       Margaret F. Sax.   Hartford, Conn.: Watkinson Library,
       Trinity College, 1980.   32p.

Includes 92 items.   Case 1: Tunesmiths and Singing Schools;
7 items, print and manuscript.   Case 2: Early 19th Century Songs and
Dances; 6 items, music and songsters.   Case 3: Shape Notes and
Revivals; 10 items.   A brief note regarding this exhibit is found in
Institute for Studies in American Music Newsletter 9/2 (May 1980),
p. 10.

228.   Bryant, Carolyn.   *And the Band Played On: 1776-1976.*
       Washington, D.C.: Smithsonian Institution Press, 1975.   54p.

"This publication accompanies an exhibition developed by the
Smithsonian Institution Traveling Exhibition Service as a
Bicentennial celebration of the colorful and varied history of
American bands."   Includes 3 chapters.   Chapter 1 focuses on "Early
American Bands," and includes facsimiles of manuscript and printed
music, such as "Yankee Doodle" (1799) from the *Bellamy Band Music
Book.*

229.   Campbell, Frank C.   "How the Music Division of the New York
       Public Library Grew—A Memoir.   Part IV: Exhibitions 1966-
       1980; Columbian Gems: American Musical Rarities in the New
       York Public Library."   *Notes* 38/1 (September 1981): 38-39.

This exhibit was held in celebration of the Bicentennial on
October 1976-February 1977 at the Vincent Astor Gallery and was
organized by Richard Jackson, John Shepard, and Tema Hecht.   "The
major portion of the exhibition, which included 150 items, was a
selection of manuscripts of American composers and early published
editions in book and sheet music form.   The books included the *Bay
Psalm Book* (1742), Billings' *New-England Psalm-Singer* (with an
engraving by Paul Revere, 1770), and the *Singing Book* of Kentucky
pioneer Joshua Watkins (1809).   Sheet music included "The Star
Spangled Banner" (first printing), and "The President's March"
(first edition, 1793).   No formal catalog exists, but a number of
items, in addition to those cited above, are listed in this article.

230.   *Catalogue of the Exhibition.*   Horticultural Hall, Boston,
       January 11 to 26, 1902.   Foreword signed "Chickering &

Sons." [Boston: Barta Press, 1902].   78p.   (Copy in Library
of Congress: ML 141.B8H8.)

Includes 1,346 items.   Mostly musical instruments and some
tunebooks, including: 111. "A View of Modern Psalmody" (ms.) by
William Cole; 118. *Columbian and European Harmony* by Bartholomew
Brown, 1804; 125. "America" (ms) by Samuel F. Smith; 131.
Massachusetts Harmony (Boston, 1803); 288. *The Minstrel* by John Cole
(Baltimore, 1812); 1241 *Christian Psalmody in Four Parts, etc.* by
Samuel Worcester (Boston, 1819); and tunebooks by Thomas Walter and
William Billings.   Photos of instruments.   Published literature on
this exhibit includes "Historical Musical Exhibition" in *Violinist*
2/7 (March 1902), p. 7, and "The Historical Musical Exhibition" in
Musical Courier 1141 (1902).

231.   *Catching the Tune: Music and William Sidney Mount.*   Ed. by
Janice Gray Armstrong.   Stony Brook, N.Y.: The Museums,
1984.   67p.

A stunning exhibition guide in the form of four essays by
Martha V. Pike, Peter G. Buckley, M. Hunt Hessler, and Laurence
Libin, describing the music and social environment of William Sidney
Mount, "America's first genre painter of international reknown."
Included are some of his paintings depicting early American music
subjects, as well as photographs of musical instruments, and
facsimiles of music and newspaper advertisements and playbills.
Bibliography.   For additional information on this exhibit, which
accompanied the conference "Music and Dance in 19th Century America:
Traditional and Popular Entertainment, 1800-1860," held at the State
University of New York at Stony Brook, see the article, "Catching
the Tune," in *Sonneck Society Newsletter* 11 (Spring 1985), pp. 7-8.

232.   Cipolla, Frank J. and Raoul F. Camus.   *Oom Pah Pah: The Great
American Band.*   Foreword by George Weissman and Mary Black.
Exhibit held at The New-York Historical Society, July 1-
November 7, 1982; Dallas Historical Society, January 5-
February 13, 1983; New York State Museum, Albany, March 7-
May 29, 1983; Milwaukee Public Museum, June 25-August 14,
1983.   16p.

A history of the band during the 18th-20th centuries.   Pre-
1820 topics include British regimental bands in American colonial
towns and Francis Johnson, leader of the Washington Guards Band in
Philadelphia.   16 illustrations.

233. *The Conservatory of Music, University of Missouri-Kansas City
      Presents Treasures from the Collection of the Institute for
      Studies in American Music.* Prepared by Jack L. Ralston for
      the Grolier Club, May 15, 1972. 20p. (Copy in Library of
      Congress: ML 141.K316.)

Includes 94 items. Organized into 12 tables covering a
broad spectrum of American music. Table 10 is titled "Colonial
America" and includes the following pre-1820 works: "Rudiments of
the Art of Playing On the Piano Forte, Containing Elements of Music,
Preliminary Remarks On Fingering with Examples, Thirty Fingered
Lessons, and a Plain Direction for Tuning. Arranged by Gottlieb
Graupner" (Boston, 1806); "Hark! from the Tombs, &c., and Beneath
the Honors, &c" by Samuel Holyoke (H. Ranlet, 1800); *Bickerstaff's
Genuine Boston Almanack; or Federal Calendar* (1768); "President's
March and Ca Ira" by Philip Phile (Philadelphia: Carr & Co., 1793 or
94); "The Star Spangled Banner" (New York: Geib & Co., 1816 or 17);
"Divertimenti, or Familiar Lessons for the Piano Forte" by Rayner
Taylor (Philadelphia: Carr, 1797?); "A Sonata for the Piano Forte
with an Accompaniment for a Violin" by Raynor Taylor (Philadelphia:
Carr, 1797). Table 12 is titled "Oblong Tune Books" and contains
the following pre-1820 items: *Federal Harmony* (5th ed.) by Asahel
Benham (Middletown, Conn.: M.H. Woodward, 1795?); *The Missouri
Harmony*, compiled by Allen B. Carden (St. Louis: Carden, 1820); *The
Northampton Collection of Sacred Harmony* by Elias Mann (Northampton,
Mass.: Daniel Wright and Company, 1797); *The Village Harmony* (11th
ed; Newburyport, Mass.: C. Norris & Co., 1813); *The Psalms of David*
by Isaac Watts (Exeter, N.H.: J.J. Williams, 1818).

234. Davison, Nancy R. *American Sheet Music Illustration:
      Reflections of the Nineteenth Century. A Guide to an
      Exhibition in the Museum of Art, October 12-November 18,
      1973.* Ann Arbor: University of Michigan, William L.
      Clements Library, 1973. 24p.

The exhibition was based on the Corning Collection of some
30,000 pieces of sheet music, dating from the 1790s to 1900. The
guide has only 4 illustrations, but does describe the works
displayed in a chronological narrative format.

235. *An Exhibit of Music and Materials on Music Early and Rare.*
      Presented in Honor of the Midwest Chapters, American
      Musicological Society and Music Library Association, April
      17-19, 1953, with the Cooperation of the Library of

Congress, the Newberry Library, the University of Illinois
Libraries, the Sibley Musical Library. Iowa City: State
University of Iowa, 1953. 39p. (Copy in the Music Library,
University of Pittsburgh: R ML 141 I6I6x.)

Includes 100 items. Section D, "Tune Books of the 17th and
18th Centuries," includes Thomas Sternhold and John Hopkins, *The
Whole Book of Psalmes* (London, 1605); William Tansur, *The Psalm-
Singer's Jewell* (London: Printed for S. Crowder, 1760; on last page
of text "Boston, March 12, 1761"); William Tansur, *The American
Harmony: or, Royal Melody Compleat* (5th ed.; Newbury-Port: D.
Bayley, 1769); Andrew Law, *A Select Number of Plaine Tunes Adapted
to Congregational Worship* (Boston: Kneeland and Adams, 1767?);
William Billings, *The Psalm-Singer's Amusement* (Boston, 1781);
William Billings, *The Continental Harmony* (Boston: Isaiah Thomas and
Ebenezer T. Andrews, 1794); *The American Musical Miscellany*
(Northampton, Mass.: Andrew Wright, 1798).

236.   Fesperman, John T. *Organs in Early America* [exhibition
             brochure]. Washington, D.C.: Division of Musical
             Instruments, Smithsonian Institution, 1968. [5p.].

237.   Filby, P.W. and Edward G. Howard. *Star-Spangled Books: Books,
             Sheet Music, Newspapers, Manuscripts, and Persons Associated
             with "The Star-Spangled Banner."* Baltimore: Maryland
             Historical Society, 1972.

        An exhibition catalog.

238.   *Four Centuries of Music: An Exhibit.* Chapin Library,
             Williams College, May 1950. Prepared by Joaquin Nin-
             Culmell. 33p. Copy in Library of Congress (ML 141.W5W5)

        Focuses primarily on European music. Annotated. Includes
Sternhold-Hopkins, *The Whole Book of Psalmes* (1604); *The Psalms, for
the Use of the Reformed Protestant Dutch Church of the City of New
York* (New York: J. Parker, 1767); Oliver Holden, *Sacred Dirges,
Hymns and Anthems, Commemorative of the Death of General Washington*
(Boston: I. Thomas and E.T. Andrews, 1800); Andrew Law, *Select
Harmony* (New Haven, 1779).

239. *The Harmonious Craft: American Musical Instruments.* Organized
      and held at the Renwick Gallery, Washington, D.C., September
      29, 1978-August 5, 1979. James M. Weaver, curator of the
      exhibit. 80 slides and audio cassette with printed guide
      (9p.). Washington, D.C.: Smithsonian Institution, 1979.

      Includes banjos, a glass harmonica, and a selection of folk
instruments. See also the article based on the exhibit "The
Harmonious Craft: American Musical Instruments" in *Guitar and Lute* 8
(January 1979), p. 33.

240. Jackson, Richard. "Musical Treasures in American Libraries:
      An Exhibition in the Vincent Astor Gallery." *Bulletin of
      the New York Public Library* 72/7 (September 1968): 428-41.

      This exhibition accompanied a joint meeting of the
International Music Council and the International Association of
Music Libraries and took place in New York July 10-September 24,
1968, and focused on a broad spectrum of musical manuscripts and
publications borrowed from 14 American libraries. Included in the
exhibit was a copy of the 9th edition of the *Bay Psalm Book* from the
Massachusetts Historical Society in Boston. The work is described
in this article. A brief description of the exhibition is printed
in *Notes* 38/1 (September 1981), p. 23.

241. Kass, Philip. "Exhibition of Pre-1900 American String
      Instruments." *Journal of the Violin Society of America* 2/4
      (Fall 1976): 70-83.

      Exhibit at the Proceedings of the Fourth Annual Convention,
Violin Society of America, Philadelphia, November 12-14, 1976. A
variety of repositories and individuals contributed to this exhibit.
The article consists of an essay on the history and background of
the manufacturing and availability of string instruments in America.
The catalog is arranged by categories: instruments, manufacturers,
music (print and manuscript), and method books. Some of the items
include: violin (Philadelphia: Peter Young, 1778); violin (Boston:
A. Smith, 1800); violin (Philadelphia: John G. Klemm, 1820s);
violoncello (Philadelphia: W.E. Wolf, 1803); "Six Duettos" and
"Overture to the Harlequin's Invasion" by Alexander Reinagle; and
"Medley Overture" by James Hewitt.

242. *Land Marks of American Music History: An Exhibit in Honor of Oscar George Sonneck, 1873-1928.* Prepared by Jack L. Ralston. The University of Missouri-Kansas City, Friends of the Library, Festival of the Book. October 13-14, 1973. 8p. (Copy in the Library of the University of Missouri-Kansas City.)

"This exhibit and annotated bibliography are based on a paper read by Mr. Irving Lowens at Old Sturbridge, Massachusetts May 5, 1973 entitled 'Early American Music: What's Left to be Done?'" Exhibited were 40 books dated 1898-1971 and considered noteworthy in American music.

243. *Music in Colonial America: An Exhibition Opened at the John Carter Brown Library, November 14, 1975.* Providence, R.I.: Brown University, 1975. 33p.

Based on holdings of the Brown Library for the period 1630s-1790s. Includes the following 8 cases: "Sacred Music and Native Sacred Music"; "Andrew Law and Sacred Music Established"; "Secular Music and Musical Theatre"; "Music in Providence and Sally Brown"; "African Music"; "Mexican Music"; "Indian Music"; and "Indian Ritual." Five panels are titled: "Instrumental Music"; "Sailors, Scots and Sports"; "Love, Ah Sweet Love"; "Love, Woeful Love"; and "Patriotic Music."

244. *Musical Instruments and Their Portrayal in Art.* Baltimore: Baltimore Museum of Art, April 26-June 2, 1946. 48p. (Copy in Library of Congress: ML 141.B15M8.)

Has 156 items covering a broad spectrum of works of art. The purpose of this exhibit was ". . . to present a survey of important musical instruments and their gradual development together with paintings and sculpture depicting them." Includes an essay on "Baltimore's Contribution to the Development of the Pianoforte." In addition to American paintings which depict musical instruments, the following are included: 120. Piano, maker James Stewart (Baltimore, ca. 1814-1820); 126-130. Five transverse flutes inscribed C.H. Eisenbrandt (1810-57); 145. Psalm Starter, used in the First Congregational Church of Williamstown, Mass. (1768); 149. Drum (ca. 1814) used at the Battle of North Point, September 12, 1814.

245.   North, Louise J.   *The Psalms and Hymns of Protestantism from the Sixteenth to the Nineteenth Century: An Introduction to the History of Protestant Hymnody as Illustrated by an Exhibition in the Library of Drew University, in June, 1936.* Madison: Drew University, 1936.   12p.

Includes a Sternhold and Hopkins psalter, the *Bay Psalm Book*, hymnbooks of Isaac Watts, Methodist hymnbooks, including Melchior Steiner's *Hymns and Spiritual Songs* (Philadelphia, 1753), and other works.

246.   Ochs, Michael.   "Musical Americana in Harvard Libraries: An Exhibition Honoring the Sonneck Society."   *Harvard Library Bulletin* 32/4 (Fall 1984): 408-426.

The catalog, for the exhibition of March 19 to April 6, 1984, was originally a typewritten list and is printed here with added introduction, footnotes, and illustrations.   "The exhibition drew upon the resources of six units of the Harvard University Library system and the Schloesinger Library on the History of Women in America, at Radcliffe College.   It showed a cross-section of the University's printed and manuscript materials that document America's musical life."   Topics include "New England Psalmody, 1640-1770" (8 items); "Sacred Music, 1752-1846" (8 items); "Patriotic Songs" (7 items); "Boston Musical Life, 1808-1825" (5 items); "Secular Publishing, 1786-1826" (6 items); "Secular Music, 1832-1878" (6 items); "Music in the Theatre, 1752-1814" (7 items); and additional 19th and 20th-century topics.   Each item cited is annotated.   Refer to a review of this exhibit in *Sonneck Society Newsletter* 12 (Spring 1986), p. 11.

247.   *The Printed Note: 500 Years of Music Printing and Engraving.* The Toledo Museum of Art, January 14-February 24, 1957. Foreword by A. Beverly Barksdale.   144p.

Includes 188 items.   "This exhibition, *The Printed Note*, attempts to show the various processes used since the second half of the 15th century for reproducing music mechanically in books and scores.   Many of the leading libraries of America and several abroad have made available items of great rarity and some which are unique."   In the section "Americana" are the following: 169.   *Bay Psalm Book* (1698 ed.), Massachusetts Historical Society; 170.   John Tufts, *An Introduction to the Singing of Psalm-Tunes* (Boston: Samuel Gerrish, 1726), Boston Public Library; 171.   Thomas Walter, *The*

Grounds and Rules of Music Explained (Boston: F. Franklin, 1721), Massachusetts Historical Society; 172. *Geistreicher Lieder* (Germantown: Christoph Saur, 1752), Historical Society of Pennsylvania; 173. Josiah Flagg, *Psalm Tunes* (Boston, 1764), Newberry Library; 174. Francis Hopkinson, *The Psalms of David* (New York: James Parker, 1767), Pierpont Morgan Library; 175. William Billings, *The New-England Psalm-Singer* (Boston: Edes and Gill, 1770), Clements Library, University of Michigan; 176. William Billings, *The Psalm Singer's Amusement* (Boston: Billings, 1781), Newberry Library; 177. William Billings, *The Suffolk Harmony* (Boston: J. Norman, 1786), Houghton Library, Harvard University; 178. Francis Hopkinson, *Seven Songs for the Harpsichord or Forte Piano* (Philadelphia: T. Dobson, 1788), Toledo Museum of Art; 179. Abraham Wood, *Divine Songs* (Boston: Isaiah Thomas, 1789), Houghton Library, Harvard University; 180. Jacob French, *The New American Harmony* (Boston: John Norman, 1789), Houghton Library, Harvard University; 181. William Cooper, "An Anthem Designed for Thanksgiving Day" (Boston: Isaiah Thomas and Ebenezer T. Andrews, 1792), Clements Library, University of Michigan; 182. William Little and William Smith, *The Easy Instructor* (New York: G. and R. Waite, 1802), Case Memorial Library, Hartford Seminary Foundation. Includes descriptions and some facsimiles of the items. Bibliography.

248.　*Ring the Banjar!: The Banjo in America from Folklore to Factory.* Robert Lloyd Webb, exhibition curator. Cambridge: MIT Museum, Massachusetts Institute of Technology, 1984. ix, 101p.

"Published in conjunction with the exhibition of the same name, 12 April-29 September 1984, in the MIT Museum Compton Gallery, Cambridge, Massachusetts." Includes photographs of a sketch of a gourd banjo drawn in 1819; four-string gourd banjo (ca. 1770?); a four-string banjo (ca. 1800?). There are descriptions of the instruments and essays, including "The Banjo Makers of Boston" by James F. Bollman; the latter are not indexed. See *Institute for Studies in American Music Newsletter* 14/1 (November 1984), p. 5, for additional information on this exhibit.

249.　Roy, G. James, Jr. "The BMI/Haverlin Archives Go Abroad." *Fontes Artis Musicae* 24/2 (April-June 1977): 76-77.

Background and description of four exhibits that commemorated the Bicentennial and were displayed in the United

States and Europe.   Themes included history, literature, and music.
Selected items are mentioned in the article.   A brochure titled *The
Carl Haverlin Collection/BMI Archives* (New York, 1976) is available
from the BMI Archives in New York.

250.   *A Souvenir of Romanticism in America; or, An Elegant
        Exposition of Taste and Fashion from 1812 to 1865.*
        Baltimore: Baltimore Museum of Art, May 10-June 10, 1940.
        [72p.]   (Copy in Library of Congress: N 6510.B3.)

        This exhibit catalog includes a brief essay on music of the
19th century, beginning with Anthony Philip Heinrich.   "A Musicale,
comprising the typical compositions, instruments, and foibles of the
Age of Romance outlined above, was presented in the Museum's
auditorium on the nights of May 13, 15 and 17, and the afternoon of
the 19th."   Also mentions a corollary exhibit at Peabody
Conservatory of Music; examples of songs of the period were
displayed.

251.   Thomas, Ruth Colby.   "Music of the Revolutionary Times."
        Daughters of the American Revolution Magazine 118/10
        (December 1984): 721, 773, 790.

        The article provides historical background information on
the exhibit, "Music in the American Home," held December-January 4,
1985 in the DAR Museum.   "This exhibit explores the tradition of
cultivated music in the home," and includes photographs of a chamber
barrel organ, ca. 1800, and a piano made by Charles Taws of
Philadelphia, ca. 1794.   The article also includes information on
William Billings, Francis Hopkinson, and James Lyon.

252.   *Wellsprings of a Nation; America before 1801: A Bicentennial
        Exhibition from the Collections of the American Antiquarian
        Society at the Worcester Art Museum, April 19-June 5, 1977.*
        Text by Rodger D. Parker.   Worcester, Mass.: American
        Antiquarian Society, 1977.   v, 141p.

        The exhibit consisted of historical documents that depicted
those aspects of a new nation that were "to be the model for the
rest of the world to emulate."   This catalog includes 264 items
representing a number of topics.   A section on music includes: *The
New-England Psalm-Singer* (Boston, 1770) and *The Continental Harmony*
(Boston, 1794) by William Billings; *The Rural Harmony* (Boston, 1793)

by Jacob Kimball; *The Art of Singing* (Cheshire, Conn., 1794) by
Andrew Law; *The Archers* (New York, 1796) by Benjamin Carr; "The
Federal Constitution and Liberty for Ever" (New York, 1798); *New
England Harmony* (Northampton, Mass., 1801) by Timothy Swan.   The
catalog contains a number of additional songs and ballads, as well
as the *Bay Psalm Book*.   Illustrations.

253.   *A Yankee Lyre: Musical Instruments by American Makers: An
        Exhibition of Instruments by 19th-Century American Makers
        with Supplementary Exhibits of Graphics, Books, and
        Furniture*.   Presented by the Yale University Collection
        of Musical Instruments.   New Haven, Conn., 1986.   xiii, 62p.

        Illustrations and bibliography.

IV. SPECIAL REFERENCE WORKS

Broadsides

Carleton Sprague Smith in his "Broadsides and Their Music in
Colonial America" in *Music in Colonial Massachusetts* (see entry 533)
defines a broadside "as a single sheet of paper, usually printed on
one side although occasionally on both." Broadsides served as a
fast means of communication, and could be either handed out to
persons in the street or tavern, or posted on public buildings. The
topics communicated were as varied as one can imagine, and included,
for example, notices of society meetings, death notices, lists of
books for sale, and song texts. Given the ephemeral nature of
broadsides, one wonders why so many have survived. It is possibly
due to the sheer quantity that were printed—perhaps many thousands
more than we know. For an essay on the value of broadsides for the
study of American music, see Gillian Anderson's "'Samuel the Priest
Gave Up the Ghost'" (see entry 754). For an article illustrating
the problems and research strategies involved in matching a tune
with a broadside text, refer to Arthur F. Schrader's "Broadside
Ballads of Boston, 1813" (see entry 217). Yet additional
information on broadsides is found in Cynthia Adams Hoover's
"Epilogue to Secular Music in Early Massachusetts," in *Music in
Colonial Massachusetts* (see entry 533). For identifying collections
of broadsides, refer to *Resources of American Music History* (see
entry 175).

254. *Catalog of Broadsides in the Rare Book Division*. Washington,
      D.C.: Library of Congress, 1972. 3 vols. Available on
      microfilm (4 reels). Boston: G.K. Hall, 1972.

      One of the truly significant collections of broadsides,
including some 27,000 items. Some interesting examples are "A New
Song on the Repeal of the Stamp-Act, Tune a Late Worthy Old Lyon"
(Philadelphia, 1766); "American Roast Beef, a Song, Composed for the
4th March, 1801"; and "Odes to be Sung at the Celebration of the
Anniversary of American Independence, July 4, 1811." The Rare Book

Room of the Library of Congress maintains a card index labeled "Broadside Collection Supplement" of items acquired since the publication of this work. Readers should also ask for vertical file material under the heading "Broadsides."

City and Trade Directories

City and trade directories are useful for identifying music teachers, manufacturers of instruments, and other musical occupations. Often such works include illustrations, advertisements, and information not found elsewhere. By the mid-nineteenth century, important regional trade directories began to appear, such as the *The American Musical Directory, 1861* (New York: Thomas Hutchinson, 1861; reprint, with a new introduction by Barbara Owen. New York: Da Capo Press, 1980) and followed by the *Complete Catalogue of Sheet Music and Musical Works, 1870* (Board of Music Trade, 1871; reprint, with a new introduction by Dena J. Epstein. New York: Da Capo Press, 1973). Listed below are the principal sources for identifying directories, as well as some early examples.

255.   Andrews, Frank D. *Directory for the City of Hartford for the Year 1799*. Vineland, N.J.: privately printed, 1910. 34p.

   This directory for Hartford, Conn. includes names and occupations, including: Mr. Allen, "dancing master"; George Catlin, "musical instrument maker"; John Hodgkinson, "actor"; Mr. Ives, "music teacher, at Mr. Joseph Lancon's dancing academy"; Joseph Laucon [*sic*], "dancing master"; Henry Priest, "music teacher at Mr. Church's on Church Street." Reprinted in *City Directories of the United States*, microfiche 505 (see entry 257).

256.   *The Boston Directory*. Boston: Rhoades and Laughton, for John West, 1798. 145p.

   Cites names, occupations, and addresses. Musicians listed include: Lewis D'hattentot, "musician No. 9 Jarvis's buildings"; Hans Gram, "musician, Belknap's lane"; Jonathan Greenleaf, "organist, Cold lane"; Francis Mallet, "musician, Orange St." Reprinted in *City Directories of the United States*, microfiche 117 (see entry 257).

257.   *City Directories of the United States in Microform.*   New
           Haven, Conn.: Research Pub., 1970.   Microfiche (to 1860) and
           microfilm.

           Directories published from the 17th-20th centuries for
selected cities and some states; for the period before 1860,
however, it includes all American city directories.   A complete list
through 1860 is available on microfiche with the collection.
Readers may also refer to Spear's *Bibliography* (see entry 265).

258.   Motte, Abraham.   *Directory and Strangers' Guide for the Year
           1816.*   Charleston, 1816.   93p.

           An example of a city directory for Charleston, S.C. that
includes names of town inhabitants, their professions, and where
they lived.   Some of the musicians listed include: John Albert,
"musician"; Jacob Eckhard, "organist"; George B. Eckhard, "organist,
St. Philips Church"; Jacob Eckhard, Jun., "organist, German Lutheran
Church"; Joseph W. Foucard, "musician"; Charles Gilfert, "music
master"; Jane Labat, "piano forte teacher"; McDonald & Bonner,
"piano forte makers"; John Mitchell, "fiddler"; John Speissegger,
"musical instrument maker"; Charles Thineman, "music master."
Reprinted in *City Directories of the United States*, microfiche 239
(see entry 257).

259.   Mullin, John.   *The Baltimore Directory, for 1799.*   Baltimore:
           Warner & Hanna, 1799.   144p.

           Cites names, occupations, and street addresses.   Includes
George Albright, "Liberty St. piano forte maker"; Joseph Carr,
"music store, 6, Gay St."; Robert Etts, "dancing master York St.
Old-town"; Henry Hupfield, "musician, Conowago St."; Robert Slaw,
"teacher of music, East St."   Reprinted in *City Directories of the
United States*, microfiche 65 (see entry 257).

260.   *The New Trade Directory, for Philadelphia, Anno 1800.*
           Philadelphia: Way & Groff, 1799.

           An example of an early trade directory that lists many kinds
of merchants and occupations arranged alphabetically under various
categories.   Each entry includes name of person and street address.
There are 14 "musicians" and 6 "musical instrument makers" cited.
Reprinted in *Early American Imprints* (see entry 43).

261.   Redway, Virginia Larkin. *Music Directory of Early New York
        City: A File of Musicians, Music Publishers, Musical
        Instrument Makers Listed in New York Directories from 1786
        through 1835, Together with the Most Important New York
        Music Publishers from 1836 through 1875.* New York: New York
        Public Library, 1941. 102p.

        Includes lists of names, addresses, and dates of musicians
and teachers, publishers, printers, music dealers, instrument makers
and dealers, and dancers and dancing masters. Also includes a list
of musical societies, 1789-99.

262.   *Robinson's Philadelphia Register and City Directory, for 1799.*
        Philadelphia: John Bioren, 1799.

        This city directory for Philadelphia includes a George
Gillingham as "professor of music," and residing at "21, North Ninth
St." Reprinted in *City Directories of the United States*, microfiche
239 (see entry 257).

263.   Romaine, Lawrence B. *A Guide to American Trade Catalogs,
        1744-1900.* New York: R.R. Bowker, 1960. Reprint, New York:
        Arno Press, 1976. xxiii, 422p.

        This guide to 180 trade catalogs is arranged topically and
has a section on "Musical Instruments & Accessories," including an
entry for John R. Parker's *A Catalog of Music and Musical
Instruments* (Boston, 1820). See also the section, "Books,
Booksellers and Publishers," which includes an entry for Robert
MacGill's *Catalog of a Small Collection of Books* (Williamsburg,
1772) that mentions some "song books." Of note is a review by
Irving Lowens in *Notes* 18/3 (June 1961), pp. 414-15.

264.   Romaine, Lawrence B. "Pictorial Records of Musical
        Instruments in 19th-Century American Trade Catalogs." *Notes*
        18/3 (June 1961): 383-96.

        Based on the author's catalog (see entry 263).

265.   Spear, Dorothea N. *Bibliography of American Directories
        through 1860.* Worcester, Mass.: American Antiquarian
        Society, 1961. 389p.

Includes 1,647 entries ("of this total the AAS has 1110"). This guide cites library holdings and is arranged alphabetically by city and then chronologically. No general index to key words in titles. Not included are registers, gazetteers, almanacs, census lists, and guide books.

266.   Thompson, [William] and [James L.] Walker. *The Baltimore Town and Fell's Point Directory.* Baltimore: Peachin & Co., 1796. 100p.

Lists names, occupations and street addresses for these two Maryland towns. Includes a listing (out of alphabetical order) for John Boyer, a "musician, Waggon Alley, West of Howard St." Reprinted in *City Directories of the United States*, microfiche 64 (see entry 257).

267.   *The Washington Directory.* Washington, D.C.: S.A. Elliot, 1827. 108p.

This Washington, D.C. directory includes the following members of the Carusi family who were musically active from the early 1800s on: G. Carusi, "proprietor Washington assembly rooms, Corner Cn and 11W"; Nathaniel Carusi, "professor of music"; Samuel Carusi, "professor of music"; Lewis Carusi, "teacher of dancing." Also listed are F. Massi, "professor of music, n side Pen av btw 9 and 10w" and Vincent Massi, "dancing master ditto." Reprinted in *City Directories of the United States*, microfiche 1519 (see entry 257).

Copyright Records

Although copyright was established in 1783, the copyright of music did not begin until 1831. Prior to 1831, however, books that included music were registered under the category of books or engravings. For a brief discussion of copyright and music, see Donald Krummel's *Guide for Dating Early Published Music* (see entry 1400).

268.   *Copyright Record Books of the District Courts, 1790-1870.*   321
        vols.   76 microfilm reels.   Washington, D.C.: Library of
        Congress Photoduplication Service, 197- .

        Copyright records microfilmed and arranged by geographical
region.   Before 1870 when the Library of Congress became the
copyright registry, works were registered with United States
district courts.   These original records, which are registered in
large folio volumes and are held in the Library of Congress's Rare
Book Division, are available on microfilm.   One needs to know the
state and approximate year a work was registered in order to locate
a specific title.   Indexes.   See also Martin Roberts, *Records in
the Copyright Office Deposited by the United States District Courts
Covering the Period 1790-1870* (Washington, D.C.: Government Printing
Office, 1939).

Diaries and Letters

To date a comprehensive analysis of American diaries and letters for
their music content has not been undertaken.   However, the
bibliographies cited below are useful for identifying diaries that
pertain to specific geographical areas.   In addition, researchers
may wish to consult various dissertations cited in the chapter
"Histories, Chronologies, and Area Studies" below.   Doctoral studies
often include lists of diaries, letters, travel journals, and the
like.   See, for example, Simon Anderson's "American Music during the
War for Independence, 1775-1783" (see entry 316) for an excellent
list for that period.

269.   Arksey, Laura, Nancy Pries, and Marcia Reed.   *American
        Diaries: An Annotated Bibliography of Published American
        Diaries and Journals.*   Detroit: Gale Research Company,
        1983.   2 vols.

        Approximately 5,000 entries.   See especially volume 1:
"Diaries Written from 1491 to 1844."   Supercedes Matthews (see entry
272).   Arranged chronologically.   Typical entry includes name of
author, title, source, and annotation.   Name, subject, and
geographic indexes.   Ten entries are cited under "Music" in the
subject index; other relevant subject headings include various
groups such as "Baptists" and "Moravians," cities and towns,
"Teachers," "Travel diaries," and "Travelers."

270.   Cameron, Kenneth Walter. *Colonial Anglicanism in New England:*
          A Guide.   Hartford, Conn.: Transcendental Books, 1984.
          Various pagination.

          "Designed to help historiographers of the American Church to
classify documents and aid researchers in the Colonial period to
carry out editorial tasks." Includes a number of "widely scattered
historical aids," which are useful for identifying letters and
documents. Part 1 includes a "chronological inventory of Colonial
letters available in certain printed sources." Part 2 consists of a
selection of letters and part 3 includes colonial letters indexed by
state. Although this work requires considerable browsing for
locating items, there are, nonetheless, references to the letters of
such 18th-century musicians as Thomas Bacon and Alexander Malcolm.

271.   Havlice, Patricia P. *And So to Bed: A Bibliography of Diaries*
          Published in English.   Metuchen, N.J.: Scarecrow Press,
          1987. viii, 698p.

          Consists of 2,509 entries, including an index to diaries in
Matthews (see entry 272). Entries are arranged chronologically.
Includes a few entries on music in the index.

272.   Matthews, William. *American Diaries: An Annotated*
          Bibliography of American Diaries Written Prior to the Year
          1861. Boston: J.S. Canner, 1959. xiv, 383p.

          About 2,400 unnumbered entries arranged chronologically,
then alphabetically by name. Name index only, which necessitates
searching through the annotated entries for relevant diaries. For
many years was the principal reference work of its type, but now
superceded by Arksey, *American Diaries* (see entry 269) which has
nearly twice the entries. One might wish to consult Matthews' work,
however, to cross-check annotations.

273.   Matthews, William. *American Diaries in Manuscript, 1580-*
          1954: A Descriptive Bibliography. Athens: University of
          Georgia Press, 1974. xvi, 176p.

          Includes 5,022 annotated entries arranged alphabetically by
names. Divided into two principal sections: "Dated Diaries" and
"Undated Diaries," the latter being relatively few in number. The
list of contributing libraries is ample evidence of the thoroughness

of this work.   The index is one of names only; therefore, readers should know the name of the person connected with music, otherwise they will have to browse through the annotations searching for musical key words.   Entries 252, 668, 739, and 888 are relevant; other diaries that are not annotated may likely contain musical information.   For example, in entry no. 218 (post-1820) Nathaniel Booth was an amateur musician as well as a merchant (see "The Diary of Nathaniel Booth: A Contemporary Account of the Antebellum Musical Culture of the Hudson Valley" by Geoffrey Miller in *Sonneck Society Newsletter* 11 (Fall 1985), pp. 75-76).   In addition, various Moravian and travel diaries may also be relevant.

Travel Accounts

Travel accounts are an important source of information for the researcher of early American music.   Typically, they consist of chronological records of what travelers experienced as they went from place to place.   Commentary on musical activities and other descriptions often include concerts, musicians, music in churches, instruments, theatrical productions, and physical descriptions of buildings in which entertainments took place.   Currently, however, there is no comprehensive study of travel accounts for their music content.   Of note, the *Harvard Guide to American History* (see entry 51) provides useful information on the value of travelers' accounts to the researcher.   Bibliographies of accounts, such as those described below, are usually compiled in a selective manner, and according to period or area visited.   Currently there are bibliographies of accounts for Virginia, Vermont, New Jersey, and the South.   See especially the list in Francis Prucha's *Handbook for Research in American History* (Lincoln: University of Nebraska Press, 1987), pp. 219-21.   Cited below are examples of individual travel diaries.   Others are included below in the section titled *"Area Studies."*

274.   Carson, Jane.   *Travelers in Tidewater Virginia, 1700-1800: A Bibliography.*   Williamsburg: Colonial Williamsburg; distributed, Charlottesville: University Press of Virginia, 1965.   xx, 237p.

Included here as an example of a regional list of travel accounts, with some references to music.   Lists, for example, Ebenezer Hazard's account of a benefit ball for Peter Pelham, a

Williamsburg musician. Begin a search in the index under the subjects "Amusements" and "Theatre." The annotations focus principally on travelers' visits to the Virginia tidewater area, although it should be noted that many of the accounts cited are relevant to other geographic areas as well.

275.   Clark, Thomas D., ed. *Travels in the Old South: A Bibliography.* Norman: University of Oklahoma Press, 1956-59. 3 vols.

Another regional list that is comprehensive in its coverage. Unfortunately music and related subjects are not included in the index. The period covered is 1527-1783. Each volume is compiled by a separate contributor. Volume 2 includes these references to music: William Priest's musical endeavors during the late 1700s in Philadelphia, and his visits to other places, and James Kirke Paulding's comments on American music in the early 19th century. See also Clark entries 110 and 111, pp. 133-35 for accounts that mention dancing activities.

276.   Cole, Garold L. *Travels in America, from the Voyages of Discovery to the Present: An Annotated Bibliography of Travel Articles in Periodicals, 1955-1980.* Norman: University of Oklahoma Press, 1984. xix, 291p.

The principal guide to travel diaries reprinted in periodicals. Arranged geographically, with an index of travelers, places, and subjects. Subject headings for music and related topics are lacking.

277.   Cox, Edward Godfrey. *A Reference Guide to the Literature of Travel.* Seattle: University of Washington, 1938. 3 vols.

The principal reference work for travel accounts. Volume 2 focuses on the "New World." Entries are arranged chronologically. Unfortunately the annotations are not extensive and readers searching for accounts having musical content will encounter some difficulty.

278.   Hamilton, Alexander. *Itinerarium Being a Narrative of a Journey. . . 1744.* Ed. by Albert B. Hart. St. Louis:

William Bixby, 1907. Reprint, New York: Arno Press, 1971. xxvii, 263p.

Included here as an example of a travel diary that includes musical information on the Philadelphia "Musick Club" not found elsewhere. Cited in Cox, *A Reference Guide to the Literature of Travel*, p. 190 (see entry 277).

279.   Mifflin, Benjamin. "Journal of My Proceeding on My Excursion in the Country." Ed. by Victor H. Paltsits in *Bulletin of the New York Public Library* 39 (June 1935): 423-38.

Mifflin visited Annapolis in June of 1761 and commented on a "fine Large Organ" in St. Anne's Church. Cited in Clark, *Travels in the Old South*, volume 1, pp. 244-45 (see entry 275).

Discographies

*   *American Music before 1865 in Print and on Records: A Biblio-Discography*. Cited above as item 82.

280.   Davis, Elizabeth A. *Index to the New World Recorded Anthology of American Music: A User's Guide to the Initial One Hundred Records*. New York: W.W. Norton, 1981. ix, 235p.

New World Records ranks among the best for an on-going series devoted exclusively to American music. Not only are the performances first-rate, but also the liner notes and essays are scholarly, often comprehensive, and deserve notice by researchers. The first 100 recordings, made possible by a grant provided by The Rockefeller Foundation, include a number of discs that focus on music before 1820. This guide includes a master index, with discs arranged numerically and full contents described. But there are also indexes to recorded material, printed material, genres and performing media. Readers may also refer to an index arranged by chronological period. Currently there are 365 albums in the series. Recordings whose topical material date before 1865 are also indexed in *American Music Before 1865* (see entry 82). See also an *Index of the Recorded Anthology of American Music* (Brooklyn College, Institute for Studies in American Music, 1980) which covers the first 100 discs.   Yet another partial listing of recordings in this series is included in entry 354.

281.   Heintze, James R.   "'American Music before 1865 in Print and on Records: A Biblio-Discography': Supplement to Music on Records." *Notes* 34/3 (March 1978): 571-80.

This supplement to entry 82 covers the period December 1975-September 1977.

282.   Heintze, James R.   "'American Music before 1865 in Print and on Records: A Biblio-Discography': Second Supplement to Music on Records." *Notes* 37/1 (September 1980): 31-36.

This supplement to entry 82 covers the period October 1977-March 1980.

Obituaries

Obituaries of musicians in early American newspapers frequently provide information not found elsewhere.   Although there are lists of obituaries compiled from a number of colonial newspapers (see entry 284), many notices have as yet to be identified and indexed.

283.   *Index of Obituaries in Boston Newspapers, 1704-1800.*   Boston: G.K. Hall, 1968.   3 vols.

Volume 1: Deaths within Boston; volumes 2-3: Deaths outside Boston.   Based on 11 newspapers from the period.   An excellent source for information not readily accessible elsewhere.   For example, includes entries for John Dupee (instrument maker in Boston, 1773), Josiah Flagg (composer, 1795), Jonas Green (French horn player in Annapolis and printer of the *Maryland Gazette*, 1767), Trille Le Barre (musician, 1797), and Alexander Malcolm (musician from Maryland, 1763).

284.   Jarboe, Betty.   *Obituaries: A Guide to Sources.*   Boston: G.K. Hall, 1982.   xv, 370p.

A principal reference work, arranged by state, that includes numerous lists of obituaries based on colonial newspapers. A useful search strategy would include checking under the name of a newspaper, such as the *Maryland Gazette* or *New Hampshire Gazette*, that pertains to a particular locale, to see if an obituary index is available. This work also refers readers to lists of obituary card files and where they are located. Author and subject indexes.

Parish and Other Church Records

Parish registers and similar church records are valuable sources for identifying organists, their salaries, and for providing information on organs and other instruments, as well as musical activities before 1820 in individual churches.

285. Kirkham, E. Kay. *A Survey of American Church Records.* 4th ed. Logan, Utah: Everton, 1978. xii, 344p.

The principal guide to parish and other church records found in archival collections. Includes surveys by denomination and by states. A typical entry includes county name, denomination or name of church, location, kind of record, years included, and location of records. Of note are the bibliographies found under each state.

Probate Records

County probate court records consist of wills, inventories, and accounts of administration for the settlement of estates and are excellent sources for the study of early American music. These documents often provide the only extant evidence that an individual was a musician. In addition, probate records can reveal what musical instruments and music were owned by an individual or family and what their value was at that time. By careful examination of records for generations of a single family, a researcher can determine if music or instruments had actually been passed down. Some county probate records are available on microfilm and some are published, but most are only available in manuscript. Entry 286 serves as a useful introduction to probate records. In addition, see Barbara Lambert's "Social Music, Musicians, and Their Musical

Instruments in and Around Colonial Boston," in *Music in Colonial Massachusetts* (see entry 533), which is based on an extensive examination of probate records for the Boston area, and includes numerous examples of household inventories.

286.   Main, Gloria L.   "Probate Records as a Source for Early American History." *William and Mary Quarterly* 32/1 (January 1975): 89-99.

Main's article is an excellent introduction to the use of these documents, what they consist of, why they are important to our understanding of the cultural activities at that time, and how to use them.   She includes numerous examples (some of which are music), and describes what a will or inventory is likely to reveal. Information is provided on the identification and location of major collections of probate documents.

287.   *Maryland Inventories and Accounts*.   Annapolis: Maryland Hall of Records.   Available on microfilm: Library of Congress "Colonial Series," control number 966.   256 microfilm reels.

Cited here as a significant example of colonial probate records that include the names of individuals who owned musical instruments.   The collection consists of court judgments and inventories and accounts, the latter for the period 1718-77.   A typical entry includes the names of persons present at the time the inventory of household effects was taken, the name of the deceased, the date, the name of the county, and a list of items identified. An index prepared by Nancy Baker under a grant from the National Endowment for the Humanites (grant no. 0067-79-0738) lists the contents of the Anne Arundel County Inventories and is available at the Maryland Hall of Records in Annapolis, Maryland.   The musical contents taken from this list are cited in David K. Hildebrand, "Musical Instruments: Their Implications Concerning Musical Life in Colonial Annapolis" (M.A. thesis, George Washington University, 1987).

Theses and Dissertations

288.   Adkins, Cecil and Alis Dickinson.   *Doctoral Dissertations in Musicology*.   Philadelphia: American Musicological Society

and International Musicological Society, 1984.   545p.   With
4 supplements to November 1987.

The principal tool, with a classified arrangement, for
doctoral dissertations completed and in progress.   Includes
references to *Dissertation Abstracts International* (see entry 292).
Subject and author indexes.

289.   *American Doctoral Dissertations.*   Vol. 1- .   Ann Arbor, Mich.:
       University Microfilms International, 1955/56- .

       Supercedes *Doctoral Dissertations Accepted by American
Universities.   Lists dissertations accepted by North American
universities.   Dissertations are reported by the universities.
Arranged by subject and then by university.

290.   Colwell, Richard J.   *Directory of International Music
       Education Dissertations in Progress.*   Urbana: Council for
       Research in Music Education, University of Illinois, 1987.
       xiii, 161p.

       Published annually, this tool is likely to include a few
works in progress not in Adkins (see entry 288).   The arrangement is
classified and included is a category index that has, for example,
sections on "Historical Studies" and "Church Music."

291.   *Comprehensive Dissertation Index, 1861-1972.*   37 vols.   Ann
       Arbor, Michigan: University Microfilms International, 1973.
       With annual supplements.   A ten-year supplement covering
       1973-82 was published in 1984.

       A comprehensive list that includes some dissertations not
included in *Dissertation Abstracts* (see entry 292), due to
supplementary reliance on varied unpublished lists.

292.   *Dissertation Abstracts International.*   Ann Arbor, Mich.:
       University Microfilms, 1938- .   V. 1- .   Monthly.

       This principal reference work for dissertations completed in
American colleges and universities is based on citations submitted
by contributing libraries and includes lengthy abstracts.   Of note,
University Microfilms publishes   *Recent Studies in Music: A Catalog*

of Doctoral Dissertations and *History: A Catalog of Selected Doctoral Dissertations*, the latter including a section on United States history, with entries on early American music.

293.   Heintze, James R.   *American Music Studies: A Classified Bibliography of Master's Theses.*   Bibliographies in American Music, 8.   Detroit: Information Coordinators, 1984.   xxv, 312p.

Includes 2,370 entries and is the principal source to 1984 for the identification of theses on a broad range of topics in American music.   The work is based on printed sources, queries sent to some 92 colleges and universities, and an examination of a number of college card catalogs.   A supplement is in progress.   Author, geographic, and subject indexes.

294.   Hoglund, A. William.   *Immigrants and Their Children in the United States: A Bibliography of Doctoral Dissertations, 1885-1982.*   New York: Garland Publishing, 1986.   xxviii, 491p.

Over 3,500 entries.   An excellent means for identifying dissertations that focus on ethnic groups in early America. Includes a number of dissertations that include information on music, but unfortunately there is no subject index.   Therefore, one needs to browse under the various headings in the "Index of Ethnic and Nationality Groups" for relevant works.

295.   *Index to Theses Accepted for Higher Degrees by the Universities of Great Britain and Ireland*, 1950- .   Vol. 1- .   London: Aslib, 1950- .   Annual.

Easy to overlook, this source occasionally includes graduate studies that focus on early American music.   See, for example, P. Sudlow's "The First New England School: An Historical Account of Sacred Music in America, 1620-1820" (M.A., University of Keele, 1977), vol. 27/1 (1979), no. 145, p. 5.   Continued in 1986 by *Index to Theses with Abstracts Accepted for Higher Degrees by the Universities of Great Britain and Ireland.*

296.   *Master's Abstracts International.*   Ann Arbor, Mich.:
           University Microfilms International, 1962- .   Vol. 1- .
           Quarterly.

       A classified arrangement of theses reported by a group of
colleges and universities.   Unfortunately, this work does not
adequately identify the number of works on American music completed
annually.   To supplement this list, readers should refer to Herbert
M. Silvey's *Master's Theses in the Arts and Social Sciences in the
United States and Canada* (see entry 298).

297.   Mead, Rita H.   *Doctoral Dissertations in American Music: A
           Classified Bibliography.*   I.S.A.M. Monographs, 3.   New York:
           Brooklyn College, Institute for Studies in American Music,
           1974.   xiv, 155p.

       This principal reference work for doctoral studies in
American music is categorically arranged and includes 1,226 entries,
many of which are taken from *Dissertation Abstracts* (see entry 292).
The cut-off date is December 1973.   Author and subject indexes.

298.   Silvey, Herbert M.   *Master's Theses in the Arts and Social
           Sciences in the United States and Canada.*   Cedar Falls,
           Iowa: Bureau of Research, University of Northern Iowa,
           1976- .   Annual.

       An excellent means for identifying recently completed works
on American music.   Many of the titles cited are not in *Master's
Abstracts International* (see entry 296).

299.   Snyder, Suzanne.   *University of Iowa Theses in American Music.*
           Iowa City: University of Iowa, 1985.   26p.

       Includes 162 entries on a wide range of topics and cites a
number of works not included in Heintze (see entry 293).

Atlases

Atlases are useful sources of information to help one understand the
geographical history of musical events, to identify the places where

musicians were known to have lived, and to help determine how musical traditions might have passed from one area to another.

300.   *Atlas of American History.*   Ed. by Kenneth T. Jackson.   New York: Charles Scribner's Sons, 1978.   xv, 294p.

This atlas has, as its editor states, "earned a well-deserved reputation for scholarship and usefulness."   Included are maps showing areas of settlement during the 17th-19th centuries, maps depicting colonies and towns, and topical maps, such as those for colonial roads, that depict routes that immigrant musicians might have travelled.   Index.

PART TWO
HISTORICAL STUDIES

V. HISTORIES, CHRONOLOGIES, AND AREA STUDIES

General Histories of Music and American History

Most general histories of music such as Donald J. Grout's *History of
Western Music*, 3rd ed., with Claude V. Palisca (New York: Norton,
1980), devote little or no coverage of American music of the 18th-
19th centuries. Cited below are a few selected histories that
include sections devoted to American music.

301. Adler, Guido. *Handbuch der Musikgeschichte.* Tutzing: Hans
        Schneider, 1961. 2 vols.

        Compared to some English language histories, this history of
western music includes a relatively substantial essay and
bibliography (pp. 1186-1200). Titled "Amerika" and written by Carl
Engel, it covers most topics, including the New England singing
school tradition, Moravians, and music in English colonial towns.

302. Borroff, Edith. *Music in Europe and the United States: A
        History.* Englewood Cliffs, N.J.: Prentice-Hall, 1971. xvi,
        752p.

        Although not comprehensive regarding American music before
1820, Borroff does cite principal events. A forthcoming second
edition promises to have additional information on American music
and will be issued with an anthology and set of recordings.

303. Heinrici, Max, ed. *Das Buch der Deutschen in Amerika.*
        Philadelphia: Walther's Buchdruckerei, 1909. vii, 974p.

A series of essays by various authors on the contribution of German culture to American society. In addition to information on the Moravians, Mennonites, and the Ephrata Cloister, musicians discussed include Johann Conrad Beissel, Johannes Kelpius, and Charles Theodore Pachelbel.

304.   Hollander, A.N.J. den and Sigmund Skard, eds. *American Civilisation: An Introduction*. London: Longman, 1968. 532p.

Chapter 10, pp. 294-313, on "Music" by H. Wiley Hitchcock, includes a discussion of sacred and secular music to 1820, and introduces William Billings as "the first major figure."

305.   Lang, Paul Henry. *Music in Western Civilization*. New York: W.W. Norton, 1941. xvi, 1,107p.

For many years the standard and best general history which incorporated music, social, and other historical events. In chapters 14 and 19, "The Peripheries of Eighteenth-Century Music and Its Practice," and "The Peripheries of Nineteenth-Century Music and Its Practice," the emphasis is on Pennsylvania Germans and New England music and the work and influence of Lowell Mason. The principal focus is on art music.

306.   Nef, Karl. *An Outline of the History of Music*. Trans. by Carl F. Pfatteicher. New York: Columbia University, 1964. xvi, 400p.

Written in 1919, this work has had 6 American printings. The purpose is to provide a scholarly text for either "classroom instruction" or for the "general reader." One of the first foreign works to include a section (pp. 333-44) on American music. Nef, however, dismisses early American music after only one paragraph and states, "Only the music composed after 1860 in America merits consideration in a work such as this." Includes a suprisingly extensive bibliography of American art and folk music sources.

307.   Pahlen, Kurt. *Music of the World: A History*. Trans. from German by James A. Galston. New York: Crown Publishers, 1949. 422p.

See "Early Music in the United States," pp. 357-60; brief survey relates persons and events in America to those in Europe.

308.   Rosenstiel, Léonie, ed. *Schirmer History of Music.* New York: Schirmer Books, 1982.   xviii, 974p.

Brief account.   See especially "Music in the English and German Colonies," pp. 860-63 and "Anglo-America: The United States to the War of 1812," pp. 874-86.

309.   Savelle, Max. *Seeds of Liberty.*   2nd ed.   Seattle: University of Washington, 1965.   Reprint, Westport, Conn.: Greenwood Press, 1981.   xvii, 618p.

Chapter 9 is titled "Of Music, and of American Singing," contributed by Cyclone Covey.   A lengthy article on many aspects of music in early America, including psalmody, hymnody, instruments, Moravian music, art music in Boston, New York, Philadelphia, and Charleston, opera, and popular music.   Based mostly on secondary sources.   Musical examples and facsimiles.

310.   Silverman, Kenneth. *A Cultural History of the American Revolution.*   N.Y.: Thomas Y. Crowell, 1976.   Reprint, New York: Columbia University Press, 1987.   xvii, 699p.

This work is a comprehensive study of the culture of the period 1763-89 and includes rather extensive essays on music.   The information, based on primary sources, was reviewed by Richard Crawford, recognized authority for music of that period.   Discusses concerts, teachers, singing schools, instruments, liberty songs, military music, and musicians such as William Billings and Andrew Law.   Excellent bibliography to 1976.   Facsimiles, photos, and index.

311.   Ulrich, Homer and Paul A. Pisk. *A History of Music and Musical Style.*   New York: Harcourt, Brace and World, 1963.   viii, 696p.

Chapter 31 is titled "Three Centuries of American Music" and includes a short summary (8p.) of principal musicians.   Of interest are the illustrations, including a facsimile page from Andrew Law's *Art of Singing* (1794).

312.   Wertenbaker, Thomas J. *The Golden Age of Colonial Culture.*
        N.Y.: New York University Press, 1949. Reprint, Westport,
        Conn.: Greenwood Press, 1980. 171p.

        Discusses the cultural centers of colonial America and
recognizes the significance of smaller towns, such as Annapolis and
Williamsburg, as compared with Boston, New York, Philadelphia, and
Charleston.

Histories of American Music

Cited below are comprehensive historical texts, monographs that
consist of historical essays, and articles that serve as general
summaries. For a recent essay on histories of American music in
light of the development of the discipline, see H. Wiley Hitchcock's
article, "Histories," in *The New Grove Dictionary of American Music,*
vol. 2, pp. 399–402 (see entry 30).

313.   Aboudara, Elizabeth S. "Development of American Music."
        Daughters of the American Revolution Magazine 89/11
        (November 1955): 1053, 1115.

        This brief survey includes a few notable events of the
English tradition in America. Although the Afro-American tradition
is mentioned, other ethnic groups go unnoticed.

314.   Ammer, Christine. *Unsung: A History of Women in American
        Music.* Contributions in Women's Studies, 14. Westport,
        Conn.: Greenwood Press, 1980. 317p.

        An extensive work, but unfortunately too little is known
about women and American music before 1820. Chapter 1, titled "The
First Flowering—At the Organ," discusses women as participants in
18th-century singing schools, English ballad opera in America, and
some early instances of women performers in Charleston, S.C. during
the 1790s, and as members of Boston's Handel and Haydn Society in
1817.

315.   Anderson, Garland. "Early American Music." *Music Clubs
        Magazine* 43/3 (1964): 8–9.

316.   Anderson, Simon Vance.   "American Music during the War for Independence, 1775-1783."   Ph.D. dissertation, University of Michigan, 1965.   298p.   UM 65-10920.   *DAI* 26/6 (December 1965): 3386-87.

     The author examines the signal-music of the Continental Army, including fife tunes and drum beats, "the musical life of only the American Revolutionists," and "the mainstream of American civilian society."   Five chapters include: "The Duty-Calls of the Fifers and Drummers"; "Socio-Economic Conditions of the Fifers and Drummers"; "'Bands of Musick'"; "Music Among the Colonial Aristocrats"; "Music of the Common Folk."   Musical examples and bibliography.

317.   Arrington, Golden Elwyn.   "Nationalism and American Music, 1790-1815."   Ph.D. dissertation, University of Texas at Austin, 1969.   *DAI* 30/12 (June 1970): 5464-65-A.   UM 70-10746.

     "The search for an American music has been restricted in this study to those works with texts or programs identified with America; those works with titles suggestive of things American; and those works whose composers have indicated their purpose to be the creation of American or national music."   Based on primary sources.

318.   Barnes, Edwin N.C.   *American Music, From Plymouth Rock to Tin Pan Alley: A Lecture on American Music.*   Washington, D.C.: Music Education Publications, 1936.   22p.

     Very brief survey, based in part on Howard's *Our American Music* (see entry 362).

319.   Bialosky, Marshall.   "A Brief History of Composers' Groups in the United States."   *College Music Symposium* 20/2 (Fall 1980): 29-40.

     Composers groups before 1820 include: 1) the New Englanders Thomas Symmes, John Tufts, and Thomas Walter; 2) the first native school with William Billings, Daniel Read, and others; 3) the first wave of immigrant composers, including James Hewitt, Alexander Reinagle, and others; 4) the Moravian composers.

320.   Borroff, Edith. "Amerikanische Musik bis 1900." In
            Amerikanische Musik seit Charles Ives. Regensberg: Laaber-
            Verlag, 1987, pp. 13-19.

        A brief survey, including commentary on the early New
England composers, and also John Antes, Benjamin Franklin, Anthony
Philip Heinrich, and Thomas Jefferson.

321.   Burk, Cassie, Virginia Meierhoffer, and Claude Anderson
            Phillips. *America's Musical Heritage.* Chicago: Laidlaw
            Bros., 1942. 368p.

        For younger audiences. The first 5 chapters discuss "Early
Music in New England," "Music in the Southern Colonies," music in
New York and Pennsylvania, and of French and Spanish colonists
(mission music), instruments, and instrumental music. Musical
examples. Index.

322.   Chase, Gilbert, ed. *The American Composer Speaks: A
            Historical Anthology, 1770-1965.* Baton Rouge: Louisiana
            State University Press, 1966. ix, 318p.

        Contains a selection of writings by American composers from
the colonial period to the present. Of note are William Billings'
"To All Musical Practitioners" (1770) and excerpts from *The
Continental Harmony* (1794); Francis Hopkinson, "Dedication to His
Excellency George Washington, Esquire" (1788); Anthony Philip
Heinrich's preface to his *The Dawning of Music in Kentucky* (1819).
Index.

323.   Chase, Gilbert. *America's Music: From the Pilgrims to the
            Present.* 3rd ed. Foreword by Richard Crawford. Urbana:
            University of Illinois Press, 1987. xxiv, 712p.

        An excellent and thorough history whose approach is not
based on theoretical analysis of significant works, but rather a
cultural approach that recognizes the pluralism of American music
and its place in American society. Index. For a comparison and
review of the three editions of this work, see *American Music* 6/4
(Winter 1988), pp. 463-64.

324. Chase, Gilbert. "America's Music: The First Century."
      American Music Teacher 26/1 (September/October 1976): 10-13,
      18.

      Highlights, with an emphasis on the period after 1800.

325. Clarke, Garry E. *Essays on American Music.* Westport, Conn.:
      Greenwood Press, 1977. xviii, 259p.

      The essays cover all periods of American musical history.
See especially "The Yankee Tunesmiths," which includes information
on singing schools, musical style, with Supply Belcher, William
Billings, and Timothy Swan as the primary composers discussed.
Musical examples.

326. Crawford, Richard A. "American Music and Its Two Written
      Traditions." *Fontes Artis Musicae* 31/1 (January-March
      1984): 79-84.

      Discusses the difference between "composers' music," and
"performers' music." For early American music, Crawford uses Rayner
Taylor and Jeremiah Ingalls as examples.

327. Crawford, Richard A. "American Music around 1776." *Musical
      Newsletter* 6/2 (1976): 3-8.

328. Crawford, Richard A. "A Historian's Introduction to Early
      American Music." *Proceedings of the American Antiquarian
      Society* 89/2 (1980): 261-98.

      A survey to 1801. Includes important dates, places, events,
and musicians.

329. Davis, Josephine K.R. "Program Music of Early America."
      Music Journal 33/5 (May 1975): 14-15, 40.

      Discusses concerts, with information on Josiah Flagg, Peter
Pelham, Jr., and William Selby.

330.   Davis, Ronald L. *A History of Music in American Life.*
       Huntington, N.Y.: Robert Krieger Publishing Company, 1980-
       82.   3 vols.

       An excellent text taking a historical non-analytical
approach; however, musical examples are lacking. The first 8
chapters of volume 1 focus on music before 1820. Most principal
topics are covered. Recommended are the "Bibliographical Notes,"
presented in a narrative format, which consist of annotations of
relevant music and general history books and articles.

331.   Despard, Mabel H. *The Music of the United States: Its Sources
       and History.* New York: J.J.H. Muirhead, 1936. 94p.

       For juvenile audiences. Perhaps useful in its day, but now
not recommended. Includes a chapter on the Afro-American heritage
and the New England tradition.

332.   Donakowski, Conrad L. *A Muse for the Masses: Ritual and Music
       in an Age of the Democratic Revolution, 1770-1870.* Chicago:
       University of Chicago, 1977. 435p.

       The author studies the relationship among the arts,
psychology, religion, and modern history, with a primary focus on
Europe. New World discussions of ritual music include Afro-American
music of slaves and American Protestant congregations. Refer to the
heading "United States of America" in the index.

333.   Eastman, Allan J. "The Beginnings of American Music: A Sketch
       of Our Musical Endeavor Up to the Early Years of the Last
       Century." *Etude* 40/3 (March 1922): 155-56.

       Brief information on the Puritans, German-Americans, musical
organizations, and William Billings and Francis Hopkinson.

334.   Eberlein, Harold Donaldson and Cortlandt Van Dyke Hubbard.
       "Music in the Early Federal Era." *Pennsylvania Magazine of
       History and Biography* 69/2 (April 1945): 103-27.

       Surveys sacred and secular music after the Revolutionary War
in Philadelphia, Baltimore, New York, and Charleston. Includes a
number of concert programs and notices from newspapers, as well as

information on Charles Taws, Francis Hopkinson, John Penn, Thomas
Pike, and Alexander Reinagle.

335.   Edwards, Arthur C. and W. Thomas Marrocco. *Music in the
          United States.* Dubuque, Iowa: Wm. C. Brown Company, 1968.
          xi, 179p.

        A well-organized concise history focusing solely on the
development of art music. Includes facsimiles and a useful
discography and bibliography. The examples provided are based on
William T. Marrocco's *Music in America: An Anthology from the
Landing of the Pilgrims to the Close of the Civil War, 1620-1865*
(see entry 374).

336.   Elson, Arthur. "Early Epochs in American Music." *Musician* 18
          (1913): 18-19.

337.   Elson, Louis C. "The Evolution of American Music." *Etude* 17
          (1900): 155-56.

338.   Elson, Louis C. *The History of American Music.* New York:
          Macmillan, 1904. xiii, 380p.; enlarged 1915. xiii, 387p.;
          enlarged by A. Elson 1925. xiii, 423p. Reprint, New York:
          Burt Franklin, 1971.

        The first three chapters, "The Religious Beginnings of
American Music," "Early Musical Organizations," and "Instrumental
Music and American Orchestras," are relevant. See also chapter 7
"National and Patriotic Music." Folk music consists mostly of
Indian music and the music of Stephen Foster.

339.   Elson, Louis C. *The National Music of America and Its
          Sources.* Boston: L.C. Page and Company, 1900. 326p.
          Reprint of 1924 ed., Detroit: Gale Research Co., 1974.
          338p.

        Elson's first American music history text is quaint and
serves primarily as a reflection of what was known at that time.
Discussed are music of the New England tradition and secular music
in the middle colonies. As was common at that time, sources are not
cited for quoted material.

340. Elson, Louis C. "Old Times in American Music." *Musician* 19
        (1914): 805, 866.

341. Elson, Louis C. "The Pioneers of American Music." *Etude* 32/3
        (March 1914): 171-72.

        Discusses some of the principal composers of the 18th and
19th centuries in the context of the first American composers,
William Billings and Francis Hopkinson, and the first American
orchestra under Gottlieb Graupner in Boston.

342. Ewen, David. *Music Comes to America.* New York: Thomas Y.
        Crowell, 1942. 319p.

        A narrative with no sources provided. Divided into two
principal parts: "Yesterday" and "Today." In part 1, chapter 2
"America's Musical Pioneers" mentions only Gottlieb Graupner in
Boston in 1810. For Ewen, America's music history begins in 1840.

343. Farwell, Arthur and W. Dermot Darby, editors. *Music in
        America.* The Art of Music, 4. New York: The National
        Society of Music, 1915. xxix, 478p.

        This work is volume 4 of *The Art of Music: A Comprehensive
Library of Information for Music Lovers and Musicians* (14 vols.).
Includes 15 chapters by 6 contributors. A chronological history
that is quite extensive for its time. Each chapter focuses on a
separate topic, including the Virginia colonists and the New England
tradition, with chapters on music in the middle colonies, "Early
Concert Life" in various cities, "Early Musical Organizations," and
the beginning of opera in America. Index.

344. Faust, Patricia. "The Musicmakers." *Early American Life* 8/4
        (1977): 39-41, 58-59.

        Brief information on music and instruments in 18th-century
America.

345. Fennell, Frederick. "The American Musical Heritage." *Music
        Educators Journal* 43/4 (February-March 1957): 28, 30, 32,
        34, 48-49.

Discusses the characteristics of Americans that gave rise to our unique heritage.

346. Fillmore, John C. "Music in North America." *Music: A Monthly Magazine* 8 (1895): 171-75, 276-80, 599-606.

347. Fitz, Adeline F. "Music of Our Forefathers." *New England Magazine* 37 (1908): 669-78.

348. Gleason, Harold and Warren Becker. *Early American Music: Music in America from 1620 to 1920*. 2nd ed. Bloomington, Ind.: Frangipani Press, 1981. ix, 201p.

A series of outlines that serve as a "guide and a resource" of American music. Covers most topics. Included are facsimile pages of various tunebooks and bibliographies for further reading.

349. Goepp, Philip H. "The American Musical Antiquary." *Etude* 17 (1899): 159.

On 18th-century American music.

350. Gunn, Glenn D. "Music in Colonial America." *National Historical Magazine* 75/9 (1941): 4-7.

351. Gusikoff, Lynne. *Guide to Musical America*. New York: Facts on File, 1984. xii, 347p.

Arranged by five geographical areas. The author's intention is "to present historic highlights of different styles of music, and where they might be heard today." The New England tradition and psalmody, Moravian music, early patriotic music, and brief comments on Afro-American music are the major topics relevant to early American music. Facsimiles from works by William Billings, William Little, and James Lyon are included. Index.

352. Hackett, Karleton. "Notes on American Music of the XVIII Century." *Music: A Monthly Magazine* 21 (1902): 129-38.

353. Hadland, F.A. "The Early Days of Music in the Colonies of North America and the United States." *Monthly Musical Record* 50 (1920): 247-48.

354. Hamm, Charles. *Music in the New World*. New York: W.W. Norton, 1983. xiv, 722p.

    One of the standard and excellent histories of American music that includes popular, folk, and classical traditions. The first 7 chapters survey music of native Americans, sacred music, Afro-American folk music, concert and operatic activities, Afro-American traditions, and popular song. Included is a discography of the series *New World Records* (see entry 280) from which many of the examples are taken. Classified bibliography and index.

355. Harrington, Alice M. "When Music Fought for Its Life in Early New England." *Musical America* 54/13 (1934): 10, 14.

356. Hartzell, Lawrence W. "American Music: 1600-1750. Part I: The Spanish Colonies." *Bach* 7/3 (1976): 3-6.

357. Hartzell, Lawrence W. "American Music: 1600-1750. Part II: The English Colonies." *Bach* 7/4 (1976): 26-30.

358. Hartzell, Lawrence W. "American Music: 1600-1750. Part III: The German Colonies." *Bach* 8/1 (1977): 18-22.

359. Haskins, James. *Black Music in America: A History through Its People*. New York: T.Y. Crowell, 1987. 198p.

    A survey, including information on slave songs.

360. Hitchcock, H. Wiley. *Music in the United States: A Historical Introduction*. 3rd ed. Englewood Cliffs, N.J.: Prentice-Hall, 1988. 365p.

    A standard work that offers a distinction between "cultivated" and "vernacular" traditions. Included are chapters on sacred and secular music in the colonies, including psalmody, the singing school movements, representative composers, concerts, operas, dance music, and more.   An excellent study.

361.   Hollister, Florence Hartman.   "An Introduction to American
        Music." *Daughters of the American Revolution Magazine* 103/5
        (May 1969): 516-19, 557.

        Discusses first instances of music in Boston, first organs,
first written music, early concerts, and early use of music by
slaves.

362.   Howard, John Tasker.   *Our American Music.*   3rd ed.   New York:
        Thomas Y. Crowell Company, 1946.   xxii, 841p.

        First published in 1931, this text is based, in part, on
Howard's contact with descendants and relatives of composers.   At
the time of its publication, it was the most extensive American
music history.   Although the facts presented are not verified by
sources, for this third edition, Howard relies on other specialists
to review "the accuracy of all statements in the light of recent
discoveries. . . ."   Perhaps Howard's real achievement is that his
work is the first systematic and logical organization of a
comprehensive body of American music history.   Despite its date, the
bibliography is still useful.   There is a 4th ed. titled *Our
American Music: A Comprehensive History* (1964).

363.   Howard, John Tasker, and George Kent Bellows.   *A Short History
        of Music in America.*   New York: Thomas Y. Crowell Company,
        1967.   xxvii, 496p.

        Howard recognizes that American music history is made up of
"an incredibly complex American musical ethos."   Nonetheless, except
for an introductory chapter on music of the American Indian, Howard
focuses primarily on the main currents in art music and does not
include folk music.   Chapters 2-5 include a survey of early music in
the colonies, followed by a chapter on Hopkinson, Lyon, and Billings
(in that order) and concluding with 2 chapters on music during the
"Years of the Revolution" and "The Turn of the Century, to the
1830s."   This book is not a shorter version of his *Our American
Music* (see entry 362).   In fact, *A Short History* contains data not
in the former work.

364.   Kaufmann, Helen L. *From Jehovah to Jazz: Music in America
        from Psalmody to the Present Day.* New York: Dodd, Mead,
        1937. Reprint, Port Washington, N.Y.: Kennikat Press, 1969.
        xiii, 303p.

        An informal, non-scholarly, and often amusing account.
Stories and statements without basis are frequently interjected.

365.   Keast, Naomi Atkins. "Music in America—1607-1800."
        Daughters of the American Revolution Magazine 85/10 (October
        1951): 781, 890.

        Cites a few facts about early American music with mention of
the various printings of the *Bay Psalm Book*.

366.   Kingman, Daniel. *American Music: A Panorama.* New York:
        Schirmer Books, 1979. xxx, 577p.

        A well-written survey appropriate for the undergraduate,
although more advanced students should find it particularly useful
for its broad perspective. Annotated bibliographies.

367.   Kinscella, Hazel Gertrude. *History Sings: Backgrounds of
        American Music.* Lincoln, Nebraska: University Publishing
        Company, 1948. xvi, 560p.

        A descriptive narrative weaving music into aspects of
society of that day. Divided into categories: "Atlantic Coast
Beginnings"; "Along Southern Borders"; "Pacific Coast Tales";
"Facing North"; "The Middle States." Frances Clark contributing the
"Foreword" informs us that the book is directed to "the glorious
youth of America."

368.   Kohn, Karl. *Music in American Life.* Chicago: Rand McNally,
        1967. 48p.

        Brief survey. See especially, the following sections: "The
Importance of Music in Colonial America," which discusses "the
Puritans' view of music, psalm-singing and the reformers, singing
schools, recreational music, music and the religious groups, and
attitudes toward music of Jefferson, Franklin, and Hopkinson," and
"Development of Early American Music," which discusses "the New

England composers, folk hymns, revival hymns and camp meetings, the African inheritance and the music of American Negroes," and other topics.   Includes facsimiles of title pages of tunebooks.   Brief bibliography.

369.   Krueger, Karl. *The Musical Heritage of the United States: The Unknown Portion.*   New York: Society for the Preservation of the American Musical Heritage, 1973.   237p.

Includes 11 chapters equally divided between a survey of the history of American music and a discography of the Society's recordings.   See especially chapter 2, "The Formative Period," which highlights secular pre-1820 composers and discusses various groups such as the Moravians.   Index.

370.   Loring, Florence B.   "Music Connected with the American Revolution."   *American Monthly Magazine* 12 (1898): 11-18.

371.   Lowens, Irving. *Music and Musicians in Early America.*   New York: W.W. Norton, 1964.   328p.

A series of 18 articles previously published in journals and books, but here revised; recommended for their scholarly content. Topics include the *Bay Psalm Book*, fuging tunes, psalmody, tunebooks compiled by William Little, John Tufts, and John Wyeth, and other composers, including Benjaming Carr, Lewis Edson and family, James Hewitt, Andrew Law, and Daniel Read.   Included also is an article on the Warrington Collection of early tunebooks in the Case Memorial Library at Hartford Seminary.   Of note, Lowens cites a few corrections for Charles Evans' *American Bibliography* (see entry 45). General and title indexes.

372.   Lowens, Irving.   "Our Neglected Musical Heritage."   *Hymn* 3/2 (April 1952): 49-56.

In this brief historical survey, Lowens calls for a thorough analysis of the history of psalmody.   He discusses "the problem areas in need of study. . . through an overview of the sociological implications and general musical content of the American tunebooks of the period."

373. Lucas, Clarence. "Music in the Time of Washington." *Musical
      Courier* 76/8 (1918): 21.

374. Luening, Otto. *Music Materials and the Public Library.* New
      York: Social Science Research Council, 1949. 87p.

      Includes 5 chapters. Produced, in part, as a SSRC study of
the "American free public library." Luening provides a historical
background of American music by way of introducing "Music and the
Public Library." He discusses briefly the New England tradition in
a section, "Church Music and the Singing Schools," with William
Billings as the principal representative.

375. Marrocco, W. Thomas and Harold Gleason. *Music in America: An
      Anthology from the Landing of the Pilgrims to the Close of
      the Civil War, 1620-1865.* New York: W.W. Norton, 1964.
      371p.

      A standard work. Consists principally of a compilation of
representative musical compositions, with each group of works
preceded by an essay. Topics for the period prior to 1820 include
psalmody, singing schools, the Ephrata Cloister and the Moravians,
native American composers, and immigrant composers in Charleston,
Philadelphia, New York, and Boston. Included is a section of
biographies, arranged alphabetically, on the composers included in
the work. General, classified, and first line indexes.

376. Mathews, William Smythe Babcock, ed. *A Hundred Years of Music
      in America.* Chicago: G.L. Howe, 1889. Reprint, New York:
      AMS Press, 1970. ix, 715p.

      Discusses psalmody from 1620 to 1750, contains a chapter on
William Billings, information on Timothy Swan, Stephen Jenks, Joel
Harmon, and others, and early musical instruments. One chapter
includes biographies of early musicians in a dictionary format.

377. Maurer, Maurer. "The Musical Life of Colonial America in the
      Eighteenth Century." Ph.D. dissertation, Ohio State
      University, 1950.

378.   Mellers, Wilfrid.   *Music in a New Found Land: Themes and
       Developments in the History of American Music.*
       New York: Oxford University Press, 1987.   xxxi, 544p.

       This 1987 edition is a reprinting of the 1964 edition with a
new introduction added.   The work is somewhat uneven in that there
is only one relatively brief chapter on early American music, and
its title is "A Pre-History of American Music: The Primitives, the
Retreat to Europe and the Conservative Tradition."   The New England
tradition is discussed with Timothy Swan, William Billings, and
Jacob Kimball as the principal examples.   A discussion of Moravian
music is brief.   Discography, bibliography, and index.

379.   Milligan, Harold V.   "Pioneers in American Music."   *American
       Scholar* 3/2 (Spring 1934): 224-37.

       Discusses musical instruments and musicians in the colonies,
including Peter Albrecht Von Hagen, John Antes, Thomas Ball, William
Billings, Oliver Holden, and Francis Hopkinson.   Supports the view
that Puritans were hostile toward music, yet contradicts himself by
describing Puritan singing activities in church.

380.   *Music in American Society, 1776-1976: From Puritan Hymn to
       Synthesizer.*   Ed. by George McCue.   New Brunswick, N.J.:
       Transaction Books, 1977.   201p.

       Consists of 12 essays contributed by various composers and
other writers in association with the Bicentennial Horizons of
American Music and the Performing Arts held in 1976.   Edward
Jablonski's article, "Music with an American Accent," discusses
musical Americanisms with examples, including the music of William
Billings and ballad opera, and Austin B. Caswell's "Social and Moral
Music: The Hymn," which discusses the significance of the hymn in
American society, focusing, in part, on New England psalmody, the
music of William Billings and 18th-century hymnody, and the early
19th-century shape note tradition.

381.   "Musical Founding Fathers."   *Pan Pipes of Sigma Alpha Iota*
       68/4 (1976): 2, 11.

       Mentions Benjamin Franklin, Francis Hopkinson, and Thomas
Jefferson.

382.   *Musical U.S.A.*   Ed. by Quaintance Eaton.   New York: Allen,
         Towne and Heath, 1949.   206p.

         Includes an essay, "Early Beginnings," by Herbert F. Peyse,
followed by 13 essays by various contributors focusing on individual
cities or geographic areas, including in this order: New York,
Boston, Philadelphia, Chicago, Baltimore, Cincinnati, Minneapolis,
St. Louis, New Orleans, Texas, San Francisco, Los Angeles, Seattle
and the Northwest Pacific.

383.   Nettl, Paul.   "Immigration and American Music."   *American-
         German Review* 9/2 (1942): 6-8, 34.

         Discusses German musicians from the 18th century on.

384.   Nicolisi, Robert J.   "Music in America."   *American Music
         Teacher* 26/5 (April-May 1977): 24-26.

         Brief notes regarding the function of music in society
during the late eighteenth and early nineteenth centuries.

385.   Peyser, Herbert F.   "The Story of Music in America, 1: Early
         Beginnings."   *Musical America* 66/3 (1946): 5, 138, 160, 370.

386.   Pfohl, Mrs. J. Kenneth.   "Our American Music."   *Daughters of
         the American Revolution Magazine* 98/9 (November 1964): 876-
         77, 931.

         Discusses some of the early New England psalters.
Illustrations.

387.   Ritter, Frédéric Louis.   *Music in America.*   New York: Charles
         Scribner's Sons, 1883.   xiv, 423p.   New ed. 1890 (New York:
         Charles Scribner's Sons.   xiv, 512p; reprint with a new
         introduction by Johannes Riedel (xviiip.), New York: Johnson
         Reprint Company, 1970).

         The first general history of American music.   For that
reason it deserves notice.   However, Ritter takes a European-
oriented view of American music by selecting and discussing those
aspects that are more closely associated with a more sophisticated

level of culture. Includes 9 chapters (161p.) devoted to American sacred and art music before 1820; popular and folk music is purposely omitted.

388. Rourke, Constance. *The Roots of American Culture.* Ed. by Van Wyck Brooks. New York: Harcourt, Brace and World, 1942. xii, 305p.

Published after Rourke died in 1941. The title of this book takes its name from the first of a series of essays by her. She was a student of folk and classical American cultural arts and presented one of the truly classic statements regarding the development of American culture: namely, America was not the victim of a "cultural lag" behind Europe, but rather had a unique culture of its own. "Whatever the gaps, the mischances, the downright inferiority of some of our early arts, they cannot be considered in the main as first fumblings of mere ambitious imitation. They sprang from a life peculiar to these shores; they were part of a fresh configuration." Her essay titled "Early American Music" is an eloquent discussion of secular and sacred music, with emphasis on William Billings and the singing school tradition.

389. Rublowsky, John. *Music in America.* New York: Crowell-Collier Press, 1967. 185p.

For juvenile audiences. The title is misleading considering the work's brevity and unevenness. Based on secondary sources.

390. Sablosky, Irving. *American Music.* Chicago: University of Chicago Press, 1969. xiii, 228p.

This book serves its purpose well as a brief introduction to the principal aspects of American musical history. Part 1, "New Beginnings," includes information on the New England tradition, ballad opera, gentlemen amateurs, including Benjamin Franklin, Thomas Jefferson, Francis Hopkinson, and other musicians, and examples of early concerts, early 19th-century folk-hymnody and black spirituals. Included is a short chronology of "Important Dates" and an annotated bibliography in narrative format.

391.   Sanjek, Russell. *American Popular Music and Its Business: The First Four Hundred Years.* New York: Oxford University Press, 1988. 3 vols.

This history of popular music covers much more than its title implies. Volume 1 focuses on the colonial period to 1790 and includes the singing school tradition, sections on William Billings and Andrew Law, musical theater in Philadelphia and Boston, music publishing, and the Afro-American tradition. Volume 2 (1790-1909) includes music publishing in Philadelphia, New York and Boston, copyright, and musical theater. Index.

392.   Shelton, Frances and Lucia McBride. "A Triptych of Colonial Music." *Daughters of the American Revolution Magazine* 114/3 (March 1980): 304-15, 327.

Surveys music in 17th-18th-century New England and Pennsylvania. Discusses Moravian music and music at New Sweden, Delaware, and music in New York and Charleston. Based on secondary sources. Illustrations.

393.   Shepard, Nelson McD. "Music of Colonial Days." *Daughters of the American Revolution Magazine* 56 (1922): 591-99.

394.   Smith, Carleton Sprague. "America in 1801-1825: The Musicians and the Music." *Bulletin of the New York Public Library* 68/8 (October 1964): 483-92.

A reprinting of the essay that constitutes Smith's introduction to Richard J. Wolfe's *Secular Music in America, 1801-1825* (see entry 126). Smith's survey cites many of the principal composers and musicians active in Boston, Philadelphia, New York, and Charleston.

395.   Smith, Gregg. "The Bi-Centennial Celebration: A Look Forward and Backward." *Choral Journal* 13/4 (December 1972): 6-11.

A brief historical sketch, including a discussion of principal events and musicians from 1620 to the present.

396. Smith, Lucy. "Music of the Early Colonies." *Daughters of the American Revolution Magazine* 93/6 (June 1959): 557-58.

Examples of musical enjoyment from a variety of traditions.

397. Sonneck, Oscar George. *Early Concert-Life in America (1731-1800).* Leipzig: Breitkopf & Härtel, 1907. Reprint, Wiesbaden: Martin Sändig, 1969. 338p.

A classic study based entirely on primary sources. Discussed are musicians, concerts, balls, and other musical events in Charleston and the South, Philadelphia, New York, and Boston. Includes numerous concert programs. Index.

398. Sonneck, Oscar George. "Early Concerts in America." *New Music Review* 5 (1906): 952-57.

The author includes this material in his *Early Concert-Life in America* (see entry 397).

399. Sonneck, Oscar George. "The History of Music in America: A Few Suggestions." In *Miscellaneous Studies in the History of Music.* New York: Macmillan, 1921. Reprint, New York: Da Capo Press, 1968, pp. 324-44.

Sonneck was the first scholar to point out the need for a systematic study of the history of American music. In this article, Sonneck explains why such a study has not been attempted. Highlights music topics before 1820 that are worthy of study.

400. Sonneck, Oscar George. *Suum Cuique: Essays in Music.* New York: Schirmer, 1916. Reprint, Freeport, N.Y.: Books for Libraries Press, 1969. 271p.

A broad range of essays on aspects of both European and American music. See especially "The Musical Side of Our First Presidents," discussing George Washington, John Adams, and Thomas Jefferson, and "Benjamin Franklin's Musical Side," the latter a pioneering effort having much information on the use of musical glasses in the colonies. (See also entries 670 and 1764.)

401. Southern, Eileen. *The Music of Black Americans: A History.*
      2nd ed. New York: W.W. Norton, 1983. xiii, 602p.

      One of the principal works for the study of the history of
Afro-American music. The topics treated are numerous and include:
Afro-American music, psalmody, hymnody, religious instruction, music
entertainments, military musicians, camp meetings, singing school
teachers, and more. Excellent bibliography. Index.

402. Southern, Eileen, ed. *Readings in Black American Music.* New
      York: W.W. Norton, 1971. xii, 302.

      Includes 37 essays by contributing authors covering a broad
spectrum of black music from the colonial period to the present.
See especially the following principal sections: "The African
Heritage," "Black Singers and Instrumentalists of Early America,"
"Slave Holidays and Festivals," "Religious Music in the Nineteenth
Century," "Music on the Plantations," and "General Characteristics
of Slave Music."

403. Spaeth, Sigmund. *A History of Popular Music in America.* New
      York: Random House, 1948. xv, 729p.

      As of 1971 was in its 12th printing. A narrative
presentation loaded with titles of works and composers names.
Spaeth had access to Harry Dichter's sheet music collection (see
entries 91-92). Chapter two (pp. 15-64) is a discussion of early
colonial Anglo-American popular songs, defined in a broad sense.
Oliver Holden's "Coronation" is discussed alongside of Francis
Hopkinson's "A Toast to Washington." Useful song title-composer
index. John Tasker Howard compiled the bibliography.

404. Spell, Lota M. "The First Half-Century of European Music in
      America." *Atlante* 1/1 (1953): 158-62.

405. Sudlow, Paul. "Early Americans." *Music and Musicians* 24/11
      (1976): 14-16.

406. Sweetman, Mrs. Laurence D. "Early American Music." *Daughters
      of the American Revolution Magazine* 91/11 (November 1957):
      1253-56, 1300.

Discusses the New England tradition and music by Francis Hopkinson.

407.   Tick, Judith. *American Women Composers before 1870.*   Ann Arbor, Mich.: UMI Research Press, 1983.   283p.

Includes a section of sources for the study of women composers in early America.   Chapter 2 focuses on the period 1770-1830 and includes a discussion of a woman's role in musical society.

408.   Tick, Judith.   "Towards a History of American Women Composers before 1870."   Ph.D. dissertation, City University of New York, 1979.   371p.   UM 79-13171.   *DAI* 39/12 (June 1979): 7049-A.

Discusses parlor music and divides the history of women composers of sheet music into two periods: 1790-1830 and 1830-70. Some 70 works by women were published before 1830, half of which were printed anonymously.

Chronologies

Currently, there is no comprehensive chronology of American musical events.   The works cited below include only a sampling of notable dates.

409.   *The Encyclopedia of American Facts and Dates.*   8th ed. by Gorton Carruth.   New York: Harper and Row, 1987.   x, 1006p.

This chronology is based on secondary sources and covers the period 1492 to the present.   Serves as a useful source for comparing historical events in various fields of interest with selected musical events.   Access to early American musical events are found under the heading "Music" in the index.   The annotations provide more information than *Timetables of American History* (see entry 412).

410.   Lahee, Henry Charles. *Annals of Music in America.* Boston:
          Marshall Jones, 1922. Reprint, New York: AMS Press, 1969;
          Freeport, N.Y.: Books for Libraries Press, 1970. vii, 298p.

          Eight chapters. Chapters 1-3 are "1640-1750"; "1750-1800";
and "1800-1825." The author proposes "to give as complete a record
as possible of the beginning and progress of music in the United
States of America." Because of the publication date of 1922 and the
fact that no sources are provided, the dates listed can serve only
as an approximate guideline. Primarily, ballad opera and other
musical events of the middle colonies are cited.

411.   Mattfeld, Julius. *Variety Music Cavalcade, 1620-1961: A
          Chronology of Vocal and Instrumental Music Popular in the
          United States.* Revised ed. Intro. by Abel Green.
          Englewood Cliffs, N.J.: Prentice-Hall, 1962. xiv, 713p.

          "Chronological check list of music." See especially "Music
of the Pilgrims"; "American Colonial Period"; "Before 1800"; and
"Around 1800." Following these is the chronology divided by year,
1800 to 1820, and includes historical, social, and musical events.
Title index.

412.   *The Timetables of American History.* Ed. by Laurence Urdang.
          New York: Simon and Schuster, 1981. 470p.

          A series of four charts citing history and politics, the
arts, science and technology, and miscellaneous. Includes only a
few significant musical events in early American history. Index.

Area Studies

This section includes studies devoted to geographic areas, states,
and cities. General histories of cities and counties are also
useful sources that may include information on musical activities.
A recent thorough list of county histories is P. William Filby's *A
Bibliography of American County Histories* (Baltimore: Genealogical
Publishing Company, 1985), which includes some 5,000 histories. See
also Joseph Nathan Kane's *The American Counties* (Metuchen, N.J.:
Scarecrow Press, 1972), which includes a history of each county with
principal historical texts cited. Another comprehensive list for

area studies is Marion J. Kaminkow's *United States Local Histories
in the Library of Congress: A Bibliography* (see entry 78).
Recommended also is Francis Prucha's list of bibliographies of state
and county history in his *Handbook for Research in American History*
(Lincoln: University of Nebraska Press, 1987), pp. 110-14.   Refer
also to articles under specific cities in *The New Grove Dictionary
of American Music* (see entry 30).

413.   Allen, Nathan H.   "Old Time Music and Musicians." *Connecticut
       Quarterly* 1 (1895): 274-79, 368-73; 2 (1896): 54-58, 153-57;
       3 (1897): 66-76, 286-93; 4 (1898): 319-28.

       On music in Connecticut from the 1600s on.

414.   Allis, Marguerite.   "Music Makers in Old New England: A Timely
       Review of Many Quaint Customs.   The First Hundred Years,
       1630-1730." *Etude* 57/8 (August 1939): 499-500, 543.

       Allis recognizes that, although musical instruments were not
permitted in early New England churches, "outside the meetinghouse
there certainly was music."   She provides examples of early
testimonies regarding secular music.

415.   Allwardt, Anton Paul.   "Sacred Music in New York City, 1800-
       1850."   S.M.D. dissertation, Union Theological Seminary,
       1950.   vii, 394p.

416.   Anderson, Edward P.   "The Intellectual Life of Pittsburgh,
       1786-1836." *Western Pennsylvania Historical Magazine* 14
       (1931): 9-27, 92-114, 225-36, 288-309.

417.   Andrus, Helen Josephine.   *A Century of Music in Poughkeepsie,
       1802-1911.*   Poughkeepsie, N.Y.: Frank B. Howard, 1912.
       xi, 275p.

       Chronological survey.   Discusses early music in
Poughkeepsie, N.Y., with information on Joseph Parker, a choir
director in 1802, the first organ in 1808, and Gideon Mosely, the
first vocal teacher in 1810.   Unfortunately, sources are not
provided.   Index.

418.   *Articles of the Handel Society.*   Salem, Mass.: W. Palfrey,
         Jr., 1817.

         The Handel Society was organized in January 1817 in Salem,
Mass. This document informs its readers that there were originally
thirty-two men and ten women members. Refer to Milton G. Hehr's
dissertation (see entry 492) for additional information on this
society.

419.   Ascher-Nash, Franzi. "Pennsylvania German Art Music."   In
         *Papers from the Third Conference on German-Americana in the
         Eastern United States, November 6-7, 1982.*   Radford, Va.:
         Radford University, 1985, pp. 129-38.

         An introduction with information on Johannes Kelpius and the
Wissahickon settlement, Johann Conrad Beissel and the Ephrata
Cloister, the Schwenkfelders, and the Moravians.

420.   Ayars, Christine Merrick. *Contributions to the Art of Music
         in America by the Music Industries of Boston: 1640 to 1936.*
         New York: H.W. Wilson, 1937.   Reprint, New York: Johnson
         Reprint Co., 1969.   xv, 326p.

         Discusses primarily music publishers and instrument
manufacturers. Arranged topically with surveys on each subject.
Includes a list of extant 18th and 19th-century instruments. Useful
for the identification of little-known musicians. Bibliography and
general index.

421.   Babcock, Mary K.D.   "Early Organists of Christ Church, Boston:
         1736-1824."   *Historical Magazine of the Protestant Episcopal
         Church* 14 (1945): 337-51.

422.   Baer, Elizabeth.   "Music: An Integral Part of Life in Ohio
         1800-1860."   *Bulletin of the Historical Society of Ohio* 65
         (July 1956): 197-210.

423.   Bagdon, Robert Joseph.   "Musical Life in Charleston, South
         Carolina, from 1732 to 1776 as Recorded in Colonial
         Sources."   Ph.D. dissertation, University of Miami, 1978.
         234p.   UM 78-18717.   *DAI* 39/4 (October 1978): 1912-13-A.

Includes 10 chapters. Discusses the historical, political,
social, and cultural background of Charleston. Music and musicians
of St. Philip's Church, including Charles Theodore Pachelbel, Edmund
Larken, Benjamin Yarnold, and Peter Valton, music at St. Michael's
Church, instruments, singing schools, concerts, opera, music
printing, the St. Cecilia Society, and music of slaves.

424.   Barck, Dorothy C. "The Columbian Anacreontic Society of New
          York, 1795-1803." *New-York Historical Society Quarterly
          Bulletin* 16 (1932): 115-23.

425.   Barnes-Ostrander, M.E. "Domestic Music Making in Early New
          York State: Music in the Lives of Three Amateurs." *Musical
          Quarterly* 68/3 (July 1982): 353-72.

The article is based on the "Maria Gansevoort Collection" in
the Library of Congress. The amateurs are Peter and Maria
Gansevoort, Micah Hawkins, and Edmond Charles Genet. The author
includes biographical information and commentary on the music in the
collection. The collection is compared with the Eleanor Parke
Custis collection, as well as others.

426.   Baron, John H. "Music in New Orleans, 1718-1792." *American
          Music* 5/3 (Fall 1987): 282-90.

Discusses Catholic music of the early 1700s and later,
military music after 1769, and professional musicians after 1778,
including Arnaud Sarramiac, Phelipe Sauvagan, and Rene Vancourt.

427.   Baynham, Edward Gladstone. "The Early Development of Music in
          Pittsburgh." Ph.D. dissertation, University of Pittsburgh,
          1944. 356p.

The period covered is from 1758 through the mid-19th
century. A useful work, based mostly on primary sources, for the
identification of musicians and information on musical societies in
early Pittsburgh. The author discusses Peter Declary, Pittsburgh's
first teacher of music, Dennis Loughey, composer, Edward Tyler,
music teacher, William Evens and other teachers, and Charles
Rosenbaum, piano maker, 1810-20, the organization of the Pittsburgh
Musical Society in 1818, and S.H. Dearborn and the Apollonian
Society in 1807.

428.   Beck, Roger Lawrence. "Military Music at Fort Snelling,
          Minnesota from 1819 to 1858: An Archival Study." Ph.D.
          dissertation, University of Minnesota, 1987. 374p. UM 88-
          05740. *DAI* 49/3 (September 1988): 373-A.

       Discusses company musicians and bandsmen.

429.   Bellows, George Kent. "The Story of Music in America:
          Baltimore." *Musical America* 68/15 (December 15, 1948): 9,
          42.

       Includes a few statements about music in Baltimore prior to
1820, including a musical society in 1799 and a piano advertised for
sale in 1814. Sources are not provided.

430.   Benes, Peter, ed. *Itinerancy in New England and New York.*
          The Dublin Seminar for New England Folklife Annual
          Proceedings 1984. Boston: Boston University, 1986. 256p.

       A collection of papers on itinerant professions in America
before 1850. Includes the following relevant articles: "Itinerant
Yankee Singing Masters in the Eighteenth Century" by Nym Cooke and
"John Griffiths, Eighteenth-Century Itinerant Dancing Master" by
Kate Van Winkle Keller.

431.   Benson, Norman Arthur. "The Itinerant Dancing and Music
          Masters of Eighteenth-Century America." Ph.D. dissertation,
          University of Michigan, 1963. vi, 474p. UM 64-7226. *DAI*
          25/4 (October 1964): 2551.

       Surveys cultural activities of Williamsburg, Charleston,
Philadelphia, New York, and Boston. Discusses itinerant musicians
and concert life. Annotated bibliography is noteworthy: included
are 18th-century travelers' accounts, letters and diaries.

432.   Beveridge, Lowell P. "Music in New England from John Cotton
          to Cotton Mather (1640-1726)." *Historical Magazine of the
          Protestant Episcopal Church* 48/2 (June 1979): 145-65.

       The use and philosophy of music in New England based on the
writings of John Cotton, Samuel Lee, Cotton Mather, Charles Morton,
Thomas Symmes, John Tufts, and Thomas Walter.

433. Bigger, William George. "The Choral Music of Charles Zeuner
(1795-1857), German-American Composer, with a Performance
Edition of Representative Works." Ph.D. dissertation,
University of Iowa, 1976. 2 vols. *DAI* 37/7 (January 1977):
3977-78-A.

Charles Zeuner was a German emigrant who settled in Boston
in 1830. The author includes a chapter on the development of choral
music in Boston to 1830.

434. Bowes, Frederick P. *The Culture of Early Charleston.* Chapel
Hill, North Carolina Press, 1942. Reprint, Westport, Conn.:
Greenwood Press, 1978. ix, 156p.

Includes some general information on music with names of
some 18th-century musicians taken from the *South Carolina Gazette*,
and information on theater at that time. Based on the author's
thesis (Princeton University, 1941).

435. Breslaw, Elaine G. "Dr. Alexander Hamilton and the
Enlightenment in Maryland." Ph.D. dissertation, University
of Maryland, 1973. 304p. UM 74-247. *DAI* 34/7 (January
1974): 4140-41-A.

Focuses on the musical Tuesday Club in colonial Annapolis.
Discusses its members, including Thomas Bacon and Alexander Malcolm.
Alexander Hamilton was the Club's secretary.

436. Breslaw, Elaine G. "An Early Maryland Music Society."
Maryland Historical Magazine 67/4 (Winter 1972): 436-37.

Two letters, herein transcribed, mention a musical society
on the Eastern Shore in Maryland in 1756. Its members were Thomas
Bacon, Henry Callister, and others.

437. Brooks, Henry M. *Olden-Time Music: A Compilation from
Newspapers and Books.* Boston: Ticknor and Company, 1888.
Reprint, New York: AMS Press, 1973. xiii, 283p.

Includes 35 chapters. Focuses on New England. Criticizes
Hood's *A History of Music in New England* (see entry 495) because it
included only psalmody, not instrumental music. Brooks surveys

sacred and secular music, the principal psalters in use, early
instruments in use in New England, concerts, musical societies, and
"music books advertised," and a separate chapter on William
Billings.   Many primary sources are provided making the book
somewhat useful today.   Index of names is helpful for identifying
little-known individuals.   A section concerning early organs and
organ builders in Massachusetts is reprinted in *Tracker* 13/4 (Summer
1969): 16-18; 14/1 (Fall 1969), pp. 10-12, 14.

438.   Broucek, Jack W.   "Eighteenth Century Music in Savannah,
          Georgia."   Ed.D. dissertation, Florida State University,
          1963.   256p.   UM 63-4381.   *DAI* 24/1 (July 1963): 321-22.

          The author's work is based on primary sources and includes a
discussion of the John Wesley mission and early church music,
musical contributions by Moravians, Salzburgers, blacks, Indians,
Scottish, Spanish and Jewish, theater, dancing assemblies, concerts,
and music education.

439.   Burnham, Collins G.   "Olden Time Music in the Connecticut
          Valley."   *New England Magazine* 24 (1901): 12-27.

          On music in Connecticut from the 1700s on.

440.   Byrnside, Ron.   "Toward a History of Music in Georgia."
          Georgia Historical Quarterly 65/1 (Spring 1981): 16-21.

          Explains the limitation of our knowledge of music in Georgia
during the colonial period.   Discusses an early psalm and hymn
collection, *Collection of Psalms and Hymns* (Charleston, 1737) by
John Wesley, which contains 72 hymns and psalms, but no music.

441.   Campbell, Jane.   "Old Philadelphia Music."   *Philadelphia
          History* 2/8 (1926): 181-206.

          Pertains to the 18th and 19th centuries.   This paper was
prepared for the City Historical Society of Philadelphia and read by
Campbell on May 8, 1907.

442.   Carden, Joy. *Music in Lexington before 1840*. Lexington,
          Ky.: Lexington-Fayette County Historic Commission, 1980.
          xi, 148p.

       Based in part on primary sources. Includes information on
concerts, singing schools, musicians and composers, including
Anthony Philip Heinrich. A series of 11 appendixes list, for
example, music and pianos advertised in Lexington newspapers.
Index.

443.   Carlson, Joyce Mangler. "Early Music in Rhode Island." *Rhode
          Island History* 23/2 (April 1964): 35-50.

       On Oliver Shaw and the Psallonian Society of Providence,
which first met on May 1, 1816. Includes a list of members. (See
also entries 461 and 524.)

444.   Carroll, Lucy Ellen. "Three Centuries of Song: Pennsylvania's
          Choral Composers 1681 to 1981." D.M.A. dissertation, Combs
          College of Music, 1982. 351p. UM 83-22500. *DAI* 44/7
          (January 1984): 1966-A.

       In addition to a list of choral composers, the author
discusses the Wissahickon Mystics, including transcriptions of two
works, the Ephrata Cloister, the Bethlehem Moravians, and composers,
including Francis Hopkinson, Benjamin Cross, Benjamin Carr, and
Rayner Taylor.

445.   Champlin, John D. "Nearly Two Centuries of Music." In *The
          Memorial History of the City of New-York*. Ed. by James
          Grant Wilson. 4 vols. New York: New-York History Company,
          1893, vol. 4, pp. 165-87.

       Discusses organ making, dealers in musical instruments,
ballad opera, and principal musicians for the period prior to 1820.
Sources are not cited.

446.   Chancellor, Paul G. "Pennsylvania's Colonial Influences on
          American Musical History: Philadelphia." *Etude* 66/2
          (February 1948): 75, 122-23.

Discusses mostly secular music and individuals, such as Francis Hopkinson and Benjamin Franklin.

447.   *Church Music and Musical Life in Pennsylvania in the
        Eighteenth Century.*   Publications of the Pennsylvania
        Society of the Colonial Dames of America, 4.   Philadelphia:
        The Society, 1926-47.   Reprint, New York: AMS Press, 1972.
        3 vols.

Despite its date this work is one of the principal sources for music in early Pennsylvania.   The range of subject matter is broad from German-American traditions, including the Mennonites, Ephrata Cloister, Schwenkfelders, and Moravians to music of English Philadelphia, Jewish music, ballad opera, music of the Roman Catholic Church, Swedish church music, and information on Justus Falckner (1672-1723), a Lutheran hymnologist.   Volume 1 has one of the better accounts of Johannes Kelpius and the Wissahickon Mystics, including a complete facsimile edition of "The Lamenting Voice of the Hidden Love."   Some of the articles include: William J. Hinke, "Lutheran and Reformed Church Hymnody in Early Pennsylvania"; Hugh T. Henry, "Music of the Roman Catholic Church in Pennsylvania in the Eighteenth Century"; Joseph Reider, "Jewish Music in Pennsylvania in the Eighteenth Century"; Herbert B. Satcher, "Music of the Episcopal Church in Pennsylvania in the Eighteenth Century"; George Vail, "Backgrounds of Welsh Music in Colonial Pennsylvania"; Thomas Ridgway, "Ballad Opera in Philadelphia in the Eighteenth Century"; Oscar George Sonneck, "Francis Hopkinson: The First American Poet-Composer and Our Musical Life in Colonial Times"; William Lichtenwanger, "Benjamin Franklin on Music"/"Songs of Freemasonry in Colonial Pennsylvania"/"The Philadelphia Dancing Assemblies and The Mischianza."   Illustrations and facsimiles.

448.   Cleveland, Pat.   "An Introductory Note on John Wayland, Joseph
        Funk, Singers Glen and Shape-Note Music."   *Sheet Music
        Exchange* 4/5 (October 1986): 23-25.

Singers Glen is located in southwestern Virginia.   The author discusses John Wayland, who wrote one of the early biographies of Joseph Funk, tunebook compiler, and includes biographical information on the latter.

449.   Cole, Ronald Fred.   "Music in Portland, Maine, from Colonial
        Times through the Nineteenth Century."   Ph.D. dissertation,

Indiana University, 1975.   405p.   UM 76-2796.   *DAI* 36/8 (February 1976): 4836-A.

Discusses the first references to music in the First Parish Church (est. 1725), singing schools held from 1785 to 1820, based on contemporary newspapers, list of tunebooks sold at bookstores and music shops, concert activity from October 2, 1788 (the first) on, and the use of musical instruments.

450.   Coleberd, Robert E., Jr.   "Journey to Pennsylvania: The Adventures of an Organist in the New World."   *Tracker* 17/1 (1972): 1, 3-4.

On Gottlieb Mittelberger's travel diary written in 1754. Also includes information on organs in Pennsylvania.   (See also entry 606.)

451.   Covey, Cyclone.   "Puritanism and Music in Colonial America." *William and Mary Quarterly* 8/3 (July 1951): 378-88.

Criticizes Percy A. Scholes' *The Puritans and Music in England and New England* (see entry 563).   Discusses the effects of Calvinism on music in New England and claims that the Puritans prohibited all forms of music.   Clifford K. Shipton published a scathing refutation of this thesis, with a reply from Covey, in "Letters to the Editor," *Notes* 9/1 (January 1952), pp. 128-33.

452.   Crain, Charles Robert.   "Music Performance and Pedagogy in Nashville, Tennessee, 1818-1900."   Ph.D. dissertation, George Peabody College for Teachers, 1975.   314p.   UM 75-22257.   *DAI* 36/4 (October 1975): 2080-A.

The author discusses community activities, musicians, the Nashville Female Academy, which included music in its curriculum.

453.   Crews, Emma Katherine.   "Early Musical Activities in Knoxville, Tennessee, 1791-1861."   *East Tennessee Historical Society's Publications* 32 (1960): 3-17.

454.   Crews, Emma Katherine.   "A History of Music in Knoxville, Tennessee, 1791-1910."   Ed.D. dissertation, Florida State

University, 1961.   236p.   UM 61-5634.   *DAI* 22/8 (February 1962): 2815-16.

Based on primary sources, the author discusses "church music, dance music, music for celebrations, music merchants and merchandise, concerts and art music, music organizations, theatre and entertainment music, music education, and general attitudes on music."

455.   Dana, Daniel. *A Discourse on Music, Addressed to the Essex Musical Association, at Their Annual Meeting at Boxford, Sept. 12, 1803.* Newburyport: E.M. Blunt, 1803. 19p.

Surveys the history of music with his opinions on each country's music. About American music he suggests that our composers have not been able to devote their lives to the art as European composers have and consequently "our country has been for years overflowing with productions, not destitute of sprightliness, perhaps, nor, in every instance, of gleams of genius, but composed to no plan, conformed to no principles, and communicating no distinct or abiding impression. . . ." He compliments the Essex Musical Association (Massachusetts) for their part in improving the performance of church music. For additional information on this work, refer to Nitz (see entry 534). Reprinted in *Early American Imprints, Second Series*, no. 4041 (see entry 44).

456.   Daniel, Oliver. "The Grass Roots." *Hi-Fi Music at Home* 5/7 (1958): 33-37.

On the music of New England.

457.   Daniel, Oliver. "Journeyman Composers of New England." *Musical America* 70/3 (February 1950): 110-11, 222, 248.

Discusses Supply Belcher, William Billings, and Jacob Kimball. Facsimiles include a page from William Billings' Bible and an extant example of his handwriting.

458.   Darling, James S. and Maureen McF. Wiggins. "A Constant Tuting: The Music of Williamsburg." *Music Educators Journal* 61/3 (November 1974): 56-61.

An introduction to music in colonial Williamsburg, with
mention of ballad opera, Peter Pelham, organist, and Robert Carter,
amateur musician.   Musical example.

459.   David, Hans T.   "Ephrata and Bethlehem in Pennsylvania: A
       Comparison."   *Papers of the American Musicological Society*
       (1941): 97-104.

       Discusses Johann Conrad Beissel in some detail and compares
his music to that of the Moravians.

460.   Davison, Marjorie Risk.   "Excerpts from the History of Music
       in the District of Columbia."   In *Records of the Columbia
       Historical Society of Washington, D.C., 1966-1968*, pp. 182-
       204.

       Contains only a few comments regarding music in Washington,
D.C. prior to 1820.

461.   Dineen, William and Joyce Ellen Mangler.   "Early Music in
       Rhode Island Churches."   *Rhode Island History* 17/1 (January
       1958): 1-9; 17/2 (April 1958): 33-44; 17/3 (July
       1958): 73-85; 17/4 (October 1958): 108-18.

       Discusses music in the following churches in Providence:
First Congregational Church, 1770-1850, First Baptist Church, 1775-
1834, King's Church (St. John's), 1722-1850, and Beneficent
Congregational Church and Richmond Street Congregational Church,
1744-1836.

462.   Dow, George F.   *The Arts & Crafts in New England, 1704-1775.*
       Topsfield, Mass.: Wayside Press, 1927.   Reprint, New York:
       Da Capo Press, 1967.   xxxii, 326p.

       A discussion of a broad range of arts and crafts, including
a section on music and musical instruments, with surprisingly useful
information.   Dow has extracted early advertisements and notices
concerning music from early newspapers and has carefully noted
titles and dates of issues.   Refer to the index under the headings
"Music" and "Musical instruments" for additional items.

463.   Drummond, Robert Rutherford. *Early German Music in Philadelphia.* New York: D. Appleton, 1910. Reprint, New York: AMS Press, 1972. xiv, 88p.

Actually a general history (to 1800) in that it includes non-German traditions as well. Discusses both sacred and secular music, teachers, dealers, concert music. Includes a separate chapter on Alexander Reinagle (includes a list of his compositions), and information on Philip Roth (Philip Phile). Some concert programs are used as examples. No index. See also the author's article, "The Early Pennsylvanian German as Musician," in *Pennsylvania-German* 12 (1911), pp. 171-72 (see entry 465).

464.   Drummond, Robert R.   "Early Music in Philadelphia with Special Reference to German Music." *German American Annals* 6 (1908): 157-79.

Discusses music during the 1700s.

465.   Drummond, Robert R.   "The Early Pennsylvanian German as Musician." *Pennsylvania-German* 12 (1911): 171-72.

466.   Dwight, John S.   "The Handel and Haydn Society." *New England Magazine* 1 (1889): 382-93.

467.   Dwight, John S.   "The History of Music in Boston." In *The Memorial History of Boston, Including Suffolk County, Massachusetts, 1630-1880.* Ed. by Justin Winsor. 4 vols. Boston: James R. Osgood, 1881, 4, pp. 415-64.

Dwight begins his history of music with Boston in 1810. Previous to that, he characterizes Puritan music as "one monotonous and barren type." For Dwight, Gottlieb Graupner, who founded a "Philo-harmonic Society" in Boston, was a significant musician during the period 1810-20.

468.   Dwight, John S.   "Our Dark Age in Music." *Atlantic* 50 (1882): 813-23.

Based principally on music in New England. Characterizes the period of music in America from 1620 to 1690 as "one of total darkness." Refers to William Billings as an "eccentric genius." Describes singing schools and a number of collections of New England tunebooks. In Dwight's view, the development of American music depended upon the importation of culture from Europe. He considers Gottlieb Graupner as the major figure who planted the seed in Boston with the formation of an orchestra that would perform European works.

469.   Eberlein, Harold D. and Cortlandt Van D. Hubbard. "The American 'Vauxhall' of the Federal Era." *Pennsylvania Magazine of History and Biography* 68/2 (April 1944): 150-74.

Mentions concerts, including some outdoor presentations, in New York, Philadelphia, and Charleston.

470.   Edwards, George Thornton. *Music and Musicians of Maine.* Portland, Maine: The Southworth Press, 1928. Reprint, New York: AMS Press, 1970. xxv, 542p.

A comprehensive work that includes biographies of musicians, names of organizations, musical events, etc. After a "Prologue" on the Indians of Maine, the author discusses the period 1640-1775, including the *Bay Psalm Book*, early instruments, and James Lyon. Chapter 2 focuses on the period 1776-1819, including a discussion of Supply Belcher, and lesser known musicians, the Hans Gram Musical Society, and tunebooks. Includes a biographical, geographical, and general index.

471.   Elson, Arthur. "Music in Old Boston." *Musician* 15/12 (December 1910): 795-96.

Discusses "the Puritan idea of music," congregational singing, instruments, teachers, and concerts. Musical example.

472.   Elson, Louis C. "Our Humble Beginnings in Music." *Etude* 31/12 (December 1913): 859-60.

Discusses principally the New England tradition of the 18th century, with information on early instruments, performance practice of psalmody, and William Billings. Remarkably, Elson lists some of the sources that he consulted.

473.   Engler, Martha C. "Boston's Era of German Music, 1800 to
       1918." In *Germans in Boston*. Ed. by Paul K. Ackermann.
       Boston: Goethe Society of New England, 1981, pp. 23-26.

       A brief popular account discussing Gottlieb Graupner and the
Handel and Haydn Society.

474.   Epstein, Dena J. "On Collecting Materials for Local Music
       Histories." *Notes* 24/1 (September 1967): 18-21.

       Materials on local history have to be collected before
general histories of music in America can be written. The author
cites where local preservation projects have been initiated by
libraries and examines technical problems encountered by libraries.

475.   Farish, Hunter Dickinson, ed. *Journal and Letters of Philip
       Vickers Fithian, 1773-1774: A Plantation Tutor of the Old
       Dominion.* Charlottesville: Dominion Books, University Press
       of Virginia, 1968. xxxii, 270p.

       A standard source for information on musicians and
instruments in colonial Virginia. Fithian was a tutor for the
Robert Carter family at "Nomini Hall." Begin a search in the index
under various headings, including "Balls," "Music," "Musical
Instruments," "Songs," and "Sonatas."

476.   Faulcon, Clarence. "A History of Musical Pennsylvania before
       1850." D.Mus. dissertation, Philadelphia Conservatory of
       Music, 1962.

477.   Fisher, William Arms. *Notes on Music in Old Boston.* Boston:
       Oliver Ditson, 1918. Reprint, New York: AMS Press, 1976.
       xvi, 105p.

       Fisher provides musical and historical background of Boston
as a basis for a history of the Oliver Ditson music publishing firm.
In so doing, he examines the New England tradition, mentions William
Billings, Oliver Holden, and Thomas Walter. Also discusses concerts
and secular music. The first three chapters are relevant. Of
special interest is his discussion, "Some Early Book and Music
Shops." Musical illustrations and facsimiles. Many sources are
provided thus making this book still useful today.

478.   Fleck, Hattie C.   "America's Christmas City, an Ideal
           Salzburg." *Musician* 47 (1942): 70, 79.

        On Bethlehem, Pa.

479.   Flexner, Beatrice Hudson.   "The Music of the Puritans."
           American Heritage 8/1 (December 1956): 65-67, 117-119.

        An introduction to principal musical activities of Puritan
sacred and secular music.   Various compositions by William Billings
are introduced.   Musical examples.

480.   Foote, Henry Wilder.   "Musical Life in Boston in the
           Eighteenth Century." *Proceedings of the American
           Antiquarian Society* 49/2 (1940): 293-313.

        Reviews the literature on the subject and discusses John
Tufts, Thomas Walter, sacred and secular concerts, instruments, and
tunebooks.

481.   Gaines, William H., Jr.   "A Constant Tuting." *Virginia
           Cavalcade* 4/4 (Spring 1955): 4-7.

        An introduction to music in colonial Williamsburg, Va.
Mentions early concerts, Peter Pelham, organist, and Robert Carter,
amateur musician.

482.   Gay, Julius. *Church Music in Farmington in the Olden Time.
           An Historical Address Delivered at the Annual Meeting of the
           Village Library Company of Farmington, Conn.* Hartford,
           Conn.: Lockwood and Brainard Co., 1891. 25p.

        Discusses their New England musical "ancestors," including
William Billings and his "strange tunes," and Timothy Swan who,
"inheriting a tinge of insanity from his mother, wrote that wild,
weird tune, 'Ocean. . . .'" Discusses the singing of psalms, and
amusing anecdotes regarding William Billings, and the controversy
regarding the correct way to sing psalms.

483.   Gerson, Robert A. *Music in Philadelphia.* Philadelphia:
          Theodore Presser, 1940. Reprint, Westport, Conn.:
          Greenwood Press, 1970. viii, 422p.

          Chronological survey. The first 3 chapters focus on
colonial music, the Revolutionary period, and "Music from 1800 to
1860." Based on both primary and secondary sources, this work
deserves reading. Includes photo of a page from a hymnal by
Johannes Kelpius, and "The New Presidents or Jefferson's March" by
Alexander Reinagle. Bibliography and index.

484.   Gerson, Robert A. "The Story of Music in America:
          Philadelphia." *Musical America* 66/15 (December 10, 1946):
          6-7, 16; 66/16 (December 25, 1946): 6-7, 33.

          An introduction, including sacred and secular music,
instruments, music teachers, with information on Johann Conrad
Beissel, Benjamin Carr, Benjamin Franklin, Francis Hopkinson,
Johannes Kelpius, and others. Illustrations.

485.   Gottesman, Rita S. *The Arts and Crafts in New York, 1777-
          1799: Advertisements and News Items from New York City
          Newspapers.* New York: New-York Historical Society, 1954.
          xix, 484p.

          The author has extracted notices and advertisements
concerning a broad range of arts and crafts from early newspapers
and has carefully noted titles and dates of issues. Included is a
rather substantial section on "Music and Musical Instruments" that
has information on a number of music teachers. Readers should refer
as well to the index which includes a surprising number of entries
under various music headings. See also the author's *The Arts and
Crafts in New York, 1726-1776* (New York: New-York Historical
Society, 1938; reprint, New York: Da Capo Press, 1970) and *The Arts
and Crafts in New York, 1800-1804* (New York: New-York Historical
Society, 1965).

486.   Hall, A. Oakley. "Memories of Early Music in New York."
          American Art Journal 56 (1890): 82-83.

          Pertaining to the early 19th century.

487. Hall, Roger L. "Singing Stoughton." *Journal of Church Music* 22/1 (January 1980): 7-10.

       Discusses the Stoughton Musical Society of Massachusetts.

488. Hamm, Charles. "The Ecstatic and the Didactic: A Pattern in American Music." In *Current Thought in Musicology*. Ed. by John W. Grubbs. Austin: University of Texas Press, 1976, pp. 41-62.

       Discusses "persistent patterns. . . in American music from the time of the Puritans." Styles and individuals used as examples include psalmody, "regular singing," and William Billings as compared to Andrew Law.

489. "The Handel and Haydn Society." *Musical Library* 1 (July 1835): 3; 2 (August 1835): 6; 3 (September 1835): 11; 5 (November 1835): 18; 7 (January 1836): 27-28.

       Discusses the history of Boston's Handel and Haydn Society, begun in 1815. Article possibly written by Lowell Mason or George Webb.

490. "The Handel and Haydn Society's Festival." *Dwight's Journal of Music* 11 (1857): 21-22.

       Includes some historical background.

491. Hehr, Milton Gerald. "Concert Life in Salem, 1783-1823." *Essex Institute Historical Collections* 100/2 (April 1964): 98-138.

       A principal study based on contemporary newspapers and diaries. Includes concert programs, information on musicians, musical societies, including the Essex South Musical Society, Salem Baptist Singing Society, Essex Musical Association, and the Handel Society.

492. Hehr, Milton Gerald. "Musical Activities in Salem, Massachusetts, 1783-1823." Ph.D. dissertation, Boston

University, 1963.   121p.   UM 63-6574.   *DAI* 24/4 (October
1963): 1643-44.

Includes a discussion of musical events, compositions, music
dealers, dancing teachers, musicians, musical organizations,
theatrical life, including operas and songs, and sacred music.
Significant personalities include Samuel Holyoke and Jacob Kimball,
Jr.   Also discusses the Essex Musical Association (founded 1797).

493.   Hindman, John Joseph.   "Concert Life in Ante Bellum
        Charleston."   Ph.D. dissertation, University of North
        Carolina, 1971.   xx, 758p.

"Chapter 1 contains background information on the general
social and cultural setting of the time.   Chapter 2 discusses
several aspects of concert life, with attendant manifold reflections
and ramifications."   Chapter 3 focuses on local musicians and
visiting artists.   Chapter 4 discusses types of music prevalent in
the period.   An appendix consists of a chronological record of 1,100
musical events.   Index.

494.   Hines, James Robert.   "Musical Activity in Norfolk, Virginia,
        1680-1973."   Ph.D. dissertation, University of North
        Carolina, 1974.   2 vols, 773p.   UM 74-26885.   *DAI* 35/6
        (December 1974): 3793-A.

Includes 19 chapters.   "Although Norfolk was founded in
1680, the major portion of this study deals with the period since
the revolution."   Based on 40,000 newspapers and other primary
sources.   Discusses concerts, instruments, teachers and musicians,
music in Norfolk churches, and the Moses Myers music collection.
Includes an anthology of works by Norfolk composers.   Has 20
appendixes.   General index.

495.   Hood, George.   *A History of Music in New England*.   Boston:
        Wilkins, Carter and Company, 1846.   Reprint, with new
        introd. (xxiiip.) by Johannes Riedel, New York: Johnson
        Reprint Corporation, 1970.   vii, 255p.

In Hood's words, "This book pretends only to be a history of
psalmody, and to extend from the settlement of New England to the
beginning of the present century."   A truly significant and
influential work in its day; a number of subsequent works cited by

Riedel were based, in part, on Hood's research.   See a review in
Choral Advocate, and Singing-Class Journal 1/2 (July 1850), p. 26.

496.   Hoogerwerf, Frank W., ed.   *Music in Georgia.*   New York: Da
        Capo Press, 1984.   xvi, 343p.

        Excellent introduction to aspects of music in Georgia.   A
series of 24 articles by contributing authors and reprinted from a
number of journals published 1934-77.   Included are the following
articles: John W. Wagner, "Some Early Musical Moments in Augusta";
Harry H. Hall, "Early Sounds of Moravian Brass Music: A Cultural
Note from Colonial Georgia"; Webb B. Garrison, "Salem Camp Meeting:
Symbol of an Era."   Index.

497.   Hoxie, Frances Alida.   "Five Decades of Concerts in Hartford,
        1800-1850."   *Connecticut Historical Society Bulletin* 41/4
        (October 1976): 119-28.

        An early concert took place in 1802 at the North
Presbyterian Church, and in May 1805, a chamber organ was installed
in the State House Museum.   In addition, in October 1805, George K.
Jackson was giving concerts, and Eli Robert was an organist and
teacher of music in 1816 at North Presbyterian Church.

498.   Hubbard, John.   *Essay on Music Pronounced before the Middlesex
        Musical Society, Sept. 9, A.D. 1807.*   Boston: Manning and
        Loring, 1808.   19p.

        Hubbard, an amateur musician, delivered this work at a
meeting of the Middlesex Musical Society in Dunstable, Mass.   An
attack against the "bombastic" uncultured style of American church
music, such as the fuging tunes in favor of European music.
According to Nitz (see entry 534), "it is probably safe to state
that this pamphlet was the single most important statement of the
reform movement prior to the major treatises of Lowell Mason and
Thomas Hastings who did not do their most important work until after
1820."   Reprinted in *Early American Imprints, Second Series*, no.
15276 (see entry 44).   See also Richard Crawford's comments on
Hubbard in an article, "Fuging-tune," in *The New Grove Dictionary of
American Music*, vol. 2, p. 176 (see entry 30).

499.   Jefferys, C.P.B.   "The Provincial and Revolutionary History of
          St. Peter's Church, Philadelphia, 1753-1783." *Pennsylvania
          Magazine of History and Biography* 48/2 (1924): 181-92.

          Includes a section titled "Music and Singing at St. Peter's,
1761-1783" that mentions instruments and John Bankson, organist.

500.   Johnson, H. Earle.   *Hallelujah, Amen!   The Story of the Handel
          and Haydn Society of Boston.*   Boston: B. Humphries, 1965.
          Reprint, with a new intro. by Richard Crawford, New York: Da
          Capo Press, 1981.   256p.

          A survey of the 150-year tenure of the Society.   An
informative, albeit "anecdotal," narrative that describes the
establishment of the Society in 1815.   No doubt based on the more
definitive *History of the Handel and Haydn Society* (see entry 542).

501.   Johnson, H. Earle.   "Music in New England (1799-1852)."
          Bulletin of the American Musicological Society (1937): 28.

          Abstract of a paper read at a meeting of the New England
Chapter of the AMS on May 21, 1937.

502.   Johnson, H. Earle.   *Musical Interludes in Boston, 1795-1830.*
          Foreword by Otto Kinkeldey.   New York: Columbia University
          Press, 1943.   Reprint, New York: AMS Press, 1967.   xv, 366p.

          One of the primary scholarly works to consult.   Topical
essays, including, for example, "Concert Life": 1800-25, and
sections on "teachers," "music dealers and manufacturers," and
"publishers."   Chronologically arranged.   The appendixes are
particularly useful and include: "Von Hagen Publications";
"Catalogue of Graupner Publications"; "Lesser Publishers in Boston";
and "Copyrighted Musical Works, Jan. 1, 1791- ."   General index.

503.   Kaufman, Charles H.   *Music in New Jersey, 1655-1860: A Study
          of Musical Activity and Musicians in New Jersey from Its
          First Settlement to the Civil War.*   Rutherford, N.J.:
          Fairleigh Dickinson University Press, 1981.   297p.

          Based on the author's dissertation "Music in New Jersey"
(New York University, 1974).   This principal study of music in New

Jersey focuses on Lutheran and Calvinist psalmody, secular music,
including music education, publications, instrument makers,
concerts, and published views on music. Includes indexes for
musicians, teachers, societies, and tradesmen.

504.   Keefer, Lubov. *Baltimore's Music: The Haven of the American
        Composer*. Baltimore: J.H. Furst, 1962. xvii, 343p.

        Survey from colonial times to the present. Based, in part,
on a variety of primary sources, but unfortunately complete
citations for those sources are not provided. Also discusses
colonial music of Maryland and, in particular, Annapolis and the
Tuesday Club.

505.   Keene, James A. *Music and Education in Vermont, 1700-1900*.
        Macomb, Ill.: Glenbridge, 1987. 214p.

        Based on his dissertation, "A History of Music Education in
Vermont 1770-1900" (University of Michigan, 1969). Discusses
geographic and economic influences on music education in Vermont.
Over 250 personal names are cited.

506.   Kiehner, Anton F. "The Performing Arts of Philadelphia, 1700
        to 1800." D.Mus. dissertation, Philadelphia Conservatory
        of Music, 1964.

507.   Kinscella, Hazel Gertrude. "Music in Colonial Philadelphia,
        1664-1776." Ph.D. dissertation, University of Washington,
        1941.

508.   Kmen, Henry A. *Music in New Orleans: The Formative Years,
        1791-1841*. Baton Rouge: Louisiana State University Press,
        1966. viii, 314p.

        A thorough study with copious notes based on primary
sources. Discusses early concerts and balls, opera, and black
musicians. Bibliography is recommended. Index.

509.   Krohn, Ernst C. *Missouri Music*. St. Louis, 1924. Reprint,
        New York: Da Capo Press, 1971. xl, 380p.

A standard work for identifying names of composers, musicians, concerts and other musical events, tunebooks and other publications, and musical instruments associated with Missouri. A comprehensive general index.

510.   Lahee, Henry C. "A Century of Choral Singing in New England." *New England Magazine* 26 (1902): 102-17.

511.   Lambert, Barbara. "The Musical Puritans." *Old-Time New England* 62 (January-March 1972): 66-75.

512.   Lansing, Richard H. "Music in Rochester from 1817 to 1909." *Rochester Historical Society Publication Fund Series* 2 (1923): 135-85.

513.   Lechford, Thomas. *Plain Dealing or News from New England.* London, 1642. Reprint, Boston: Wiggin and Lunt, 1867; New York: Johnson Reprint Corporation, 1969 (Foreword by Darrett B. Rutman). 211p.

An early source describing theological practices in New England. Lechford describes a typical worship service and the practice of psalm singing. He also notes the poor state of musical knowledge by parishioners at that time.

514.   Lippincott, Horace Mather *Philadelphia.* Philadelphia: Macrae Smith, 1926. Reprint, Port Washington, N.Y.: Kennikat Press, 1970. 259p.

Includes chapters on theater and dancing assemblies. Dancing masters discussed include Theobald Hackett and John Ormsby.

515.   Livermore, Solomon Kidder. *On the Practice of Music: A Discourse Pronounced at Pepperell, Massachusetts, May 17th, 1809, before the Middlesex Musical Society.* Amherst, N.H.: Joseph Cushing, 1809. 15p.

An attack against most American composers who he considered "quacks"; however, he recognized that a number of Americans "have made diligent and laborious application to the study of harmony."

For additional information on this work, refer to Nitz (see entry
534).   Reprinted in *Early American Imprints, Second Series*, no.
17923 (see entry 44).

516.   Lowens, Irving.   "Music Awakening in Old Sturbridge."
       Washington Sunday Star (13 May 1973): H-4.

       Discusses a conference on early American music titled
"Joyful Sounds" at Sturbridge, Mass., and organized by Alan
Buechner, Arthur F. Schrader, and Nicholas Tawa.   Mentions the
participants and the papers presented, as well as the music
performed.

517.   Lowens, Irving.   "Music in the American Wilderness."   *Etude*
       74/7 (September 1956): 13, 20.

       On music in New England during the 1600s.   Reprinted in
Lowens, *Music and Musicians in Early America* (see entry 371).

518.   McCausland, Susan A. Arnold.   "A Running Glance Over the Field
       of Music in Missouri."   *Missouri Historical Review* 8/4 (July
       1914): 206-10.

       A brief introduction to music in Missouri, including mention
of musical instruments used there as early as 1778 and a music club
in St. Louis in 1814.

519.   McDaniel, Stanley Robert.   "Church Song and the Cultivated
       Tradition in New England and New York."   D.M.A.
       dissertation, University of Southern California, 1983.   UM
       number not cited.   *DAI* 44/5 (November 1983): 1237-A.

       "This study details aspects of choral organization, the
training and employment of choirs, choirmasters, and organists, and
the theological trends which helped to shape music in the church.
Compositional styles of a variety of composers are examined.   During
the post-Revolutionary War years, *ad hoc* groups of singers from
local singing schools argued for the privilege of sitting together
and usually won.   Primitive modes of conducting and accompanying
these ensembles were soon introduced."

520.   MacDougall, Hamilton C.   *Early New England Psalmody.*
         Brattleboro, Vermont: Stephen Daye Press, 1940.   Reprint,
         New York: Da Capo Press, 1969.   viii, 179p.

         Scholarly treatment of the subject to about 1800; includes a
section on performance practice.   Useful for its facsimiles of works
from various tunebooks.   Includes a series of appendixes, including
a list of "Tunes from Ainsworth, the *Bay Psalm Book*, Tufts and
Walter in Modern Hymnals."   Index.

521.   Madeira, Louis C.   *Annals of Music in Philadelphia and History
         of the Musical Fund Society from Its Organization in 1820 to
         the Year 1858.*   Philadelphia: J.B. Lippincott, 1896.
         Reprint, New York: Da Capo Press, 1973.   202p.

         The first three chapters discuss pre-1820 music
entertainments, church music, instruments, and musicians, including
Benjamin Carr, Benjamin Franklin, Alexander Reinagle, George
Schetky, Rayner Taylor, and others.

522.   Mahan, K.H.   "Music in Colonial Williamsburg."   *Music Clubs
         Magazine* 66/1 (1986): 4.

523.   Mahar, William J.   "Music in Pennsylvania."   In *Pennsylvania
         1776.*   Ed. by Robert Secor.   University Park: Pennsylvania
         State University Press, 1975, pp. 253-63.

         A popular account and introduction to fife and drum music,
music of various Pennsylvania-German sects, a section on David
Tannenberg, organ builder, and music in colonial Philadelphia,
including a section on Francis Hopkinson.   Particularly appealing
are the facsimiles and other illustrations in this work.

524.   Mangler, Joyce E.   *Rhode Island Music and Musicians, 1733-
         1850.*   Detroit Studies in Music Bibliography, 7.   Detroit:
         Information Service, 1965.   90p.

         Includes a list of personal names of organists, singers,
teachers, dancing teachers, dealers of music and instruments, and a
section on church music, concert life, music education, and music
trades.   Bibliography.   (See also entry 443.)

525.   Marks, Harold K.   "Early Music and Musicians of Allentown."
       Proceedings of the Lehigh County Historical Society (1939):
       37-47.

       Allentown, Pennsylvania.

526.   "'Mattachusetts Musick' a Century Ago."   *Dwight's Journal of
       Music* 3 (1853): 155-56.

       Includes information on Thomas Walter's *The Grounds and
       Rules of Musick* (Boston, 1721).

527.   Metcalf, Frank J.   "History of Sacred Music in the District of
       Columbia."   *Records of the Columbia Historical Society* 28
       (1926): 175-202.

       Books and articles on music in early Washington, D.C. are
       scarce, so despite its date, this work is still useful.   The article
       includes a number of short biographies of individual musicians, and
       plates of title pages of early Washington music hymnbooks.

528.   Milligan, Harold V.   "An Old Choral Society."   *New Music
       Review* 23 (1924): 191-94.

       On the Stoughton Musical Society in Massachusetts.

529.   Milligan, Harold V.   "Pilgrim and Puritan."   *New Music Review*
       20 (1921): 271-73.

530.   Molnar, John W.   "Art Music in Colonial Virginia."   In *Art and
       Music in the South*.   Ed. by Francis B. Simkins.   Farmville,
       Va.: Longwood College, 1961, pp. 63-108.

       Molnar was one of the first scholars to research music of
       early Virginia.   Discusses musicians, concerts, and instruments.
       Well documented.

531.   "Music and Dancing."   *William and Mary Quarterly* 5/1 (January
       1925): 63-65.

Includes extracts for advertisements of music teachers and dancing masters from the *Virginia Argus* (1803-04) and *Richmond Enquirer* (1812).

532.   *Music in Boston: Readings from the First Three Centuries.*
        Comp. and ed. by John C. Swan.   Boston: Trustees of the
        Public Library of Boston, 1977.   viii, 99p.

        Includes excerpts from 13 sources.   See especially readings
from the *Bay Psalm Book*, Cotton Mather's *Magnalia Christi Americana*
(1702) and *The Accomplished Singer* (1721), Thomas Symmes' *Utile
Dulci* (1723), William Billings' preface to *The New-England Psalm-
Singer* (1770) and *Singing Master's Assistant* (1778), John Hubbard's
An Essay on Music (1808), and John Rowe Parker's *Euterpeiad* (1820-
22).

533.   *Music in Colonial Massachusetts, 1630-1820.*   Ed. by Barbara
        Lambert.   Publications of the Colonial Society of
        Massachusetts, 53-54.   Boston: The Colonial Society of
        Massachusetts, 1980-85.   2 vols.

        This work is a spinoff from a conference held by the
Colonial Society of Massachusetts, May 17-18, 1973, and is a
principal source of study for music of that period.   Includes the
following contributions: Joy van Cleef and Kate van Winkle Keller,
"Selected American Country Dances and Their English Sources"; Raoul
Camus, "Military Music of Colonial Boston"; Arthur F. Schrader,
"Songs to Cultivate the Sensations of Freedom"; Carleton Sprague
Smith, "Broadsides and Their Music in Colonial America"; Barbara
Lambert, "Social Music, Musicians, and their Musical Instruments in
and Around Colonial Boston"; Phyllis Braff, "A *Musical Gathering*:
Investigative Steps and Preliminary Conjectures"; Irving Lowens,
"Eighteenth-Century Massachusetts Songsters"; Richard Crawford,
"Massachusetts Musicians and the Core Repertory of Early American
Psalmody"; Sinclair Hitchings, "The Musical Pursuits of William
Price and Thomas Johnston"; Barbara Owen, "Eighteenth-Century Organs
and Organ Building in New England"; Cynthia Adams Hoover, "Epilogue
to Secular Music in Early Massachusetts."   Facsimiles and general
index.

534.   Nitz, Donald A.   "Community Musical Societies in Massachusetts
        to 1840."   D.M.A. dissertation, Boston University, 1964.
        413p.

An excellent work that discusses 13 societies before 1800, starting with the first association, the Musical Society in Newburyport (1774), and 30 societies representing the years 1800-20, as well as other societies between 1820 and 1840. Included in the discussion is a historical survey of each society, based on primary sources, its musical activities, publications, and performance practices. There are musical examples, and a complete photocopy edition of *Musica Spiritualis, or Sacred Music as Performed on Tuesday the 23d of April, 1782 at the Stone Chapel, Boston* ([Boston]: Benjamin Edes & Sons, [1782]).

535.   Nutter, Charles S.   "What the Pilgrim Fathers Sang."   *New England Magazine* 10 (1894): 201-03.

536.   O'Connell, L.   "Music in 'Mayflower' Days."   *Musician* 11/9 (September 1906): 435-37.

Discusses music in early New England, including psalmody, instruments, and music teachers.   Illustrations.

537.   Olson, Ivan Walter, Jr.   "Music and Germans in Nineteenth Century Richmond."   *Journal of Research in Music Education* 14/1 (Spring 1966): 27-32.

Based on the author's doctoral dissertation (see entry 538).

538.   Olson, Ivan Walter, Jr.   "The Roots and Development of Public School Music in Richmond, Virginia, 1782-1907."   Ed.D. dissertation, University of Michigan, 1964.   248p.   UM 64-12655.   *DAI* 26/10 (April 1966): 6091-92.

Chapter 2 focuses on music instruction before 1855.   The author's findings reveal that music instruction before 1830 was primarily a private affair for the benefit of young ladies.

539.   Osburn, Mary H.   *Ohio Composers and Musical Authors.* Columbus: F.J. Heer, 1942.   238p.

Although this book is principally a biographical dictionary of composers in Ohio for the latter half of the 19th and 20th centuries, the author does include an essay, "Development of Music

in Ohio: A Historical Sketch," in which names and musical events
before 1820 are mentioned.

540.   Osterhout, Paul Ragatz. "Music in Northampton, Massachusetts
        to 1820." Ph.D. dissertation, University of Michigan, 1978.
        405p. UM 78-22981. *DAI* 39/6 (December 1978): 3215-A.

        Two principal parts: "musical activity in Northampton from
1654 to 1820" and "the music publishing business that thrived in the
town between the years 1797 and 1812." Topics include instruments,
military music, singing, dancing, sacred music (psalmody), and
singing schools. Included is a list of all pre-1820 Northampton
music imprints.

541.   Oyler, Edna B. "Early American Music." *Musician* 10/8 (August
        1905): 330-31.

        A few words about music in early Boston.

542.   Perkins, Charles C. and John S. Dwight. *History of the Handel
        and Haydn Society of Boston, Massachusetts: 1815-1890.*
        Boston: Alfred Mudge, 1883-1913. Reprint, New York: Da Capo
        Press, 1977. 2 vols.

        The introduction discusses psalmody in New England, followed
by a history of the establishment of the Handel and Haydn Society,
whose purpose originally it was for the "selection, practice, and
improvement in the mode of performing sacred music." Discusses the
concerts and provides a source for names of musicians
(alphabetically arranged, pp. 61-69) and the identification of other
musical societies at that time, including the Stoughton Musical
Society, the Massachusetts Musical Society, and others.

543.   Pichierri, Louis. *Music in New Hampshire: 1623-1800.* New
        York: Columbia University Press, 1960. xv, 297p.

        This study has valuable information based to a large extent
on primary sources. Discussed are instruments, sacred and secular
music, musical events, including concerts and opera, teachers,
singing schools, and separate chapters on John Hubbard, Benjamin
Dearborn, and Samuel Holyoke. Appendixes include a list of

teachers' advertisements, opera programs, and "John Hancock and the Anti-Theatre Law of 1750."

544.   Ping-Robbins, Nancy R.   "Music in Antebellum Wilmington and the Lower Cape Fear of North Carolina."   Ph.D. dissertation, University of Colorado, 1979.   xviii, 794p.

545.   Ping-Robbins, Nancy R.   "Music in the Antebellum Southeast." In *Report of Proceedings: Ph.D. in Music Symposium*.   April 5-7, 1985.   Ed. by William Kearns and William Reeves. Boulder: University of Colorado, 1988, pp. 51-61.

A good introduction to musicians of the area, although most of the emphasis is on the period after 1820.   (See also entry 544.)

546.   Pratt, Waldo S.   "The Earliest New England Music." *Proceedings of the Unitarian Historical Society* 1/2 (1928): 28-47.

547.   Price, Robert Bates.   "A History of Music in Northern Louisiana until 1900."   D.M.A. dissertation, Catholic University of America, 1977.   300p.   UM 78-00902.   *DAI* 38/9 (March 1978): 5116-A.

Includes a discussion of the first recorded accounts of music from 1706-1803, including music by French explorers, a Spanish hymn, "Alabado," by Fray Antonio Margil, a Franciscan missionary. Other chapters discuss folk songs, music of slaves, singing schools and campmeetings, and "music of the planters."

548.   Prime, Alfred C.   *The Arts & Crafts in Philadelphia, Maryland, and South Carolina*.   N.p.: Walpole Society, 1929-33. Reprint, New York: Da Capo Press, 1969.   2 vols.

Despite its date, Prime's work is still useful, as it is based on advertisements and notices (herein reprinted) for a variety of arts and crafts taken from early newspapers.   Although a category for music is not included in the table of contents, begin a search in the indexes (Part 1, 1721-85; Part 2, 1786-1800) under "Music books," "Musical instruments," "Music engraving," "Music teacher," and "Musical clock."

549.   Raddin, George G., Jr.   "The Music of New York City, 1797-
          1804." *New-York Historical Society Quarterly* 38 (1954):
          478-99.

550.   *Records of the Tuesday Club of Annapolis, 1745-56.*   Ed. by
          Elaine G. Breslaw.   Urbana: University of Illinois Press,
          1988.   xxxvii, 599p.

          The Tuesday Club of Annapolis, Maryland was a significant
literary and musical club in its day.   The *Records*, faithfully
compiled by the club's founder, Alexander Hamilton, offer a wealth
of information on its members, many of whom were amateur musicians,
and serves as a principal source of study on Annapolis.   Hamilton's
chronology is here transcribed and includes an introductory essay
with bibliographical sources for further reading, and an index of
members and visitors of the club.

551.   Redway, Virginia Larkin.   "A New York Concert in 1736."
          Musical Quarterly 22/2 (April 1936): 170-77.

          The first recorded concert in New York took place on January
21, 1736.   The author proposes that Charles Theodore Pachelbel was
the performing artist.

552.   Reines, Philip.   "A Cultural History of the City of Winston-
          Salem, North Carolina: 1766-1966."   Ph.D dissertation,
          University of Denver, 1970.   649p.   UM 71-10240.   *DAI* 31/10
          (April 1971): 5569-A.

          For the period prior to 1820, the principal discussion is on
the Moravians in Salem, especially "the musical talents of the
inhabitants and their propensity for the education of their
children."

553.   "Reminiscences of the Handel and Haydn Society."   *American Art
          Journal* 55 (1890): 173-74.

554.   Rieder, Kathryn S.   "Music That Came on the Mayflower."   *Etude*
          63 (1945): 383, 412.

555. Rogers, Delmer D.   "Public Music Performances in New York City
        from 1800 to 1850." *Yearbook for Inter-American Musical
        Research* 6 (1970): 5-50.

        Discusses both sacred and secular music. Includes numerous
concert programs and notices and is based, in part, on newspapers
from the period.

556. Rohrer, Gertrude Martin. *Music and Musicians of Pennsylvania.*
        Philadelphia: Theodore Presser, 1940. vi, 127p.

        A series of essays by contributing authors on a wide variety
of topics. See especially Harvey Gaul, "Three Hundred Years of
Music in Pennsylvania," including Francis Hopkinson, the Moravians,
Benjamin Carr, and early music in Pittsburgh; no sources provided,
however. A notable feature of this work is its biographical
dictionary of Pennsylvania musicians (pp. 95-121), which includes a
number of early American musicians.

557. Rosenberry, M. Claude. "The Pennsylvania German in Music."
        Pennsylvania German Society Proceedings 41 (1933): 29-44.

        An introduction to Germans in Pennsylvania, including
Johannes Kelpius and the Wissahickon Mystics, Mennonites, Ephrata
Cloister, Schwenkfelders, Moravians, and early instruments.

558. Runner, David Clark. "Music in the Moravian Community of
        Lititz." D.M.A. dissertation, Eastman School of Music,
        1976. 100p. UM 77-8312. *DAI* 37/10 (April 1977): 6134-A.

        Discusses communal standards, musical activities and
instruments in Lititz, Pa. Personalities include Rev. Bernard
Grube, who organized the Collegium Musicum there, Jeremiah Dencke,
Johann Frederick Peter, David Tannenberg, Johannes Herbst, George
Godfrey Müller, John Antes, and John Bechler. Discusses the music
held in the Moravian Archives and the instruments in the Lititz
Church museum.

559. Saerchinger, Cesar. "Musical Landmarks in New York." *Musical
        Quarterly* 6/1 (January 1920): 69-90.

Despite its date of publication, this is still a useful
article. Includes information on concerts and operatic performances
in 18th and early 19th centuries. Illustrations.

560. Sandford, Gordon. "A Sermon on Music from 1771." *Colorado
      Journal of Research in Music Education* 4 (1968): 4-5.

      The sermon was presented by Zabdiel Adams in 1771.

561. Scholes, Percy A. "The Earliest Americans and Their Music:
      Some New Light." *Etude* 52/7 (July 1934): 399-400.

      Discusses music of the Puritans. According to the author,
no "Blue Laws" ever existed prohibiting the use of instruments in
New England, and further the Puritans likely enjoyed secular music.

562. Scholes, Percy A. "Music in Seventeenth-Century New England."
      Monthly Musical Record 63 (1933): 25-27.

563. Scholes, Percy A. *The Puritans and Music in England and New
      England*. New York: Russell & Russell, 1962. xxii, 428p.

      A useful work at the time of its first publication in 1934.
Discusses instrumental music and psalmody. Perhaps the most
interesting chapter is that on the "Blue Laws" of Connecticut, which
were supposedly against music and dance.

564. Scholes, Percy A. "The Puritans Enjoyed Music." *Educational
      Music Magazine* 15/2 (1935): 1-17.

565. Scholes, Percy A. "The Truth About the New England Puritans
      and Music." *Musical Quarterly* 19/1 (January 1933): 1-17.

      Proposes that the Puritans did not hate music and forbid its
use as has been commonly believed. Based on primary sources,
including diaries and court records.

566. Scholes, Percy A. "Why Malign Your Forefathers?" *Musical
      Courier* 106/7 (1933): 6.

Thesis is similar to entry 565 above in that the Puritans were not intolerant to music.

567.   Schwartz, G.F.   "Music in America during Revolutionary Times."
          Etude 34/8 (August 1916): 559-60.

A survey of major musical activities in Boston and Philadelphia.   Includes a photo of an organ once owned by Thomas Brattle in 1713 and located, according to the author, in St. John's Church in Portsmouth, N.H.

568.   Sears, Donald.   "Music in Early Portland." *Maine Historical Society Quarterly* 16/3 (Winter 1977): 131-60.

An excellent introduction to the early music in this Maine town from 1785 on.   Discusses various tunebooks, including those of Supply Belcher and Abraham Maxim, and early concerts and musical societies.   Based on primary sources.

569.   Seip, Oswell J.   "Pennsylvania German Choral Books."
          Proceedings of the Lehigh County Historical Society (1944):
          39-43.

570.   Simons, Elizabeth P.   *Music in Charleston from 1732 to 1919.*
          Charleston, S.C.: J. Furlong and Sons, 1927.   86p.

A quaint study that discusses concerts and other musical activities, and musicians.   Of note, the copy of this work in the Library of Congress was owned by Sonneck and was presented to him by Simons, who acknowledges in her hand-written dedication that she could not have written the work without his help.

571.   Singleton, Esther.   "Music in New York in the Days of Fulton."
          Musical Courier 59/13 (1909): 21-24.

On the early 19th century.

572.   Singleton, Esther.   "The Progress of Music in New York from
          1800." *Musical Courier* 38/19 (1899): [24 pp.].

573.   Sonneck Oscar G.   "A Contemporary Account of Music in
         Charleston, S.C., of the Year 1783." *New Music Review* 11
         (1912): 373-76.

         Reprint of a letter written by a German visitor to
Charleston.   Reprinted in *Oscar Sonneck and American Music*.   Ed. by
William Lichtenwanger (Urbana: University of Illinois Press, 1983),
pp. 94-99.

574.   Spaeth, Sigmund, ed.   *Music and Dance in the New England
         States, Including Maine, New Hampshire, Vermont,
         Massachusetts, Rhode Island & Connecticut.*   New York: Bureau
         of Musical Research, 1953.   347p.

         Consists of articles contributed by various authors on music
and dance in New England.   An introduction by Spaeth focuses on the
history of music there from the 1600s on.

575.   Spalding, Walter Raymond.   *Music at Harvard: A Historical
         Review of Men and Events.*   New York: Coward-McCann, 1935.
         xiv, 310p.

         Includes a general discussion of the music of New England in
chapter 1 as a backdrop for the first musical events, and the
historical development of music at Harvard.   Appendix 3 lists music
teachers in 18th-century Boston.   Index.

576.   Spaner, Richard.   "The History of Music in St. Louis." *Papers
         and Proceedings of the Music Teachers National Association*
         13 (1919): 40-50.

577.   Sprague, Laura F., ed.   *Agreeable Situations: Society,
         Commerce, and Art in Southern Maine, 1780-1830.*   Kennebunk,
         Me.: Brick Store Museum, 1987.   289p.

         Includes information on a guitar, located in the York
Institute Museum, that was bought by Eunice Cutts from William Selby
in 1797.   Includes photo.

578.   Standish, Lemuel W., ed.   *The Old Stoughton Musical Society:
         An Historical and Informative Record of the Oldest Choral*

Society in America. Stoughton, Mass.: The Society, 1929.
188p.

Discusses the establishment of the Society on November 7,
1786 by 25 singers in Stoughton. "An Historical Address" by Samuel
Bradley Noyes provides a brief history of psalmody in New England,
including information on William Billings. Discussed in Nitz (see
entry 534).

579. Steel, David Warren. "Sacred Music in Early Winchester."
      Connecticut Historical Society Bulletin 45/2 (April 1980):
      33-44.

Discusses psalmody in Winchester, Conn. during the 18th
century, the "regular way" versus the "usual way" of singing
psalmody, and town choirs during the 1770s. Cites names of
musicians not readily found in other sources. Includes a list of
Winchester choristers, 1769-98.

580. Stevens, Harry R. "Adventure in Refinement: Early Concert
      Life in Cincinnati, 1810-1826." *Bulletin of the Historical
      and Philosophical Society of Ohio* 5/3 (1947): 8-22; 5/4: 22-
      32.

581. Stevens, Harry R. "The Haydn Society of Cincinnati, 1819-
      1824." *Ohio State Archaeological and Historical Quarterly*
      52 (1943): 95-119.

582. Stoudt, John J. *Early Pennsylvania Arts and Crafts.* New
      York: Bonanza, 1964. 364p.

Includes a brief discussion of music and musical instruments
of the German communities. Illustrations include an organ (1776) by
John J. Dieffenbach and a number of examples of illuminations from
music manuscripts of Ephrata.

583. Stoutamire, Albert. *Music of the Old South: Colony to
      Confederacy.* Rutherford, N.J.: Fairleigh Dickinson
      University Press, 1972. 349p.

Based on the author's doctoral dissertation titled "A History of Music in Richmond, Virginia from 1742 to 1865" (Florida State University, 1960). Chapters 1-3 of 6 chapters are: "Music in Colonial Virginia," "The Emergence of a New Center of Music Culture, 1780-1799," and "Richmond as a Center for Music: The Early Years, 1800-1825." Discussed are concerts, church music, theater productions, and "Music Merchantry and Instruction." Sources are provided. "In my writing I make the assumption that these two cultural centers [Williamsburg and Richmond] also reflect the cultural tastes and pursuits, from the best to the worst, of a larger area, the South."

584.   Stoutamire, Albert T. "Musical Life in Late Eighteenth Century Richmond." *Journal of Research in Music Education* 11/2 (Fall 1963): 99-109.

Taken from the author's dissertation (see entry 583), this article is based on primary sources and includes information on balls, concerts, church music, music instruction, and opera.

585.   Stutsman, Grace M. "The Story of Music in America, 3: Boston." *Musical America* 66/11 (1946): 6-7, 26; 66/12 (1946): 8-9.

From the 1700s on.

586.   Sunderman, Lloyd Frederick. "The Beginning of Singing in America." *Journal of Musicology* 3/2 (Fall 1941): 101-19.

A history, including the New England tradition, use of psalters, with excerpts based on primary sources taken from Robert F. Seybolt's *The Private Schools of Colonial Boston* (Cambridge: Harvard University Press, 1935; reprint, New York: Arno Press, 1969). Includes a list of singing-school teachers and information on singing societies in the early 19th century.

587.   Talley, John Barry. *Secular Music in Colonial Annapolis: The Tuesday Club, 1745-56.* Urbana: University of Illinois Press, 1988. xvi, 312p.

Based on the author's dissertation with the same title (D.M.A. dissertation, Peabody Institute of the Johns Hopkins

University, 1983. 461p. UM 83-21625. *DAI* 44/5 (November 1983):
1239-A). Tuesday Club members consisted of several amateur
musicians, including Alexander Malcolm, Jonas Green, and others.
The author also discusses theater, songs and dances, and
instruments. Included is music by Thomas Bacon, and from John
Ormsby's manuscript book of minuets (1758), transcribed by Talley.
An excellent study.

588. Taricani, Jo Ann. "Music in Colonial Philadelphia: Some New
        Documents." *Musical Quarterly* 65/2 (April 1979): 185-99.

        Discusses instruments and concerts, music teachers and
musicians, including Benjamin Franklin, Michael Hillegas, and John
Palma.

589. Tawa, Nicholas E. "Buckingham's Musical Commentaries in
        Boston." *New England Quarterly* 51/3 (1978): 333-47.

        Joseph Tinker Buckingham (1779-1861), a New England editor
and music critic for a number of magazines and publisher of
Harmonia Sacra (1812) and other works, commented on musical events
in Boston in the early 1800s. (See also entry 590.)

590. Tawa, Nicholas E. "Musical Criticism and the Terrible Mr.
        Buckingham." *New-England Galaxy* 20/1 (1978): 3-11.

591. Teal, Mary Evelyn Durden. "Musical Activities in Detroit from
        1701 through 1870." Ph.D. dissertation, University of
        Michigan, 1964. 621p. UM 64-12691. *DAI* 28/4 (October
        1967): 1462-A.

        Although this study focuses on the years 1850-70, the author
provides a survey of musical life prior to that. An appendix
includes a list of "local musicians, music dealers, instrument
manufacturers, music societies, and instrumental organizations."

592. Thompson, J. William. "Change in the Church Music of New
        England (c. 1800)." *Hymn* 14/1 (1963): 17-21.

593.   Thompson, James William. "Music and Musical Activities in New
        England, 1800-1838." Ph.D. dissertation, George Peabody
        College for Teachers, 1962. 685p. UM 63-1899. *DAI* 23/9
        (March 1963): 3409-10.

        Discusses both sacred and secular music. Based on primary
sources. Includes a list of concerts presented by the Boston Handel
and Haydn Society in 1815-38, selected concert programs,
instruments, concerts, and singing schools. A survey of music in
New England before 1800 is also presented.

594.   Thrasher, Herbert Chandler. *Two Hundred and Fifty Years of
        Music in Providence, Rhode Island, 1636-1886: Rhode Island
        Composers Native and Adopted.*   Providence, R.I.: Federation
        of Music Clubs, 1942. 31p.

        A brief survey, with information on Oliver Shaw, organs and
organists, and a list of Rhode Island composers, including brief
notes on each.

595.   *Two Centuries of Nazareth, 1740-1940.* Nazareth, Pa.:
        Nazareth, Pennsylvania, Bi-Centennial, 1940. xiii, 276p.

        Mentions a few musical events during the colonial period.

596.   Wagner, John W. "New York City Concert Life, 1801-5."
        American Music 2/2 (Summer 1984): 53-69.

        Includes a chronological checklist of concerts presented.

597.   Wagner, John W. "Some Early Musical Moments in Augusta."
        Georgia Historical Quarterly 56 (1972): 529-34.

        On the early 19th century in Augusta, Ga., and includes
information on James Hewitt.

598.   Wakeling, Arthur. "Old-Time Music: New York before the
        Revolution." *Musician* 15 (1910): 810.

599. Warner, Thomas E. "European Musical Activities in North
      America before 1620." *Musical Quarterly* 70/1 (Winter 1984):
      77-95.

      Discusses early explorers Jacques Cartier, Hernando de Soto,
Sebastián Vizcaino, and Sir Francis Drake, and musical activities at
Fort Caroline and St. Augustine, Florida, New Mexico (Spanish
mission music), North Carolina, and Jamestown, Virginia.

600. Webster, Philip J. "Happy Birthday to the Handel & Haydn
      Society." *Music Journal* 23/3 (March 1965): 54, 66.

      Includes a chronology from its founding in 1815.

601. Whipple, George M. "A Sketch of the Musical Societies of
      Salem." *Essex Institute Historical Collections* 23 (1886):
      72-80, 113-33.

      On Salem, Mass., from the early 1800s on.

602. Williams, George W. "Charleston Church Music, 1562-1833."
      Journal of the American Musicological Society 7/1 (Spring
      1954): 35-40.

      Discusses music at St. Philip's Church, St. Andrew's Church,
St. Michael's Church, St. Mary's Church, Independent Congregational
Church, and Synagogue Beth Elohim. Principal musicians discussed
are Jacob Eckhard and Charles Theodore Pachelbel.

603. Williams, George W. "Early Organists at St. Philip's,
      Charleston." *South Carolina Historical Magazine* 53/3 (July
      1952): 146-54, 212-22; 54 (1953): 83-87.

      Organists discussed include, from 1761 on, in this order:
Frederick Hoff, Frederick Grunsweig, Benjamin Yarnold, John Stevens,
Ann Windsor, George Harland Hartley, Peter Valton, Jervis Henry
Stevens, William Yarnold, and Samuel Rodgers. Includes facsimiles
of music by Valton, Stevens, and Benjamin Yarnold.

604. Wilson, Ruth Mack with Kate Van Winkle Keller. *Connecticut's
      Music in the Revolutionary Era.* Hartford: American

Revolution Bicentennial Commission of Connecticut, 1979.
142p.

A scholarly work (sources provided) divided into four
chapters that serve as a chronological history. Facsimiles include:
title page of Oliver Brownson's *Select Harmony* (1783); "Advice to
the Fair Sex" from Benjamin Trumbull's Music Book; "The 108th Psalm"
from "Samuel Whitman His Book" (1768); "The Dead March" from Giles
Gibbs' "Music Book." Index includes names and titles associated
with that locale that are not found in other printed sources.

605.   Wister, Frances A. "Church Music in 1700 Used to Lure Indians
       to Become Civilized." *Diapason* 30/10 (1939): 20.

The discussion focuses on music in Philadelphia during the
18th and 19th centuries.

606.   Wolf, Edward C. "Sequel to 'Journey to Pennsylvania.'"
       Tracker 17/3 (Spring 1973): 12, 16.

On Gottlieb Mittelberger's travel diary, written in 1754,
which includes information on an organ in St. Michael's Church in
Philadelphia. See also entry 450.

607.   Woods, Leonard. *A Discourse on Sacred Music, Delivered before
       the Essex Musical Association at Their Anniversary Meeting,
       Boxford, Sept. 19, 1804.* Salem: Joshua Cushing, 1804.   16p.

A speech before the Essex Musical Association in
Massachusetts in which Woods asks that the Association "dure [sic]
the false, extravagant taste, which has prevailed in America and
give currency to ideas and compositions suited to the end of sacred
music." For additional information on this work, refer to Nitz (see
entry 534). Reprinted in *Early American Imprints, Second Series*,
no. 7798 (see entry 44).

608.   Woodward, Henry. "February 18, 1729: A Neglected Date in
       Boston Concert Life." *Notes* 33/2 (December 1976): 243-52.

The date of the first concert in the colonies was noted in
the *Boston Gazette.* Discusses the musical environment surrounding

this concert and includes a list of concerts in Boston from 1729-
36.

609.   Yellin, Victor F.   "Musical Activity in Virginia Before 1620."
       Journal of the American Musicological Society 22/2 (Summer
       1969): 284-89.

       Presents evidence based on primary sources that Virginians
were likely "transporters of English music in Virginia before 1620."

610.   Yerbury, Grace H.   "Concert Music in Early New Orleans."
       Louisiana Historical Quarterly 40 (1957): 95-109.

VI. TOPICAL STUDIES

Sacred Music

611. Anderson, Gillian B. "The Funeral of Samuel Cooper." *New England Quarterly* 50/4 (December 1977): 644-59.

Discusses William Billings' anthem, "Samuel the Priest Gave Up the Ghost" and his hymn, "Eden," composed for the funeral of Samuel Cooper, who died in 1784. Includes information on funeral practices in New England.

612. Blume, Friedrich. *Protestant Church Music: A History.* New York: W.W. Norton, 1974. xv, 831p.

Although most of this work focuses on European church music, Robert Stevenson has contributed chapter 7, "Protestant Music in America," an excellent study from colonial times to the present. Includes facsimiles, musical examples, and a discussion of New England and German-American traditions, and some information on music and explorers in America prior to 1609.

613. Cappers, Paul Kenwood. "The Anthems of Connecticut Composers Contained in Connecticut Sacred Music Imprints from 1778 to 1801." D.M.A. dissertation, University of Hartford, 1983.

614. Covey, Cyclone. "Religion and Music in Colonial America." Ph.D. dissertation, Stanford University, 1949.

615. Daniel, Ralph T. *The Anthem in New England before 1800.* Evanston: Northwestern University Press, 1966. Reprint, New York: Da Capo Press, 1979. xvi, 282p.

A standard work. After presenting a survey of church music in England and New England, the author discusses various composers of England and America, their works and stylistic traits. Two appendixes list anthems by non-American composers and native composers published in New England before 1800. Supplies biographical information. Musical examples and index.

616.   Daniel, Ralph T.   "English Models for the First American Anthems." *Journal of the American Musicological Society* 12/1 (Spring 1959): 49-58.

New England anthems were modelled after those by William Knapp, Joseph Stephenson, William Tansur, and Aaron Williams. Proposes that Americans Josiah Flagg and Daniel Bayley were the principal individuals to introduce English anthems to New England.

617.   Earle, Alice Morse. *The Sabbath in Puritan New England*. New York: Scribner, 1891. viii, 334p.

Earle describes a number of aspects regarding sacred practice in New England, including the use of psalters, church music, with separate chapters on the *Bay Psalm Book* and Sternhold and Hopkins' psalter, and the controversy regarding correct singing. Many quotes are cited but, unfortunately, no sources are given. Index.

618.   Edmunds, John. "Two Funeral Compositions in Memory of George Washington." *Bulletin of the New York Public Library* 61 (1957): 59-62.

619.   Ellinwood, Leonard. "English Influences in American Church Music." *Proceedings of the Royal Musical Association 80-83* (1953-54): 1-13.

Discusses psalmody, organs and organists in New England, Philadelphia, and Charleston.

620.   Ellinwood, Leonard Webster. *The History of American Church Music*. New York: Morehouse-Gorham, 1953. Reprint, New York: Da Capo Press, 1970. xiv, 274p.

Much ground is covered in this work but not the comprehensive study the title might suggest. Some 7 chapters focus on music before 1820, including California mission music, singing schools, composers, churches, and instruments. Of note is a fairly extensive appendix of "Biographies of American Church Musicians."

621. Ellinwood, Leonard. 'Religious Music in America' in "Religious Perspectives in American Culture," *Religion in American Life.* Princeton, N. J.: University Press, 1961, vol. 2, pp. 289-359.

An overview of the following topics focusing primarily on the English colonial traditions: "Colonial Psalmody"; "Singing Schools and Early Choirs"; "Musical Instruments"; "Hymns"; "Campmeeting Songs"; "Negro Spirituals." Based mostly on secondary sources.

622. Etherington, Charles L. *Protestant Worship Music: Its History and Practice.* New York: Holt, Rinehart and Winston, 1962. x, 278p.

Includes one brief chapter on "Worship Music in the American Colonies," including "Roman Catholic Settlements," "Protestant Communities," and "The *Bay Psalm Book.*"

623. Foote, Henry Wilder. *Three Centuries of American Hymnody.* Cambridge: Harvard University Press, 1940. Reprint, Hamden, Conn.: Archon Books, 1968. With supplement *Recent American Hymnody* (1952). xi, 418p.

Discusses the New England tradition and various psalters in use during the 17th century, an extended discussion of the decline in singing in New England during the 18th century, Pennsylvania-Germans, a chapter on "The Transition of Psalmody to Hymnody," and music of the early 19th century. The author does not consistently provide citations for sources consulted.

624. Frank, Mortimer. "Music for Funeral Services for George Washington." *Guitar Review* 23 (June 1959): 14-15.

On the "Dead March and Monody" by Benjamin Carr performed December 1799. Includes a facsimile of original edition, with a transcription.

625.   Goodell, Abner C.   "The Progress of Sacred Music in New England from Its Earliest Settlement to the Beginning of the Present Century." *Proceedings of the Essex Institute* 5 (1886-87): 188-90.

626.   Gould, Nathaniel Duren.   *Church Music in America.*   Boston: Gould and Lincoln, 1853.   Reprint, microfiche, Louisville, Ky.: Lost Cause Press, 1975.   240p.   (Joseph Sabin, *Bibliotheca Americana. Selected Americana.*)   Boston: A.N. Johnson, 1853; reprint, New York: AMS Press, 1972.

Although the author refers to early American music as a "dark age," he nonetheless has many complimentary remarks about early New England composers. Cited are principal tunebook collections and composers, some of whom are little known. Although somewhat removed, the author presents a detailed explanation as to the decline in congregational singing from the 17th century on. Includes a list of tunebooks published from 1810-53 and a list of early 19th-century singing schools.

627.   Hammond, Paul Garnet.   "Music in Urban Revivalism in the Northern United States, 1800-1835."   D.M.A. dissertation, Southern Baptist Theological Seminary, 1974.   199p.   UM 74-22660.   *DAI* 35/4 (October 1974): 2319-A.

Discusses music in revivalism as found in "larger population centers," and is based on a textual and musical analysis of certain hymnbooks.

628.   Krehbiel, Henry E.   "Church Music in New York: Some Phases in Its Development." *Church Music Review* 3 (1903-04): 329-30, 349-51, 368-70, 388-90, 409-11, 429-31, 450-52, 472-75.

629.   Lorenz, Ellen Jane.   *'76 to '76: A Study of Two Centuries of Sacred Music in America.*   Dayton, Oh.: Lorenz Publishing Co., 1975.   64p.

A brief study of the development of sacred music based on
Lorenz's collection of tunebooks, hymnals, and other books. Of
particular note are facsimile pages from works by William Billings,
Lewis Edson, Jeremiah Ingalls, and Oliver Holden from early American
tunebooks. No index.

630.   Lowens, Irving. "The American Tradition of Church Song: A
        Lecture Given at Westminster Choir College in 1963."
        Unpublished paper, 8p.

        Copy in Kent State University Library.

631.   Lutkin, Peter Christian. *Music in the Church*. Milwaukee:
        Young Churchman Co., 1910. Reprint, New York: AMS Press,
        1970. xii, 274p.

        Although most of this book focuses on music of England and
Europe, there is a brief discussion of psalmody in New England, with
William Billings as the principal composer.

632.   McKenzie, Wallace. "Anthems of the *Sacred Harp* Tunesmiths."
        American Music 6/3 (Fall 1988): 247-63.

        Discusses the tradition of anthems during the 19th cnetury.
The author discusses anthems by William Billings, Justin Morgan, and
others. Includes a list of 18th-century anthems found in "Sacred
Harp" tunebooks.

633.   Messiter, A.H. *A History of the Choir and Music of Trinity
        Church, New York from Its Organization, to the Year 1897*.
        New York: E.S. Gorham, 1906. Reprint, New York: AMS Press,
        1970. xi, 324p.

        Includes a discussion of William Tuckey, organist at Trinity
Church during the 1750s. Lacks sources. No index.

634.   Peabody, Herbert C. "Pioneer Days of Our American Church
        Music." *Musical America* 22/8 (1915): 30; 22/10 (1915): 23;
        22/14 (1915): 8; 22/21 (1915): 30; 22/22 (1915): 15.

635.   Pratt, Waldo Selden. *The Music of the Pilgrims: A Description of the Psalm-Book Brought to Plymouth in 1620.* Boston: Oliver Ditson Company, 1921. 80p.

Discusses primarily the 1612 Ainsworth psalter. The second half of the book are transcriptions with texts of the psalms. Facsimiles. Sources are not provided.

636.   Stevenson, Robert M. *Protestant Church Music in America: A Short Survey of Men and Movements from 1564 to the Present.* New York: W.W. Norton, 1966. xiii, 168p.

A standard work, although somewhat dated, not including some of the more recent research. Includes an excellent account of music and explorers, New England tradition, Pennsylvania-Germans, "Native-Born Composers in the Middle Colonies," and "the South before 1800." Other topics include music of slaves, singing school teachers, with most of the major musicians mentioned. Facsimiles and index.

637.   Stuart, Angela. "'That Part of the Publick Worship Called Singing.'" *Yankee* 34/12 (1970): 110-11, 114-15, 136-40, 143.

638.   Taylor, Phyllis J. "Non-Keyboard Instrumental Music in the Worship of Certain Congregational Churches in Connecticut from 1636 to 1900." Ph.D. dissertation, Graduate Theological Union, 1987. 181p. UM 87-17012. *DAI* 48/5 (November 1987): 1052-53-A.

In addition to organs, instruments such as bass viols were used in 18th-19th-century Connecticut churches. The author has studied documents of 24 churches.

639.   Wienandt, Elwyn A. and Robert H. Young. *The Anthem in England and America.* New York: The Free Press, 1970. xiii, 495p.

A broad study from the 17th century to the present. The author discusses English and American practice, including the following topics: "Regular Singing vs. Lining-Out," James Lyon's *Urania* (1761), English anthems found in American collections, choral singing, William Billings, "American Compilers and Borrowers," and Moravian composers. Musical examples, bibliography, and index.

Secular Music

640.   Antrim, Doron K.   "Great Presidents of Music." *International
       Musician* 39/8 (1941): 1, 22.

       Concerns music and George Washington.

641.   Antrim, Doron K.   "Our Musical Presidents." *Etude* 58/5 (May
       1940): 299, 337, 349.

       Includes a brief discussion of Thomas Jefferson.

642.   Britt, Judith S.   "Lessons for Martha's Children: Music in
       George Washington's Family." *Virginia Cavalcade* 35 (Spring
       1986): 172-83.

       Based on the author's book, *Nothing More Agreeable* (see
entry 643), this work includes a number of plates and beautiful
illustrations in a different arrangement and size than the parent
volume.   Musical examples.

643.   Britt, Judith S.   *Nothing More Agreeable: Music in George
       Washington's Family.*   Mount Vernon, Va.: Mount Vernon
       Ladies' Association, 1984.   120p.

       An excellent, carefully researched study of music of the
Washington family, including Nelly Custis and Bushrod and Anne
Washington.   The author discusses musical instruments, music
lessons, and other musicians such as John J. Frobel and Alexander
Reinagle.   Includes a number of beautiful illustrations.   Musical
examples and index.

644.   Fisher, William Arms.   "Music in Washington's Day: A
       Historical Sketch." *Etude* 50/2 (February 1932): 87-88; 50/3
       (March 1932): 169-70, 220.

       Based, in part, on the author's work, *The Music That
Washington Knew* (see entry 645).   A survey of mostly secular musical
activities in the colonies at that time.   Much of the discussion
focuses on patriotic and other popular songs, some from ballad
operas.

645.   Fisher, William Arms.   *The Music That Washington Knew, with an Historical Sketch.*   Boston: Oliver Ditson, 1931. xxiv, 44p.

Includes a number of works written in dedication of Washington, as well as other works popular at that time.   There is also a discussion of composers active at that time, with emphasis on Francis Hopkinson, and information on popular songs, Washington marches, songs from English operas, and dance music.   Much of this work is based on primary sources.

646.   Haverlin, Carl.   "Washington and Lincoln in Music."   *Music Journal* 16/2 (February 1958): 10, 37.

Mention's Francis Hopkinson's *Seven Songs* (1788) dedicated to Washington.

647.   Hoover, Cynthia Adams.   "Musical Ensembles in Eighteenth-Century American Life."   *Repertoire International d' Iconographie Musicale Newsletter* 4/2 (June 1979): 17-20.

A summary of a paper presented at the eighth annual meeting of the American Musical Instrument Society on April 20, 1979 in Chicago.   The author discusses music-making by amateur groups and the instruments that were used.   Individuals mentioned include Robert Carter, Michael Hillegas, Charles Theodore Pachelbel, and others.

648.   Howard, John Tasker.   *The Music of George Washington's Time.*   Preface by Sol Bloom.   Washington, D.C.: United States George Washington Bicentennial Commission, 1931.   96p.

The first part consists of an essay focusing primarily on secular music as might be heard in English towns such as Boston and Philadelphia.   Discusses concert life, popular songs, instruments, dances, and "Military Bands of the Revolution."   Includes musical illustrations.   The second part is "A Catalogue of Authentic Eighteenth-Century Music in Modern Editions."   This is a useful guide to publishers and music issued by them for the "celebration of the Two Hundredth Anniversary of the Birth of George Washington." No general index and not all sources provided.

649.   Huggins, Harold C.   "President John Quincy Adams' Picturesque
        Musical Impressions."   *Etude* 60 (1942): 581, 630.

650.   Johnson, H. Earle.   "The Adams Family and Good Listening."
        Journal of the American Musicological Society 11/2-3
        (Summer-Fall 1958): 165-76.

        Although most of this article is on the music that John and
Abigail Adams heard while in Paris, the author also mentions music
they heard at a concert in 1798 in Philadelphia.

651.   Kirk, Elise K.   "George Washington's Agreeable Pastime."
        American Music Teacher 38/4 (February-March 1989): 12-15,
        77.

        Discusses music in the life of George Washington, who
apparently did not play a musical instrument, but enjoyed music as
witnessed by the number of concerts he attended.   Individuals
discussed include Alexander Reinagle, Nelly Custis, and others.

652.   Kirk, Elise K.   *Music at the White House: A History of the
        American Spirit.*   Urbana: University of Illinois Press,
        1986.   xviii, 457p.

        A major study based on primary sources and devoted to music
of the presidents and the White House.   Part 1 covers the period
1789-1865 with chapters on George Washington and John Adams, Thomas
Jefferson, James Madison, and James Monroe.   Illustrations and
musical examples.   Index.

653.   Lawrence, Vera Brodsky.   *Music for Patriots, Politicians, and
        Presidents: Harmonies and Discords of the First Hundred
        Years.*   New York: Macmillan, 1975.   480p.

        An excellent folio-size work with numerous illustrations,
facsimiles, and musical examples that depicts the socio-musical
history of America from 1764 to 1876.   The material is taken from
newspapers, sheet music, broadsides, almanacs, songsters, and
pamphlets.   Index.

654.   Lowens, Irving. "Music in 1776: A Dearth of Diversion, an End
        to Entertainment?" *High Fidelity/Musical America* 26/7 (July
        1976): 46-51.

        Cites information on the last concerts to take place in the
colonies before the outbreak of the Revolutionary War. Discusses
the absence of concerts during 1776.

655.   Mackie, Shirley. "Secular Music in America." *American Music
        Teacher* 17/1 (September-October 1967): 30-32.

        Discusses concerts in Boston, Philadelphia, Charleston, and
New York. Musicians discussed include John Salter of Charleston,
Giovanni Gualdo of Philadelphia, and William Selby and Gottlieb
Graupner of Boston.

656.   Maurer, Maurer. "The Library of a Colonial Musician, 1755."
        William and Mary Quarterly 7/1 (January 1950): 39-52.

        Discusses the library of Cuthbert Ogle who died in April
1755 in York County, Va.

657.   Maurer, Maurer. "A Musical Family in Colonial Virginia."
        Musical Quarterly 34/3 (July 1948): 358-64.

        Discusses musical activities of the Robert Carter family at
Nomini Hall around 1775. Music in Williamsburg is also described.
Musicians mentioned include Philip Fithian, Cuthbert Ogle, and Peter
Pelham.

658.   Maurer, Maurer. "The 'Professor of Musick' in Colonial
        America." *Musical Quarterly* 36/4 (October 1950): 511-24.

        Discusses secular and sacred musical activities in the
American colonies, beginning with Jamestown, Va. Musicians include
James Bremner, Peter Pelham, and H.B. Victor. Includes a photo of
the manuscript of the first movement of a work from Giovanni
Gualdo's *Six Easy Entertainments*.

659.   Meyer, Eve R. "Benjamin Carr's *Musical Miscellany*." *Notes*
        33/2 (December 1976): 253-65.

The *Musical Miscellany in Occasional Numbers* (1812-25) includes both vocal and instrumental music and is representative of the secular music enjoyed at that time. The author discusses the principal aspects of the collection. Musical examples.

660. Molnar, John W. "A Collection of Music in Colonial Virginia: The Ogle Inventory." *Musical Quarterly* 49/2 (April 1963): 150-62.

An essay on Cuthbert Ogle, who taught keyboard in Williamsburg, Va. in 1755. Includes a list of the music he owned and is based on a report in the Research Department of Colonial Williamsburg.

661. Murray, Sterling E. "A Checklist of Funeral Dirges in Honor of General Washington." *Notes* 36/2 (December 1979): 326-44.

Includes 69 entries arranged by categories, including instrumental music, original music by immigrant composers, adaptations of George Frideric Handel, music by German composers adapted by American Moravian composers, and original music by native Americans. The music dates mostly from 1799 to 1802.

662. Murray, Sterling E. "Weeping and Mourning: Funeral Dirges in Honor of General Washington." *Journal of the American Musicological Society* 31/2 (Summer 1978): 282-308.

A description with musical examples of works composed in Washington's memory by Benjamin Carr, Uri K. Hill, Oliver Holden, George K. Jackson, and others. Discussed also are Moravian adaptations of European works.

663. Olsen, Dale A. "Public Concerts in Early America." *Music Educators Journal* 65/9 (May 1979): 48-59.

Discusses secular concerts in homes and public places, including theaters and concert halls in 18th-century Boston, New York, and Philadelphia. Illustrations.

664.   Redway, Virginia Larkin.   "Handel in Colonial and Post-
        Colonial America (to 1820)." *Musical Quarterly* 21/2 (April
        1935): 190-207.

        Discusses concerts in New York on March 18, 1756, in
Charleston, October 16, 1765, and in Philadelphia, news about Handel
in contemporary newspapers, and works by Handel in various
tunebooks.   Musical examples.

665.   Rensch-Erbes, R.   "Mrs. John Quincy Adams as Harpist."
        American Harp Journal 10/3 (1986): 27-28.

666.   Rose, Kenneth.   "Our Patriotic Music"   *Hobbies* 48/5 (1943):
        22-24.

        Discusses early American music and songs to the early 1800s.

667.   Rose, Kenneth.   "Patriotic Music, Part III: the War of 1812
        through the Mexican War—1846." *Hobbies* 48/11 (1944): 23-
        24.

668.   Schonberg, Harold C.   "Jefferson and the Piano." *Piano
        Teacher* 4/6 (July-August 1962): 11-12.

        Originally published in the *New York Times* (November 19,
1961).   Although Jefferson did not play the piano, he was interested
in it as evidenced in a number of letters to Thomas Adams, Francis
Hopkinson, and Martha Jefferson, reprinted here.   Also includes
information on the metronome and Jefferson.

669.   Sonneck, Oscar George.   *George Washington as a Friend and
        Patron of Music.*   Washington, D.C.: United States George
        Washington Bicentennial Commission [1931].   15p.

        "Taken from 'The Musical Side of Our First Presidents,'
contained in 'Essays in Music' by the late O.G. Sonneck. . . ."
Discusses instruments, theater, "The Armonica by Benjamin Franklin,"
concerts, and Nelly Custis, an amateur musician.   Photos.

670. Sonneck, Oscar George. "The Musical Side of Our First
          Presidents." *New Music Review* 6 (1907): 311-14, 382-85.

          Published also in *Suum Cuique: Essays in Music* (New York:
Schirmer, 1916; reprint, Freeport, New York: Books for Libraries
Press, 1969). (See entry 400.)

671. Stevenson, Robert. "The Music that George Washington Knew:
          Neglected Phases." *Inter-American Music Review* 5/1 (Fall
          1982): 19-77.

          A substantial and recommended article that reviews previous
literature and offers some corrections. Discusses early
instruments, music in Williamsburg, with information on Peter
Pelham, Jr., musical instruments at Mount Vernon, the music that
Washington heard on his sojourns, and music in Savannah and Salem.
There is also information on Francis Hopkinson and James Bremner.
Musical examples.

672. Tawa, Nicholas E. "Music in the Washington Household."
          Journal of American Culture 1 (1978): 19-43.

          A well-researched study of music in the Washington family,
including George and Martha, Eleanor Parke Custis, Patsy Custis,
Jenny Washington, Hariot Washington, and Anne and Bushrod
Washington.

673. Tawa, Nicholas E. "Secular Music in the Late-Eighteenth-
          Century American Home." *Musical Quarterly* 61/4 (October
          1975): 511-27.

          Discusses amateur-musician Eleanor Custis of Mount Vernon,
the John Adams family, the Robert Carter family of Virginia, and
Thomas Jefferson. Also focuses on popular songs of the period.

674. Upton, William T. "Secular Music in the United States 150
          Years Ago." *Papers of the American Musicological Society*
          (1941): 105-11.

          Discusses a number of composers and works associated with
vocal and instrumental music in Philadelphia, New York, and

Baltimore. Includes a list of ballad operas and their performances for the years 1767-96.

675.   Watson, Dorothy D. and R.M. Knerr. "Washington Set Fashion in Music for Presidents, and Art Is Ever Welcome in the White House." *Musical America* 41/2 (1924): 5, 19, 26.

Instrumental Music

676.   Anderson, Garland. "Alexander Reinagle and the 'Philadelphia' Sonatas." *Music Journal* 24/2 (February 1966): 50, 74, 94.

The keyboard sonatas were composed between 1786-94. The author describes the original manuscripts and provides a brief analysis of the works.

677.   Anderson, Simon V. "The Unofficial Bands of the American Revolution." *Music Educators Journal* 61/4 (December 1974): 26-33.

Contains excerpts from diaries and journals regarding bands and fife and drum music. Bands include Crane's Band of Music, Second New York Regiment Band, and others. Illustrations.

678.   Bakken, Howard Norman. "The Development of Organ Playing in Boston and New York, 1700-1900." D.M.A. dissertation, University of Illinois at Urbana-Champaign, 1975. 166p. UM 75-24252. *DAI* 36/5 (November 1975): 2473-A.

"American organ playing from ca. 1700-1800 was restricted to improvisational voluntaries, hymn and psalm accompaniments, transcriptions of vocal and choral works, and several Handel and other unidentified concertos. Despite continued theological resistance in the early 19th century, organ playing activity increased and several concert organists became prominent."

679.   Bly, Leon Joseph. "The March in American Society." Ph.D. dissertation, University of Miami, 1977. 323p. UM 78-08235. *DAI* 38/12 (June 1978): 7010-11-A.

A history of the march from colonial times to the present.
Eighteenth-century marches discussed include slow marches, "also
known as the parade march, grand march, and processional march," and
funeral marches. "An attempt was made to identify the composers
whose marches were included in the study."

680.   Camus, Raoul F.   "The Heritage: Band Music of Colonial
        America." *Music Journal* 29/6 (June 1971): 18-20.

        Serves as a brief introduction to military and band music of
the period.   Illustrations.

681.   Camus, Raoul F.   "The Military Band in the United States Army
        Prior to 1834."   Ph.D. dissertation, New York University,
        1969.   558p.   UM 70-15955. *DAI* 31/3 (September 1970): 1305-
        06-A.

        Camus is an authority on this subject.   Discussed are the
instruments and military bands in use during the 18th century, the
Revolutionary War, and the Ante-bellum period, including the War of
1812.   Although some of this information is repeated in his later
publication below (see entry 682), researchers should refer to both
works.

682.   Camus, Raoul F.   *Military Music of the American Revolution.*
        Chapel Hill: University of North Carolina, 1976.   xii, 218p.

        The author's meticulous research on this topic makes this a
valuable work.   Discussed are the colonial militia, British Army,
Continental Army, various military campaigns and bands of music, and
performance practice.   Included is a chronology of British
regimental bands, fife tutors, drum manuals, and various "published
collections suitable for military bands."   Index.

683.   Camus, Raoul F.   "A Re-Evaluation of the American Band
        Tradition." *Journal of Band Research* 7/1 (Fall 1970): 5-6.

        Corrects some misconceptions about colonial band music in
John C. Fitzpatrick's "The Bands of the Continental Army" (see entry
703) and William C. White's *A History of Military Music in America*
(see entry 751).   Camus states, "The band preceding Colonel Benjamin
Franklin of the volunteer regiment of Philadelphia on March 18,

1756, is the earliest instance so far recorded of military music in America."

684.   Camus, Raoul F. "A Source for Early American Band Music: *John Beach's Selection of Airs, Marches, Etc.*" *Notes* 38/4 (June 1982): 792-809.

From the early 1800s. Located in the Spencer Library, University of Kansas. Includes an annotated table of contents of the collection and information on Samuel Holyoke.

685.   Carpenter, Kenneth William. "A History of the United States Marine Band." *Journal of Band Research* 7/2 (1971): 23-29.

Based on the author's dissertation (see entry 686).

686.   Carpenter, Kenneth William. "A History of the United States Marine Band." Ph.D. dissertation, University of Iowa, 1970. 272p. UM 71-5721. *DAI* 31/9 (March 1971): 4813-A.

A history from 1800 to 1970. Discusses military bands of the Revolutionary War. "At first the band played only popular and patriotic airs for the government, the military, and the city, but after 1850 more serious music became part of its repertoire."

687.   Carroll, George. "The Band of Musick of the Second Virginia Regiment, 1779-83." *Journal of Band Research* 2/1 (Spring 1966): 16-18.

Discusses the establishment of the band, their dress, and cites musicians' names.

688.   Carroll, Thomas. "Bands and Band Music in Salem." *Essex Institute Historical Collections* 36/4 (October 1900): 265-84.

The first band mentioned is the Massachusetts Band of Boston, which performed in Salem in 1783. Others include the Brigade Band, 1805-06 and the Cadet Band in 1813. The paper focuses, however, on mostly mid-19th-century Salem. Sources are not provided.

689. Clark, J. Bunker. "American Organ Music before 1830: A
        Critical and Descriptive Survey." *Diapason* 72/11 (November
        1981): 1, 3, 7.

      Organ pieces by Benjamin Carr, Benjamin Cross, Francis
Linley, Thomas Loud, Jr., William Selby, and Charles Zeuner are
discussed.

690. Clark, J. Bunker. *The Dawning of American Keyboard Music.*
        Contributions to the Study of Music and Dance, 12.
        Westport, Conn.: Greenwood Press, 1988. xxii, 411p.

      Discusses keyboard music in the United States for the period
1787-1830 and includes both native-American and immigrant composers.
The organization is by type of composition and other categories,
including sonata, rondo, variations, medley, battle music, and organ
music. Includes over 200 musical examples of works published
originally as sheet music.

691. Clark, J. Bunker. "The Renaissance of Early American Keyboard
        Music: A Bibliographic Review." *Current Musicology* 18
        (1974): 127-32.

      Discusses available publications and editorial principles of
early American keyboard music. Updated in the author's *The Dawning
of American Keyboard Music* (see entry 690).

692. Clark, J. Bunker. "The Solo Piano Sonata in Early America:
        Hewitt to Heinrich." *American Music* 2/3 (Fall 1984): 27-46.

      Composers discussed include Benjamin Carr, Anthony Philip
Heinrich, James Hewitt, Mr. Newman, Alexander Reinagle, and Rayner
Taylor.

693. Compton, Benjamin Richard. "Amateur Instrumental Music in
        America, 1765 to 1810." Ph.D. dissertation, Louisiana State
        University, 1979. 282p. UM 79-21959. *DAI* 40/4 (October
        1979): 1737-38-A.

      Includes 2 principal parts: 1) "Amatuer players and their
teachers" with a discussion of "itinerant music masters among the
plantations of Tidewater Virginia, the instrumental clubs of Essex

County, Massachusetts, and musical instruction in urban area"; 2)
"an examination of the music, instruments, and books available to
the American amateur players."

694.   Curtis, Prudence B.   "American Organ Music North of
            Philadelphia before 1860: Selected Problems and an Annotated
            Bibliography."   D.M.A. dissertation, Manhattan School of
            Music, 1981.   2 vols., 559p.   UM 81-20913.   *DAI* 42/4
            (October 1981): 1362-63-A.

            Some 35 composers are represented.   The period dates from
ca. 1800.   Brief biographies are included.

695.   Danner, Peter.   "Notes on Some Early American Guitar
            Concerts."   *Soundboard* 4 (1977): 8-9, 21.

696.   Dichter, Harry.   "Benjamin Carr's *Music Journal*."   *Music
            Journal* 15/1 (January 1957): 17, 60.

            Volume 1 of Carr's *Musical Journal for the Piano Forte* was
published in 1800.   Includes biographical information on Carr,
citations for advertisements for his publications, and a photograph
of Carr.

697.   Ellison, Ross W.   "The Piano Sonatas of Alexander Reinagle."
            American Music Teacher 25/5 (April-May 1976): 23.

            A brief introduction to the sonatas.

698.   Ellison, Ross W.   "Reinagle's Piano Sonatas in the Musico-
            Historical Context."   *Dissonance* 7/1 (1975): 1-15.

699.   Erwin, Paul Francis.   "Bands, Bandmasters and Bandstands: A
            Search for Public Support in Democracy."   *Journal of
            American Culture* 9/3 (Fall 1986): 55-60.

            Discusses Moravian music and Revolutionary War bands.

700. Fain, Samuel Samson. "A Study of the Community Symphony
      Orchestra in the United States, 1750 to 1955." D.M.A.
      dissertation, University of Southern California at Los
      Angeles, 1956.

701. Ferguson, Allan J. "The Military Music Scene in Plattsburg,
      NY: Fifes, Drums and Bands in 1814 and 1819." *Military
      Collector & Historian* 35/3 (Fall 1983): 112-13.

      A brief discussion of musical bands during the period
studied. The article is based on little-known sources.

702. Ferguson, Allan J. "Trumpets, Bugles, and Horns in North
      America, 1750-1815." *Military Collector & Historian* 36/1
      (Spring 1984): 2-7.

      Defines and describes those instruments, how they were used,
and by which military bands. Mentions a powder horn, dated 1759, on
display at Fort Ontario State Historic Site in Oswego, N.Y. An
excellent introduction to this topic.

703. Fitzpatrick, John Clement. "The Bands of the Continental
      Army." *Daughters of the American Revolution Magazine* 57/4
      (April 1923): 187-97.

704. Gee, Harry. "Early American Clarinet Music." *Woodwind World*
      2/8 (1958): 9.

      Mentions Gottlieb Graupner.

705. Gibbs, Giles. *Giles Gibbs Jr., His Book for the Fife,
      Ellington, Connecticut, 1777.* Ed. by Kate Van Winkle
      Keller. Hartford: Connecticut Historical Society, 1974.
      40p.

706. Gilbert, Donald K. "Military Drumming During the American
      Revolution, 1775-1783." *Percussionist* 9/1 (Fall 1971): 1-5.

      Describes various drum patterns used by the American army
and major manuals from the period.

707.   Grenander, M.E.   "Benjamin Franklin's String Quartet."   *Early
       American Literature* 7/2 (Fall 1972): 183-86.

       Brief article describing the original manuscript, which was
discovered in 1941.

708.   Grenander, M.E.   "Reflections on the String Quartet(s)
       Attributed to Franklin."   *American Quarterly* 27/1 (March
       1975): 73-87.

       Lists and compares the 5 manuscript and 2 printed versions
of Benjamin Franklin's string quartet and offers hypotheses
regarding the authorship.

709.   Hamblen, David.   "Early Boston Bands."   *Music Journal* 24/10
       (December 1966): 32-34.

       Discusses British regimental bands and American colonial
bands and musicians, including, for example, Salem Brigade Band,
Boston Brigade Band, and Daniel Simpson, drummer.   Article
originally published in *Daughters of the American Revolution
Magazine* 100 (1966), pp. 228-30.

710.   Hazen, Margaret Hindle.   *The Music Men: An Illustrated History
       of Brass Bands in America, 1800-1920.*   Washington, D.C.:
       Smithsonian Institution Press, 1987.   225p.

       Includes a chronology of American band history.   Discusses
some scattered instances of colonial bands, including information on
the Moravian Salem Band and the formation of the Marine Band.
Illustrations and index.

711.   Hennig, Julia A.   "Battle Pieces for the Pianoforte Composed
       and Published in the United States between 1795 and 1820."
       D.M.A. dissertation, Boston University, 1968.   132p.

       Includes historical background of keyboard battle pieces,
American battle pieces, their composers, the battle described, and
an analysis of the following pieces: James Hewitt, *The Battle of
Trenton, Military Sonata* and *The Fourth of July*; Peter Ricksecker,
The Battle of New Orleans; Francesco Masi, *The Battles of Lake
Champlain and Plattsburg*; Denis-Germain Etienne, *The Battle of New*

Orleans; Philip Laroque, *The Battle of the Memorable 8th of January 1815*; and Benjamin Carr, *The Siege of Tripoli.* Appendixes include photocopies of the pieces discussed.

712.   Herbert, James W. "The Italian Musicians of the Early US
          Marine Band." *School Musician, Director, and Teacher* 50/3
          (1978): 49, 51.

713.   Hermann, Myrl Duncan. "Chamber Music by Philadelphia
          Composers, 1750-1850." Ph.D. dissertation, Bryn Mawr
          College, 1977. 334p. UM 78-01379. *DAI* 38/9 (March 1978):
          5114-A.

          Discusses Philadelphia composers, including John Gualdo,
Jean Gehot, John Christopher Moller, Rayner Taylor, Benjamin Carr,
Benjamin Franklin, Philippo Trajetta, Leopold Meigner, Charles
Hommann, and others.

714.   Hinson, Maurice. "Keyboard Music in the Colonies and the
          United States of America to 1800." *Piano Quarterly* 31/123
          (Fall 1983): 40-42.

          A brief summary of instruments, including reference to the
earliest keyboard instrument in the colonies (virginals, Boston in
1699), and various composers. Includes an insert disc recording of
works by William Brown, James Hewitt, John Christopher Moller, and
Alexander Reinagle.

715.   Hopkins, Robert. "An Edition of Four Sonatas and Two Sets of
          Variations for Piano by Alexander Reinagle." Ph.D.
          dissertation, University of Rochester, 1959.

          See also entry 1955.

716.   Horton, Charles Allison. "Serious Art and Concert Music for
          Piano in America in the 100 Years from Alexander Reinagle to
          Edward MacDowell." Ph.D. dissertation, University of North
          Carolina at Chapel Hill, 1966. 225p. UM 67-999. *DAI* 27/10
          (April 1967): 3481-A.

Includes a history of the period, the piano music analyzed by forms such as fugue, sonata, theme and variation, etc., a list of solo piano works by form, and a chronological compendium of American composers before 1865 who wrote for the piano.

717.   Housewright, Wiley L.   "Chamber Music in America before 1800." *Bulletin of the American Musicological Society* (1946): 76-78.

Abstract of a paper read at a meeting of the Texas Chapter of the AMS, November 16, 1946.

718.   Johnson, H. Earle.   *First Performances in America to 1900: Works with Orchestra.*   Bibliographies in American Music, 4. Detroit: Information Coordinators, 1979.   xxiv, 446p.

Includes information on works by Mozart, Haydn, and Beethoven performed during the late 18th and early 19th century in Philadelphia, Boston, and New York.   See also the author's article "Some First Performances in America," in *Journal of the American Musicological Society* 5 (1952), pp. 235-47.

719.   Jones, Stuart E.   "The President's Music Men."   *National Geographic* 116/6 (December 1959): 752-66.

Includes brief information on the act of Congress in 1798 that established the band.

720.   Kinkeldey, Otto.   "Beginnings of Beethoven in America." *Musical Quarterly* 13/2 (April 1927): 217-48.

Discusses early performances and publications of Beethoven's works in America, including the likelihood that Gottlieb Graupner performed arrangements of two symphonies as early as 1819 in Boston. Also mentions a Beethoven Society active in Portland, Maine in 1819.

721.   Kochan, James L.   "Notes on the 1821 Pattern Musician's Coatee."   *Military Collector & Historian* 33/2 (Summer 1981): 81-84.

Includes additional information with photographs of the uniform of an enlisted musician in the United States infantry. Refer also to an article by Stephen E. Osman (see entry 738).

722. Kolman, Barry H. "Early American Wind Music in General Instrumental Tutors, 1800-1836." *Journal of Band Research* 23/1 (1987): 61-77.

723. Kolman, Barry H. "The Origins of American Wind Music and General Instrumental Tutors." D.A. dissertation, University of Northern Colorado, 1985. 172 pp. UM 86-03223. *DAI* 46/12 (June 1986): 3529-A.

Discusses the following eight tutors from the post-Revolutionary War period: Samuel Holyoke's *The Instrumental Assistant* (2 volumes), Joseph Herrick's *The Instrumental Preceptor*, Timothy Olmsted's *Martial Music*, Oliver Shaw's *For the Gentlemen*, William Whiteley's *The Instrumental Preceptor*, Ezekiel Goodale's *The Instrumental Director*, and Henry Moore's *Merrimack Collection of Instrumental and Martial Musick*.

724. Krauss, Anne McClenny. "The First Keyboard Pieces Published in America?" *Piano Quarterly* 130 (Summer 1985): 62-63.

Brief. Late 1700s. Mentions William Brown and Alexander Reinagle.

725. Kroeger, Karl. "Victor Pelissier's Masonic March." *Sonneck Society Bulletin* 13/3 (Fall 1987): 96-98.

The *Masonic March* was first performed in Philadelphia in 1811.

726. Krohn, Ernst C. "Alexander Reinagle as Sonatist." *Musical Quarterly* 18/1 (January 1932): 140-49.

Discusses and compares Reinagle's *Six Sonatas for the Piano-Forte or Harpsichord* (London, ca. 1780) and his later American sonatas with similar works by European composers. Refer to M.D. Herter Norton's article, "Haydn in America (before 1820)" (see entry 735), where an error made by Krohn regarding the authorship of a

Haydn keyboard work ("Andante") is corrected. Krohn comments on the
writing of this article in his *Music Publishing in St. Louis*, p. xvi
(see entry 1397).

727.   Lowens, Irving. *Haydn in America.* Bibliographies in American
         Music, 5. Detroit: Information Coordinators, 1979. x,
         134p.

         The author discusses American imprints for Haydn's works
from 1789 to 1809 as well as some 247 concerts in which the name of
Haydn is cited. Included is a catalog of works with full imprint
data and library locations, a list of performances of Haydn's works,
many from contemporary newspapers, and a list of copies of Haydn's
manuscripts acquired in the Moravian towns of Salem, N.C., and
Bethlehem and Lititz, Pa. Other lists include works in the
Monticello Music Collection at the University of Virginia, and an
essay by Otto E. Albrecht, "Haydn Autographs in the United States."
Index.

728.   McClellan, Major Edwin North. "How the Marine Band Started."
         United States Institute Proceedings 49/4 (Whole no. 242,
         April 1923).

729.   Mangler, Joyce E. "The 'Early American' Repertoire." *Harp
         News* 3/1 (1960): 6-7.

         Discusses music for harp for the period 1794-1860.

730.   Marrocco, W. Thomas. "The String Quartet Attributed to
         Benjamin Franklin." *Proceedings of the American
         Philosophical Society* 116 (1972): 477-85.

731.   Metz, Charles Jonathan, II. "Keyboard Duets Belonging to the
         Washington Family: A Performance Practice Study." Ph.D.
         dissertation, Washington University, 1981. 157p. UM 81-
         22750. *DAI* 42/4 (October 1981): 1366-67-A.

         Twelve keyboard duets belonging to the wife of a nephew of
George Washington are discussed. An appendix consists of
reproductions of the duets.

732. Morehen, John. "Masonic Instrumental Music of the Eighteenth Century: A Survey." *Music Review* 42/3-4 (August-November 1981): 215-24.

Although the main focus is on European music, the author cites a number of Masonic works composed in America during the 18th century by William Dubois, Samuel Holyoke, Alexander Reinagle, and Peter Valton. Also discusses the *Bellamy Band Book* (1799), which is held in the Library of Congress.

733. Nelson, Larry L. "Two Military Bands of Music on the Northwest Frontier during the War of 1812." *Military Collector & Historian* 36/2 (Summer 1984): 67-69.

The bands are the band of Granville, Ohio and the Band of the Independent Volunteers, which performed at Fort Meigs in 1813.

734. Nettl, Paul. "Early Mozartiana in America." In *Paul Nettl: Selected Essays*. Ed. by Ralph T. Daniel. Indiana University, [1975], pp. 9-21.

First published in *Mozart-Jahrbuch* (1954), pp. 78-88, and translated here by Ralph T. Daniel. Early performance of a Mozart symphony took place in Charleston, S.C. in 1794. Additional works were performed in Philadelphia, New York, and Boston.

735. Norton, M.D. Herter. "Haydn in America (before 1820)." *Musical Quarterly* 18/2 (April 1932): 309-37.

Discusses the earliest instance of a symphony by Haydn performed in New York on April 27, 1782. Other early performances of works by Haydn took place in Boston, New York, and Bethlehem, Pa. Musicians discussed include Gottlieb Graupner, John Frederick Peter, and Alexander Reinagle. The author also discusses early publications of Haydn in America.

736. Norton, Pauline Elizabeth Hosack. "March Music in Nineteenth-Century America." Ph.D. dissertation, University of Michigan, 1983. 447p. UM 83-14339. *DAI* 44/2 (August 1983): 319-A.

A study of "form, style, and function" of marches in
America, based on some 1,800 marches published in sheet music
format. Includes a discussion of the quickstep in the early 19th
century. The author examines the relationship between the march,
dance, and music.

737. Olson, Kenneth E. *Music and Musket: Bands and Bandsmen of the
        American Civil War.* Contributions to the Study of Music and
        Dance, 1. Westport, Conn.: Greenwood Press, 1981. xx,
        299p.

        Includes a chapter on military bands in the United States
before 1820. Based on the author's dissertation, "Yankee Bands of
the Civil War" (University of Minnesota, 1971).

738. Osman, Stephen E. "Two Regular Army Musician's Coatees of the
        1821 Pattern." *Military Collector & Historian* 32/2 (Summer
        1980): 78-81.

        Includes a discussion with photographs of an enlisted
musician's uniform from that period.

739. Owen, Barbara J. "American Organ Music and Playing, from
        1700." *Organ Institute Quarterly* 10/3 (1963): 7-13.

740. Owen, Barbara J. "Early American Keyboard Music: Some
        Sources." *Tracker* 19/2 (1975): 11.

        Discusses early organs, including the first recorded use of
an organ in 1703, Moravian music, and music in Philadelphia.

741. Peeples, Georgia Kay. "The Bassoon in America, 1800-1840, as
        Depicted in Contemporary Pedagogic Sources." D.M.A.
        dissertation, University of Maryland, 1981. 87p. UM 82-
        14397. *DAI* 43/1 (July 1982): 13-A.

        Discusses general method books and tutors. Includes an
"overview of bassoonists and bassoon playing in the United States
during the period 1775-1840." Sources include: Ezekial Goodale's
The Instrumental Director, Joseph Herrick's *The Instrumental
Preceptor*, Samuel Holyoke's *The Instrumental Assistant*, Part 2,

Henry E. Moore's *Merrimack Collection of Instrumental and Martial Music*, William Whiteley's *The Instrumental Preceptor*, W.W. Jones' *The Bassoon Preceptor*, and G.E. Blake's *An Introduction to the Art of Playing the Bassoon*.

742.   Phelps, Roger Paul.   "The History and Practice of Chamber Music in the United States from Earliest Times Up to 1875." Ph.D. dissertation, University of Iowa, 1951.   2 vols., 991p.

743.   Schaffner, Anne.   "The Modern String Quartet in America Before 1800."   *Music Review* 40/3 (August 1979): 165-67.

Discusses the performance of string quartets in the colonies during the 1790s.   Musicians mentioned include John Antes, Thomas Jefferson, and others.

744.   Selden, Margery Stomne.   "Schubert and 'Yankee Doodle.'" *Sonneck Society Bulletin* 13/3 (Fall 1987): 94-96.

Proposes that a piano arrangement of "Yankee Doodle" by "F. Schubert" is actually the famous Franz Schubert and not some other composer with the same name.

745.   Simmons, David.   "The Band of Music in the American Army of 1797."   *Military Collector & Historian* 37/3 (Fall 1985): 135-36.

Discusses the instruments ordered for the band by Brigadier General James Wilkinson.

746.   Sonneck, Oscar George.   "Washington's March."   *Zeitschrift der internationalen Musikgesellschaft* 7 (1906): 273-74.

Discusses "Washington's March" as cited in the *Massachusetts Spy* on May 27, 1784, and the plausibility of Francis Hopkinson as the tune's composer.

747.   Spalding, Dan C.   "The Evolution of Drum Corps Drumming." *Percussionist* 17/3 (Spring-Summer 1980): 116-39.

Discusses drumming in the American army during the Revolutionary War period, and early drum instruction books printed in the United States, to present-day drumming.

748.   Strauss, John Felix.   "An Annotated Edition of Two Pianoforte Sonatas by Alexander Reinagle."   D.M.A. dissertation, University of Texas at Austin, 1976.   94p.   UM 76-26582. *DAI* 37/6 (December 1976): 3261-62-A.

Includes the D major and F major sonatas, and is based on the originals in the Library of Congress.   Included is "A Biographical Sketch of Alexander Reinagle," "The Pianoforte of Reinagle's Time," and "A Description of the Reinagle Sonata Manuscripts in the Library of Congress."

749.   Warburton, Thomas.   "Historical Perspective of the String Quartet in the United States."   *American Music Teacher* 21/3 (January 1972): 20-22, 37.

Mentions the string quintets of the Moravian Johann Friedrich Peter, the playing of string quartets by Thomas Jefferson at Monticello, and an early quartet in Philadelphia in 1816.

750.   Weaver, Philip D.   "More on Those Coats of 1775: The Coats of Musick."   *Military Collector & Historian* 37/1 (Spring 1985): 2-7.

Supplies evidence as to what the musicians' uniform of the New York Provincial Forces of 1775 looked liked.

751.   White, William Carter.   *A History of Military Music in America*.   New York: Exposition Press, 1944.   Reprint, Westport, Conn.: Greenwood Press, 1975.   272p.

Includes a survey of military music of the Continental Army, bands of the army from 1792-1848, and early bands in New England, New York, and Pennsylvania.   Musical examples, including a few transcriptions from Joshua Cushing's *Fifers Companion* (1803).

752.   Wolverton, Byron Adams.   "Keyboard Music and Musicians in the Colonies and United States of America before 1830."   Ph.D.

dissertation, Indiana University, 1966.   503p.   UM 67-3728.
DAI 27/11 (May 1967): 3899-A.

Discussed in terms of chronological and geographical
divisions.   Focuses on harpsichords, clavichords, and organs in the
colonies.   Musicians include Edward Enstone, Charles Theodore
Pachelbel, John Rice, James Bremner, William Selby, Benjamin
Yarnold, Peter Valton, Francis Hopkinson, William Brown, Alexander
Reinagle, George K. Jackson, Gottlieb Graupner, James Hewitt,
Charles Gilfert, Benjamin Carr, Rayner Taylor, John Christopher
Moller, Christopher Meineke, Peter K. Moran, Philip Anthony Corri
(Arthur Clifton), Jacob Eckhard, Jr., Oliver Shaw, and Anthony
Philip Heinrich.

Vocal Music

753.   Anderson, Gillian B.   *Freedom's Voice in Poetry and Song.*
        Wilmington, Del.: Scholarly Resources, Inc., 1977.   xxxiv,
        888p.

This is a collection of song texts taken from colonial
American newspapers representing the 13 colonies for the years 1773-
83.   Part 1 consists of the inventory arranged by colony, city, and
newspaper.   The lyrics are arranged chronologically.   Included are
first line, title, author, tune, and 18th-century source indexes.
Part 2 consists of a song book containing "92 songs and 8 poems,
arranged chronologically, selected to give both a representative
sampling of sentiments and music."

754.   Anderson, Gillian B.   "'Samuel the Priest Gave Up the Ghost'
        and 'The Temple of Minerva': Two Broadsides." *Notes* 31/3
        (March 1975): 493-516.

Contains information on the value of broadsides for the
study of American music.   "Samuel the Priest" refers to Rev. Samuel
Cooper, Boston minister, who died in 1783.   The work was written by
William Billings.   The second broadside is actually the words for
"America Independent: An Oratorical Entertainment," composed by
Francis Hopkinson.

755.   Bartlett, Homer N. "About Our National Anthem." *Musical Courier* 65/5 (1912): 26-28.

756.   Bean, Helen J. "Our American Christmas Carols." *American Music Teacher* 4/2 (1954): 10, 12.

Mentions William Billings.

757.   Behrend, Jeanne. "Early American Choral Music." *Choral & Organ Guide* 8/9 (1955): 22, 30.

758.   Blanck, Jacob. "The Star Spangled Banner." *Papers of the Bibliographical Society of America* 60 (1966): 176-84.

759.   Brant, Cyr de. "America and the Christmas Carol. *Etude* 63/12 (December 1945): 681, 721.

Brief remarks and some examples of the New England tradition and Spanish mission music.

760.   Browne, C.A. "The Story of 'Yankee Doodle.'" *Musician* 15 (1910): 444.

761.   "Circumstances under Which Famous Patriotic Songs Were Written." *American Art Journal* 71 (1898): 195-96.

762.   Darcy, Capt. Thomas F., Jr. "The Star Spangled Banner: This Is How It Happened." *Music Journal* 8/4 (September 1950): 8-9, 35-38.

Information on the battle and Francis Scott Key's mission.

763.   Davis, Harold. "On the Origin of Yankee Doodle." *American Speech* 13 (1938): 93-96.

764. Delaplaine, Edward W.   "Francis Scott Key and the National
         Anthem." *Records of the Columbia Historical Society* 46-47
         (1944-45): 13-26.

      Recounts the conditions under which the song was written.

765. Engel, Lehman. "Songs of the American Wars." *Modern Music*
         19/3 (March-April 1942): 147-52.

      Discusses songs associated with the Revolutionary War,
including William Billings' "Chester," Andrew Law's "The American
Hero," and of the War of 1812, including the "American Star."

766. Flood, W.H. Grattan. "The Air of the 'Star Spangled Banner':
         A Reply." *Records of the American Catholic Historical
         Society of Philadelphia* 25 (1914): 97-102.

767. Foner, Philip S. *American Labor Songs of the Nineteenth
         Century.* Urbana: University of Illinois Press, 1975. xvii,
         356p.

      A unique, excellent, and extensive study. Chapter 1,
"Colonial, Revolutionary, and Early National Period," discusses
colonial workers and slaves. Included is a number of workers' song
texts and Revolutionary War song texts. Facsimiles.

768. Gray, Leon Wilbur. "The American Art-Song: An Inquiry into
         Its Development from the Colonial Period to the Present."
         643p. Ed.D. dissertation, Columbia University, 1967. UM
         70-12516. *DAI* 31/2 (August 1970): 785-A.

      Based on an examination of several hundred art songs. The
author concludes that songs from the colonial period were mostly a
reflection of European influence.

769. "Hail Columbia: Mr. M'Master's Account of the Origin of the
         National Song in 1798." *Brainard's Musical World* 22 (1885):
         271.

770.   Hall, Roger L.   "Early Performances of Bach and Handel in America."   *Journal of Church Music* 27/5 (May 1985): 4-7.

Portions of Handel's *Messiah* were performed as early as 1756 in New York.   Works by Bach were first performed in the 19th century.   Facsimiles.

771.   Hart, Charles Henry.   "'Hail Columbia' and Its First Publication: A Critical Inquiry."   *Pennsylvania Magazine of History and Biography* 34/2 (1910): 162-65.

Disagrees with Oscar George Sonneck regarding the facts regarding the original edition of "Hail Columbia."   The song was written by Joseph Hopkinson for performance in Philadelphia in 1798.   Illustration.

772.   Hazen, Margaret H.   "Songs of Revolutionary America."   *New England Historical and Genealogical Register* 130 (1976): 179-95.

773.   Henry, Hugh T.   "The Air of the 'Star-Spangled Banner.'"   *Records of the American Catholic Historical Society of Philadelphia* 24 (1913): 289-335.

774.   Hill, Richard S.   "The Melody of 'The Star Spangled Banner' in the United States before 1820."   In *Essays Honoring Lawrence C. Wroth.*   Ed. by Frederick R. Goff.   Portland, Me., 1951, pp. 151-93.

775.   Hill, Thomas C.   "'The Star-Spangled Banner': Yesterday and To-Day."   *Musical America* 28/10 (1918): 11, 13.

776.   Holl, Herbert.   "Some Versions of Pastoral in American Music." Ph.D. dissertation, University of Texas at Austin, 1980. 301p.   UM 81-09180.   *DAI* 41/11 (May 1091): 4535-A.

The author defines "pastoral" as "an idyllic or rustic environment" and "a single, idealized lifestyle."   Discusses the British-American tradition of pastoral song between 1790 and 1820 in chapter 1 and also works by Anthony Philip Heinrich.

777.   "How Not to Set Words to Music." *High Fidelity/Musical America* 26/7 (1976): 48-49.

Benjamin Franklin's letter to his brother on setting song texts.

778.   Howard, John T. "Philadelphia Collectors Claim Discovery of Hewitt Star Spangled Banner Setting." *Musical Courier* 101/23 (1930): 7.

779.   "John Dickinson's 'Liberty Song.'" *Daughters of the American Revolution Magazine* 86/8 (August 1952): 876-77.

A reprinting of the text.

780.   Keast, Laury S. "The Songs of America, 1775-1840: The First 65 Years of America's Popular Music." *Music Journal Annual-Anthology* (1969): 50-51, 114-16.

781.   Keets, Alfred. "'Yankee Doodle': Its Origin and Significance." *Musical Courier* 75/4 (1917): 32.

782.   Kidson, Frank. "Some Guesses about Yankee Doodle." *Musical Quarterly* 3/1 (January 1917): 98-103.

An early attempt at establishing the provenance of the tune. Also discusses the derivation of the term "Yankee Doodle." Musical examples.

783.   Kidson, Frank. "The 'Star-Spangled Banner': An Exhaustive Official Inquiry." *Musical Times* 56 (1915): 148-50.

784.   Kimball, Frank W. "The Star Spangled Banner." *Etude* 53 (1935): 390, 434.

785.   Klamkin, Marian. *Old Sheet Music: A Pictorial History.* New York: Hawthorn Books, 1975. 214p.

A survey of the history of sheet music publication in
America with each chapter devoted to a specific topic such as
"patriotic and political music," "early publishers and
lithographers," etc.   Although the bulk of this work focuses on the
1820s and after, there is a chapter on the "care and repair of old
sheet music."

786.   Kouwenhoven, John A. and Lawton M. Patten.   "New Light on 'The
       Star Spangled Banner.'"   *Musical Quarterly* 23/2 (April
       1937): 198-200.

       Reviews various theories regarding whether or not Key's
verses were intended to be sung.   The authors contend that Key had
the Anacreontic tune in mind when he wrote those famous words.

787.   Kroeger, Karl.   "William Billings' 'Anthem for Easter': The
       Persistance of an Early American 'Hit.'"   *Proceedings of the
       American Antiquarian Society* 97/1 (1987): 105-28.

       Includes historical background of anthems and the publishing
history of Billings' work, including a list of printings from 1787-
1986.   Musical examples.

788.   Lawrence, Vera Brodsky.   "The Earliest Performances of 'The
       Creation' in the United States."   *Moravian Music Journal*
       27/4 (Winter 1982): 90-91.

       Franz Joseph Haydn's work was first performed in 1811 by the
Collegium Musicum in Nazareth, Pa.

789.   Lax, Roger and Frederick Smith.   *The Great Song Thesaurus.*
       New York: Oxford University Press, 1984.   665p.

       Includes a few song titles arranged by date for the period
before 1820.   Presented chronologically with major social and
historical events cited (see pp. 9-13).   Not comprehensive.

790.   LeMassena, C.E.   "Evolution of a National Anthem."   *Musician*
       47 (1942): 90-91.

       On the "Star Spangled Banner."

791.   Lemay, J.A. Leo.   "The American Origins of 'Yankee Doodle.'"
        William and Mary Quarterly 33/3 (July 1976): 435-64.

        The author proposes that the text is an American folksong
from the late 1740s.   Examines the earliest texts of "Yankee Doodle"
and discusses Oscar Sonneck's theories regarding its origin.
Particularly valuable for its extensive citations of literature on
the tune.

792.   Levy, Lester S.   *Flashes of Merriment: A Century of Humorous
        Songs in America, 1805-1905.*   Norman: University of Oklahoma
        Press, 1971.   xiv, 370p.

        Includes a broad range of songs here transcribed for voice
alone, but with facsimiles of sheet music covers, some of which are
not reprinted in other sources.   Short essays precede each category
of songs.

793.   Levy, Lester S.   *Picture the Songs: Lithographs from the Sheet
        Music of Nineteenth-Century America.*   Baltimore: Johns
        Hopkins University Press, 1976.   x, 213p.

        Although all of the lithographs contained in this
compilation are dated after 1826, the author provides information on
lithography and music for the period 1819-26.

794.   Levy, Lester S. and James J. Fuld.   "Unrecorded Early
        Printings of *The Star Spangled Banner*." *Notes* 27/2
        (December 1970): 245-51.

        Includes 15 printings not in Muller's bibliography, *The Star
Spangled Banner* (see entry 805).

795.   Lichtenwanger, William.   "The Music of 'The Star Spangled
        Banner,' Whence and Whither?" *College Music Symposium* 18/2
        (Fall 1978): 34-81.

        Discusses the origin of the tune, the controversy regarding
John S. Smith, the composer of the tune, Ralph Tomlinson, author of
the text, and the Anacreontic Society.   Originally printed in
Quarterly Journal of the Library of Congress (July 1977).

796.   Lichtenwanger, William.   "Richard S. Hill and the 'Unsettled'
       Text of The Star Spangled Banner."   In *Richard S. Hill:
       Tributes from Friends*.   Comp. and ed. by Carol June Bradley
       and James B. Coover.   Detroit Studies in Music Bibliography,
       58.   Detroit: Information Coordinators, 1987, pp. 71-184.

       Discusses Hill's research on this famous song by Francis
Scott Key and 45 subsequent versions of text found in songsters and
other sources.   Includes a chart which compares texts, musical
examples, and other illustrations.   (See also entry 774.)

797.   Lichtenwanger, William.   "Star-Spangled Bibliography."
       College Music Symposium 12 (Fall 1972): 94-102.

       A narrative account of major studies of "The Star-Spangled
Banner."

798.   Lindsay, Bryan Eugene.   "The English Glee in New England,
       1815-1845."   Ph.D. dissertation, George Peabody College for
       Teachers, 1966.   405p.   UM 67-3616.   *DAI* 27/12 (June 1967):
       4285-A.

       This work focuses on Boston and Salem, Mass., and
Providence, R.I., and is based on primary sources.   "The study found
that English glee performance began in America during the last
decade of the eighteenth century, and that glee clubs similar to
those active in England were organized in the United States before
1800."

799.   Lippencott, Margaret E.   "'O'er the Land of the Free.'"   *New-
       York Historical Society Quarterly Bulletin* 25 (1941): 28-36.

       On the "Star Spangled Banner."

800.   Lossing, Benson J.   "The Origin of Yankee Doodle."   *Dwight's
       Journal of Music* 19 (1861): 107.

801.   Lowens, Irving.   "The Songster and the Scholar."   *Proceedings
       of the American Antiquarian Society* 76/1 (April 1966): 59-
       70.

Defines and discusses American songsters. According to Lowens, 28 pre-1821 songsters have been identified; includes titles, excerpts, and some brief comments on a number of them. This article serves as an excellent introduction to songsters of that period. (See also entries 127-128.)

802.   Lowens, Irving. "'Yankee Doodle' in Connecticut: A Musical Controversy Ends as Macaroni." *Sonneck Society Newsletter* 4/2 (1978): 13-14.

803.   McNeil, Anna W. "The Star Spangled Banner." *Etude* 55 (1937): 432, 480, 488.

804.   "Mrs. Washington's Song Book." *Annual Report of the Mount Vernon Ladies' Association of the Union* (1964): 11-13.

805.   Muller, Joseph. *The Star Spangled Banner: Words and Music Issued Between 1814-1864.* New York: G.A. Baker & Co., 1935. Foreword by John Tasker Howard. Reprint, New York: Da Capo Press, 1973. 223p.

A standard reference work, which despite the date, is still valuable. Subtitle: "An Annotated Bibliographical List With Notices of the Different Versions, Texts, Variants, Musical Arrangements, and Notes on Music Publishers in the United States. Illustrated with 108 Portraits, Facsimiles, etc." Index.

806.   Myers, Gordon. "Songs of Early Americans." *Music Journal* 27/9 (September 1969): 36-37.

Mentions works by William Billings and other New England composers, Francis Hopkinson, and the Moravians.

807.   Nathan, Hans. "United States of America." In *A History of Song*. Ed. by Denis Stevens. New York: Norton, 1970, pp. 408-60.

An essay on the history of song in America, beginning with a discussion of the New England tunebook tradition, songs by Francis

Hopkinson and various Moravians; however, most of this study focuses on the 19th and 20th centuries.

808.   "Origin of 'Hail Columbia.'"   *Brainard's Musical World* 28
         (1891): 93.

809.   "Origin of the 'Star-Spangled Banner.'"   *Music: A Monthly
         Magazine* 1 (1892): 469-71.

810.   "'Origin' of Yankee Doodle."   *Musical Reporter* 1 (1841): 207-
         09.

         Gives examples of texts set to the tune and where the tune
was played.   Musical examples.   Reprinted in *American Periodicals,
1800-1850*, reel 840 (see entry 131).

811.   "Our National Song."   *Brainard's Musical World* 31 (1894): 339,
         361.

812.   Owen, Barbara.   "Our Choral Heritage: The Legacy of Colonial
         America."   *Journal of Church Music* 22/8 (October 1980): 10-
         11.

         Mentions major composers of choral music and includes a list
of modern editions.

813.   Potter, Warren H.   "American Choral Music in the 1700's: A
         Survey of Colonial Singing Societies."   *Musical America* 63/5
         (March 1943): 6-7, 14.

         Includes information on Boston, New York, Philadelphia,
Baltimore, and Charleston.   Musicians mentioned include William
Billings, Josiah Flagg, William Selby, and others.   Illustrations.

814.   Puissegur, Jo Ann Theresa.   "An Analysis of a Selected
         Collection of Secular Early American Vocal Literature."
         Ph.D. dissertation, Louisiana State University and
         Agricultural and Mechanical College, 1986.   190p.   UM 87-
         10583.   *DAI* 48/4 (October 1987): 864-A.

Four chapters. Discusses secular songs of native-born and immigrant composers, 1759-1800, and a brief survey of vocal music in the United States before 1800. Chapter 3 has biographical information on each composer and an analysis of one song by each composer.

815.   Robinson, Albert F. "Choral Music and Choirs in Early America." *Journal of Church Music* 18/2 (February 1976): 2-5.

816.   Salisbury, Stephen. "The Star Spangled Banner and National Airs." *American Historical Record* 1 (1872): 550-54.

Also printed in Dwight's *Journal of Music* 32 (1872), pp. 332-33.

817.   Scott, John Anthony. *The Ballad of America: The History of the United States in Song and Story.* Carbondale: Southern Illinois University Press, 1983. xiii, 439p.

Includes music and text for ballads, songs, and Psalm 100. Chronologically arranged. Discography, index of titles and first lines, and general index. Refer to a review in *American Music* 4/1 (Spring 1986), pp. 110-12. See also the author's article, "Ballads and Broadsides of the American Revolution," in *Sing Out!* 16/2 (1966).

818.   Shedlock, John S. "The Star-Spangled Banner." *Monthly Musical Record* 47 (1917): 121-22.

819.   Shippen, Rebecca Lloyd. "'The Star-Spangled Banner.'" *Pennsylvania Magazine of History and Biography* 22/3 (1898): 321-25.

An extract from a letter written in 1856 by Robert B. Taney, brother-in-law of Francis Scott Key, which explains the writing and setting to music of the song.

820.   Smith, Alice T. "The Star-Spangled Banner." *Music Clubs Magazine* 44/3 (February 1965): 12.

Brief history with mention of Public Law #823 making it the official national anthem. See also *Music Clubs Magazine* 64/4 (April 1965), p. 19.

821.   Sonneck, Oscar G.   "Critical Notes on the Origin of 'Hail Columbia.'" *Sammelbände der internationalen Musikgesellschaft* 3 (1901): 139-66.

822.   Sonneck Oscar G.   "The First Edition of 'Hail Columbia.'" *Pennsylvania Magazine of History and Biography* 40 (1916): 426-35.

Discusses the physical characteristics of the original edition. Comments on Charles Hart's article (see entry 771). Reprinted in *Miscellaneous Studies in the History of Music* (see entry 399).

823.   Sonneck, Oscar George.   *Report on "The Star-Spangled Banner"; "Hail Columbia"; "America"; "Yankee Doodle."* Washington, D.C.: Government Printing Office, 1909. Reprint, Dover Publications, 1972.   203p.

A principal source for the study of these works. Included are facsimiles, musical examples, and index. See also "The Star-Spangled Banner" in *Instrumentalist* 29/5 (1974), pp. 39-41.

824.   Sonneck, Oscar George.   *"The Star Spangled Banner."* Washington, D.C.: Government Printing Office, 1914.   115p.

An expanded version of Sonneck's earlier study (see entry 823). A detailed study, including musical examples and facsimiles, the original broadside of Key's poem, and other documents. Index.

825.   "The Star-Spangled Banner." *American Art Journal* 37 (1882): 502-03.

826.   "The Star Spangled Banner." *Dwight's Journal of Music* 19 (1861): 37, 39, 46.

827.   Steers, Katherine V. "Patriotic Songs." *American Monthly
        Magazine* 42 (1913): 120-23.

828.   Svejda, George J. *History of the Star-Spangled Banner from
        1814 to the Present.* Washington, D.C.: Division of History,
        Office of Archeology and Historic Preservation, 1969. 525p.

        A major study based to a large extent on newspapers and
other primary sources. Discusses the tune and musical arrangements.
Includes facsimiles and an extensive bibliography for further study.

829.   Tawa, Nicholas E. "The Performance of Parlor Songs in
        America, 1790-1860." *Yearbook for Inter-American Musical
        Research* 11 (1975): 69-81.

        Discusses performance practice, the composers, some
performers, and a sampling of characteristic songs.

830.   Tawa, Nicholas E. *Sweet Songs for Gentle Americans: The
        Parlor Song in America, 1790-1860.* Bowling Green, Ohio:
        Bowling Green University Popular Press, 1980. 273p.

        A history and definition of parlor songs, treated topically,
not chronologically. Subjects include, for example, types of songs,
topics, sales, and musical characteristics. Included is a list of
"the most popular songs in the extant collections of music," musical
examples, and facsimiles.

831.   Upton, William Treat. *Art-Song in America: A Study in the
        Development of American Music.* Boston: Oliver Ditson, 1930.
        Reprint, New York: Johnson Reprint Corporation, 1969. xi,
        279p.

        Until recently, this study was the major work for this
medium. Chapters 1-2 focus on the period from 1750-1825, including
the work of James Bremner, Benjamin Carr, Gottlieb Graupner, James
Hewitt, Francis Hopkinson, Victor Pelissier, Alexander Reinagle,
William Selby, and Rayner Taylor. Unfortunately, sources are not
provided. Musical examples and index.

832.   Urkowitz, Steven and Lawrence Bennett.   "Early American Vocal
       Music." *Journal of Popular Culture* 12/1 (Summer 1978): 5-
       10.

       Discusses the New England singing school tradition and the
early 19th-century controversy regarding American composition.
Includes excerpts from a letter written by Elkanah Kelsey Dare to
Andrew Law in 1811.

833.   Van Camp, Leonard. "Some Modern Editions of 18th-Century
       American Choral Music." *Church Music*, 1976, no. 2: 13-22.

834.   Washington, Eugenia. "Origin of 'Yankee Doodle.'" *American
       Monthly Magazine* 10 (1897): 53-54.

835.   Winslow, Ola Elizabeth. *American Broadside Verse.* New Haven,
       Conn.: Yale University Press, 1930. xxvi, 224p.

       An excellent collection of 101 facsimiles depicting a
variety of broadsides held by various historical societies and
libraries. The collection is arranged by category, including
funeral verses and memorials, meditations, comments on local
incidents, and more. Index of titles and first lines and names.

836.   Yerbury, Grace Helen. *Song in America from Early Times to
       about 1850.* Metuchen, N.J.: Scarecrow Press, 1971. 305p.

       Based on the author's dissertation, "Styles and Schools of
Art-Song in America (1720-1850)" (Indiana University, 1953). The
author begins her study of art song by including the early New
England composers of psalmody as the first school, then discusses
three additional schools based on location, including the
Philadelphia, New York, and Boston schools. Yet other schools are
classified by individual composers' styles, including, for example,
that of Benjamin Carr. Refer to a review in *Notes* 29/2 (December
1972), pp. 241-42.

Psalmody and Singing Schools

The following list does not include tunebooks. For a bibliography
of tunebooks published in the United States before 1800, refer to
Britton, "Theoretical Introductions in American Tune-Books to 1800"
(see entry 83). For a list of tunebooks published in 1800-10, refer
to Lindsley, "Early Nineteenth-Century American Collections of
Sacred Choral Music, 1800-1810" (see entry 108). A list of
tunebooks in reprint editions is found in Chapter 8 below, and in
American Music before 1865 (see entry 82) and Miller's *Folk Music in
America*, pp. 284-91 (see entry 112). Readers should note that a
number of these facsimile editions include informative essays by
recognized scholars. Included below is a selection of noteworthy
sermons and discourses on psalmody and singing schools published in
the United States during the 18th and early 19th centuries. For a
list of 32 sermons and other writings on this subject published
during the years 1760-1800, see De Jong, "Both Pleasure and Profit"
(see entry 865). For an excellent article by Richard Crawford on
early American psalmody, refer to *The New Grove Dictionary of
American Music*, vol. 3, pp. 635-43 (see entry 30).

837.   Anderson, John. *A Discourse on the Divine Ordinance of
        Singing Psalms. . . .* Philadelphia: William Young, 1791.
        112p.

        Anderson was minister of the Mill-Creek and Herman's Creek
congregations near Pittsburgh. He presents a definition of
psalmody, and discusses its justification and importance in worship.
He believes that the "style and manner of a composition" has to be
varied according to the subject of the psalm. Anderson also speaks
about a "Synod of New York and Philadelphia," which appointed a
committee to examine "the different versions of the Book of Psalms."
Reprinted in *Early American Imprints*, no. 23123 (see entry 43).

838.   Anderson, John. *Vindiciae Cantus Dominici; or, A Vindication
        of the Doctrine Taught in a Discourse on the Divine
        Ordinance of Singing Psalms.* Philadelphia: William Young,
        1793. 184p.

        Anderson speaks of "the scheme of singing human composures
in our solemn worship," and refers to it as a "new scheme." He
defends the use of biblical scriptures as the proper form of
psalmody in public worship. Other subjects include the effect of

music in religious worship and the use of instrumental music in church.   Reprinted in *Early American Imprints*, no. 25110 (see entry 43).

839.   Appel, Richard G.   "The Bay Psalm Book and Its Music, 1640-1773."   *Consort* 30 (1974): 72-76.

A general discussion, including facsimile pages from the 1698 edition.

840.   Atkins, Charles L.   "William Billings: His Psalm and Hymn Tunes."   *Papers of the Hymn Society of America* 24 (1962) 3-27.

841.   Balch, William.   *An Address on Music, Delivered to the Salisbury and Amesbury* [Massachusetts] *Singing Societies, Convened at Salisbury, April 3, 1812.*   Newburyport, Mass.: W. and J. Gilman, 1812.   12p.

Persons should improve their abilities to sing properly. Balch preferred European music, especially Handel and Arne: "It is from these models that a correct musical taste is to be formed." Reprinted in *Early American Imprints, Second Series*, no. 24679 (see entry 44).

842.   Barbour, J. Murray.   "Billings and the Barline."   *American Choral Review* 18/4 (October 1976): 37-49.

Includes numerous musical examples from various tunebooks by Billings.

843.   Barbour, J. Murray.   "The Texts of Billings' Church Music."   *Criticism: A Quarterly for Literature and the Arts* 1 (1959): 49-61.

844.   Becker, Laura L.   "Ministers vs. Laymen: The Singing Controversy in Puritan New England, 1720-1740."   *New England Quarterly* 55 (March 1982): 79-96.

Discusses the controversy regarding the correct way of singing psalmody. Includes a bibliography of local histories that has information on this debate for the years 1722-44. An appendix includes a list of 31 clergymen known to have supported the approved way of singing psalms.

845.   Benson, Louis F. "The American Revisions of Watts's
         'Psalms.'" *Journal of the Presbyterian Historical Society*
         2/1 (June 1903): 18-34; 2/2 (September 1903): 75-89.

         Researchers interested in this topic will want to refer to this work, despite its date of publication. Includes a partial listing of revisions, with full imprint data noted.

846.   Birge, Edward Bailey. *History of Public School Music in the
         United States.* Philadelphia: Oliver Ditson Company, 1939.
         Reprint, Washington, D.C.: Music Educators National
         Conference, 1973. 323p.

         Chapter 1 is titled "The Development of the Singing-School," and focuses primarily on New England with most principal musicians mentioned. Discusses the decline of proper singing. The one musical example included is Oliver Holden's "Coronation." Index.

847.   *A Brief Discourse Concerning Regular Singing.* Boston: B.
         Green for John Eliot, 1725.

         Written in 1722, this tract discusses what is meant to sing psalms "with skill."

848.   Britton, Allen P. "The Here and Why of Teaching Singing
         Schools in Eighteenth-Century America." *Council for
         Research in Music Education Bulletin* 99 (Winter 1989): 23-
         41.

849.   Britton, Allen. P. "Music in Early American Public
         Education: A Historical Critique." In *Basic Concepts in
         Music Education.* The Fifty-Seventh Yearbook of the National
         Society for the Study of Education. Ed. by Nelson B. Henry.
         Chicago: University of Chicago Press, 1958, pp. 195-211.

Includes a brief survey of the early American singing school, attempts at early music instruction, and early instruction books, including those by John Tufts and Thomas Walter. The bibliography is worthy of note and includes German-American sources.

850.   Britton, Allen P.   "The Musical Idiom in Early American Tunebooks." *Journal of the American Musicological Society* 3/3 (Fall 1950): 286.

Abstract of a paper presented at a meeting of the Midwestern Chapter of the AMS in St. Louis on April 14, 1950.

851.   Britton, Allen P.   "The Singing School Movement in the United States."   In *Report of the Eighth Congress, New York, 1961* [of the International Musicological Society].   2 vols.   New York: Bärenreiter, 1961, vol. 1, pp. 89-99.

An excellent introduction to the singing school, its singing masters and tunebooks.   However, much more is known about this movement today than when Britton wrote on the subject some twenty-nine years ago.

852.   Brown, Robert Benaway and Frank X. Braun.   "The Tunebook of Conrad Doll." *Papers of the Bibliographical Society of America* 42/3 (1948): 229-38.

Doll of Lancaster, Pa., compiled and published his *Sammlung geistlicher Lieder nebst Melodien von verschiedenen Dichtern und Componisten* (1798).   Includes biographical information on Doll, an organist in Lancaster, Pa.

853.   Buechner, Alan Clark.   "Yankee Singing Schools and the Golden Age of Choral Music in New England, 1760-1800."   Ed.D. dissertation, Harvard University, 1960.

854.   Carpenter, Edmund J.   "The Bay Psalm Book." *New England Magazine* 15 (1897): 575-84.

855. Chauncey, Nathaniel. *Regular Singing Defended and Proved to
      be the Only True Way of Singing the Songs of the Lord.* New
      London: T. Green, 1728. 54p.

         Perhaps the first tract on the subject published in Conn.
Cited in Steel, "Sacred Music in Early Winchester" (see entry 579).
Reprinted in *Early American Imprints*, no. 3006 (see entry 43).

856. Cheek, Curtis Leo. "The Singing School and Shaped-Note
      Tradition: Residuals in Twentieth-Century American Hymnody."
      D.M.A. dissertation, University of Southern California,
      1968. 306p. UM 69-5046. *DAI* 29/9 (March 1969): 3167-A.

         Discusses the psalters brought to America by the colonists,
the decline in congregational singing in New England in the 17th and
18th centuries, and the transition to 19th-century practice.
Discussed also is Ananias Davisson's tunebook, *Kentucky Harmony*
(1816).

857. Cheek, Curtis Leo. "The Singing Schools in America:
      Backgrounds." *Hymn* 13/1 (1962): 5-11.

         Refer also to the author's dissertation (see entry 855).

858. Covey, Cyclone. "Did Puritanism or the Frontier Cause the
      Decline of Colonial Music?" *Journal of Research in Music
      Education* 6/1 (Spring 1958): 68-78.

         In the form of a mock debate, Covey's emphasis is on William
Billings and New England psalmody.

859. Crawford, Richard. "A Hardening of the Categories:
      'Vernacular,' 'Cultivated,' and Reactionary in American
      Psalmody." In *American Studies and American Musicology: A
      Point of View and a Case in Point.* I.S.A.M. Monographs, 4.
      New York: Brooklyn College, Institute for Studies in
      American Music, 1975, pp. 16-33.

         Discusses "the American as a composer, the style of music
appropriate for sacred use, and the idiom of sacred music," based on
an examination of various 18th- and early 19th-century tunebooks by

William Billings, Supply Belcher, Joel Harmon, James Newhall, and
others.

860.   Crawford, Richard, and David P. McKay.   "Music in Manuscript:
            A Massachusetts Tune-Book of 1782." *American Antiquarian
            Society Proceedings* 84 (April 1974): 43-64.

861.   Crawford, Richard and David P. McKay.   "The Performance of
            William Billings' Music." *Journal of Research in Music
            Education* 21/4 (Winter 1973): 318-30.

        Based, in part, on the writings of Billings.   The author
discusses the musical elements to consider in performing Billings'
music, and, interestingly, the placement of the choir in a manner
similar to likely practice during the colonial period.

862.   Crawford, Richard.   "Watts for Singing: Metrical Poetry in
            American Sacred Tunebooks, 1761-1785." *Early American
            Literature* 11/2 (Fall 1976): 139-46.

        An excellent introduction to metrical psalms and hymns from
a music historian's vantage point.   Composers discussed include
William Billings, Andrew Law, Daniel Read, and others.

863.   Daniel, Ralph T.   "Handel Publications in 18th-Century
            America." *Musical Quarterly* 45/2 (April 1959): 168-74.

        Discusses works by Handel in the following publications:
Josiah Flagg, *Sixteen Anthems* (1766); Isaiah Thomas, *The Worcester
Collection of Sacred Harmony* (1786); Daniel Read, *Columbian
Harmonist* (1795); and Oliver Holden, *Massachusetts Compiler* (1795).

864.   Davis, Josephine K.R.   "Early American Singing Schools."
            Music Journal 20/3 (March 1962): 46, 94-95.

        A brief introduction to the role of the singing school in
society, its teachers, and examples of landmark tunebooks.

865. De Jong, Mary Gosselink. "'Both Pleasure and Profit': William
       Billings and the Uses of Music." *William and Mary Quarterly*
       42/1 (January 1985): 104-16.

       Discusses Billings' musical writings, and the controversy
concerning regular singing. Lists 32 sermons and other writings on
vocal music published between 1760 and 1800. Yet additional
commentary centers on Billings' fuging tunes.

866. Dorenkamp, J.H. "The *Bay Psalm Book* and the Ainsworth
       Psalter." *Early American Literature* 7/1 (Spring 1972): 3-
       16.

       A description of both psalters and how they were used, with
a comparison of texts.

867. Dwight, Josiah. *An Essay to Silence the Outcry That Has Been
       Made in Some Places Against Regular Singing.* Boston: John
       Eliot, 1725.

       Explains that it is young persons who are mostly in favor of
regular singing. Also describes the practice of usual singing.

868. Eames, Wilberforce. *A List of Editions of the Bay Psalm Book
       or New England Version of the Psalms.* Bound with a
       facsimile reprint of the 1640 ed. of the *Bay Psalm Book.*
       New York: the author, 1885. Reprint, New York: Burt
       Franklin, 1973. 297p.

       The first edition in 1640 did not contain music.
Wilberforce includes full imprint data and describes its contents.

869. Ellis, Ferdinand. *An Address on Music, Delivered to the First
       Baptist Singing Society, Boston, Thursday Evening, May 15,
       1806.* Boston: Russell and Cutler, 1806. 22p.

       The author preached about "the value of sacred music in
general, the importance of a good church choir, and the necessity of
having a good balance between men and women singers" (quote from
Nitz dissertation, p. 105; see entry 534). Reprinted in *Early
American Imprints, Second Series*, no. 10348 (see entry 44).

870.   Engelke, Hans.   "A Study of Ornaments in American Tune Books,
       1760-1800."   Ph.D. dissertation, University of Southern
       California, 1960.   217p.   UM 60-558.   *DAI* 20/10 (April
       1960): 4130.

       Includes a "categorical breakdown of the tune books and
their sources for the ornaments," and "various interpretations, how
they were to be learned, the proper places for their use, and a
short historical background of each."   Also discusses performance
practice.

871.   Eskew, Harry B.   "Joseph Funk's 'Allgemein nützliche Choral-
       Music' (1816)."   *Journal of German-American History* 32
       (1966): 38-46.

872.   Eskew, Harry.   "Using Early American Hymnals and Tunebooks."
       Notes 27/1 (September 1970): 19-23.

       Discusses the difference between a hymnal and tunebook,
shape note tunebooks, and the acquisition, processing and cataloging
of them.

873.   Farnsworth, H.   *An Oration on Music.*   Cooperstown: Elihu
       Phinney, 1795.   21p.

       Presented at the court house in Cooperstown in 1794 "at the
conclusion of a singing school, taught by Nathaniel Billings."
Presents a discourse on the advantages of learning music and its
value in religious worship.   Reprinted in *Early American Imprints*,
no. 28650 (see entry 43).

874.   Finney, Theodore M.   "Bibliographical Note: William Billings'
       The Continental Harmony."   *Journal of Research in Music
       Education* 18/4 (Winter 1970): 418-19.

       Mentions printer errors in the publication of the tunebook,
which was published in 1794.

875.   Finney, Theodore M.   "The Third Edition of Tufts' *Introduction
       to the Art of Singing Psalm-Tunes.*"   *Journal of Research in
       Music Education* 14/3 (Fall 1966): 163-70.

Describes the contents of the third edition of 1723 held in the library of the Pittsburgh Theological Seminary.   Facsimile.

876.   Fisher, James L.   "The Roots of Music Education in Baltimore."
       Journal of Research in Music Education 21/3 (Fall 1973):
       214-24.

Discusses early singing schools beginning with Ishmael Spicer and his school, November 1789.   Tunebooks examined include the *Baltimore Collection of Sacred Music* (1792), John Cole's *Beauties of Psalmody* (1804), Wheeler Gilet's *Maryland Selection of Sacred Music* (1809), and Samuel Dyer's *New Selection of Sacred Music* (1817).

877.   Fisher, William Arms.   *Ye Olde New-England Psalm-Tunes: 1620-
       1820.*   Boston: Oliver Ditson, 1930.   56p.

Includes an essay on the history of psalmody in New England beginning with the Ainsworth psalter and the *Bay Psalm Book*, and based, in part, on Metcalf's *American Writers and Compilers of Sacred Music* (see entry 1682).   The author mentions most of the principal tunebook compilers.   Also includes a series of 25 biographical sketches.   The second half of this study has some 42 pieces, including "Hints on the Performance of the Music."

878.   Foote, Henry Wilder.   *An Account of the Bay Psalm Book.*
       Papers of the Hymn Society of America, 7.   Hymn Society of
       America, 1940; reprint, 1980.   18p.

Discusses the various editions, including the 1698 edition, the first to include music.

879.   Foote, Henry Wilder.   "The Bay Psalm Book and Harvard
       Hymnody."   *Harvard Theological Review* 33/3 (July 1940): 225-
       37.

Discusses circumstances surrounding the publication of the first edition and its impact on society at that time.   Also mentions subsequent editions, and the controversy regarding the proper manner of singing psalms.

880.   Fouts, Gordon E.   "Music Instruction in America to Around 1830
        as Suggested by the Hartzler Collection of Early Protestant
        American Tune Books."   Ph.D. dissertation, University of
        Iowa, 1968.   352p.   UM 68-798.   *DAI* 29/6 (December 1968):
        1915-A.

        Based, in part, on 120 books published before 1831 and owned
by the Hartzler family.   Discusses music education after the
Revolutionary War, and the system of teaching developed by the
English Joseph Lancaster and Andrew Bell but adapted by Ezra Barrett
for teaching music in the United States.   An appendix includes an
annotated catalog of the Hartzler Collection, now in the library at
Goshen College in Indiana.

881.   Freeman, Jonathan.   *A Discourse on Psalmody: Delivered at
        Newburgh, before the Presbytery of Hudson, September, 1801.*
        Newburgh, N.Y.: Dennis Coles, 1801.   31p.

        Presents arguments that it is the duty of Christians to sing
psalms, and that the subjects should be derived from the gospel.
Talks about different versions of psalms that are sung by various
denominations, and argues against the Scottish Rouse version in use.
Regarding Rouse, Freeman states, "We are often obliged to sing two
syllables to one note which makes an unpardonable jar in the music."
Reprinted in *Early American Inprints, Second Series*, no. 520 (see
entry 44).

882.   Garrett, Allen M.   "Performance Practices in the Music of
        William Billings."   *Journal of the American Musicological
        Society* 5/2 (Summer 1952): 147.

        Includes a list of 9 elements related to the performance of
Billings' music.

883.   Gates, J. Terry.   "A Comparison of the Tune Books of Tufts and
        Walter."   *Journal of Research in Music Education* 36/3 (June
        1988): 169-93.

        Presents an analysis and comparison of John Tufts' *An
Introduction to the Singing of Psalm-Tunes* (1726) and Thomas
Walter's *The Grounds and Rules of Musick Explained* (1721), with
information on the 1698 edition of the *Bay Psalm Book*.   Includes
tables and facsimiles.

884. Grashel, John W. "The Gamut and Solmization in Early British
and American Texts." *Journal of Research in Music Education*
29/1 (Spring 1981): 63-70.

Discusses British models for American practice, and
"American adaptations" by John Tufts, Thomas Walter, William
Billings, and Andrew Law. Illustrations.

885. Gryc, Stephen M. "Explicating William Billings's 'Jargon.'"
In Theory Only 3/1 (April 1977): 22-28.

An analysis of this short and unusually dissonant work
written in 1778 by Billings as his response to those who accused him
of not using seventh or ninth chords in his music.

886. Hall, James William, Jr. "The Tune-Book in American Culture:
1800-1820." Ph.D. dissertation, University of Pennsylvania,
1967. 426p. UM 67-12749. *DAI* 28/5 (November 1967): 1743-
44-A

Confirms the thesis that the 19th-century tunebooks
"fulfilled important religious, educational, recreational, and
artistic needs," and that they were at that time a reflection of
musical reform, in that native works were being replaced with
European compositions. The author includes a bibliography of
tunebooks for the period studied, and constructs a list of 193 tunes
most frequently printed.

887. Hamm, Charles. "Patent Notes in Cincinnati." *Ohio Historical
and Philosophical Society Bulletin* 16 (October 1958): 293-
310.

888. Haraszti, Zoltan, ed. *The Bay Psalm Book: A Facsimile Reprint
of the First Edition of 1640.* Chicago: University of
Chicago Press, 1956. 148p.

Includes a separate section, "Notes on the Reproduction."

889. Haraszti, Zoltan. *The Enigma of the Bay Psalm Book.* Chicago:
University of Chicago Press, 1956. xiii, 144p.

Discusses the historical background, text, authorship, printing, and extant copies of the work. Chapter 8 focuses on "The Psalm-Singing of the Puritans," and is based on a variety of primary and secondary sources. Index of names.

890.   Horn, Dorothy. "Sacred Music of the Singing-Schools." *Church Music*, 1976, no. 1, 11-15.

Discusses psalmody and the introduction of character notes. Musical examples.

891.   Horn, Dorothy. "Shape-Note Hymnals and the Art Music of Early America." *Southern Folklore Quarterly* 5/4 (December 1941): 251-56.

The author discusses the connection between folk music and tunes in shape note hymnals. Includes a list of 18th-century tunes found in 19th-century collections.

892.   Inserra, Lorraine and H. Wiley Hitchcock. *The Music of Henry Ainsworth's Psalter.* I.S.A.M. Monograph, 15. New York: Brooklyn College, Institute for Studies in American Music, 1981. vii, 126p.

A facsimile and transcription of this psalter, which was published in Amsterdam in 1612, but which was used extensively in 17th-century New England. Commentary includes an essay on "Early Protestant Psalmody," Henry Ainsworth, and the text and music in his psalter.

893.   Irwin, Joyce. "The Theology of Regular Singing." *New England Quarterly* 51/2 (June 1978): 176-92.

According to the author, the movement for the establishment of regular singing was related to a "new theological basis for music in worship." Reviews discourses by John Cotton, Cotton Mather, Thomas Symmes, and Thomas Walter.

894.   Jackson, George Pullen. "Buckwheat Notes." *Musical Quarterly* 19/4 (October 1933): 393-400.

Brief survey of the use of shape notes in American tunebooks, beginning with John Tufts and Thomas Walter. Includes examples from William Little and William Smith, *The Easy Instructor* (1802) and Andrew Law, *The Art of Singing* (1803).

895.   Jones, Matt B.   "Bibliographical Notes on Thomas Walter's 'Grounds and Rules of Musick Explained.'" *Proceedings of the American Antiquarian Society* 42/2 (October 1932): 235-46.

896.   Jones, Matt B.   "Some Bibliographical Notes on Cotton Mather's 'The Accomplished Singer.'" *Publications of the Colonial Society of Massachusetts* 28 (December 1931): 186-93.

897.   Kaufman, Lee Jack.   "A Historical Study of Seven Character Shaped Note Music Notation."   Ed.D. dissertation, University of Virginia, 1970.   159p.   UM 71-6669.   *DAI* 31/9 (March 1971): 4818-A.

This study "describes the nature of the system and documents those facts which reveal its design and development."

898.   Kaufmann, Helen Stewart.   "John Cole's *Rudiments of Music*: Performance Practice in Early American Church Music." *American Choral Review* 18/4 (October 1976): 50-65.

An introductory study of this Baltimore musician and his *Rudiments of Music* (Baltimore, 1810).   Also includes information on Cole's *Songs of Zion* (Baltimore, 1818) and other works.

899.   Keene, James.   *A History of Music Education in the United States.*   Hanover, N.H.: University Press of New England, 1982.   ix, 399p.

Discusses music of the 18th-century singing school movement.

900.   Kegerreis, Richard I.   "The Handel Society of Dartmouth." *American Music* 4/2 (Summer 1986): 177-93.

Discusses concerts by the Musical Choir from 1771 on. Also mentions the composer John Hubbard, the Amherst Handelian Society, and the Central Musical Society of Concord, N.H.

901.   Kinne, Aaron. *Alamoth: An Address Delivered to the Singing Schools in the First and Second Societies in Groton.* Brattleborough, Vt.: William Fessenden, 1812. 11p.

Mentions a Levi Redfield, music "instructor," and how he came to teach in Groton. Also discusses the nature of musical expression as based on biblical teachings.

902.   Klocko, David Grover. "Jeremiah Ingalls' *The Christian Harmony: Or, Songster's Companion* (1805)." Ph.D. dissertation, University of Michigan, 1978. 3 vols., 1,332p. UM 78-15962. *DAI* 39/3 (September 1978): 1182-A.

Consists of 4 principal parts, including a survey of all references to Ingall and his tunebook; information on the author, and printing sources for the tunebook; sources of the melodies with an analysis of the musical aspects; and information on the publication of the work.

903.   Kouwenhoven, John A. "Some Unfamiliar Aspects of Singing in New England, 1620-1810." *New England Quarterly* 6 (September 1933): 567-88.

Discusses the singing of psalms and the decline of its proper practice. Both primary and secondary sources are consulted.

904.   Kroeger, Karl. "Dynamics in Early American Psalmody." *College Music Symposium* 26 (1986): 97-105.

The author proposes that, although most examples of psalmody published in the 18th century appeared "without any dynamic indications at all," dynamics were nonetheless important to composers at that time.

905.   Kroeger, Karl. "Errors in the Facsimile Edition of William Billings' The Continental Harmony." *Sonneck Society Bulletin* 14/3 (Fall 1988): 126-28.

Kroeger provides an errata list for the tunebook in preparation for a critical edition to be published in the *Complete Works* of William Billings (see entry 1932). Mentions Hans Nathan's facsimile edition of the tunebook (see entry 1933).

906. Kroeger, Karl. "The Music of William Billings: A Summary of Research." In *Report of Proceedings: Ph.D. in Music Symposium.* April 5-7, 1985. Ed. by William Kearns and William Reeves. Boulder: University of Colorado, 1988, pp. 131-33.

Focuses principally on the republication of the complete works of Billings by the American Musicological Society and the Colonial Society of Massachusetts.

907. Kroeger, Karl. "Slur and Tie in Anglo-American Psalmody." *American Choral Review* 28/2 (April 1986): 17-29.

The author discusses William Billings' use of the slur and tie. Includes musical examples and excerpts from theoretical introductions to collections by Oliver Holden, Elias Mann, and others.

908. Kroeger, Karl. "William Billings's Music in Manuscript Copy and Some Notes on Variant Versions of His Pieces." *Notes* 39/2 (December 1982): 316-45.

An analysis and list of contents of the manuscript. Musical examples.

909. Kroeger, Karl. "The Worcester Collection of Sacred Harmony and Sacred Music in America, 1786-1803." Ph.D. dissertation, Brown University, 1976. 708p. UM 77-14148. *DAI* 38/1 (July 1977): 18-19-A.

This study discusses the "history, repertory, and problems" of this significant late 18th-century tunebook compiled by Isaiah Thomas. Chapters 1-2 are on the musical background of New England at that time. Other chapters are devoted to the analysis of the collection with discussions on fuging tunes, anthems, set pieces, and the texts. An appendix lists all surviving copies of the collection.

910.   Kroeger, Karl.   "Word Painting in the Music of William
       Billings."   *American Music* 6/1 (Spring 1988): 41-64.

       The author pulls together a number of examples of word
painting from pieces found in Billings' tunebooks as the basis for
an essay on the subject.   Includes a table of Billings' works that
contain examples of word painting and cites tune name, location, and
type of word painting.

911.   Kroeger, Karl.   "A Yankee Tunebook from the Old South: Amos
       Pilsbury's *The United States Sacred Harmony*."   *Hymn* 32/3
       (1981): 154-62.

       Pilsbury's tunebook was published in 1799 in Boston, but
compiled in Charleston, S.C.   Includes tables of sources, composers,
and contents.   Musical examples.

912.   Krohn, Ernst C.   "A Checklist of Editions of 'The Missouri
       Harmony.'"   *Bulletin of the Missouri Historical Society* 6
       (1949-1950): 23-33, 374-99.

       This tunebook was compiled and published in 1820 by Allen
Carden.

913.   Landon, Esther Abrams.   "Seventeenth and Eighteenth Century
       English and Colonial American Music Texts: An Analysis of
       Instructional Content."   Ph.D. dissertation, University of
       California at Los Angeles, 1977.   238p.   UM 78-06503.   *DAI*
       38/11 (May 1978): 6389-90-A.

       Includes a discussion of "innovative teaching devices and
unorthodox notations" in 19th-century America.

914.   Latta, James.   *A Discourse on Psalmody: In Which It Is Clearly
       Shewn That It Is the Duty of Christians to Take the
       Principal Subjects and Occasions of Their Psalms, Hymns, and
       Spiritual Songs from the Gospel of Christ*.   4th ed.
       Philadelphia: William W. Woodward, 1801.   107p.

       Discusses the subjects and sources of biblical writings from
which psalmody should be derived.   Also expresses his concerns about

the introduction of instrumental music in public worship.   Reprinted
in *Early American Imprints, Second Series*, no. 797 (see entry 44).

915.   Lee, William.   "Instructions in Psalmody in Boston before
          1750." *New England Historical and Genealogical Register* 42
          (1888): 197-98.

          The instructions were written by John Lee (1717-1761).   This
is a unique document in that it is actually an article of agreement
for members of a singing school, whose teacher was Samuel Holbrook.

916.   Lindsley, Charles Edward.   "Scoring and Placement of the 'Air'
          in Early American Tunebooks." *Musical Quarterly* 58/3 (July
          1972): 365-82.

          Reviews previous literature and bases his information on the
prefaces of a number of tunebooks.   Facsimiles.

917.   Link, Eugene P.   "The Republican Harmony (1795) of Nathaniel
          Billings." *Journal of Research in Music Education* 18/4
          (Winter 1970): 414-18.

          The author discusses his search for information on this
little-known composer and the location of this tunebook which
previously had been cited as unlocated.   Refer to Allen P. Britton
and Irving Lowens, "Unlocated Titles in Early Sacred American Music"
(see entry 84).

918.   Loessel, Earl Oliver.   "The Use of Character Notes and Other
          Unorthodox Notations in Teaching the Reading of Music in
          Northern United States during the Nineteenth Century."
          Ed.D. dissertation, University of Michigan, 1959.   571p.   UM
          59-4951. *DAI* 20/5 (November 1959): 1820.

          The first 8 chapters discuss four-character and seven-
character notations, numeral notation, and other notations.
Following is a bibliography of 109 hymnbooks and tunebooks, with
full imprint data and library locations.   Includes two 18th-century
books.

919. [Lorenz, Ellen J.] "A Folio of Pages from Early American
        Songbooks." *Church Music*, 1976, no. 1, 38-40.

        Includes facsimiles from 19th-century sacred collections.

920. Lowens, Irving. "Amphion: Another Piracy from Andrew Law?"
        In *Richard S. Hill: Tributes from Friends*. Comp. and ed. by
        Carol June Bradley and James B. Coover. Detroit Studies in
        Music Bibliography, 58. Detroit: Information Coordinators,
        1987, pp. 185-98.

        A discovery by Lowens that a British tunebook, *Amphion or
the Chorister's Delight* (ca. 1789), was based, in part, on Andrew
Law's *Select Harmony* (1779).

921. Lowens, Irving. "Andrew Law and the Pirates." *Journal of the
        American Musicological Society* 13/1-3 (1960): 206-23.

        Discusses Law's various tunebooks and a collection by an
unknown compiler, *New Collection of Psalm Tunes Adapted to
Congregational Worship* (ca. 1781), which was pirated from Law's *A
Select Number of Plain Tunes Adapted to Congregational Worship*
(1781). Daniel Bayley and William Little are included in this
discussion. Includes photos of title pages. Reprinted in Lowens,
Music and Musicians in Early America (see entry 371).

922. Lowens, Irving. "The Bay Psalm Book in 17th-Century New
        England." *Journal of the American Musicological Society* 8/1
        (Spring 1955): 22-29.

        Traces the publication of the various editions. Reprinted
in Lowens, *Music and Musicians in Early America* (see entry 371).

923. Lowens, Irving and Allen P. Britton. "Daniel Bayley's 'The
        American Harmony': A Bibliographical Study." *Papers of the
        Bibliographical Society of America* 49/4 (1955): 340-54.

        Discusses 11 editions of William Tansur's *The Royal Melody
Complete* issued occasionally under the title *The American Harmony*,
printed by Daniel Bayley. Compares contents of the various editions
from 1767 on.

924.   Lowens, Irving and Allen P. Britton.   *"The Easy Instructor*
            (1798-1831): A History and Bibliography of the First Shape
            Note Tune Book."   *Journal of Research in Music Education* 1/1
            (Spring 1953): 31-55.

        Includes a checklist of the various editions and issues of
this tunebook compiled by William Little and William Smith.   Also
includes library locations.   Illustrations.

925.   Lowens, Irving.   "John Tufts' *Introduction to the Singing of*
            Psalm-Tunes (1721-1744): The First American Music Textbook."
            Journal of Research in Music Education 2/2 (Winter 1954):
            89-102.

        Reprinted in Lowens, *Music and Musicians in Early America*
(see entry 371).

926.   Lowens, Irving.   "John Wyeth's *Repository of Sacred Music,*
            Part Second: A Northern Precursor of Southern Folk Hymnody."
            Journal of the American Musicological Society 5/2 (Summer
            1952): 114-31.

        Wyeth's tunebook was first published in 1813.   The author
traces the publication history of the compilation, compares it to
other tunebooks of the period 1815-44, and includes an appendix of
tunes.   Photos.   Reprinted in Lowens, *Music and Musicians in Early*
America (see entry 371).

927.   Lowens, Irving.   "The Origins of the American Fuging Tune."
            Journal of the American Musicological Society 6/1 (Spring
            1953): 43-52.

        Defines and discusses the origin and development of the
fuging tune, mentioning American composers who wrote in this style.
Musical examples.   Reprinted in Lowens, *Music and Musicians in Early*
America (see entry 371).

928.   Lowens, Irving.   "Shape Notes, New England Music, and White
            Spirituals."   *Etude* 75/1 (January 1957): 15, 64; 75/2
            (February 1957): 20, 52.

This two-part article includes a brief survey of tunebooks, including those by William Little and William Smith, John Cole, Andrew Law, John Wyeth, and others.

929.   Lowens, Irving.   "Tune Books, Tunesmiths, and Singing
         Schools." *Etude* 74/9 (November 1956): 20, 59.

Selects Nehemiah Shumway's *American Harmony* (1793) as a "typical" tunebook of the period.   Discusses the difference between a hymnbook and tunebook.

930.   McGraw, Hugh.   "The Shape Note Singing Tradition."   In *College
         Music Society Proceedings: The National and Regional
         Meetings, 1983-84.*   Ed. by Roger E. Foltz.   Boulder, Col.:
         College Music Society, 1985, p. 48.

An abstract of a paper presented at the 27th annual meeting of the College Music Society, Oct. 4-7, 1984.   Discusses the principal shape note publications, beginning with the *Bay Psalm Book.*

931.   McKay, David P.   "Cotton Mather's Unpublished Singing Sermon."
         New England Quarterly 48/3 (September 1975): 410-22.

The sermon was published April 18, 1721 in Boston, and is a discussion of psalmody.   Includes full text of the sermon.

932.   Marrocco, W. Thomas.   "The Notation in American Sacred Music
         Collections."   *Acta Musicologica* 36 (1964): 136-42.

Discusses John Tufts' *Introduction to the Singing of Psalm-Tunes* (1721), Benjamin Dearborn's *A Scheme for Reducing the Science of Music to a More Simple State* (1785), and works by Andrew Adgate, Francis Hopkinson, Andrew Law, William Smith and William Little, and Charles Woodward.   Facsimiles.

933.   Marrocco, W. Thomas.   "The Set Piece."   *Journal of the
         American Musicological Society* 15/3 (Fall 1962): 348-52.

Discusses the derivation of the term and lists tunebooks that include set pieces, including Stephen Jenks' *Delights of*

Harmony (1805) and the *New Brunswick Collection of Sacred Music* (1818), among others.

934.   Mellen, John. *Religion Productive of Music: A Discourse Delivered at Marlborough, March 24th, 1773 at a Singing Lecture.* Boston: Printed and sold by Isaiah Thomas, 1773. 34p.

Discusses the proper way to sing psalms and notes preferences regarding the different versions of psalms. Also an interesting call for "grammar school masters" to teach "the first rudiments of singing, as they teach them the art of reading, writing, etc." Reprinted in *Early American Imprints*, no. 12867 (see entry 43).

935.   Metcalf, Frank J. "*The Easy Instructor*: A Bibliographic Study." *Musical Quarterly* 23/1 (January 1937): 89-97.

This tunebook was compiled by William Little and William Smith in 1798. The author compares the earliest surviving copies of 1802 and 1806. Includes photos of title pages.

936.   Mills, Samuel J. *The Nature and Importance of the Duty of Singing Praise to God, Considered.* Hartford, Conn.: Ebenezer Watson, 1775. 19p.

A sermon espousing the merits of "regular" singing delivered March 22, 1775 in Litchfield, Conn. For more information on this work, refer to Steel, "Sacred Music in Early Winchester" (see entry 579). Reprinted in *Early American Imprints*, no. 14260 (see entry 43).

937.   Murray, Sterling E. "Performance Practice in Early American Psalmody." *American Choral Review* 18/4 (October 1976): 9-26.

Serves as an excellent introduction to the subject. Based on contemporary writings.

938.   Music, David W. "Alexander Johnson and the *Tennessee Harmony*." *Current Musicology* 37/38 (1984): 59-73.

Johnson (1791-1832) published his tunebook in 1818. The author provides biographical information, an analysis of the tunebook and comparison with other similar works, and a list of tunes by Johnson. Of note, the 3rd edition (1824) is not cited in Richard J. Stanislaw's *A Checklist of Four-Shape Shape-Note Tunebooks* (see entry 120).

939.   Music, David W. "Ananias Davisson, Robert Boyd, Reubin Monday, John Martin, and Archibald Rhea in East Tennessee, 1816-26." *American Music* 1/3 (Fall 1983): 72-84.

Biographical. Davisson was the compiler of the tunebook *Kentucky Harmony* (1816).

940.   Music, David W. "The Meyer Manuscript: An 18th-Century American Tunebook." *Current Musicology* 29 (1980): 31-40.

The manuscript dates from the 1770s.

941.   "Music in Churches." *New Englander* 7 (July 1844): 335-46.

Discusses the value of music in church services, but contends that it must be improved. Mentions the practice of altering old tunes in recently published tunebooks.

942.   Myers, Gordon. "The Precentor: Early America's Unsung Hero." *Music Journal* 30/1 (January 1972): 28-29, 32.

Discusses the deterioration of the proper way to sing psalms occuring during the 17th and 18th centuries, various sermons preached at the time, the practice of lining-out, and information on Thomas Walter and John Tufts.

943.   Nathan, Hans. "William Billings: *The Continental Harmony* (1794)." *American Choral Review* 18/4 (October 1976): 27-36.

An introduction to notes regarding performance practice and other key elements in Billings' compilation. Musical examples.

944.   Nitz, Donald.   "The Norfolk Musical Society 1814-1820: An
       Episode in the History of Choral Music in New England."
       Journal of Research in Music Education 16/4 (Winter 1968):
       319-28.

       Discusses the reform movement in singing schools in New
England, and the influence of the Boston Handel and Haydn Society on
the Norfolk Musical Society, the latter founded in Dedham, Mass.
Also discusses the "transition from psalm tunes to oratorios" in the
performance repertoire.

945.   Noble, Oliver.   *Regular and Skilful Music in the Worship of
       God, . . . Shewn in a Sermon Preached at the North Meeting-
       House, Newbury-Port, at the Desire of the Church and
       Congregation, February 8th, 1774.*   Boston: Mills and Hicks,
       for Daniel Bayley, 1774.   46p.

       The earliest record of a musical organization in
Newburyport, Mass.   Discusses the advantage for the establishment of
a singing school and that the skills necessary for proper or
"regular" performance of psalmody be promoted.   Refer to Nitz for
additional information on this study (see entry 534).   Reprinted in
Early American Imprints, no. 13503 (see entry 43).

946.   "On Psalmody."   *Churchman's Magazine* 5/4 (April 1808): 141-44.

       On the value of singing psalms and encourages members of
congregations to join in singing them.   Signed "S.S."   Reprinted in
American Periodicals, 1800-1850 (see entry 131).

947.   Osterhout, Paul R.   "Note Reading and Regular Singing in
       Eighteenth-Century New England."   *American Music* 4/2 (Summer
       1986): 125-44.

       Discusses the parishes at Farmington, Hartford, Windsor, and
East Windsor, Connecticut.

948.   Perrin, Phil Daniel.   "Pedagogical Philosophy, Methods, and
       Materials of American Tune Book Introductions: 1801-1860."
       Journal of Research in Music Education 18/1 (Spring 1970):
       65-69.

Although most of this article focuses on the period after 1820, the author mentions Jeremiah Ingalls' *Christian Harmony* (1805).

949.   Perrin, Phil Daniel.   "Theoretical Introductions in American Tune-Books from 1801 to 1860."   D.M.A. dissertation, Southwestern Baptist Theological Seminary, 1968.   v, 227p.

Discusses systems of scale notation, including shape, numeral, and letter notation, meter, tempo, philosophy and methodology.   Includes a list of tunebooks by title, and a chronological list by system of scale notation.

950.   Pierce, Edwin Hall.   "The Rise and Fall of the 'Fugue-Tune' in America."   *Musical Quarterly* 16/2 (April 1930): 214-28.

Discusses the origins and nature of the fuging tune in America.   Includes information on John Tufts' *An Introduction to the Singing of Psalm-Tunes* (1721) and William Billings.   Note that because of its date of publication, this article should be used for its historical perspective of what was known about fuging tunes at that time.

951.   Poladian, Sirvart.   "Rev. John Tufts and Three-Part Psalmody in America."   *Journal of the American Musicological Society* 4/3 (Fall 1951): 276-77.

Abstract of a paper read at a meeting of the Greater New York Chapter of the American Musicological Society on February 17, 1951.   Consists of a discussion of Tufts' *An Introduction to the Singing of Psalm-Tunes* (1721).

952.   Riedel, Johannes.   "Early American Music."   *Journal of Church Music* 5/10 (November 1963): 2-4.

A brief discussion of composers and compilers of early tunebooks.

953.   Rogers, Samuel Kirby.   "The Social and Pedagogical Function of *The Worcester Collection*, *The Village Harmony* and *The Easy Instructor* in the Early-American Singing School."   Ph.D.

dissertation, Florida State University, 1969. 219p. UM 70-11158. *DAI* 30/12 (June 1970): 5473-74-A.

Discusses the music education movement during the 1700s, the link between the tunebook and the singing school, and the social nature and popularity of the movement.

954. Rosewall, Richard Byron. "Singing Schools of Pennsylvania, 1800-1900." Ph.D. dissertation, University of Minnesota, 1969. 439p. UM 69-16442. *DAI* 30/4 (October 1969): 1591-92-A.

Based on primary sources, this work discusses the historical development of the singing school in Pennsylvania, including German schools. The author divides his study into three periods: 1800-40, 1840-75, and 1875-1900.

955. Sanders, Robert L. "Notes on the Tune 'Albion.'" *Hymn* 12/3 (1961): 81-82.

The tune is found in Carden's *The Missouri Harmony* (1820).

956. Schwartz, Charles. "Development of Music Education in the United States." *National Association of Schools of Music: Proceedings of the 52nd Annual Meeting* 65 (1977): 124-28.

957. Sherman, Elna. "Ravenscroft's Psalter, 1621, and Its Place in the Early New England Scene." *Bulletin of the American Musicological Society*, nos. 11-13 (September 1948): 32-34.

958. Silver, Rollo G. "Prologue to Copyright in America: 1772." *Studies in Bibliography: Papers of the Bibliographical Society of the University of Virginia* 11 (1958): 259-62.

A brief study of William Billings' attempt to secure copyright for his *New-England Psalm-Singer* (1770). Based on primary sources.

959. "The Singing School." *Missouri Historical Review* 38 (1944): 325-30.

960.   Sluder, Claude K.   "The Ketcham Tune-Book: Examples of 18th-
       Century Hymnody in Indiana." *Current Musicology* 23 (1977):
       79-89.

       John Ketcham's tunebook is dated 1802. The author includes
a list of its musical contents and discusses a few of the works.
Musical examples.

961.   Smith, Carleton Sprague.   "Music of the *Ainsworth Psalter* and
       Bay Psalm Book." *Bulletin of the American Musicological
       Society* (1939): 8.

       Abstract of a paper read at a meeting of the Greater New
York Chapter of the AMS, April 18, 1939.

962.   Smith, Timothy Alan.   "Congregational Singing in Colonial New
       England." *Journal of Church Music* 26/7 (September 1984):
       10-15, 46-48.

       A survey of psalmody with mention of principal composers.
Facsimiles.

963.   Sollinger, Charles Edmond.   "The Music Men and the
       Professors—A History of String Class Methods in the United
       States, 1800-1911." Ed.D. dissertation, University of
       Michigan, 1970. 219p. UM 71-4549. *DAI* 31/8 (December
       1970): 4208-A.

       "This study reveals that instruments were taught in classes
as early as the 1840s (and perhaps as early as 1800) in isolated
parts of the country."

964.   Spell, Lota May Harrigan.   "Musical Education in North America
       during the Sixteenth and Seventeenth Centuries." Ph.D.
       dissertation, University of Texas, 1923.

965.   Stanislaw, Richard John.   "Choral Performance Practice in the
       Four-Shape Literature of American Frontier Singing Schools."
       D.M.A. dissertation, University of Illinois at Urbana-
       Champaign, 1976. 479p. UM 77-9200. *DAI* 37/10 (April
       1977): 6135-A.

Discusses tunebooks having four-shape notation, campmeetings and singing schools where they were used, performance practice then, and how these hymns and fuging tunes can be performed today.

966.   Stanislaw, Richard J.   "The Part Assignments in Nineteenth Century Four Shape Tune Books." *Choral Journal* 18/6 (February 1978): 14-21.

Discusses the placement of the "air" and performance practice.   Early tunebooks referred to include those by Ananias Davisson, John Wyeth, and several others for the period after 1820.

967.   Stearns, Charles. *A Sermon: Preached at an Exhibition of Sacred Musick, in Lincoln, on the Nineteenth of April, 1792.* Boston: Isaiah Thomas and Ebenezer T. Andrews, 1792. 15p.

"Musick. . . will claim preeminence to many other arts." Discusses the importance of music and mentions the musical qualities of the choir and that they established a "revival of sacred musick in this place." Names Isaac Lane of Bedford, Mass. as the singing school teacher. Reprinted in *Early American Imprints*, no. 24816 (see entry 43).

968.   Steinberg, Judith T.   "Old Folks Concerts and the Revival of New England Psalmody." *Musical Quarterly* 59/4 (October 1973): 602-19.

Discusses 19th and 20th-century attempts at reviving the music of the 18th-century singing school tradition.   Included is a list of early composers.

969.   Strickling, George F.   "The Bay Psalm Book." *Choral & Organ Guide* 7/1 (1954): 25-26.

970.   Strong, Joseph. *The Duty of Singing.* New Haven, Conn.: T. and S. Green, n.d.

Based on a singing lecture of March 18, 1773 in Simsbury, Conn.   Discusses the reform method or "regular way" of singing.   For

more on this work and the Simsbury Society, refer to Steel, "Sacred
Music in Early Winchester" (see entry 579).

971.   Stroud, William Paul.   "The Ravenscroft Psalter (1621): The
            Tunes, with a Background on Thomas Ravenscroft and Psalm
            Singing in His Time."   D.M.A. dissertation, University of
            Southern California, 1959.   592p.   UM 59-1865.   *DAI* 20/2
            (August 1959): 690-91.

        The Ravenscroft Psalter was used in New England in the 17th
century.   The author discusses the 179 pieces of music in the
collection and determines the provenance of individual tunes.

972.   Sunderman, Lloyd F.   "Early Music Education in Massachusetts."
            Education 72/1 (September 1951): 45-67.

        A brief survey beginning with the late 1700s through the
19th century.   Discusses psalmody and the singing school.   Sunderman
states, "The dark ages of American music education may be considered
as the period prior to 1815."

973.   Sunderman, Lloyd F.   "Sign Posts in the History of American
            Music Education."   *Education* 62/9 (May 1942): 515-50.

        Discusses significant events in chronological order of the
history of music education beginning with the New England singing
school tradition.

974.   Symmes, Thomas.   *The Reasonableness of Regular Singing.*
            Boston: B. Green and Samuel Gerrish, 1720.   24p.

        Although not the first to comment on the decline of singing
and musical knowledge in 17th and early 18th-century New England,
Symmes' statement was was of the strongest and most descriptive of
the problem.   He discusses how tunes were altered due to
parishioners having "laid aside" their "singing-books" in favor of
learning tunes by ear only.   Reprinted in *Early American Imprints*,
no. 2183 (see entry 43).

975.   Symmes, Thomas.   *Utile Dulci or, a Coco-Serious Dialogue,
            Concerning Regular Singing: Calculated for a Particular*

Town, (Where It Was Publickly Had, on Friday Oct. 12, 1722).
Boston: B. Green for Samuel Garrish, 1723.   59p.

Singing by rule or regular singing.   Presents what
apparently were, at that time, the reasons why some people preferred
to sing the usual way, that is, by not reading music.   A lengthy
description of the usual practice.

976.   Tallmadge, William.   "Folk Organum: A Study of Origins."
American Music 2/3 (Fall 1984): 47-65.

Reviews the theories regarding the origins of organum and
discusses the first instance of organum and its relation to lining-
out and psalm tunes in America in 1724 in the *New England Courant.*

977.   Temperley, Nicholas and Charles G. Manns.   *Fuging Tunes in the
Eighteenth Century.*   Detroit Studies in Music Bibliography,
49.   Detroit: Information Coordinators, 1983.   xi, 493p.

A principal work that discusses and compares both British
and American fuging tunes, the latter divided into 2 periods: 1761-
82 and 1783-1800.   The catalog is comprehensive and is based on an
extensive list of 18th-century tunebooks.   Each entry includes tune
incipit, number of voices in earliest source, analysis of structure,
and additional information.   Included is a list of tunes in modern
editions and indexes for names of tunes and persons.

978.   Temperley, Nicholas.   "The Old Way of Singing: Its Origins and
Development." *Journal of the American Musicological Society*
34/3 (Fall 1981): 511-44.

Traces the development of the "usual" way of singing in
Europe and the United States.   Discusses psalmody in Boston and
music associated with the Mennonites.

979.   Thacher, Peter, John Danforth and Samuel Danforth.   *An Essay
Preached by Several Ministers of the Gospel for the
Satisfaction of Their Pious and Consciencious Brethren, as
to Sundry Questions and Cases of Conscience, Concerning the
Singing of Psalms.* Boston: S. Kneeland for S. Gerrish,
1723.   22p.   Reprinted in Samuel Hopkins Emery, *The Ministry*

of Taunton, with Incidental Notices of Other Professions (Boston: J.P. Jewett, 1853).

Discusses the value of singing psalms and singing them "skilfully," including "keeping time, number and measure, aptly, with a sweet, tunable, musical voice." Includes substantial information on the usual versus the regular way of singing. Lists the churches that "sing by rule."

980.   Thorndike, S. Lothrop. "The Psalmodies of Plymouth and Massachusetts Bay." *Publications of the Colonial Society of Massachusetts* 1 (1895): 228-38.

981.   "Thoughts on the Singing of Psalms and Anthems in Churches." *Churchman's Magazine* 5/5 (May-June 1808): 175-87.

Written in Philadelphia in 1808. Discusses the proper way of singing anthems; singers should be "masters of their respective parts before they perform in the presence of the congregation," and there should be proper decorum in performance. Only one tune should be assigned to a psalm, so that only those words will be associated with the tune. Discusses the use of organs in church. Includes a rare note on the practice and use of interludes and voluntaries in church services. A substantial article. Reprinted in *American Periodicals, 1800-1850* (see entry 131).

982.   Tufts, John. *An Introduction to the Singing of Psalm-Tunes.* Boston: Printed for Samuel Gerrish, 1726.

A first edition, published in 1721, is unlocated. One of the first music education manuals in colonial America using letter notation to teach individuals how to sing by reading music. Among the tunes included in the collection is "100 Psalm Tune New," which is possibly the first composition by an American composer. The complete text of this manual is transcribed in Lowens, *Music and Musicians in Early America* (see entry 371) and reprinted in *Early American Imprints*, no. 39856 (see entry 43), and as a separate text (Philadelphia: Musical Americana, 1954).

983.   Turner, Maxine Thompson. "A History of the *Bay Psalm Book*." Ph.D. dissertation, Auburn University, 1971. 124p. UM 71-20212 *DAI* 32/3 (September 1971): 1424-A.

Discusses the use of the *Bay Psalm Book* in New England from 1640, the date of the first edition, through the subsequent editions to the period prior to the Revolution.

984. Van Camp, Leonard. "Choral Balance and the Alto Part in Early American Choral Music." *Choral Journal* 15/9 (May 1975): 7-9.

Includes information on singing school performance practice and on choral balance based, in part, on a number of tunebooks from the period, including William Billings' *The New-England Psalm-Singer* (1770), Oliver Holden's *The Union Harmony* (1793), and Amos Bull's *The Responsary* (1795).

985. Van Camp, Leonard. "Dynamics in Performing Early American Choral Music." *Choral Journal* 26/4 (1985): 13-25.

Based, in part, on information in early tunebooks.

986. Van Camp, Leonard and John Haberlen. "On Performing the Music of William Billings." *Choral Journal* 14/3 (November 1973): 18-22; 14/4 (December 1973): 16-17, 20.

This two-part article discusses Billings' style, assignment of vocal parts, instruments, accents, bar lines, rhythm, tone quality, dynamics, and phrasing.

987. Walter, Thomas. *The Grounds and Rules of Musick Explained.* Boston: Printed by J. Franklin for S. Gerrish, 1721. 24p.

Walter's first-hand experience in hearing psalmody sung in a chaotic manner led him to compile this instruction book, considered a landmark work, which teaches individuals to sing by reading music. Reprinted in *Early American Imprints*, no. 2303 (see entry 43).

988. Walter, Thomas. *The Sweet Psalmist of Israel, a Sermon Preach'd at the Lecture Held in Boston, by the Society for Promoting Regular & Good Singing.* Boston: J. Franklin for S. Garrish, 1722. 28p.

A discussion of the doctrine of music.   Reprinted in
American Culture Series, reel 50 (see entry 31).

989.   Weiss, Joanne Grayeski.   "The Relationship between the 'Great
        Awakening' and the Transition from Psalmody to Hymnody in
        the New England Colonies."   D.A. dissertation, Ball State
        University, 1988.   216p.   UM 88-20744.   *DAI* 49/8 (February
        1989): 2018-19-A.

The author examines the "ecclesiastical structure" of the
Congregationalists, Presbyterians, and Baptists and how it
influenced the reform movement.   This work traces the movement to
1770.

990.   Weld, Ezra.   *A Sermon Preached at a Singing Lecture: in
        Braintree May 21st, MDCCLXXXVIII.*   Springfield, Mass.: Ezra
        W. Weld, 1789.   28p.

Discusses subject matter of psalms and its relation to the
selection of a psalm-tune, and an appropriate key.   Prefers simple
set pieces to more complicated fuging tunes for pleasing the heart.
Persons who have singing ability should exercise their devotion to
God by singing psalms.   Reprinted in *Early American Imprints*, no.
22264 (see entry 43).

991.   Wentworth, E.   "My First Singing School."   *Musical Herald* 4/5
        (May 1883): 124.

Discusses his singing school experiences in Connecticut
around 1820, and his use of Thomas Hastings' *Musica Sacra* (1819).
An excellent source worth reviewing for its information on how a
singing school was conducted at that time.

992.   Wetzel, Richard D.   "Some Music Notation Systems in Early
        American Hymn-Tune Books."   *Keystone Folklore Quarterly* 12/4
        (Winter 1967): 247-60.

Pre-1820 musical examples include: William Little and
William Smith, *The Easy Instructor* (1807); Andrew Law, *Musical
Primer* (1812); *The American Harmonist* (1821); Andrew Adgate, *The
Philadelphia Harmony* (1811); Charles Woodward, *Ecclesiae Harmonia*
(1809).

993.   Willard, Samuel. *The Expediency and Proper Application of
        Sacred Music: A Discourse, Preached at Heath, Feb. 21, 1816,
        as a Musical Lecture.* Deerfield, Mass.: Graves and Wells,
        1816.   16p.

        Discusses the proper way of singing psalms and hymns and
that for children proper singing should be considered an
"indispensible part of education; no more to be omitted, than
arithmetic or writing." For additional information on this work,
refer to Nitz (see entry 534). Reprinted in *Early American
Imprints, Second Series*, no. 39826 (see entry 44).

994.   Willard, Samuel. *The Use and Design of Sacred Music, in a
        Discourse Preached March 19, 1811, as a Musical Lecture in
        Greenfield.* Greenfield, Mass.: n.p., 1811.   28p.

        Willard, who was a clergyman in Deerfield, Mass. and who
apparently in addressing a singing school class, discussed the newer
style of performing psalmody and expressed his dislike for fuging
tunes in that the congregation is "more occupied in imagining or
observing how the parts, falling in one after another, as they do,
are brought out together, than they are the sentiment the tune is
trying to express." For additional information on this work, refer
to Nitz (see entry 534).

995.   Williams, Albert S.   "America's First Book Was Musical."
        Music Journal 17/3 (March 1959): 60-61.

        Brief mention of the *Bay Psalm Book.*

996.   Williams, Thomas. *A Discourse, at a Public Meeting of the
        Singers, in the North Parish in Wrentham, 13th May, 1817.*
        Dedham, Mass.: Abel D. Alleyne, 1817.   22p.

        Discusses the "effort to promote the proper performance of
psalmody" which he says is the "object of the Norfolk Musical
Society." Refer to Nitz (see entry 534) for additional information
on this study. Reprinted in *Early American Imprints, Second Series*,
no. 42917 (see entry 44).

997.   Willman, Frederick R.   "A Brief Historical Study of the
        Singing Schools and Shape Notes and Implications for Music

Education Today." *Missouri Journal of Research in Music Education* 3/5 (1976): 91-111.

998.   Winchell, James Manning.   *An Address on Music, Delivered before the Singing-Society of the Second Baptist Church in Boston, 7th April, 1814.*   Boston: Manning and Loring, 1814.   16p.

Speaks about the reform movement in singing and that "the style of music introduced is so much superior to that which has prevailed in New England in years past."   Reprinted in *Early American Imprints, Second Series*, no. 33701 (see entry 44).

999.   Winslow, Ola Elizabeth.   *Meeting House Hill, 1630-1783.*   New York: W.W. Norton, 1972.   x, 344p.

Focuses on religion in colonial America, based on events in the colonial meetinghouse of New England.   Includes an interesting chapter (pp. 150-70) on the usual versus regular singing of psalmody Based on primary sources.

1000.   Winslow, Ola E.   "Victory in the 'Singing Seats.'"   *New-England Galaxy* 3/4 (1962): 3-14.

Discusses psalmody during the 17th and 18th centuries in New England.

1001.   Wolf, Edward C.   "Ehrenfried's Pennsylvania German Tunebook."   *Der Reggeboge: Journal of the Pennsylvania German Society* 19 (1965): 15-17.

1002.   Woodbridge, Timothy.   *The Duty of God's Professing People in Glorifying Their Heavenly Father, Preached at a Singing-Lecture in Hartford East Society, June 28, 1727.*   New London: T. Green, 1727.   16p.

Discusses reasons why the "regular way" for singing was best.   Cited in Steel, "Sacred Music in Early Winchester" (see entry 579).   Reprinted in *Early American Imprints*, no. 2979 (see entry 43).

1003.   Woodall, William L.   "Early American Psalm Singers." *Church
        Musician* 13/9 (September 1962): 15-16.

        Brief discussion of 17th-century psalters in use in New
England.

1004.   Worst, John William.   "New England Psalmody 1760-1810:
        Analysis of an American Idiom."   Ph.D. dissertation,
        University of Michigan, 1974.   564p.   UM 75-857,   *DAI* 35/7
        (January 1975): 4605-06-A.

        Discusses the New England singing school tradition, its
tunebooks, composers, and contains an analysis and setting of 174
"mostly four-part settings of psalms and hymns."   Included is an
index of tunes by titles.

1005.   Wright, Edith A.   "James Lyon's 'Friendship.'" *Notes* 4/3
        (June 1947): 293-95.

        Discusses a book of tunes discovered in Newburyport, Mass.,
in which is included Lyon's work.

1006.   York, Terry W.   "Lining-Out in Congregational Singing." *Hymn*
        28/3 (July 1977): 110-17.

        Brief review of the practice, including present renditions.

Hymnody

*Readers will find the following reference works of use for the study
of hymnody of the period:*

1007.   *Bibliography of American Hymnals.*   Ed. by Leonard Ellinwood
        and Elizabeth Lockwood.   Produced by the Hymn Society of
        America.   New York: University Music Editions, 1983.   27
        microfiche 4" by 6" (98 frames per fiche).

        Consists of 7,500 entries.   Includes title of hymnal,
imprint, year of publication, compiler (individual or organization),

pagination, location of copy indexed, the denomination for which the hymnal is intended, and the name of the indexer. Serves as a companion to Ellinwood's *Dictionary of American Hymnology* (see entry 1009).

1008.   Clark, Keith C.   *A Selective Bibliography for the Study of Hymns, 1980.*   2nd ed.   Papers of the Hymn Society, 33.   Springfield, Ohio: Hymn Society of America, 1980.   42p.

Includes principal works arranged topically.   Books, periodical articles, and unpublished items.   Lacking are annotations and index.

1009.   *Dictionary of American Hymnology: First-Line Index.*   Ed. by Leonard Ellinwood.   Produced by the Hymn Society of America.   New York: University Music Editions, 1984.   179 microfilm reels and printed *User's Guide* (26p.)

Includes some 1 million first-line citations covering 192,000 hymns.   Information includes: first lines of hymns, refrains, titles, original first lines of translated hymns, authors, translators, and additional details.   Location for the hymnals from which the hymns are extracted are provided, a complete list of contributors, and psedonymns and maiden names of hymn authors as well.   Yet included are a number of essays on hymns having confused authorship.   Refer also to Ellinwood's *Bibliography of American Hymnals* (see entry 1007).

1010.   Diehl, Katherine.   *Hymns and Tunes, an Index.*   New York: Scarecrow Press, 1966.   iv, 1,185p.

Includes 5 indexes based on 78 hymnals: first lines, authors, tune names, composers, and melodies.   Arrangement is alphabetical.   Includes a list of hymnals arranged chronologically.

1011.   McCutchan, Robert Guy.   *Hymn Tune Names: Their Sources and Significance.*   New York: Abingdon Press, 1957.   Reprint, St. Clair Shores: Scholarly Press, 1974.   206p.

Includes some 2,000 hymn tune names.   Each entry includes a melodic scheme, poetic meter, derivation, composer, and additional relevant information.   Alphabetical list of tunes; melodic index;

names not included in the alphabetical list; index of first words or
lines of hymns.

1012. McDormand, Thomas B. and Frederic S. Crossman. *Judson
          Concordance to Hymns.* Valley Forge, Pa.: Judson Press,
          1965. 375p.

       A subject index to some 2,342 hymns found in 27
denomination hymnals in the United States and Canada. Included is a
table of first lines, and in the line index, key words from lines of
hymns refer the reader to the appropriate entry in the table of
first lines.

1013. Messenger, Ruth Ellis and Helen Pfatteicher. *A Short
          Bibliography for the Study of Hymns.* New York: The Hymn
          Society of America, 1964. 31p.

       A classified list of books. Identifies and describes hymn
book collections in the United States.

1014. Rogal, Samuel J. "A Bibliographical Survey of American
          Hymnody, 1640-1800." *Bulletin of the New York Public
          Library* 78 (1975): 231-52.

1015. Voigt, Louis and Ellen Jane L. Porter. *Hymnbook Collections
          of North America.* Springfield, Ohio: Hymn Society of
          America, 1979. 32p.

       Includes 179 entries. "The names of collectors and
collections, both public and private, are assembled in one
alphabetic listing with references from collection titles to the
institution or present proprietor." The author acknowledges that
not all collections are included. The index includes personal
names, associations, and subjects.

1016. Breed, David R. *The History and Use of Hymns and Hymn-Tunes.*
          Chicago: Fleming H. Revell, 1903. 364p.

       Although the emphasis is on British hymnody, included is a
section on "American Psalmody" that discusses briefly the psalters
in use during the 17th and 18th centuries in New England.

1017.   Brobston, Stanley Heard.   "A Brief History of White Southern
          Gospel Music and a Study of Selected Amateur Family Gospel
          Music Singing Groups in Rural Georgia."   Ph.D.
          dissertation, New York University, 1977.   614p.   UM 78-
          08451.   *DAI* 39/2 (August 1978): 532-A.

          Includes historical background of early religious music,
campmeeting hymns, singing schools, and shape note notation.

1018.   Bruce, Dickson Davies, Jr.   *And They All Sang Hallelujah:
          Plain-Folk Camp-Meeting Religion, 1800-1845.*   Knoxville:
          University of Tennessee Press, 1974.   xii, 155p.

          An excellent discussion of campmeetings and music and
tunebooks used at services.   Based on the author's dissertation with
the same title (University of Pennsylvania, 1971).   Facsimiles.

1019.   Bultmann, Phyllis W.   "Everybody Sing: The Social
          Significance of the Eighteenth-Century Hymn."   Ph.D.
          dissertation, University of California at Los Angeles,
          1950.   278p.

1020.   Christ-Janaer, Albert, Charles W. Hughes, and Carleton
          Sprague Smith.   *American Hymns Old and New.*   New York:
          Columbia University Press, 1980.   2 vols.

          Volume 1 is a "history of the development of American
religious song by examples" arranged principally by centuries.
Includes Anglo-American psalters such as Sternhold and Hopkins,
Ainsworth, Tate and Brady, and the *Bay Psalm Book*, and hymnbooks and
psalters representing the Dutch, Swedes, and Germans in America as
well as denominational hymns.   Volume 2, prepared by Charles W.
Hughes, includes provenance data and "information about the hymns
and their authors and the tunes and their composers."   Includes
320 pages of biographies of authors and composers and is
particularly valuable for   information not found in other
sources.   Extensive bibliography.   See also a review in *Choice* 18/8
(April 1981), p. 1113.

1021.   Crawford, Richard.   "'Much Still Remains to Be Undone':
          Reformers of Early American Hymnody."   *Hymn* 35/4 (October
          1984): 204-08.

Discusses Andrew Law, Thomas Hastings, and other later reformers.

1022.   Cross, Virginia Ann.   "The Development of Sunday School Hymnody in the United States of America, 1816-1869." D.M.A. dissertation, New Orleans Baptist Theological Seminary, 1985.   701p.   UM 85-23087.   *DAI* 46/8 (February 1986): 2120-21-A.

Chapter 1 discusses campmeetings, urban revivals, popular song, and Sunday school hymnody.   Chapter 2 includes a survey of "words-only hymnbooks from 1816 to 1869."   Chapters 3-5 discuss hymnody after 1826.

1023.   Downey, James C.   "The Music of American Revivalism."   Ph.D. dissertation, Tulane University, 1968.

1024.   Dubbs, Joseph H.   "Early German Hymnology of Pennsylvania." *Reformed Quarterly Review* 29 (1882): 584-610.

1025.   Ellington, Charles Linwood.   "The Sacred Harp Tradition of the South: Its Origin and Evolution."   Ph.D. dissertation, Florida State University, 1969.   172p.   UM 70-6294.   *DAI* 30/10 (April 1970): 4476-A.

Discusses the tradition of Benjamin Franklin White's *Sacred Harp* to the early 19th-century shape note tradition.

1026.   Ellinwood, Leonard.   "Revolutionary Hymnody."   *Hymn* 27/2 (April 1976): 37-42.

Discusses Isaac Watts' hymn texts, works by Billings, and presents the thesis that Billings' "Chester" was not that popular, a falsehood started, according to Ellinwood, by Nathaniel Gould in his *Church Music in America* (see entry 626) during the Revolutionary War.   Originally printed in *Journal of Church Music* 17/9 (1975), pp. 2-5.

1027.   England, Martha W.   "Emily Dickinson and Isaac Watts: Puritan
        Hymnodists."   *Bulletin of the New York Public Library* 69
        (1965): 83-116.

1028.   Eskew, Harry L.   "American Folk Hymnody."   *Hymn Society of
        Great Britain and Ireland Bulletin* 7 (1971): 142-55.

1029.   Eskew, Harry Lee.   "Shape-Note Hymnody in the Shenandoah
        Valley, 1816-1860."   Ph.D. dissertation, Tulane University,
        1966.   182p.   UM 67-3821.   *DAI* 27/10 (April 1967): 3479-A.

        Discusses 13 tunebooks in shape-note notation in 31
editions before the Civil War beginning with Ananias Davisson's
Kentucky Harmony (1816).

1030.   Haussman, William A.   "German-American Hymnology, 1683-1800."
        Ph.D. dissertation, Johns Hopkins University, 1895.

        See also the author's article under the same title in
Americana Germanica 2/3 (1898), pp. 1-61.

1031.   Hinton, Sam.   "The Shape-Note Hymns: An American Choral
        Tradition."   *Choral Journal* 13/5 (January 1973): 7-11.

        Reviews some of the literature on the subject.   Discussed
briefly are representative collections by Samuel Holyoke, Jeremiah
Ingalls, John Wyeth, and others.

1032.   Horn, Dorothy D.   "A Study of the Folk Hymns of Southeastern
        America."   Ph.D. dissertation, Eastman School of Music of
        the University of Rochester, 1953.

1033.   Hulan, Richard Huffman.   "The American Revolution in
        Hymnody."   *Hymn* 35/4 (October 1984): 199-203.

        Discusses the revival and hymn singing at Cane Ridge,
Kentucky, in August 1801.

1034.   Hulan, Richard Huffman.   "Camp-Meeting Spiritual Folksongs: Legacy of the 'Great Revival in the West.'"   Ph.D. dissertation, University of Texas at Austin, 1978.   246p.

Includes the "repertoire found in camp-meeting songsters, 1800-1805."

1035.   Hunnicutt, Judy.   "Music for the Bicentennial: A Heritage of American Hymnody: Part 8."   *Journal of Church Music* 18/4 (April 1976): 17-18.

Consists of a list of hymn-text authors and composers born in the United States before Dec. 3, 1830, and a brief list of European-born authors and composers.

1036.   Jackson, George Pullen.   *White Spirituals in the Southern Uplands*.   Chapel Hill, N.C.: University of North Carolina, 1933.   Reprint, Hatboro, Pa.: Folklore Associates, 1964. 444p.

One of the first general studies of tunebooks and the shape-note movement of the 19th century, and is frequently referred to in the literature.   Includes chapters on the early New England singing school movement, its "spread to the West and South," with separate chapters on particular tunebooks and the movement in the Shenandoah Valley, Kentucky, and Tennessee.   Discussed also are songs of the campmeeting movement, with a comparison of white and black spirituals.

1037.   Keith, Edmond D.   *Christian Hymnody*.   Nashville: Convention Press, 1956.   xii, 147p.

A brief general history that includes a chapter on American hymnody.   Discussed are the New England psalters (Ainsworth and *Bay Psalm Book*), and the "transition from psalmody to hymnody," with information on early American hymn writers, including Samuel Davies (1723-61), Samson Occum (1723-92), Timothy Dwight (1752-1817), Oliver Holden (1765-1844), Thomas Hastings (1784-1872), and others.

1038.   Kroeger, Karl.   "William Billings and the Hymn-Tune."   *Hymn* 37/3 (July 1986): 19-26.

Provides information on Billings and his tunebooks and "Billing's literary tastes" for his selection of texts. Includes a discussion of performance practice.

1039.   Marini, Stephen A.   "Hymnody in the Religious Communal Societies of Early America." *Communal Societies* 2 (Autumn 1982): 1-25.

1040.   Metcalf, Frank J.   "Cut Hymn Books." *American Collector* 3 (1926-27): 159-61.

Mentions an early 19th-century example.

1041.   Metcalf, Frank J.   "Early Hymn Books Printed in Washington, D.C." *American Collector* 5 (1927-28): 144-50.

1042.   Music, David W.   "Wesley Hymns in Early American Hymnals and Tunebooks." *Hymn* 39/4 (October 1988): 37-42.

A brief history of the use of Wesley's hymns in America, and publications, including *Hymns and Sacred Poems* (Philadelphia, 1740), *Hymns and Spiritual Songs* (Philadelphia, 1756), James Lyon's *Urania* (Philadelphia, 1761), Josiah Flagg's *A Collection of the Best Psalm Tunes* (Boston, 1764), George Whitefield's *A Collection of Hymns for Social Worship* (Philadelphia, 1768), Samson Occum's *A Choice Collection of Hymns and Spiritual Songs* (New-London, 1774), *A Collection of Psalms and Hymns* (Philadelphia, 1781), and Robert Spence's *A Pocket Hymn Book* (New York, 1786).

1043.   Ninde, Edward S.   *The Story of the American Hymn.*   New York: Abingdon Press, 1921. Reprint, New York: AMS Press, 1975. 429p.

Discusses the *Bay Psalm Book* and the New England tradition of psalmody in the 18th century with emphasis on Oliver Holden, the use of Isaac Watts' hymns, and "Pioneer Hymn Writers," including Mather Byles, Samuel Davies, and William B. Tappan.

1044.   Porter, Ellen Jane (Lorenz). *Glory, Hallelujah! The Story
        of the Campmeeting Spiritual.* Nashville: Abingdon, 1980.
        144p.

        A quaint discussion of the evangelical camp meetings in the
early 1800s, but nonetheless based on some significant primary
sources. Additional information is provided on hymns and spirituals
sung at those meetings and tunebooks and other songbooks in use by
the Methodists. Index. A brief bibliography worthy of notice.

1045.   Porter, Ellen Jane Lorenz. "A Treasure of Campmeeting
        Spirituals." Ph.D. dissertation, Union Graduate School,
        1978. 458p. UM 79-16965. *DAI* 40/2 (August 1979): 531-32-
        A.

        Although the bulk of this work focuses on mid-nineteenth-
century campmeeting spirituals as published in northern hymnbooks,
the author supplies some information on campmeetings and revivals of
the early nineteenth century.

1046.   Reynolds, William Jensen. *A Joyful Sound: Christian Hymnody.*
        2nd ed. New York: Holt, Rinehart and Winston, 1978. xii,
        308p.

        Discusses early American singing schools, hymn singing,
campmeeting songs, with a survey of the development of hymnody in
America with mention of various denominations. Includes 159 hymns
(music and text). General index.

1047.   Rogal, Samuel J. "Noted Hymn Writers of New York State."
        Hymn 23/2 (1972): 54-63.

        Concerns the 18th and 19th centuries.

1048.   Rogers, James A. "From Israel to England to America; or,
        Watts a Nice Psalm Like You Doing in a Country Like This?"
        Hymn Society of Great Britain and Ireland Bulletin 8
        (1974): 57-67.

1049.   Ruth, John Landis. "English Hymn-Writing in America, 1640-
        1800." Ph.D. dissertation, Harvard University, 1968.

1050. Sims, John Norman. "The Hymnody of the Camp-Meeting
       Tradition." D.S.M. dissertation, Union Theological
       Seminary, 1960. 181p.

1051. Smith, Timothy Alan. "The Southern Folk-Hymn, 1800-1860:
       Notes on Performance Practice." *Choral Journal* 23/7 (March
       1983): 23-29.

       Based on the author's master's thesis, this work
investigates the following performance suggestions in introductions
to tunebooks from the period studied: ensemble singing, balance,
tone, dynamics, ornamentation, tempi, and more. Includes excerpts
from Ananias Davisson's *Kentucky Harmony* (1816).

1052. Steel, David Warren. "John Wyeth and the Development of
       Southern Folk Hymnody." In *Music from the Middle Ages
       through the Twentieth Century: Essays in Honor of Gwynn
       McPeek*. Ed. by Carmelo P. Comberiati and Mathew C. Steel.
       New York: Gordon and Breach Science Publishers, 1988, pp.
       357-74.

       Focuses on the first edition of Wyeth's *Repository of
Sacred Music* (1810), "the sources of its music and its influence on
later tunebooks." Also discusses *Wyeth's Repository of Sacred
Music, Part Second* (1813).

1053. Stevenson, Arthur Linwood. *The Story of Southern Hymnology*.
       Roanoke, Va.: Stone Printing Co., 1931. Reprint, New York:
       AMS Press, 1975. vi, 187p.

       Although most of this work falls within the latter part of
the 19th century, the author does include a number of short
biographies of hymn writers active before 1820, including Joseph B.
Cook, Robert T. Daniel, William Dorsey, Richard Furman, Jesse
Mercer, George C. Sedgwick, and others.

1054. Stevenson, Robert. "The Eighteenth-Century Hymn Tune."
       Inter-American Music Review 2/1 (Fall 1979): 1-33.

       Discusses a broad range of tunes popular in the colonies,
and includes musical examples and other illustrations. Describes
Deacon Story's "Singing Book" (Durham, Conn., 1740).

1055. Stevenson, Robert. "Jeremiah Clarke Hymn Tunes in Colonial
          America." *Hymn* 29/1 (January 1978): 15-18.

          Based on 3 works by this English composer discovered in the
Deacon Story Music Book manuscript (ca. 1740) held in the Newberry
Library, Chicago. Published also in *Inter-American Music Review* 2/1
(Fall 1979), pp. 35-39.

1056. Stevenson, Robert. "Watts in America: Bicentenary
          Reflections on the Growth of Watts' Reputation in America."
          Harvard Theological Review 41/3 (July 1948): 205-11.

          Discusses the introduction and influence of Watts' hymn
texts in America from the 1700s on.

1057. Stoughton, Marion Wilberforce. "The Influence of the
          Kirchenlied of the Reformation on Protestant Hymnody in
          England and America." Ph.D. dissertation, Northwestern
          University, 1934. 140p.

1058. Weadon, David A. "A Hymnal Tour in Protestant America."
          Journal of Church Music 29/3 (March 1987): 9-12, 30.

          A brief survey of major hymnals in America from the
colonial period. Includes a list of 19th-century hymnals published
in the United States.

1059. Westermeyer, Paul. "German Reformed Hymnody in the United
          States." *Hymn* 31/2 (1980): 89-94; 31/3 (1980): 200-04,
          212.

1060. Wilhoit, Melvin Ross. "A Guide to the Principal Authors and
          Composers of Gospel Song of the Nineteenth Century."
          D.M.A. dissertation, Southern Baptist Theological Seminary,
          1982. 360p.

          Includes hymnal location guide, and index of first lines
and song titles.

1061.   Wolf, Edward C.   "Two Divergent Traditions of German-American
        Hymnody in Maryland circa 1800."   *American Music* 3/3 (Fall
        1985): 299-312.

        Discusses the Zion Lutheran Church and tunebooks compiled
by Adam Arnold, Joseph Doll, Frederick S. Weiser, and others.
Includes a list of chorales in Arnold's *Geistliche Ton-Kunst* (1803).

Music of Ethnic and Religious Groups

A number of excellent articles can be found under ethnic headings in
The New Grove Dictionary of American Music (see entry 30).   See also
articles by various contributors under the heading "European-
American Music," vol. 2, pp. 64-86.

Afro-American

1062.   Allen, William Francis, Charles Pickard Ware and Lucy McKim
        Garrison.   *Slave Songs of the United States*.   New York: A.
        Simpson, 1867.   Reprint, New York: Peter Smith, 1951.
        xlviii, 115p.

        Includes 136 songs with text.   Of particular value is the
introductory essay.   Written in 1867, this compilation provides
information on the derivation, performance practice, and other
characteristics of slave songs at that time.   Indexes.

1063.   Bastin, Bruce.   "Black Music in North Carolina."   *North
        Carolina Folklore Journal* 27 (1979): 3-19.

        Focuses on the 18th and 19th centuries.

1064.   Brooks, Tilford Uthratese.   "A Historical Study of Black
        Music and Selected Twentieth-Century Black Composers and
        Their Role in American Society: A Source Book for
        Teachers."   Ed.D. dissertation, Washington University,
        1972.   802p.   UM 74-22513.   *DAI* 35/4 (October 1974): 2315-
        A.

Discusses Afro-American music with a historical perspective of the major characteristics of the music before 1900.

1065.   Courlander, Harold.   *Negro Folk Music, U.S.A.*   New York: Columbia University Press, 1963.   x, 324p.

Discusses African and European elements that have contributed to music of blacks.   The music is discussed topically, and includes anthems and spirituals, cries and calls, blues, and other songs.   Musical examples and index.

1066.   Ekwueme, Lazarus E.N.   "African-Music Retentions in the New World."   *Black Perspective in Music* 2/2 (Fall 1974): 128-44.

Discusses musical elements, such as melody, rhythm, and form.   Musical examples.

1067.   Epstein, Dena J.   "African Music in British and French America."   *Musical Quarterly* 59/1 (January 1973): 61-91.

Discusses music, dance, and musical instruments, based on contemporary accounts, and the gradual adoption of European influences.

1068.   Epstein, Dena J.   "Documenting the History of Black Folk Music in the United States: A Librarian's Odyssey."   *Fontes Artis Musicae* 23/4 (October-December 1976): 151-57.

Discusses, in part, the lack of primary documentation for the study of music of blacks before 1800, and the influence and acculturation of African instruments and dancing.

1069.   Epstein, Dena J.   *Sinful Tunes and Spirituals: Black Folk Music to the Civil War.*   Chicago: University of Illinois Press, 1977.   xix, 433p.

Compares favorably as a comprehensive and thorough work to Southern's *The Music of Black Americans* (see entry 401).   Based mostly on primary sources.   Discussion of music prior to 1820 includes "Early Report of African Music in British and French

America," instruments, music in the daily lives of blacks, and
acculturation of musical style.   Bibliography and index.

1070.   Epstein, Dena J.   "Slave Music in the United States before
            1860: A Survey of Sources." *Notes* 20/2 (Spring 1963): 195-
            212; 20/3 (Summer 1963): 377-90.

            Part 1 focuses on the period before 1800.   Part 2 is also
relevant and includes information on boat songs and instruments.
Based on primary sources.

1071.   Fauley, Leonore Lynne.   "Black Dance in the United States,
            from 1619 to 1970."   Ph.D. dissertation, University of
            Southern California, 1971.   502p.   UM 71-21454.   *DAI* 32/2
            (August 1971): 770-A.

            "Arranged chronologically and geographically, Afro-American
dance was studied in the southern plantations, in the north and in
New Orleans.   Dance in minstrelsy and the theatre was also
investigated.   Both secular and sacred dance were examined."

1072.   Fisher, Miles Mark.   *Negro Slave Songs in the United States*.
            Ithaca, N.Y.: Published for the American Historical
            Association by Cornell University Press, 1953.   Reprint,
            New York: Russell and Russell, 1968.   xv, 223p.

            A general survey discussing African musical influences,
types of songs, music of slaves, including musical practices and
instruments, and early 19th-century campmeeting songs.   Based on the
author's dissertation, "The Evolution of Slave Songs in the United
States" (University of Chicago, 1949).

1073.   Hare, Maud Cuney.   *Negro Musicians and Their Music*.
            Washington, D.C.: Associated Publishers, Inc., 1936.
            Reprint, New York: Da Capo Press, 1974.   xii, 439p.

            Discusses "African influences in America," and includes
music of slaves.

1074.   Jackson, Irene V.   "Music Among Blacks in the Episcopal
            Church: Some Preliminary Considerations."   In *More than*

Dancing: Essays on Afro-American Music and Musicians.   Ed. by Irene V. Jackson.   Contributions in Afro-American and African Studies, 83.   Westport, Conn.: Greenwood Press, 1985, pp. 107-25.

A few pages are devoted to black Episcopalians and music during the 18th and early 19th centuries.

1075.   Jerde, Curtis D.   "Black Music in New Orleans: A Historical Overview."   *Black Music Research Newsletter* 9/1 (Spring 1987): 1-4.

Reviews previous literature and includes information on music from 1799 on.

1076.   Katz, Bernard, ed.   *The Social Implications of Early Negro Music in the United States.*   New York: Arno Press, 1969. xiii, 146p.

A series of essays by contributing authors on a variety of topics, including Black songs, spirituals, campmeeting melodies, and plantation hymns.   Includes some 150 songs.   Song index.

1077.   Levine, Lawrence W.   "Slave Songs and Slave Consciousness: An Exploration in Neglected Sources."   In *The Private Side of American History.*   2nd edition.   New York: Harcourt Brace Jovanovich, 1979, pp. 303-29.

An excellent introduction to slave songs.   The author reviews the literature on this subject and discusses the differences between black and white religious music and the creation and transmission of the songs.   A 4th (1987) edition is available.

1078.   Lovell, John, Jr.   *Black Song: The Forge and the Flame: The Story of How the Afro-American Spiritual Was Hammered Out.*   New York: Macmillan, 1972.   xviii, 686p.

Explores the origins and development of the Afro-American spiritual and the influence of Africa and white America on it.   An excellent source for explanations to problematic questions, theories, and evidence regarding Afro-American spirituals.   Includes a general index and index to spirituals.

1079.   Maultsby, Portia Katrenia.   "Africanisms Retained in the
          Spiritual Tradition."   In *IMS Report, Berkeley 1977*.
          Kassel: Bärenreiter, 1981, pp. 75-82.

          Discusses the origin of black spirituals in the context of
southern slaves for the period 1619-1861.

1080.   Maultsby, Portia Katrenia.   "Afro-American Religious Music:
          1619-1861, Part I: Historical Development.   Part II:
          Computer Analysis of One Hundred Spirituals."   Ph.D.
          dissertation, University of Wisconsin at Madison, 1974.
          460p.   UM 75-7597.   *DAI* 35/11 (May 1975): 7343-A.

          Discusses African tribal origins and their influence on
Afro-American music, European influences on Afro-American music, and
a definition of musical elements of the black sacred music
tradition.   The analysis of spirituals includes "textual and melodic
structures," "phrase structures," "scale structures," and pitch,
range, melodic intervals, and rhythm.

1081.   Maultsby, Portia Katrenia.   "Afro-American Religious Music: A
          Study in Musical Diversity."   *Papers of the Hymn Society
          of America*, 35.   Springfield, Ohio: Hymn Society of
          America, 1981.   19p.

          Discusses the influence of African culture on black music
in America, black preachers, music of slaves, folk spirituals, and
performance practices.

1082.   Maultsby, Portia Katrenia.   "Influences and Retentions of
          West African Musical Concepts in U.S. Black Music."
          Western Journal of Black Studies 3/3 (Fall 1979).

1083.   Maultsby, Portia Katrenia.   "Music of Northern Independent
          Black Churches during the Ante-Bellum Period."
          Ethnomusicology 19/3 (September 1975): 401-20.

          Discusses both the white and black traditions of the 1700s,
with a review of the previous literature.

1084.   Maultsby, Portia Katrenia. "West African Influences and
          Retentions in U.S. Black Music: A Sociocultural Study."   In
          *More than Dancing: Essays on Afro-American Music and
          Musicians*. Ed. by Irene V. Jackson.   Contributions in
          Afro-American and African Studies, 83.   Westport, Conn.:
          Greenwood Press, 1985, pp. 25-57.

          Includes a discussion of the social environment and musical
traditions of blacks before 1865.

1085.   Metcalfe, Ralph H., Jr.   "The Western African Roots of Afro-
          American Music." *Black Scholar* 1/8 (1970): 16-25.

1086.   Moore, John H. "A Hymn of Freedom—South Carolina, 1813."
          Journal of Negro History 50 (1965): 50-53.

1087.   Ping, Nancy R. "Black Musical Activities in Antebellum
          Wilmington, North Carolina." *Black Perspective in Music*
          82/2 (Fall 1980): 139-60.

          Discusses songs, dances, and other musical activities.
(See also entries 544-545.)

1088.   Putney, Martha S. "Historical Note: A Proposal for a Black
          Military Band during the War of 1812." *Negro History
          Bulletin* 38/8 (1975): 490-91.

1089.   Roach, Hildred. *Black American Music: Past and Present.*
          Malabar, Fla.: Robert E. Krieger Publishing Company, 1985.
          2 vols.

          Volume 1 discusses "the black man in colonial America," his
"African heritage," "early folk music," and "spirituals" for the
period 1619-1870s.

1090.   Southern, Eileen. "Musical Practices in Black Churches of
          New York and Philadelphia, ca. 1800-1844." *Journal of the
          American Musicological Society* 30/2 (Summer 1977): 296-312.

Discusses Methodist hymnbooks, musical instruction, and concerts. Musicians named include William Appo, Morris Brown, Jr. Isaac Hazard, James Hemmenway, Francis Johnson, Darius E. Jones, Jacob A. Stans, and William C. Webster.

1091. Stevenson, Robert. "The Afro-American Musical Legacy to 1800." *Musical Quarterly* 54/4 (October 1968): 475-502.

Although most of this article deals with Latin America, the author mentions a few facts concerning music and blacks in colonial America.

1092. Waterman, Richard Alan. "African Influence on the Music of the Americas." In *Acculturation in the Americas: Proceedings and Selected Papers of the XXIXth International Congress of Americanists.* Ed. by Sol Tax. New York: Cooper Square, 1967, pp. 207-18.

Examines hypotheses regarding musical scales, harmony, and rhythm in African music and European influences on these elements in Afro-American music.

Baptists

1093. Burkitt, Lemuel. *A Concise History of the Kehukee Baptist Association, from Its Original Rise Down to 1803.* Philadelphia: Lippincott and Grambo, 1850. Reprint, New York: Arno Press, 1980. xxix, 351p.

The churches in the Association were located in North Carolina. Includes a discussion of musical practices during church services and Elder Burkitt's hymnbooks (see pp. 148-49, 153). The lack of an index requires some browsing for locating those portions on music.

1094. Drummond, Robert Paul. "A History of Music among Primitive Baptists Since 1800." D.A. dissertation, University of Northern Colorado, 1986. 428p. UM 86-21958. *DAI* 47/7 (January 1987): 2360-A.

"The purpose of this study was to portray, as comprehensively as possible, a history of the musical life of the Primitive Baptists and to determine the influence of their music on the choral art. Techniques of musical analysis, biographical and bibliographical description, and an informal survey of Primitive Baptist churches were utilized in gathering information for the study."

1095.   Duncan, Curtis Daniel. "A Historical Survey of the Development of the Black Baptist Church in the United States as a Study of Performance Practices Associated with Dr. Watts Hymn Singing: A Source Book for Teachers." Ed.D. dissertation, Washington University, 1979. 286p. *DAI* 40/2 (August 1979): 730-31-A.

Traces the development of lined hymn singing in the 17th-18th centuries, slaves and plantations, musical survivals from Africa, characteristics of Black singing, and the relationship of these characteristics to 20th-century practice.

1096.   Eskew, Harry L. "Southern Baptist Contributions to Hymnody." *Baptist History and Heritage* 19 (January 1984): 27-35.

1097.   Hooper, William L. "The Story of Baptist Hymnody in Colonial America." *Church Musician* 15/3 (March 1964): 10-12.

Discusses the New England tradition and the collection, *Hymns and Spiritual Songs* (1766). Includes a list of Baptist hymnbooks for the period 1766-93.

1098.   Murrell, Irvin Henry, Jr. "An Examination of Southern Ante-Bellum Baptist Hymnals and Tunebooks as Indicators of the Congregational Hymn and Tune Repertories of the Period with an Analysis of Representative Tunes." D.M.A. dissertation, New Orleans Baptist Theological Seminary, 1984. 145 pp. UM 85-09624. *DAI* 46/4 (October 1985): 836-A.

Chapter 1 presents a historical look at the hymnals and tunebooks studied. Chapter 2 lists the libraries' holdings of these works and a catalog of the works, and chapter 3, the results of the analysis of the tunes and hymns. Appendixes include biographical

information on the compilers of the hymnals and tunebooks and a list
of the authors and composers of the compositions.

1099.   Music, David.   "The First American Baptist Tunebook."
        Foundations 23 (July-September 1980): 267-73.

        The tunebook is titled *The Christian Harmonist* and was
published in 1804 in Boston by Samuel Holyoke.   Also discusses tunes
used by Baptists before 1804.

1100.   Music, David.   "Music in the First Baptist Church of Boston,
        Massachusetts, 1665-1820."   *Quarterly Review: A Survey of
        Southern Baptist Progress* 42/3 (1982): 37 ff.

1101.   Reynolds, William J.   "Our Heritage of Baptist Hymnody in
        America."   *Baptist History and Heritage* 11 (1976): 204-07.

1102.   Singer, David.   "God and Man in Baptist Hymnals, 1784-1844."
        Mid-Continent American Studies Journal 9/2 (1968): 14-26.

1103.   Sutton, Brett.   "Shape-Note Tune Books and Primitive Hymns."
        Ethnomusicology 26/1 (January 1982): 11-26.

        Discusses current singing tradition of Primitive Baptist
hymn singing in view of a number of published works.   Perhaps this
evidence allows one to understand what the musical practices of the
early 1800s was in those areas studied.

1104.   Wicks, Sammie Ann.   "Life and Meaning: Singing, Praying, and
        the Word among the Old Regular Baptists of Eastern
        Kentucky."   Ph.D. dissertation, University of Texas at
        Austin, 1983.   vi, 182p.

Brethren Church

1105.   Fisher, Nevin W.   *The History of Brethren Hymnbooks.*
        Bridgewater, Va.: Beacon Publishers, 1950.   153p.

Discusses the various printings of *Das Kleine Davidische Psalterspiel* by Christopher Sower (Saur), Germantown, Pa., beginning in 1744. Includes a first-line index of all principal hymnbooks, and information on the Mennonite compiler Joseph Funk.

1106.   Hinks, Donald R. *Brethren Hymn Books and Hymnals, 1720-1884.* Gettysburg, Pa.: Brethren Heritage Press, 1986. 205p.

Ten chapters describe the German and English hymnbooks in use during the period studied. Includes 50 photographs from the major hymnbooks. Refer to a review by Robert M. Copeland in *American Music* 6/3 (Fall 1988), pp. 320-23.

1107.   Howe, Roland L. *The History of a Church (Dunker) with Comments Featuring the First Church of the Brethren of Philadelphia, Pa., 1813-1943.* Philadelphia: privately printed, 1943. xvii, 706p.

Includes citations regarding musical matters from an early church ledger for 1818.

1108.   Saltzman, Herbert. "A Historical Study of the Function of Music among the Brethren in Christ." D.M.A. dissertation, University of Southern California, 1964.

Catholics

1109.   Henry, Hugh T. "A Philadelphia Choir Book of 1787." *Records of the American Catholic Historical Society* 26 (1915): 208-23.

Discusses John Aitken's *A Compilation of the Litanies and Vespers, Hymns and Anthems* (1787).

1110.   Henry, Hugh T. "Philadelphia Choir Books of 1791 and 1814." *Records of the American Catholic Historical Society* 28 (1915): 311-27.

1111.   Higginson, J. Vincent.   "Foreign Influences in Early American
        Catholic Hymnody."   *Hymn* 17/1 (January 1966): 16-20.

        Discusses the French and English influence, and mentions
John Aitken's publications.   Also discusses the *Pious Guide to
Prayer and Devotion* (1808), which had some 28 English hymns
included, and a later edition, which included French hymns.

1112.   Higginson, J. Vincent.   *History of American Catholic Hymnals:
        Survey and Background.*   Springfield, Ohio: Hymn Society of
        America, 1982.   xi, 286p.

1113.   Higginson, J. Vincent.   "John Aitken's Compilations—1787 and
        1791."   *Hymn* 27/3 (July 1976): 68-75.

        John Aitken, who was not a Catholic, published his *A
Compilation of the Litanies and Vespers, Hymns and Anthems* in 1787
and later editions in 1791 and 1814.   The author compares the
editions and provides sources for some of the pieces.

1114.   King, Percy.   "Some Early Catholic Hymnals."   *Caecilia:
        Monthly Magazine of Catholic Church and School Music* 66
        (1939): 61-64.

1115.   Mitchell, Nathan.   "Old Hymnal Illuminates Roots of Catholic
        Music."   *Pastoral Music* 1/6 (August-September 1977): 30-32.

        Discusses John Aitken's *A Compilation of the Litanies and
Vespers, Hymns and Anthems* (1787).   Facsimiles.

1116.   Montani, Nicola A.   "Early Church Music in America."
        Catholic Choirmaster 14/1 (January 1928): 7-11.

        Discusses the collection *Litanies, Vespers, Chants, Hymns
and Anthems as Used in the Catholic Churches of Philadelphia and
Throughout the United States* (Philadelphia: Charles Taws, 1814).
Musical examples.

1117. Nemmers, Erwin E. "Early American Catholic Church Music (Revised Bibliography)." *Catholic Choirmaster* 40 (1954): 158-59, 190.

1118. Nemmers, Erwin E. "The History of American Catholic Church Music." *Catholic Choirmaster* 32/1 (March 1946): 6-9, 43-44, 46; 32/2 (June 1946): 54-56, 88; 32/3 (September 1946): 133-35, 138.

An excellent introduction, including information on Spanish mission music in the west, and eastern seaboard colonies. Includes information on collections, including *Anthems, Hymns, Etc. Usually Sung at the Catholick Church in Boston* (Boston, 1800), compiled by John Cheverus, and *A Compilation of the Litanies and Vespers, Hymns and Anthems* (1787), compiled by John Aitken, and information on the Joseph and Thomas Carr family of publishers. There is also a list of church music published in the United States, 1787-1860, and a bibliography for further study.

1119. Weller, Philip T. "Early Church Music in the United States." *Caecilia: Monthly Magazine of Catholic Church and School Music* 66 (1939): 297-304.

Dutch

1120. Kenney, Alice P. "Hudson Valley Dutch Psalmody." *Hymn* 21/1 (January 1974): 15-26.

Discusses the psalters and offers reasons why the tradition was "disrupted" at the time of the Revolutionary War.

1121. Smith, Carleton Sprague. "The 1774 Psalm Book of the Reformed Protestant Dutch Church in New York City." *Musical Quarterly* 34/1 (January 1948): 84-96.

The author presents the historical background that led to the publication of this book, which is not listed in Evans (see entry 45). Also discusses *The Psalms of David* (New York, 1767) edited by Francis Hopkinson.

1122.   Weegar, Carlton E.   "The First School Music in New York
         State." *Music Educators Journal* 45/3 (January 1959): 62-
         63.

         Discusses the presence of a schoolmaster in New Netherland
as early as 1638, and that the singing of psalms was likely a part
of the curriculum.

Ephrata Cloister

The following bibliography is worthy of note:

1123.   Doll, Eugene E. and Anneliese M. Funke.   *The Ephrata
         Cloister: An Annotated Bibliography.*   Philadelphia: Carl
         Schurz Memorial Foundation, 1944.   139p.

         Includes sources for the history of the Cloister, and
sources regarding the printing press for the years 1745-94.

1124.   Alderfer, E. Gordon.   *The Ephrata Commune: An Early American
         Counterculture.*   Pittsburgh: University of Pittsburgh
         Press, 1985.   xiii, 273p.

         A history based on original manuscripts and secondary
sources.   Discusses music manuscripts, the singing school, and
Johann Conrad Beissel as composer.   Includes an excellent
bibliography.   Index.

1125.   Aurand, A. Monroe, Jr.   *Historical Account of the Ephrata
         Cloister and the Seventh Day Baptist Society.*   Harrisburg,
         Pa.: the author, 1940.   24p.

         Discusses hymns and Johann Conrad Beissel's rules for
singers.   Includes excellent photographs of the Ephrata buildings.

1126.   Blakely, Lloyd G.   "Johann Conrad Beissel and Music of the
         Ephrata Cloister." *Journal of Research in Music Education*
         15/2 (Summer 1967): 120-38.

Includes only a little biographical information on Beissel, but much more information on the musical activities of the Cloister, including singing, a translation of Beissel's treatise from the *Turtel-Taube* (1747), and performance practice.

1127.   Brumbaugh, Martin Grove. *A History of the German Baptist Brethrens in Europe and America.* Mount Morris, Ill.: Brethren Publishing House, 1899. Reprint, New York: AMS Press, 1971. xxii, 559p.

Includes a chapter on the Ephrata Cloister. Discussed is singing in a service in the "Saal," or chapel, and a brief comment on the hymnbook, *Paradisisches Wunder-Spiel* (1766).

1128.   Carlson, Charles Howard. "The Ephrata Cloister's Music of Yesteryear." *Music Journal* 22/1 (January 1964): 52, 118-22.

An introduction to Ephrata and Johann Conrad Beissel.

1129.   Chancellor, Paul G. "Pennsylvania 'Dutch' Music at Ephrata: A Musical Anomaly." *Etude* 66/3 (March 1948): 147, 186.

An introduction with emphasis on Johann Conrad Beissel and his various hymnbooks.

1130.   David, Hans T. "Hymns and Music of the Pennsylvania Seventh-Day Baptists." *American-German Review* 9/5 (1943): 4-6, 36.

1131.   David, Hans T. "Musical Composition at Ephrata." *American-German Review* 10/5 (1944): 4-5.

1132.   Doll, Eugene E. *The Ephrata Cloister: An Introduction.* Ephrata, Pa.: Ephrata Cloister Associates, 1958. 32p.

Although brief, this work is recommended for its excellent photographs of buildings. Musical examples.

1133.   Dubbs, Joseph Henry.   "Ephrata Hymns and Hymn-Books."
        Lancaster County Historical Society Papers 13/2 (1909): 21-
        37.

        Includes information on Johann Conrad Beissel and a general
description of the hymns, with mention of books published by
Benjamin Franklin, Christopher Saur, and the brotherhood at Ephrata.

1134.   Engel, Carl.   "Views and Reviews."   *Musical Quarterly* 14/2
        (April 1928): 297-306.

        Discusses the contents of the collection, *Das Gesäng der
einsamen und verlassenen Turtel-Taube* (1747) and how the Library of
Congress acquired it.   Facsimile.

1135.   Erb, Peter C.   *Johann Conrad Beissel and the Ephrata
        Community: Mystical and Historical Texts.*   Studies in
        American Religion, 14.   Lewiston, N.Y.: Edwin Mellen Press,
        1985.   393p.

        The introduction includes a brief discussion on the music.
See also, pp. 323-26.   Of note is a chronological list of published
and unpublished works by members of the community.   No index.

1136.   Getz, Russell P.   "Music in the Ephrata Cloister."   *Communal
        Societies* 2 (Autumn 1982): 27-38.

1137.   Henry, Thomas L.   "The Singing School at the Ephrata
        Cloister."   *Keystone Folklore Quarterly* 11 (1966): 203-06.

1138.   Lamech, Brother and Brother Agrippa.   *Chronicon Ephratense: A
        History of the Community of Seventh Day Baptists at
        Ephrata, Lancaster County, Penn'a.*   Trans. by J. Max Hark.
        Lancaster: S.H. Zahm, 1889.   Reprint, New York: Burt
        Franklin, 1972.   ix, 288p.

        This early work includes information on Johann Conrad
Beissel.

1139.   Martin, Betty Jean.   "The Ephrata Cloister and Its Music,
          1732-1785: The Cultural, Religious, and Bibliographical
          Background."   Ph.D. dissertation, University of Maryland,
          1974.   400p.   UM 75-9499.   *DAI* 35/10 (April 1975): 6754-A.

          This work's purpose is "to provide an accurate account of
the music and musicians of the Ephrata Cloister, to make available a
representative collection of hymns and choral works, and to furnish
bibliographical information for further research."   Includes a
discussion of the hymnals, an analysis of the music, information on
the hymn texts, Johann Conrad Beissel, and performance practice.   An
excellent work.   Musical examples.

1140.   Richards, Henry M.M.   "The Ephrata Cloister and Its Music."
          Publications of the Lebanon County Historical Society 8
          (1921-24): 279-99.

1141.   Sachse, Julius Friedrich.   *The German Sectarians of
          Pennsylvania, 1708-1800: A Critical and Legendary History
          of the Ephrata Cloister and the Dunkers.*   Philadelphia:
          Printed for the author, 1899-1900.   Reprint, New York: AMS
          Press, 1971.   2 vols.

          Despite its date of publication, this work remains one of
the principal studies of the Ephrata Cloister.   Information on the
music and Johann Conrad Beissel's musical influence on the community
is introduced in various places in this work.   Refer to the index in
each volume under the heading "Music."   See especially chapter 6,
"The Music of the Cloister," in volume 2.   Includes transcriptions
and facsimiles not easily found elsewhere.

1142.   Sachse, Julius Friedrich.   *The Music of the Ephrata Cloister.*
          Lancaster, Pa.: the Society, 1903.   Reprint, New York: AMS
          Press, 1971.   108p.

          A standard work for the study of Ephrata music.   Sachse
discusses the music and hymns in use at the Cloister, and includes a
facsimile of parts of Johann Conrad Beissel's preface to his *Das
Gesäng der einsamen und verlassenen Turtel-Taube* (1747).   Included
are other music facsimiles with transcriptions.   Index.

1143.   Seilhamer, Larry.   "Remnants of Conrad Beissel's Church."
        Brethren Life and Thought 26 (Summer 1981): 152-53.

1144.   Viehmeyer, L. Allen.   "A Report on the Development of an
        Index to Ephrata Hymnology."   In *Papers from the Third
        Conference on German-Americana in the Eastern United
        States, November 6-7, 1982.*   Radford, Va.: Radford
        University, 1985, pp. 1-10.

        Reviews previous literature on this topic and discusses
current research on Ephrata imprints and manuscripts.   According to
Viehmeyer, "18 different titles of printed and manuscript
collections of hymn texts published by the Ephrata Cloister have
been identified.   In all, some 222 copies of these titles have been
located in the United States and Great Britain."

<u>Episcopalians</u>

1145.   Douglas, Charles W.   "Early Hymnody of the American Episcopal
        Church."   *Historical Magazine of the Protestant Episcopal
        Church* 10 (1941): 202-18.

1146.   Gable, Martin D., Jr.   "The Hymnody of the Church, 1789-
        1832."   *Historical Magazine of the Protestant Episcopal
        Church* 36 (1967): 249-70.

1147.   Rasmussen, Jane E.   "Churchmen Concerned: Music in the
        Episcopal Church, 1804-1859: A Study of Church Periodicals
        and Other Ecclesiastical Writings."   Ph.D. dissertation,
        University of Minnesota, 1983.   2 vols., 433p.   UM 84-
        04224.   *DAI* 44/11 (May 1984): 3202-A.

        Based upon "viewpoints of clergy and/or laymen, rather than
musicians."

1148.   Rasmussen, Jane.   *Musical Taste as a Religious Question in
        Nineteenth-Century America.*   Studies in American Religion,
        20.   Lewiston, N.Y.: E. Mellen Press, 1986.   xxvi, 603p.

Deals with the music of the Protestant Episcopal Church during 1804-59.   Useful for its survey of documents.

1149.   Satcher, Herbert B.   "Music of the Episcopal Church in Pennsylvania in the Eighteenth Century." *Historical Magazine of the Protestant Episcopal Church* 18 (1949): 372-413.

1150.   West, Edward N.   "History and Development of Music in the American Church." *Historical Magazine of the Protestant Episcopal Church* 14 (1945): 15-37.

1151.   West, Edward N.   "The Music of Old Trinity." *Historical Magazine of the Protestant Episcopal Church* 16 (1947): 100-27.

1152.   Wilson, Ruth M.   "Episcopal Music in America: The British Legacy." *Musical Times* 124/1685 (July 1983): 447-50.

Focuses on the period 1780-1820s.   Discusses Rayner Taylor, George K. Jackson, and Benjamin Carr and their contributions to Episcopal music.   Publications discussed include *The First Verse of Every Psalm of David* (1808) by John Cole, *A Churchman's Choral Companion to His Prayer Book* (1809) by William Smith, and *Episcopalian Harmony* (ca. 1802-03) by Israel Terril.

French

1153.   Jones, Howard Mumford.   *America and French Culture 1759-1848.* Chapel Hill: University of North Carolina Press, 1927. Reprint, Westport, Conn.: Greenwood Press, 1973.   xvi, 615p.

Contains section on music and includes a general bibliography.

1154.   Kendall, Raymond.   "French Music in America." *Boletin Latino-Americano* 5 (1939).

Harmonists

1155.   Arndt, Karl J.R.   "George Rapp's Harmony Society."
          Communities (Winter 1985): 20-26.

1156.   Arndt, Karl J.R. and Richard D. Wetzel.   "Harmonist Music and
          Pittsburgh Musicians in Early Economy." *Western
          Pennsylvania Historical Magazine* 54/2 (April 1971): 391-
          413.

          A principal study of Harmonist music from 1811 on, with
information on Johann Christoph Müller.   Musical examples.

1157.   Brewster, Paul G.   "Three Songs from New Harmony." *Indiana
          Magazine of History* 47 (1951): 261-64.

          New Harmony, Indiana.

1158.   Hahn, Ruth, S.   "Music and the Harmonists." *Sonneck Society
          Bulletin* 14/3 (Fall 1988): 119-20.

          Brief history, with an overview of materials available to
the researcher at Old Economy Village.

1159.   Kring, Hilda Adam.   "The Harmonists—A Folk-Cultural
          Approach." Ph.D. dissertation, University of Pennsylvania,
          1969.   308p.   UM 69-21385.   *DAI* 30/6 (December 1969): 2439-
          A.

          Studies the three settlements of Harmony, Pa., New Harmony,
Ind., and Economy, Pa.   Based on contemporary primary sources such
as travel diaries, 71 letters translated by the author, and other
materials.   The author has translated 25 hymn texts.

1160.   Spear, Lee S.   "Vocal Music in the Harmonist Society, 1804-
          1832."   D.M.A. dissertation, University of Cincinnati,
          1979.   2 vols.

          Volume 1 consists of text; volume 2 is a thematic catalog.

1161.   Wetzel, Richard Dean.   "Frontier Music-Makers."   *Carnegie
        Magazine* 42 (1968): 343, 345-47.

1162.   Wetzel, Richard Dean.   "The Hymnody of George Rapp's Harmony
        Society."   *Hymn* 23/1 (1972): 19-29.

1163.   Wetzel, Richard Dean.   "The Music of George Rapp's Harmony
        Society: 1805-1906."   Ph.D. dissertation, University of
        Pittsburgh, 1970.   569p.   UM 71-3529.   *DAI* 31/8 (December
        1970): 4210-A.

        A major study of the Harmonists.   The author discusses the
Harmonist communities, musical works, musicians, including W.C.
Peters.

Italians

1164.   Marraro, Howard R.   "Italian Music and Actors in America
        During the Eighteenth Century."   *Italica* 23 (1946): 103-
        117.

1165.   Schiavo, Giovanni Ermenegildo.   *Italian-American History*.
        New York: Vigo Press, 1947.   Reprint, New York: Arno Press,
        1975.   2 vols.

        Volume 1 includes substantial information on "Italian Music
and Musicians in America," and covers the colonial period to the
present.   Discusses Italian musicians, musicians who played Italian
music, with information on the compositions, for various cities.
Includes a useful and fairly comprehensive "Dictionary of Musical
Biography," with little-known musicians cited.   Recommended.

Jews

1166.   Binder, Abraham W.   "Synagogue Music in America."   *Journal of
        Church Music* 6 (1964): 2-4.

1167.   Marcus, Jacob R.   *The Colonial American Jew, 1492-1776.*
        Detroit: Wayne State University Press, 1970.   3 vols.

        Includes a discussion of Nathan Levy, a violinist in the
Philadelphia Musick Club, and David Franks, an amateur musician in
Philadelphia.

Lutherans

*The following bibliography serves as an excellent introduction to
works published prior to 1820:*

1168.   Wolf, Edward C.   "Lutheran Hymnody and Music Published in
        America, 1700-1850: A Descriptive Bibliography."   *Concordia
        Historical Institute Quarterly* 50/4 (Winter 1977): 164-85.

        Two parts describe hymnals and hymn collections without
music, and chorale books and tunebooks.   Each entry includes imprint
data and a description.

1169.   Schalk, Carl.   "Lutheran Hymnody in America: Problems and
        Possibilities."   *Church Music*, 1976, no. 1, 16-19.

        Discusses some of the early Lutheran publications and
compilers in Pennsylvania, including J.C. Kunze (1744-1807) "whose
Hymn and Prayer Book of 1795 was the first English Lutheran
collection of hymns prepared and published in America. . . ."

1170.   Smith, Carlton York.   "Early Lutheran Hymnody in America,
        from the Colonial Period to the Year 1850."   Ph.D.
        dissertation, University of Southern California, 1956.
        302p.

1171.   Steimle, A.   "Church Music in the Lutheran Church of
        America."   *New Music Review* 4 (1905); 109-10, 203-04, 255-
        56, 302-03, 355-56, 494-95.

1172.   Tappert, Theodore G.   "The Place of Music in Colonial
        Lutheran Worship."   *Bulletin* (Gettysburg Theological
        Seminary) 48 (1968): 15-20.

1173.   Wolf, Edward C.   "America's First Lutheran Chorale Book."
        Concordia Historical Institute Quarterly 46/1 (Spring
        1973): 5-17.

        The first chorale book proposed was *Erbauliche Lieder-
Sammlung* (Germantown, 1786).   Discusses the publication of the work
and John Christopher Moller's assistance in that effort.   However,
the work was never published.   The first chorale book published was
the *Choral-Buch fuer die Erbauliche Lieder-Sammlung der deutschen
Evangelisch-Lutherischen Gemeinden in Nord Amerika* (Philadelphia:
Conrad Zentler and George Blake, 1813).   Justus H.C. Helmuth (1745-
1825) was instrumental in the latter publication.

1174.   Wolf, Edward Christopher.   "Lutheran Church Music in America
        during the Eighteenth and Early Nineteenth Centuries."
        Ph.D. dissertation, University of Illinois, 1960.   473p.
        UM 61-218.   *DAI* 21/10 (April 1961): 3118-19.

        Discusses musical programs and congregational singing, and
Lutherans who wrote hymn, anthem, and cantata texts, including Rev.
Justus Henry Christian Helmuth, pastor at St. Michael's and Zion
Church in Philadelphia from 1779-1825.   Discusses a David Tannenberg
organ in Zion Church, and music and singing in Ebenezer, Georgia in
1739.

1175.   Wolf, Edward Christopher.   "Music in Old Zion, Philadelphia,
        1750-1850."   *Musical Quarterly* 58/4 (October 1972): 622-52.

        Focuses on the musical activities of St. Michael's and Zion
German Lutheran Congregation, including various publications, the
instruments, and individuals associated with Old Zion, including
David Ott, music teacher, David Tannenberg, organ builder, Johann
Christopher Moller, musician, and Benjamin Carr, music dealer.

1176.   Worner, William F.   "Music in Trinity Church Steeple."
        Lancaster County Historical Society Papers 32 (1928): 135-
        37.

On music in Lutheran Trinity Church in Lancaster, Pa., in 1809.

Mennonites

The following bibliographies are worthy of note:

1177.   Hostetler, John A.   *Annotated Bibliography on the Amish.*
        Scottdale, Pa.: Mennonite Publishing House, 1951.   xx,
        100p.

        Although dated, provides a comprehensive listing of
published and unpublished materials on the Old Order Amish
Mennonites to June 1950.   Included are books, pamphlets, articles,
theses and dissertations, and unpublished primary materials,
including letters and documents.   Refer to the "Analytical Subject
Index" under "Hymnology" where items concerning hymns, music, and
songs are listed.

1178.   Ressler, Martin E.   *A Bibliography of Mennonite Hymnals and
        Songbooks, 1742-1972.*   Quarryville, Pa.: Ressler, 1972.
        30p.

        Includes 76 items.   "The following bibliography is an
attempt to compile accurately a chronological record of all hymnals
and songbooks published by the (Old) Mennonite Church in America
. . . ."   Provides known reprints and commentary on each item.
First 4 items pre-date 1820.

1179.   Springer, Nelson P. and A.J. Klassen.   *Mennonite
        Bibliography: 1631-1961.*   Scottdale, Pa.: Herald Press,
        1977.   2 vols.

        Includes 28,155 numbered entries.   The principal
international source for identifying periodicals and articles,
books, pamphlets, dissertations, festschrifts, symposia, and
encyclopedia articles on all aspects of Mennonite history.   Volume 2
includes a substantial section on North America.   Begin a search
under basic terms, "Music" and "Hymns" (cross-references to other
musical subjects are provided), in the subject index.   Other

subjects include, for example, "Church Music," "Music in Churches," and "Musical Instruments." There is an author index as well.

1180. *Ausbund, Das ist: Etliche schöne Christliche Lieder.*
          Germantown: Christoph Saur, 1742. Reprint, Amsterdam:
          Frits Knuf, 1972.

          The *Ausbund* was the principal hymn book for the Mennonites in America.

1181. Barbour, J. Murray. "The Unpartheyisches Gesang-Buch." In
          Cantors at the Crossroads. Ed. by Johannes Riedel. St.
          Louis, Mo.: Concordia Publishing House, 1967, pp. 87-93.

          The *Unpartheyisches Gesang-Buch*, first published in 1804,
was an important psalm and hymn collection which ran through some 15
editions. The author also discusses a number of other Mennonite
collections.

1182. Bender, Harold S. "The First Edition of the Ausbund."
          Mennonite Quarterly Review 3/2 (April 1929): 147-50.

          A short introduction to *Ausbund, Das ist* including an
"exact reproduction of the table of contents."

1183. Bender, Harold S. "The Literature and Hymnology of the
          Mennonites of Lancaster County, Pennsylvania." *Mennonite
          Quarterly Review* 6 (1932): 156-68.

1184. Burkhart, Charles. "Church Music of the Old Order Amish and
          Old Colony Mennonites." *Mennonite Quarterly Review* 27
          (1953): 34-54.

          Very concise description of music in worship services;
includes a history of the music and a discussion of various
hymnbooks, performance practice, and an analysis of the music.
Musical examples.

1185. Burkhart, Charles. "Music of the Old Colony Mennonites."
          Mennonite Life 7 (1952): 20-21, 47.

1186.   Hohmann, Rupert Karl.   "The Church Music of the Old Order
         Amish of the United States."   Ph.D. dissertation,
         Northwestern University, 1959.   262p.   UM 60-436.   *DAI* 20/9
         (March 1960): 3769-70.

         Includes a historical survey of the Old Order Amish, a
study of the music in use today, and a description and analysis of
the tunes.

1187.   Jackson, George Pullen.   "The Strange Music of the Old Order
         Amish."   *Musical Quarterly* 31/3 (July 1945): 275-88.

         Although this work focuses primarily on 20th-century field
work on the Amish, the author includes brief background information
on them as well as a photo of the title page of a later edition of
their principal hymnbook, *Ausbund, Das ist* (Lancaster, 1834).

1188.   Jost, Walter James.   "The Hymn Tune Tradition of the General
         Conference Mennonite Church."   D.M.A. dissertation,
         University of Southern California, 1966.   318p.   UM 66-
         8792.   *DAI* 27/4 (October 1966): 1072-73-A.

         Discusses the various Mennonite hymnbooks from the
publication of *Ausbund* in the 16th century.   The author states that
"Few original Mennonite tunes or texts can be found after the
Reformation.   Mennonite hymnody became a borrowed hymnody."

1189.   Kadelbach, Ada.   *Die Hymnodie der Mennoniten in Nordamerika
         (1742-1860): Eine Studie zur Verpflanzung, Bewahrung und
         Umformung europäischer Kirchenliedtradition.*   Mainz: the
         author, 1971.   viii, 285p.

         Includes background information and a discussion of the
various tunebooks in use.   Contains numerous facsimiles and musical
examples.

1190.   Kadelbach, Ada.   "Hymns Written by American Mennonites."
         Mennonite Quarterly Review 48 (1974): 343-70.

1191.   Ressler, Martin E.   "A History of Mennonite Hymnody."
         Journal of Church Music 18/6 (June 1976): 2-5.

Includes a discussion with facsimiles of the hymnals published in America. Also mentions the influence of Joseph Funk's *A Compilation of Genuine Church Music* (1832).

1192.   Ressler, Martin E.   "Hymnbooks Used by the Old Order Amish."
         Hymn 28/1 (1977): 11-16.

1193.   Schreiber, William I.   "The Hymns of the Amish Ausbund in
         Philological and Literary Perspective." *Mennonite
         Quarterly Review* 36/1 (January 1962): 36-60.

         Used today by the Old Order Amish, the *Ausbund* has been abandoned by all other Mennonite groups. The author gives a history of its publication and a literary analysis.

1194.   Umble, John S.   "Recent Research in Amish Hymn Tunes."
         Mennonite Quarterly Review 24 (1950): 91-93.

1195.   Wohlgemuth, Paul William.   "Mennonite Hymnals Published in
         the English Language."   D.M.A. dissertation, University of
         Southern California, 1956.   424p.

1196.   Yoder, Paul Marvin.   "Nineteenth Century Sacred Music of the
         Mennonite Church in the United States."   Ph.D.
         dissertation, Florida State University, 1961.   vii, 180p.
         UM 61-3653.   *DAI* 22/4 (October 1961): 1207-08.

         Includes 5 chapters: "Music in the Early Settlements" during the 18th century; "German Hymnals of the Mennonites"; "Music in the Sunday School"; "Mennonite Singing School Books"; "Summary and Conclusions." Topics focusing on the early tradition include Christopher Dock, and Mennonites in Ohio and Pennsylvania. The appendix is noteworthy: "Chronological Listing of Mennonite Music Publications," which includes all of the principal hymnals and editions.

Methodists

1197.   Baldridge, Terry L.   "Evolving Tastes in Hymntunes of the
        Methodist Episcopal Church in the Nineteenth Century."
        Ph.D. dissertation, University of Kansas, 1982.   494p.   UM
        83-01665.   *DAI* 43/8 (February 1983): 2485-A.

        Covers the period 1808-78.   Discusses early tunebooks, and
includes a classification of tunes and an analysis of successive
versions of tunes.

1198.   *Companion to the Hymnal: A Handbook of the 1964 Methodist
        Hymnal*.   Nashville: Abingdon Press, 1964.   766p.

        Includes an annotated list of texts and tunes arranged
alphabetically by title, including provenance, and biographies of
the author and composers.   Useful for biographical information not
found elsewhere.   Bibliography and general index.

1199.   Ellinwood, Leonard W.   "Wesley's First Hymnal Was Never
        Officially Condemned!"   *Hymn* 12/2 (1961): 56-59.

        On *A Collection of Psalms and Hymns* (Charleston, 1737).

1200.   England, Martha W.   "The First Wesley Hymn Book."   *Bulletin
        of the New York Public Library* 68 (1964): 225-38.

        Discusses *A Collection of Psalms and Hymns* (Charleston,
1737).

1201.   Hill, Double E.   "A Study of Tastes in American Church Music
        as Reflected in the Music of the Methodist Episcopal Church
        to 1900."   Ph.D. dissertation, University of Illinois at
        Urbana-Champaign, 1962.   890p.

1202.   Morgan, Catharine.   "Methodist Folk-Hymnody."   *Music Ministry*
        1/5 (February 1960): 9-10, 27; 1/6 (March 1960): 2-3.

        Brief survey of hymnody, beginning with *A Collection of
Psalms and Hymns* (Charleston, 1737).

1203.   Rogal, Samuel J.   *Guide to the Hymns and Tunes of American
        Methodism.*   Westport, Conn.: Greenwood Press, 1986.   xxii,
        318p.

        Serves as a reference guide to six major hymnals.   In the
first section, 2,005 hymns are listed.   The second section has short
biographies of hymnodists, composers, and arrangers, many of which
are not found elsewhere.   First-line index and tune-names index.

1204.   Stevenson, Robert M.   "John Wesley's First Hymnbook."   *Review
        of Religion* 14 (January 1950): 140-60.

        On *A Collection of Psalms and Hymns* (Charleston, 1737).

1205.   Van Burkalow, Anastasia.   "Expanding Horizons: Two Hundred
        Years of American Methodist Hymnody."   *Hymn* 17/3 (July
        1966): 77-84.

        Brief article that mentions musical practice of Methodists
in New York in 1766, and the first American hymnal, which was
adopted in Baltimore in 1784, *A Collection of Psalms and Hymns.*
Discusses Wesley hymns.

<u>Moravians</u>

1206.   Anderson, Thomas Jerome.   "The Collegium Musicum Salem, 1780-
        1790: Origins and Repertoire."   Ph.D. dissertation, Florida
        State University, 1976.   261p.   UM 76-29414.   *DAI* 37/7
        (January 1977): 3977-A.

        Includes 7 chapters.   Discusses the vocal and instrumental
music in Salem, its Collegium Musicum, and Johann Friedrich Peter.
Of note is an extensive catalog consisting of 256 incipits of the
instrumental repertoire of the Collegium Musicum in Salem, N.C.   Two
appendixes include indexes of composers and copy-dates found in the
catalog.

1207.   Asti, Martha Secrest.   "The Moravian Music of Christian
        Gregor (1723-1801): His Anthems, Arias, Duets, and

Chorales." Ph.D. dissertation, University of Miami, 1982. 236p. UM 83-13070. *DAI* 44/2 (August 1983): 315-16-A.

Although Christian Gregor's life was spent in Herrnhut, Saxony (now in East Germany), "this study of Gregor deals specifically with his anthems, arias, and duets as contained in the Herbst Collection and the Salem Congregation Music, plus the Gregor chorales in his 1784 edition of *Choral-Buch*. . ., housed in the Moravian Music Foundation in Winston-Salem, North Carolina."

1208.   Austin, Raymond. "The Moravian Trombone Choir." *Instrumentalist* 22/5 (December 1967): 38-39.

Very brief history of the trombone choir to the present.

1209.   Beck, Herbert H. "Lititz as an Early Music Center." *Lancaster County Historical Society Papers* 19 (1915): 71-81.

On Moravian music in Lititz, Pa.

1210.   Behrens, Edith. "Thor Johnson Discusses Moravian Music." *Music Clubs Magazine* 31/3 (January 1952): 5-6, 23.

1211.   Birney, Allan D. "Four Unpublished Anthems by David Moritz Michael, Moravian Composer (1751-1827): Edited and Provided With a Biographical Sketch." Ph.D. dissertation, Juilliard School of Music, 1971.

Discusses Thor Johnson's early research into Moravian music, and includes information on Johann Friedrich Peter.

1212.   Boeringer, James. "Handel and the Moravians." *Journal of Church Music* 27/2 (February 1985): 6-9.

Includes a description and list of works by George Frideric Handel copied by hand by American Moravians. These works are located in the Moravian Archives in Bethlehem, Pa. Musical examples.

1213.   Boeringer, James.   "Moravian Influence on Music in
            Philadelphia." *Moravian Music Journal* 27/3 (Fall 1982):
            66-69.

        Discusses composers, collections of music, musical
instrument makers, and musicians.

1214.   Branstine, Wesley R.   "The Moravian Church and Its Trombone
            Choir in America. . . ." D.M.A. dissertation, North Texas
            State University, 1984. 58p. UM 84-23857. *DAI* 45/7
            (January 1985): 1906-A.

        A general overview of the musical heritage of the Moravian
Church, history of the trombone choir and its use in Bethlehem, Pa.

1215.   Chancellor, Paul G.   "Our Astonishing Musical Beginnings at
            Bethlehem." *Etude* 66/4 (April 1948): 221, 256, 266.

        Brief introduction mentioning instrumental and vocal music
by composers John Antes and Johann Friedrich Peter.

1216.   Claypool, Richard D.   "A Manuscript with Two Sketches of
            Bethlehem's Musical History." *Moravian Music Foundation
            Bulletin* 22/1 (Spring-Summer 1977): 8-9.

        Discusses the manuscript copy of Rufus A. Grider's
*Historical Notes on Music in Bethlehem, Pennsylvania, from 1741 to
1871* (see entry 1231), which contains additional information not in
the book. Also discusses a manuscript, "The Annals of the Music of
Bethlehem, Pennsylvania, with an Historical Introduction of the
Music of the Moravian Church," dated 1859, by Lewis H. Weiss.

1217.   Crawford, Richard.   "The Moravians and Eighteenth-Century
            American Musical Mainstreams." *Moravian Music Foundation
            Bulletin* 21/2 (Fall-Winter 1976): 2-7.

        An introduction to Moravian musical life and a comparison
with the New England tradition.

1218.   Cummock, Frances.   "The Lovefeast Psalm: Questions and a Few
        Answers."   *Moravian Music Foundation Bulletin* 23/1 (Spring-
        Summer 1978): 2-8.

        Discusses the use of the psalm in the worship service
"shortly before the food was served."   Also discusses the texts, the
composers, the use of certain psalms, including, for example, the
fifty-year jubilee psalm for the Single Sisters Choir celebrated on
May 4, 1780.

1219.   Cumnock, Frances.   "The Salem Congregation Music: Problems
        Then and Now."   *Moravian Music Foundation Bulletin* 19/2
        (Fall-Winter 1974): 1-4.

        Discusses the development of the collection during the
period 1780-1810, including the composers and their music.

1220.   David, Hans Theodore.   "Background for Bethlehem: Moravian
        Music in Pennsylvania."   *Magazine of Art* 32 (1939): 222-25,
        254.

1221.   David, Hans T.   "Music of the Early Moravians in America."
        Musical America 59/14 (1939): 5, 33.

1222.   David, Hans T.   *Musical Life in the Pennsylvania Settlements
        of the Unitas Fratrum.*   Moravian Music Foundation
        Publications, 6.   Foreword by Donald M. McCorkle.   Winston-
        Salem: Moravian Music Foundation, 1959.   44p.

        David, one of the first to study American Moravian music in
depth, presents a survey of his findings.   Discussed are musicians,
instruments, and musical events.   The article was originally
published in *Transactions of the Moravian Historical Society* 13
(1942), pp. 19-58.

1223.   Falconer, Joan O.   "The Second Berlin Song School in
        America."   *Musical Quarterly* 49/3 (July 1973): 411-40.

        Includes historical background of Moravians in America,
their music, especially vocal music.   The principal composer

discussed is Johannes Herbst, including his life and manuscripts. Musical examples.

1224.   Findley, Rowe.   "Old Salem, Morning Star of Moravian Faith."
        National Geographic 138/6 (December 1970): 818-37.

        A popular introduction to a lovefeast in Old Salem, N.C. interspersed with historical facts.   Includes an excellent schematic drawing of historic landmarks, and a photograph of a reenactment of the 1783 Independence Day celebration.

1225.   Fleming, Shirley.   "The Music-Making Moravians."   *High
        Fidelity/Musical America* 16/9 (September 1966): MA 16-17.

        Music in colonial Winston-Salem, N.C.   Introduces manuscripts and principal musicians.

1226.   Fries, Adelaide L.   *Funeral Chorals of the Unitas Fratrum or
        Moravian Church*.   Winston-Salem, N.C.: privately printed,
        1905.   23p.

        Includes information on the tradition of the trombone music used at funeral services, and a group of works to be used at such services.

1227.   Frost, Ruth G.   "Concerning Moravian Music."   *Music Journal*
        18/8 (November 1960): 34, 76-77.

        Brief introduction to musical activities and instruments of the Moravians.

1228.   Geisler, John H.   "Musical Ministers of the Moravian Church."
        Hymn 29/1 (January 1978): 6-14, 28.

        Includes information on John Antes, John Christian Bechler, Jacob Van Vleck, Peter Wolle, and others.

1229.   Gombosi, Marilyn.   *A Day of Solemn Thanksgiving: Moravian
        Music for the Fourth of July, 1783, in Salem, North*

Carolina.   Chapel Hill: University of North Carolina Press, 1977.   x, 215p.

Consists of essays, "The Moravian Church and Its Music" and "Music in Salem Prior to the Fourth of July, 1783," copious notes on the music for the Fourth of July celebration of 1783 as performed by Moravians, and a full and edited score.   The photos are especially worthy of note.   Index.

1230.   Gombosi, Marilyn.   "Guardians of a Heritage."   *Music Ministry* 6/8 (April 1965): 4-7, 36.

An introduction to the Moravians and their music, with Jeremiah Dencke, John Antes, David Tannenberg, and others presented as principal musicians.

1231.   Grider, Rufus A.   *Historical Notes on Music in Bethlehem, Pennsylvania, from 1741 to 1871.*   Philadelphia: Printed by John L. Pile for J. Hill Martin, 1873.   Reprint, Winston-Salem: Moravian Music Foundation, 1951.   Moravian Music Foundation Publications, 4.   41p.

One of the earliest accounts of music, this work is still useful today for its list of musicians active in Bethlehem.   Thanks to Grider's forethought, many of these names were related to him from "old living musicians, who depended alone upon their memory, except as to the dates, which were taken from the tablets in the grave yard."

1232.   Griffin, Francis.   "The Moravian Musical Heritage."   *Hymn* 19/4 (October 1968): 101-03.

A popular brief account mentioning the early chamber music, composers, collections, and performances.   Published also in *Moravian Music Foundation Bulletin* 12/2 (Spring 1968), pp. 1-3.

1233.   Grubb, Marion.   "Trombone Town, Pennsylvania."   *Etude* 60/6 (June 1942): 378, 424.

Introduction to the use of trombones by the Moravians in Lititz, Pa.   Photographs.

1234.   Hall, Harry H. "The Columbian Band: Bethlehem Moravians in the Early Nineteenth Century Pennsylvania Militia." *Journal of Band Research* 20/2 (Spring 1985): 40-49.

        The Columbian Band, 97th Regiment, was likely formed in 1815. Discusses the musicians and performances. This article appeared originally in *Moravian Music Journal* 29/4 (Winter 1984), pp. 98-105.

1235.   Hall, Harry H. "Early Sounds of Moravian Brass Music in America: A Cultural Note from Colonial Georgia." *Moravian Music Foundation Bulletin* 15/1-2 (Fall-Winter 1970): 1-4.

        An introduction, with emphasis on the Georgia settlement. Discusses information on the first trombones in America, based on a letter by Peter Bohler (1712-1775) written in 1739.

1236.   Hall, Harry H. "Early Sounds of Moravian Music in America: A Cultural Note from Colonial Georgia." *Brass Quarterly* 7/3 (Spring 1964): 115-23.

        Discusses Johann Böhner (1710-1785), who was apparently "the first individual thus far specifically identified with American Moravian music." The discussion centers on the brass ensemble in the Georgia settlement and corrects some previous errors by other writers concerning instrumentation of the brass ensemble.

1237.   Hall, Harry H. "The Moravian Trombone Choir: A Conspectus of Its Early History and the Traditional Death Announcement." *Moravian Music Journal* 26/1 (Spring 1981): 5-8.

        Records in Bethlehem, Pa. show that the practice of playing a distinctive hymntune to announce the death of a Moravian individual was established there on April 4, 1757. The author provides a history of this practice.

1238.   Hall, Harry H. "The Moravian Wind Ensemble: Distinctive Chapter in America's Music." Ph.D. dissertation, George Peabody College for Teachers, 1967. 2 vols., 568p. UM 67-15007. *DAI* 28/7 (January 1968): 2712-13-A.

A comprehensive discussion of the history of trombone choirs and collegia musica in use in Bethlehem, Pa., Salem, N.C., and other settlements. Of special note is the earliest woodwind music by David Moritz Michael.

1239.   Hall, Harry H. "The Moravian Wind Ensemble Tradition in America." *Moravian Music Foundation Bulletin* 9/2 (Spring 1965): 1-2, 4.

An introduction to the tradition in Nazareth, Bethlehem, and Lititz, Pa. and Salem, N.C., with a list of representative works. Reprinted in *Journal of Band Research* 1/2 (1965), pp. 27-29.

1240.   Hall, Harry H. "The Salem Band: Its Early Nineteenth-Century Military Image." *Journal of Band Research* 17/2 (Spring 1982): 1-14.

Provides a brief history of the band of Salem, N.C. Most of the article focuses on the period after 1831.

1241.   Hamilton, Kenneth G. "The Bethlehem Christmas Hymn." *Transactions of the Moravian Historical Society* 14 (1947-51): 11-23.

The hymn was composed in 1742 in Bethlehem, Pa.

1242.   Hartzell, Lawrence W. *Ohio Moravian Music*. Winston-Salem, N.C.: Moravian Music Foundation Press, 1988. 201p.

The principal study of Moravian music in Ohio. Includes a survey of music in the Ohio Indian missions, 1772-1823, and music in the congregations, 1799-1842. Musicians discussed include David Peter, Heinrich Keller, Abraham Luckenbach, Jacob Blickensderfer, Abraham Ricksecker, and Johnathan Winsch. Index.

1243.   Hartzell, Lawrence W. "Trombones in Ohio." *Moravian Music Journal* 28 (Winter 1983): 72-74.

1244. Hellyer, Roger. "The Harmoniemusik of the Moravian
          Communities in America." *Fontes Artis Musicae* 27/2 (April-
          June 1980): 95-108.

     Reviews previous research. Discusses David Moritz Michael,
and includes a list of wind music by foreign-born composers that was
performed in the colonies. Illustrations and musical examples.

1245. Holder, Edward M. "Social Life of the Early Moravians in
          North Carolina." *North Carolina Historical Review* 11
          (1934): 167-84.

1246. Hoople, Donald Graham. "Moravian Music Education and the
          American Moravian Music Tradition." Ed.D. dissertation,
          Columbia University Teachers College, 1976. 230p. UM 77-
          6715. *DAI* 37/10 (April 1977): 6335-A.

     A history of Moravian music education in Bethlehem, Pa. and
Salem, N.C. during the 18th and 19th centuries and based on primary
sources such as diaries, journals, financial statements, etc. Early
composers discussed include John Frederik Peter and David Moritz
Michael.

1247. Howe, M.A. DeWolfe. "'Venite in Bethlehem': The Major
          Chord." *Musical Quarterly* 28/2 (April 1942): 174-85.

     Although the focus of this article is on the musical
tradition in Bethlehem, Pa. during the late 19th and early 20th
centuries, the author includes brief background information on the
earlier period.

1248. Hudson, Arthur Palmer. "The Singstunde in Old Wachovia."
          North Carolina Folklore 14/2 (November 1966): 4-11.

     Survey of Moravian music, especially singing in the church
services, in old Salem, N.C.

1249. Huebener, Mary A. "Bicentennial History of the Lititz
          Moravian Congregation." *Transactions of the Moravian
          Historical Society* 14 (1947-51): 199-271.

Includes information on music of the Moravians in Lititz, Pa.

1250. Ingram, Jeannine. "Moravians and Music in America." In *Southern Humanities Conference: Winston-Salem, 1977*. Ed. by W.E. Ray. Winston-Salem, N.C.: 1977, p. 54+

1251. Ingram, Jeannine. "The Moravians in America: Preservers of a Musical Heritage." *Moravian Music Foundation Bulletin* 22/2 (Fall-Winter 1977): 2-6.

Discusses works by European Moravian composers that were likely copied in America. Includes a checklist of rare music in the Salem Collegium Musicum Collection.

1252. Ingram, Jeannine. "Music in American Moravian Communities: Transplanted Traditions in Indigenous Practices." *Communal Societies* 2 (Autumn 1982): 39-51.

1253. Ingram, Jeannine. "A Musical Potpourri: The Commonplace Book of Johann Friedrich Peter." *Moravian Music Foundation Bulletin* 24/1 (Spring-Summer 1979): 2-7, 12.

Discusses a commonplace book, compiled by Peter, as a means for copying music requested by members of the Moravian community. The author includes a list of 214 items in the book, and notes composer and title with text incipit for each entry.

1254. Ingram, Jeannine. "Reflections on the Salem Collegium Musicum." *Moravian Music Foundation Bulletin* 20/1 (Spring-Summer 1975): 8-11.

A historical introduction, with information on its various directors, including Johannes Reuz, Gottlieb Schober, C.G. Reichel, C.L. Benzien for the period prior to 1822.

1255. Ingram, Jeannine. "Repertory and Resources of the Salem Collegium Musicum, 1780-1790." *Fontes Artis Musicae* 26 (October-December 1979): 267-81.

Includes biographical information on Johann Friedrich Peter, information on the composers represented in the collection, and lists of musical works.

1256.   Johansen, John H.   "The Hymnody of the Moravian Church." *Hymn* 8/2 (1957): 41-46, 59.

1257.   Johansen, John H.   "Moravian Hymnody."   *Hymn* 30/3 (1979): 167-77, 195; 30/4 (1979): 230-39, 242.

1258.   Jueckstock, John Douglas.   "The Complete Works of Jeremias Dencke (1725-1795)."   D.M.A., Southwestern Baptist Theological Seminary, 1984.   UM number not cited.   *DAI* 45/4 (October 1984): 982-A

All of the 152 works of Dencke have been edited and transcribed here, with a comparative study of the scores.

1259.   Kolb, Margaret Leinbach.   "The 'History of Moravian Music in America' Project." *Moravian Music Journal* 26/2 (Summer 1981): 27-28.

A report on a project that will document the history of musical activity in Bethlehem, Pa. during 1741-61 and Salem, N.C. during 1766-90.

1260.   Konig, Linda.   "Our Musical Heritage from the Moravians." *Church Musician* 27/9 (June 1976): 40-45.

A popular article introducing the reader to John Antes and other composers, and special service music the Moravians used in Bethlehem, Pa. and Salem, N.C.

1261.   Kortz, Edwin W.   "The Liturgical Development of the American Moravian Church." *Transactions of the Moravian Historical Society* 18 (1961-62): 267-302.

1262.   Kroeger, Karl.   "A Core Repertory of American Moravian Hymn-Tunes." *Moravian Music Journal* 31/1 (Spring 1986): 2-8.

Includes background information on significant sources, and
a list of the tunes. Also includes facsimiles from part-books
compiled in the 1780s by Johann Friedrich Peter.

1263. Kroeger, Karl. "David Moritz Michael's Psalm 103: An Early
       American Sacred Cantata." *Moravian Music Foundation
       Bulletin* 21/2 (Fall-Winter 1976): 10-11.

On the work and its first performance, which took place on
November 8, 1805 in Nazareth, Pa. Musical examples.

1264. Kroeger, Karl. "John Hutton's Tunebook in 1744: An Early
       Source of Moravian Chorales." *Hymn* 31/2 (1980): 108-17,
       126.

1265. Kroeger, Karl. "The Moravian Choral Tradition: Yesterday and
       Today." *Choral Journal* 19/5 (January 1979): 5-9, 12.

Brief survey, discussing performance practice and modern
editions. Includes a photograph of a Tannenburg organ in Winston-
Salem, N.C., and a list of modern editions of Moravian choral music.

1266. Kroeger, Karl. "Moravian Music in America: A Survey." In
       Unitas Fratrum: Herrnhuter Studien. Ed. by Mari P. van
       Buijtenen and others. Utrecht: Rijksarchief, 1975, p. 387-
       400

A brief, but well written summary of musical activities,
musicians, and instruments in the various Moravian settlements.

1267. Kroeger, Karl. "Moravian Music in 19th Century American
       Tunebooks." *Moravian Music Foundation Bulletin* 18/1
       (Spring-Summer 1973): 1-3.

Discusses the tunebooks and Moravian tunes in them. The
earliest piece of music by a Moravian in an American tunebook is in
Samuel Dyer's *A New Selection of Sacred Music* (Baltimore, 1817).
The piece is "Hosanna" by Christian Gregor.

1268.   Kroeger, Karl.   "The Moravian Tradition in Song." *Moravian Music Foundation Bulletin* 20/2 (Fall-Winter 1975): 8-10.

Discusses works by Jeremiah Dencke, Johannes Herbst, and others.

1269.   Kroeger, Karl.   "New Light on Early Bethlehem Music." *Moravian Music Foundation Bulletin* 19/1 (Spring-Summer 1974): 4-5.

On Bethlehem, Pa., and a letter written by Eliza S. Bowne on August 9, 1803 regarding musical activities there.

1270.   Kroeger, Karl.   "New Moravian Manuscript Discoveries." *Moravian Music Foundation Bulletin* 22/2 (Fall-Winter 1977): 8-9.

Discusses works copied by Johannes Herbst and a volume of songs, dated 1796, owned by Theodora S. Eyerly of Bethlehem, Pa.

1271.   Kroeger, Karl.   "On the Early Performance of Moravian Chorales." *Moravian Music Foundation Bulletin* 24/2 (Fall-Winter 1979): 2-8.

Based on primary sources, both European and American.

1272.   Kroeger, Karl.   "A Singing Church: America's Legacy in Moravian Music." *Journal of Church Music* 18/3 (March 1976): 2-4, 32.

Discusses the early settlements, musical activities, and composers, including a photo of Johann Christian Till (1742-1844), composer and organist.

1273.   LaRue, Jan P.   "English Music Papers in the Moravian Archives of North Carolina." *Monthly Musical Record* 89/995 (September-October 1959): 185-88.

Discusses some of the earliest and rarest copies of works by Boccherini, Haydn, Pergolesi, and others.

1274.   Lawson, Charles Truman.   "Musical Life in the Unitas Fratrum
        Mission at Springplace, Georgia, 1800-1836."   Ph.D.
        dissertation, Florida State University, 1970.   180p.   UM
        70-16335.   *DAI* 31/3 (September 1970): 1311-A.

        The research is based on a set of diaries kept by Moravian
missionaries in Springplace, Georgia.   The author investigates the
use of music in school and church and what effect it had on the
Cherokee Indians.   Extracts from the diaries are included in an
appendix.   Musicians named include Christian Burckhardt, Gottlieb
Byhan, Henry Clauder, Anna Rosina Kliest Gambold, Karsten Petersen,
and Jacob Wohlfarth.

1275.   Leaman, Jerome.   "The Trombone Choir of the Moravian Church."
        Moravian Music Foundation Bulletin 20/1 (Spring-Summer
        1975): 2-7.

        A historical introduction to the use of these choirs in
American Moravian communities.

1276.   Lowens, Irving.   "Haydn in America."   In *Haydn Studies;
        Proceedings of the International Haydn Conference,
        Washington, D.C., 1975.*   Ed. by Jens Peter Larsen, Howard
        Serwer, and James Webster (New York: Norton, 1981), pp 35-
        48.

        Discusses the performance preservation of some works by
Haydn by the American Moravians.

1277.   Lowens, Irving.   "Moravian Music—Neglected American
        Heritage."   *Musical America* 78/3 (February 1958): 30-31,
        122, 124, 126.

        An excellent introduction that reviews previous literature
and includes illustrations of several Moravian musicians and
examples of rare musical discoveries in the holdings of the Moravian
Archives.

1278.   McCorkle, Donald M.   *The "Collegium Musicum Salem": Its
        Music, Musicians and Importance.*   Moravian Music Foundation
        Publications, 3.   Winston-Salem: Moravian Music Foundation,
        1956.   20p.

Originally published in the *North Carolina Historical Review* 33/4 (October 1956), this work includes information on early chamber music in Salem, N.C., Johann Friedrich Peter, and other musicians. Included is a portrait of Wilhem Ludwig Benzien, one of the directors of the Collegium Musicum in Salem.

1279.   McCorkle, Donald M.   "Early American Moravian Music." *Music Journal* 13/9 (November 1955): 11, 45-47.

An introduction to Moravian music with principal composers mentioned, including John Antes, David Moritz Michael, and Johann Friedrich Peter. Includes information on European works held in the Moravian Archives.

1280.   McCorkle, Donald M.   "In a Nutshell: American Moravian Music." *Moravian Music Foundation Bulletin* 5/3 (Fall 1961): 1, 6.

An introduction to principal musicians.

1281.   McCorkle, Donald M.   *The Moravian Contribution to American Music.*   Moravian Music Foundation Publications, 1. Winston-Salem: Moravian Music Foundation, 1956.   20p.

Originally published in *Notes* 13/4 (September 1956), McCorkle describes briefly the Collegium Musicum and trombone choir in use, musical instruments, and secular and sacred music in Lititz and Bethlehem, Pa. and Salem, N.C.

1282.   McCorkle, Donald Macomber.   "Moravian Music in Salem: A German-American Heritage."   Ph.D. dissertation, Indiana University, 1958.   431p.   UM 59-333.   *DAI* 20/2 (August 1959): 688-89.

The first extensive study of Moravian music in Salem, N.C., with emphasis on the composer Johann Friedrich Peter. The musical heritage of Salem is compared to that of Bethlehem, Pa.

1283.   McCorkle, Donald M.   "Musical Life in Salem."   *Antiques* 88 (1965): 65-68.

A brief article on Moravian music in Salem, N.C.

1284.   McCorkle, Donald M.   "The Unknown Century of American
        Classical Music." *Moravian Music Foundation Bulletin* 4/2
        (Spring-Summer 1960): 1, 3, 6.

An introduction to the Moravians in Bethlehem, Pa., and
Salem, N.C.

1285.   Mack, Elmer L.   "They Called It Bethlehem."   *Music Journal*
        16/8 (November 1958): 12, 47-48.

Introduction to Moravian music in Georgia and Bethlehem,
Pa.

1286.   Maurer, Joseph A.   "America's Heritage of Moravian Music:
        Contributions of Early Pennsylvania Composers." *Historical
        Review of Berks County* 18 (April-June 1953): 66-70, 87-91.

1287.   Maurer, Joseph A.   "Moravian Church Music—1457-1957."
        American Guild of Organists Quarterly 2/1 (January 1957):
        3-6, 16-17, 30-32.

1288.   Maurer, Joseph A.   "Moravian Music."   *Music Journal* 17/2
        (February 1959): 6-7.

Very brief overview of Moravian music.

1289.   Maurer, Joseph A.   "The Moravian Trombone Choir, Bicentennial
        of Bethlehem's Historic Music Ensemble." *Historical Review
        of Berk's County* 20/1 (October-December 1954): 2-8.

A brief account of the brass ensemble in Bethlehem, Pa.

1290.   Maurer, Maurer.   "Music in Wachovia, 1753-1800."   *William and
        Mary Quarterly* 8/2 (April 1951): 214-27.

Discusses hymnbooks, instruments, and musical activities in
Bethlehem, Pa.

1291. Media, Jay. "Christmas Music in the Little Town of
       Bethlehem, Pennsylvania." *Etude* 58/12 (December 1940):
       801-02, 856.

       A popular introduction to Moravian music.

1292. Media, Jay. "A Remarkable American Musical Tradition, the
       Moravian Funeral Chorals [*sic*] at Salem." *Etude* 51/9
       (September 1933): 573.

       Brief account of the trombone choir in Salem, N.C. Based
on information given to the author by Howard E. Rondthaler, then
president of Salem College. Musical examples.

1293. Mellin, Ted. "Christmas in Bethlehem." *Music Journal* 11/12
       (December 1953): 10-11, 44.

       A popular article introducing the reader to the music and
musicians that were associated with traditional Moravian Christmas
festivities in Bethlehem, Pa.

1294. Myers, Richmond E. "Two Centuries of Trombones." *Etude* 73/4
       (April 1955): 12, 45.

       Discusses the use of trombones by the Moravians in
Bethlehem, Pa.

1295. Nolte, Ewald V. "Early Moravian Music in America." *Journal
       of Church Music* 8/4 (1966): 2-4.

       A brief introduction and definition of Moravian music.

1296. Nolte, Ewald V. "Sacred Music in the Early American Moravian
       Communities: An Introduction." *Church Music*, 1971, no. 2,
       16-25.

1297. Ottenberg, June C. "Two Odes by Jeremias Dencke: Eighteenth-
       Century American/Moravian Style." *Music Review* 45/2 (May
       1984): 112-21.

Dencke composed the odes during the period August 1765-December 1768 at Bethlehem, Pa. Includes biographical information, an analysis, and musical examples.

1298.   Pfohl, Bernard J.   "The Salem Band: The Trombone Choir of the Moravian Church." *Moravian Music Foundation Bulletin* 18/1 (Spring-Summer 1973): 5-8.

Discusses the history and use of brass music in Salem, N.C., and notes performance practice concerning an Easter morning service in 1911. See also the author's *The Salem Band* (Winston-Salem: Winston Printing Co., 1953), which includes photographs of early instruments.

1299.   Rau, Albert F.   "Development of Music in Bethlehem, Pennsylvania." *Transactions of the Moravian Historical Society* 13 (1942): 59-64.

On Moravian music.

1300.   Reynolds, Jeff.   "The Moravian Trombone Choir." *Newsletter of the International Trombone Association* 8/1 (1980): 24-25.

1301.   Rierson, Charles Frederick, Jr.   "The Collegium Musicum Salem: The Development of a Catalogue of Its Library and the Editing of Selected Works." Ed.D. dissertation, University of Georgia, 1973. 288p. UM 74-4872. *DAI* 34/9 (March 1974): 6028-29-A.

A catalog of the instrumental published edition housed in the Moravian Music Foundation Archives in Winston-Salem, N.C. Information includes composer, title, form, publisher, plate number, movement with key signature, time signature and number of measures, and instrumentation.

1302.   Rothrock, Donna K.   "Moravian Music Education: Forerunner to Public School Music." *Bulletin of Historical Research in Music Education* 8/2 (July 1987): 63-82.

        Discusses Bethlehem, Pa. and Salem, N.C. and the Moravian
practice of requiring recitation of hymns and instruction on the
piano as part of a sound education. An excellent introduction to
this subject.

1303.   Schwarze, W.N.   "Early Hymnals of the Bohemian Brethren."
        Transactions of the Moravian Historical Society 13 (1944):
        163-73.

1304.   Serwer, Howard.   "Händel in Bethlehem."   *Händel-Jahrbuch* 27
        (1981): 107-16.

        Discusses 13 choral works by Handel preserved in the
Moravian Music Foundation in Bethlehem, Pa. Discusses the
performance of this music in Lititz, Pa. from 1790 to ca. 1840.

1305.   Serwer, Howard.   "Handel in Bethlehem."   *Moravian Music
        Foundation Bulletin* 25/1 (Spring-Summer 1980): 2-7.

        Describes and lists compositions by G.F. Handel extant in
the Moravian Archives, Bethlehem, Pa.

1306.   Snyder, Robert P.   "Our Moravian Forefathers Were Pioneers in
        American Music."   *Moravian* 95 (1950): 3-4.

1307.   Steelman, Robert.   "A Cantata Performed in Bethlehem in the
        1740s."   *Moravian Music Foundation Bulletin* 20/2 (Fall-
        Winter 1975): 2-7.

        Reviews previous literature on it and provides new evidence
on this work.

1308.   Steelman, Robert.   "The First Trombone Choir of Lititz."
        Moravian Music Journal 27/1 (Spring 1982): 4-6.

        The first trombones were acquired in Lititz, Pa. in 1771.
Discusses some of the musicians active at that time.

1309.   Steelman, Robert. "A Source of Some Early Moravian Chorale
        Melodies." *Moravian Music Foundation Bulletin* 21/2 (1976):
        7-9.

1310.   Stoudt, John J. "The Pennsylvania Christmas Hymn of 1742."
        Pennsylvania History 22 (1955): 69-73.

        Concerning Bethlehem, Pa.

1311.   Strauss, Barbara. "The Concert Life of the Collegium
        Musicum, Nazareth, 1796-1845." *Moravian Music Foundation
        Bulletin* 21/1 (Spring-Summer 1976): 2-7.

        Reviews previous literature and includes a concert program
dated October 28, 1796.

1312.   Walters, Raymond. "Bach at Bethlehem, Pennsylvania."
        Musical Quarterly 21/2 (April 1935): 179-89.

        Although the article is primarily on the Bach Choir at
Bethlehem, the author includes some information on the 18th-century
Moravian's love for European composers' works.

1313.   Walters, Raymond. *The Bethlehem Bach Choir: An Historical
        and Interpretive Sketch.* Boston: Houghton Mifflin Co.,
        1918. Reprint, New York: AMS Press, 1971. xi, 289p.

        Includes 10 chapters. Although this work deals primarily
with the Bach Choir and Moravian music of the 19th century, Walters
does discuss music of 18th-century Bethlehem, Pa. He utilizes
original sources, but fails to cite locations and precise
information for identifying them. Includes a facsimile of the 1811
Bethlehem score of Franz Joseph Haydn's *Creation*.

1314.   Walters, Raymond. "From Pioneer Days to the Era of Steel: A
        Sketch of Bethlehem's Musical History." *Musical Courier*
        74/20 (1917): 38-40.

        Brief information on the music of the Moravians.

1315.   Weidman, Wanda.   "The Moravian Church's Contribution to
        Music."   *Dissonance* 7/1 (1975): 16-24.

1316.   Weinlick, John R.   "Moravian Music a Way of Life."   *Moravian
        Music Foundation Bulletin* 14/2 (Spring 1970): 1-5.

        An introduction based on Rufus A. Grider's *Historical Notes
on Music in Bethlehem, Pennsylvania, from 1741 to 1871* (see entry
1231).

1317.   Williams, Henry L.   "The Development of the Moravian Hymnal."
        Transactions of the Moravian Historical Society 18 (1962):
        239-66.

1318.   Wolf, Jean K. and Eugene K. Wolf.   "Musical Staff-Liners at
        Old Salem: A Unique Treasure."   *Moravian Music Journal* 28/2
        (Summer 1983): 28-30; 28/4 (Winter 1983): 76.

        Discusses extant staff-liners and the value they have in
providing information on the music of the Moravians.   Photographs.

<u>Presbyterians</u>

The following bibliography is of interest:

1319.   Trinterud, Leonard J.   *A Bibliography of American
        Presbyterianism during the Colonial Period.*   Philadelphia:
        Presbyterian Historical Society, 1968.   Unpaginated.

        Includes 1,129 numbered entries.   Printed sources based, in
part, on Evans' *American Bibliography* (see entry 45).   Full imprint
data based on the Readex micro-cards with Evans numbers cited.   A
number of items not found in Evans are included.   The index and
cross-references do not cite items that refer to music, although
John Tufts and Thomas Walter are indexed.   There is some overlap
between Hixon (see entry 99) and Heard (see entry 97).   Examples of
items that refer to music are nos. 649 and 850-54.

1320.   Doughty, Gavin Lloyd.   "The History and Development of Music
in the United Presbyterian Church in the United States of
America."   Ph.D. dissertation, University of Iowa, 1966.
421p.   UM 66-7196.   *DAI* 27/5 (November 1966): 1393-94-A.

A history of the Presbyterian Church from 1800, including
the development of psalmody and hymnody, and a consideration of
American hymn and tune writers.

1321.   Hinke, William J.   "The Early German Hymn Books of the
Reformed Church in the United States."   *Journal of the
Presbyterian Historical Society* 4/4 (December 1907): 147-
61.

Includes background and short sketch of the principal
publications starting with the first Presbyterian hymnbook
publication, *Neu-vermehrt-und vollständiger Gesang-Buch* (Germantown:
Christopher Saur, 1753).

1322.   Martin, Raymond Jones.   "The Transition from Psalmody to
Hymnody in Southern Presbyterianism, 1753-1901."   S.M.D.
dissertation, Union Theological Seminary, 1963.   173p.   UM
63-7852.   *DAI* 24/6 (December 1963): 2512-12.

The transition was begun by Samuel Davies, and other
English clergymen who introduced Isaac Watts' psalm paraphrases and
hymns to colonial America.   "A real and serious struggle over
psalmody as opposed to hymnody set in."   The author discusses the
ensuing struggle and transition.

1323.   Worner, William F.   "Music in a Rural Church."   *Lancaster
County Historical Society Papers* 34 (1930): 137-38.

On a concert which took place in the Upper Octorara
Presbyterian Church on March 19, 1812.

Quakers

1324.   Carroll, Kenneth L.   "Singing in the Spirit in Early
Quakerism."   *Quaker History* 73/1 (Spring 1984): 1-13.

Contrary to the popular notion that the Quakers did not
allow the practice of music among their following, the author
presents evidence that in New York and New England singing did
occur.

Schwenkfelders

1325.   Furcha, Edward J.   "Schwenckfelder Hymns and Theology."
        Mennonite Quarterly Review 46 (1972): 280-89.

1326.   Gottschall, Robert J.   "Christopher Schultz and
        Schwenckfelder Hymnology."   *Schwenckfeldiana* 1/1 (1940):
        33-37.

1327.   Kriebel, Howard Wiegner.   *The Schwenkfelders in Pennsylvania:
        A Historical Sketch.*   Lancaster: Pennsylvania-German
        Society, 1904.   Reprint, New York: AMS Press, 1971.   xiv,
        232p.

        Discusses hymnology of the group and musical elements in
public worship.

1328.   Seipt, Allen A.   *Schwenkfelder Hymnology and the Sources of
        the First Schwenkfelder Hymnbook Printed in America.*
        Philadelphia: American German Press, 1909.   Reprint, New
        York: AMS Press, 1971.   112p.

        A list of manuscripts and printed hymnbooks, with
information on George Weiss of Philadelphia.   Includes information
on *Neu-Eingerichtetes Gesang-Buch*, the first Schwenkfelder hymnbook
printed in American in 1762.

Shakers

The following reference works and collections are noteworthy:

1329. Pike, Kermit J. *A Guide to Shaker Manuscripts in the Library of the Western Reserve Historical Society: With an Inventory of Its Shaker Photographs.* Cleveland: The Society, 1974. xiii, 159p.

See also entry 212.

1330. Richmond, Mary L. *Shaker Literature: A Bibliography.* Hancock, Mass.: Shaker Community, 1977. 2 vols.

Includes 3,986 entries. A significant publication. Volume 1 lists books, pamphlets, broadsides, and periodical articles by the Shakers; items in volume 2 are about the Shakers. Each entry is fully annotated and is arranged alphabetically under types of materials. Included is a section on "Music Leaflets"; yet other music items are found in the title and joint author index.

1331. *Shaker Collection, 1723-1952.* Ann Arbor, Mich.: UMI Research Collection, 19- . Manuscripts; microfilm; 123 reels. 35 mm. Printed materials: 1,187 microfiches; 105 x 148 mm. With *The Shaker Collection of the Western Reserve Historical Society: A Reel List to the Manuscripts and a Short Title List of the Printed Materials Contained in the Microform Collection.* Ed. by Marie T. Stefani.

Included are "official documents, correspondence, financial records, journals, testimonies and sermons, music, photographs, and inspired writings." The printed section includes books, pamphlets, and some 25 books about the Shakers.

1332. Thomason, Jean Healan. *Shaker Manuscript Hymnals from South Union, Kentucky.* Bowling Green: Kentucky Folklore Society, 1967. v, 56p.

Discusses 15 manuscript hymnals in the library of Western Kentucky University.

1333. *Western Reserve Historical Society Shaker Collection.* Sanford, N.C.: Microfilming Corporation of America, 1977. 1,186 microfiches; 11 x 15.

Includes 820 monographs, 420 broadsides, 2 periodicals, and a number of manuscript materials representing a broad spectrum of Shaker communal life during the 1780s to the 1920s, including religious practices, music, and other cultural aspects. A short title list of the materials in print is provided in Mary Richmond's *Shaker Literature: A Bibliography* (see entry 1330).

1334.　Andrews, Edward D.　"Shaker Songs." *Musical Quarterly* 23/4 (October 1937): 491–508.

Includes historical background of the Shakers. Musical examples.

1335.　Christenson, Donald E.　"A History of the Early Shakers and Their Music." *Hymn* 39/1 (January 1988): 17–22.

Includes biographical information on Ann Lee, founder of the sect, and information on the establishment of the communities in America. Illustration.

1336.　*A Collection of Millenial Hymns, Adapted to the Present Order of the Church.* Canterbury, N.H.: Printed in the United Society, 1847. Reprint, New York: AMS Press, 1975. 200p.

1337.　Cook, Harold E.　*Shaker Music: A Manifestation of American Folk Culture.* Lewisburg, Pa.: Bucknell University Press, 1973. 312p.

Based, in part, on the author's dissertation (Western Reserve University, 1947). Includes a historical background of the Shakers, development of their hymnody and notation, discussion of tunebooks, musical practice, and performance of the music. Also includes a list of the printed and manuscript hymnals held in the Western Reserve Historical Society in Cleveland. Musical examples, illustrations, and index.

1338.　Evans, Frederick William.　*Shaker Music: Inspirational Hymns and Melodies Illustrative of the Resurrection Life and Testimony of the Shakers.* Albany: Weed, Parsons and Co., 1875. Reprint, New York: AMS Press, 1974. 67p.

Includes Shaker songs in 2-4 parts. See also Evans' *Shaker Music: Original Inspirational Hymns and Songs Illustrative of the Resurrection Life and Testimony of the Shakers* (New York: W.A. Pond, 1884).

1339. Hall, Roger L. "Shaker Hymnody: An American Communal Tradition." *Hymn* 27/1 (January 1976): 22-29.

Discusses the first Shaker hymnal, *Millennial Praises* (Hancock, Mass., 1813). Originally appeared in *Journal of Church Music* 17/8 (1975), pp. 2-6.

1340. Patterson, Daniel W. "A Ballad by Elder Issachar Bates." *Shaker Quarterly* 2 (1962): 60-66.

1341. Patterson, Daniel W. "Shaker Music." *Communal Societies* 2 (Autumn 1982): 53-64.

1342. Patterson, Daniel W. "The Shakers' 'Sundry Strange' Tunes." *Shaker Quarterly* 1 (1961): 4-9.

1343. Patterson, Daniel W. "Word, Song, and Motion: Instruments of Celebration among Protestant Radicals in Early Nineteenth-Century America." In *Celebrations: Studies in Festivity and Ritual*. Ed. by Victor Turner. Washington, D.C.: Smithsonian Institution, 1982, pp. 220-30.

Brief survey mentioning the Shakers, but also Baptists and tunebooks. Illustrations.

1344. Smith, Harold Vaughan. "Oliver C. Hampton and Other Shaker Teacher-Musicians of Ohio and Kentucky." D.A. dissertation, Ball State University, 1981. 255p. UM 82-01910. *DAI* 42/8 (February 1982): 3344-A.

Includes a historical background of the Shakers and an appendix having 30 musical examples transcribed by the author.

1345.   Terri, Salli.   "The Gift of Shaker Music."   *Music Educators Journal* 62/1 (September 1975): 22-35.

A survey that includes facsimiles, musical examples, and other illustrations.

Spanish Mission Music

The following bibliographies are noteworthy:

1346.   Beers, Henry Putney.   *Spanish and Mexican Records of the American Southwest: A Bibliographical Guide to Archive and Manuscript Sources.*   Tucson: University of Arizona Press, 1979.   493p.

An excellent means for identifying manuscript sources for various missions.

1347.   Keim, Betty.   "Comparative Study of the Music of the Indians and the Spanish in Arizona and New Mexico: A Selective Bibliography."   *Current Musicology* 19 (1975): 117-21.

1348.   Bakkegard, B.M.   "Music in Arizona Before 1912."   *Journal of Research in Music Education* 8/1 (Spring 1960): 67-74.

Includes a brief section on "Music in the Indian Missions."

1349.   Benson, Norman A.   "Music in the California Missions: 1602-1848."   *Student Musicologists at Minnesota* 3 (1968-69): 128-67; 4 (1970-71): 104-25.

1350.   Boeringer, James.   "Early American Church Music in California."   *Journal of Church Music* 18/5 (May 1976): 2-4.

Brief introduction to the missions and padres.   Facsimiles.

1351.   Crouch, Margaret L.   "An Annotated Bibliography and
        Commentary Concerning Mission Music of Alta California from
        1769 to 1834: In Honor of the American Bicentennial."
        Current Musicology 22 (1976): 88-99.

        A short essay discussing mission music in general, and the
mission period at Alta California from 1769 to 1834.   The
bibliography is recommended for its citations not easily identified
elsewhere.

1352.   Cudworth, Charles.   "The Californian Missions: 1769-1969."
        Musical Times 110/1512 (February 1969): 194-96.

        A brief introduction to the missions and their musical
practices.

1353.   Da Silva, Owen Francis.   *Mission Music of California: A
        Collection of Old California Mission Hymns and Masses.*   Los
        Angeles, 1941.   Reprint, New York: Da Capo Press, 1978.
        xv, 132p.

        Includes an extended essay on mission music and the
following musicians, in this order: Junipero Serra, Fermin de
Lasuen, Estevan Tapis, Felipe Arroyo de la Cuesta, Florencio Ibaniz,
Juan Sancho, José Vinals, Narciso Durán, and Pedro Font.   Included
are transcriptions of a number of compositions.   Facsimiles and
index.

1354.   Geiger, Maynard.   "Harmonious Notes in Spanish California."
        Southern California Quarterly 57 (1975): 243-50.

        A description of Fray Durán who taught Indians singing and
instruments during the early 19th century.

1355.   Göllner, Theodor.   "Two Polyphonic Passions from California's
        Mission Period." *Yearbook for Inter-American Musical
        Research* 6 (1970): 67-76.

        Probably written during the latter part of the 18th
century.   Includes an analysis of the music and notation.

1356. Hahn, Henry. "Music of the Early North American West."
       Pacific Historian 15 (1971): 25-38.

       Discusses California missions.

1357. Halpin, Joseph. "Musical Activities and Ceremonies at
       Mission Santa Clara de Asís." *California Historical
       Quarterly* 50/1 (March 1971): 35-42.

       Father José Viader was conductor of the small orchestra at
the mission. Also discusses Father Narciso Durán, who was at the
mission San José de Guadalupe. Includes a facsimile page from the
"Gloria In Excelsis Deo."

1358. Hartzell, Lawrence W. "Early Organs in the American
       Southwest." *Tracker* 23/1 (Fall 1978): 9-11, 21.

       Organs in the missions in New Mexico.

1359. Higgins, Ardis O. "Revival of Early California Mission
       Music." *Music: The A.G.O./R.C.C.O. Magazine* 10/1 (1976):
       28-31.

1360. Higginson, J. Vincent. *Hymnody in the American Indian
       Missions.* Papers of the Hymn Society of America, 18.   New
       York: Hymn Society of America, 1954.   39p.

       Includes a brief section on the music of the California
missions.   Also published in *Catholic Choirmaster* 40 (1954), pp.
161-76.

1361. Joan of Arc, Sister M. "Mission Music of the Southwest."
       Catholic Choirmaster 26 (1940): 102-04.

1362. Laine, Juliette. "Music in Early California." *Music Journal*
       14/10 (December 1956): 20-24.

       Includes only a few comments regarding mission music.

1363. McGill, Anna Blanche. "Old Mission Music." *Musical Quarterly* 24/2 (April 1938): 186-93.

Includes general information on Spanish missions in what is now Texas and New Mexico. Musical examples.

1364. Rouse, Father Warren. "Mission Music of California." *Musart* 14/3 (1962): 4-5, 34-36; 14/5 (1962): 6, 48-49.

1365. Shaver, Lillie T. "Spanish Mission Music." *Papers and Proceedings of the Music Teachers National Association* 12 (1919): 204-08.

1366. Spell, Lota. "Music Teaching in New Mexico in the 17th Century." *New Mexico Historical Review* II (1927): 27-36.

One of the first articles on music of the missions in New Mexico.

1367. Spiess, Lincoln B. "Benavides and Church Music in New Mexico in the Early 17th Century." *Journal of the American Musicological Society* 17/2 (Summer 1964): 144-56.

A significant article that reviews the published literature on music and New Mexico to 1964. Discusses music and instruments of the mission music during the 17th century.

1368. Spiess, Lincoln B. "Church Music in Seventeenth-Century New Mexico." *New Mexico Historical Review* 40/1 (January 1965): 5-21.

An excellent article discussing missionary music, instruments, the liturgical books in use, including 2 missals dating from ca. 1690 and 1726, and others. Musical examples.

1369. Spiess, Lincoln B. "Instruments in the Missions of New Mexico: 1598-1680." In *Essays in Musicology: A Birthday Offering for Willi Apel*. Ed. by Hans Tischler. Bloomington: Indiana University, 1968, pp. 131-36.

Includes citations of a number of excellent general works
for the study of mission music in New Mexico.

1370.   Stevenson, Robert.   "California Music 1806-1824; Russian
        Reportage." *Inter-American Music Review* 4/2 (Spring-Summer
        1982): 59-64.

        Concerns information on a California mission reported by a
Russian who visited California in the early 19th century.   Musical
examples.

1371.   Summers, William.   "The Organs of Hispanic California."
        Music: The A.G.O./R.C.C.O. Magazine 10/11 (1976): 50-51.

1372.   Summers, William.   "Spanish Music in California, 1769-1840, a
        Reassessment." In *IMS Report, Berkely, 1977*.   Kassel:
        Bärenreiter, 1981, pp. 360-80.

        Discusses Spanish music brought to California by Franciscan
missionaries.   The compositions, some of which were previously
unknown, range from 2-part works to extended masses.

1373.   Warkentin, Larry.   "The Rise and Fall of Indian Music in the
        California Missions." *Latin American Music Review* 2/1
        (Spring-Summer 1981): 45-65.

        Discusses the music of the Spanish Catholic tradition as
utilized by the Indians in the Franciscan missionaries between 1769
and 1846.   Mentions the choirs and instruments used.

1374.   Whitinger, Julius Edward.   "Hymnody of the Early American
        Indian Missions." Ph.D. dissertation, Catholic University
        of America, 1971.   344p.   UM 71-25237.   *DAI* 32/4 (October
        1971): 2126-A.

        Discusses the work of Spanish Jesuits in the Southwest in
establishing music schools, choirs, and instrumental ensembles as
part of their Indian missionary activity, and French Jesuits in the
Great Lakes basin and their use of music as an instructional aid.

Unitarian

For an introduction to the history of Unitarianism and music in early America, refer to Walter Klauss' article, "Unitarian Universalist Church," in *The New Grove Dictionary of American Music*, vol. 4, pp. 436-37 (see entry 30).

The following bibliography is worthy of note:

1375.   Foote, Henry W.   "A Descriptive Catalogue of American Unitarian Hymn Books." *Proceedings of the Unitarian Historical Society* 6/1 (1938): 31-49.

Wissahickon Mystics

1376.   Bornemann, Robert.   "Johannes Kelpius, Mystic Hymn Writer." *Journal of Church Music* 18/6 (June 1976): 13-14.

Introduces Johannes Kelpius (1673-1708) and his hymnbook.

1377.   Hess, Albert G.   "Observations on 'The Lamenting Voice of the Hidden Love.'" *Journal of the American Musicological Society* 5/3 (Fall 1952): 211-23.

A significant article for the study of Johannes Kelpius and the Wissahickon group. "The Lamenting Voice" is a manuscript of tunes whose composer and scribe is unknown. Contains, possibly, the earliest known "practical example of a continuo realization in mensural notation."

1378.   Hess, Albert G.   "Observations on the MS 'The Lamenting Voice of the Hidden Love,' (Ac. 189, Historical Society of Pennsylvania)." *Journal of the American Musicological Society* 4/3 (Fall 1951): 274-75.

Abstract of a paper presented at a meeting of the Western New York Chapter of the AMS in Ithaca on April 28, 1951.

1379. Sachse, Julius Friedrich. *The German Pietists of Provincial
        Pennsylvania, 1694-1708.* Philadelphia: Printed for the
        author, 1895. Reprint, New York: AMS Press, 1970. xviii,
        504p.

        An early yet principal work for the study of Johannes
Kelpius and the Wissahickon Mystics. Discusses the Kelpius
manuscript hymn book, "The Lamenting Voice of the Hidden Love"
(1765). Facsimile.

1380. Seidensticker, Oswald. "The Hermits of the Wissahickon."
        Pennsylvania Magazine of History and Biography 11/4 (1887):
        427-41.

        Discusses the original members of the group that arrived in
the colonies, and a translation of a letter describing their voyage.
Written by a companion of Johannes Kelpius, the letter is dated
August 7, 1694, and mentions hymn singing and the use of instruments
on board ship.

Printing and Publishing

For an excellent introduction to this subject, refer to "Publishing
and Printing of Music" by Donald W. Krummel in *The New Grove
Dictionary of American Music*, vol. 3, pp. 650-54 (see entry 30).

The following bibliography is worthy of note:

1381. Winans, Robert B. *A Descriptive Checklist of Book Catalogues
        Separately Printed in America 1693-1800.* Worcester,
        Mass.: American Antiquarian Society, 1981. xxxi, 207p.

        Includes 285 numbered entries. A useful tool for
identifying catalogs issued by "booksellers, publishers, book
auctioneers, circulating libraries, social libraries, college
libraries, and private libraries." Provides a means of identifying
music and books on music, psalms, hymns, etc. and where they were
published and likely sold. Begin a search under the heading "Music"
in the index where additional cross-references are provided for
other musical topics. See also "Psalmody." Each entry includes

full imprint data with references to library holdings, and other descriptive commentary. The earliest cited item herein, which includes music, is dated 1786.

1382.   Brown, H. Glenn, and Maude O. Brown. "A Directory of the Book-Arts and Book Trade in Philadelphia to 1820, Including Painters and Engravers." *Bulletin of the New York Public Library* 53 (1949): 211-26, 290-98, 339-47, 387-401, 447-58, 492-503, 564-73, 615-22; 54 (1950): 25-37, 89-92, 123-45.

Includes music engravers and publishers.

1383.   Carey, John Thomas. "The American Lithograph from Its Inception to 1865 with Biographical Considerations of Twenty Lithographers and a Check List of Their Works." Ph.D. dissertation, Ohio State University, 1954. 466p. UM 59-2547. *DAI* 20/2 (August 1959): 634-36.

Although this is a general study of lithography, many lithographers worked with music sheet covers. Mentions Henry Stone, who worked in Washington, D.C. in 1823.

1384.   Crawford, Richard and D.W. Krummel. "Early American Printing and Engraving." In *Printing and Society in America*. Ed. by William Leonard Joyce, and others. Worcester, Mass.: American Antiquarian Society, 1983, pp. 186-227.

An excellent comprehensive article that includes information on the use and impact of imported music type, as well as the beginning of the sheet music industry. Also discusses early American tunebook production.

1385.   Demarest, Alison. "Paul Revere's Music Engraving." *Music Journal* 22/3 (March 1964): 58-59, 89.

A discussion of the collaboration between Paul Revere, engraver, and Josiah Flagg, compiler, on *A Collection of the Best Psalm Tunes* (Boston, 1764). Facsimiles.

1386.   Dolmetsch, Christopher L.   "German Printing Among North
           Carolina Moravians." *Moravian Music Journal* 29/4 (Winter
           1984): 93-98.

         Discusses various printers, including Lemuel Bingham,
Francis Coupee (1773-1814), Philo White, and others.   Facsimiles.

1387.   Duncan, Barbara.   "American Sheet Music in the Early 19th
           Century." *Bulletin of the American Musicological Society*
           (1937): 16-17.

         Abstract of a paper read at a meeting of the Western New
York Chapter of the AMS, October 30, 1937.

1388.   Epstein, Dena J.   "Music Publishing in the Age of Piracy: The
           Board of Trade and Its Catalogue." *Notes* 31/1 (September
           1974): 7-29.

         A revised version of the introduction in the reprint
edition of *Complete Catalogue of Sheet Music and Musical Works, 1870*
(N.Y.: Da Capo Press, 1973).   Also includes information on copyright
during the early 1800s.

1389.   Fisher, William Arms.   *One Hundred and Fifty Years of Music
           Publishing in the United States: An Historical Sketch with
           Special Reference to the Pioneer Publisher, Oliver Ditson
           Company, Inc., 1783-1933.*   Boston: Oliver Ditson, 1933.
           Reprint, St. Clair Shores, Mich.: Scholarly Press, 1977.
           xvi, 146p.

         General survey worth examining; not all sources are
provided, however.   Encompasses the 17th-19th centuries.   Topics
include the New England tradition, music publishers of Philadelphia,
Baltimore, and New York, and "Early Boston Book and Music-Shops."
Facsimiles of newspaper advertisements and music.

1390.   Gates, J. Terry.   "Samuel Gerrish, Publisher to the 'Regular
           Singing' Movement in 1720s New England." *Notes* 45/1
           (September 1988): 15-22.

         Includes only a little biographical information, but more
on Gerrish's role in the Boston singing movement.   Also has a number

of userful tables, including a list of printers and booksellers in the Boston area and a list of extant music publications, 1700-50.

1391.   Grimes, Calvin Bernard.   "American Music Periodicals, 1819-1852: Music Theory and Musical Thought in the United States."   Ph.D. dissertation, University of Iowa, 1974. 312p.   UM 75-13756.   *DAI* 35/12 (June 1975): 7943-A.

Discusses 34 literary musical magazines for the period under study.   The first such work was the *Literary and Musical Magazine* (1819).

1392.   Holibaugh, Ralph W. and Donald W. Krummel.   "Documentation of Music Publishing in the U.S.A. in the 19th Century." Twelfth International Congress of Music Libraries, Archives and Documentation Centres Cambridge/England. 3-8 August. *Fontes Artis Musicae* 28/1-2 (January-June 1981): 94-97

Discusses music publishing in America from 1698 to 1950. Includes a table of "estimated production of musical editions in the U.S.A."   Includes an excellent survey of reference works available for identifying music published during the 18th-19th centuries.

1393.   Howe, Mabel Almy.   *Music Publishers in New York City before 1850*.   New York: New York Public Library, 1917.   18p.

Lists some 48 publishing firms, including engravers, music printers, and dealers from 1776 on.   Cites names and addresses.

1394.   Jackson, George Pullen.   "Buckwheat Notes."   *Boletin Latino-Americano* 5 (1939).

Originally a paper read at the Inter-American Conference on Music held at the Library of Congress, and conducted by the United States State Department in October 1939.   (Refer also to entry 894.)

1395.   Johnson, H. Earle.   "Music Publishing in New England."   In *Richard S. Hill: Tributes from Friends*.   Comp. and ed. by Carol June Bradley and James B. Coover.   Detroit Studies in Music Bibliography, 58.   Detroit: Information Coordinators, 1987, pp. 199-210.

A general discussion starting with the publication of the *Bay Psalm Book* in 1640. Focuses on psalmody, popular songs, broadsides, and discusses Joseph Tinker Buckingham, Gottlieb Graupner, and John Tufts.

1396. Kroeger, Karl D. "Isaiah Thomas as a Music Publisher." *Proceedings of the American Antiquarian Society* 86/2 (1976): 321-41.

1397. Krohn, Ernst C. *Music Publishing in St. Louis.* Completed and ed. by J. Bunker Clark. Bibliographies in American Music, 11. Warren, Mich.: Harmonie Park Press for the College Music Society, 1988. xxiii, 126p.

An excellent introduction, including information on early publications such as *The Missouri Harmony* (1820).

1398. Krummel, Donald W. "Counting Every Star; Or, Historical Statistics on Music Publishing in the United States (American Music Bibliogrpahy, IV)." *Yearbook for Inter-American Musical Research* 10 (1974): 175-93.

1399. Krummel, Donald W. "Graphic Analysis: Its Application to Early American Engraved Music." *Notes* 16/2 (March 1959): 213-33.

Discusses musical characteristics for determining the date of a manuscript. Publishers discussed include George Blake, George Willig, and included are a number of musical plates.

1400. Krummel, Donald W. *Guide for Dating Early Published Music: A Manual of Bibliographical Practices.* Hackensack, N.J.: Joseph Boonin, 1974. 268p.

Arranged by country, the section under the United States includes a list of the major publishers for the 1790s and early 1800s and plate numbers used by them. Also included is a short essay on copyright practices at that time. Facsimiles of title pages of sheet music.

1401.   Krummel, Donald W.   "Philadelphia Music Engraving and
         Publishing, 1800-1820: A Study in Bibliography and Cultural
         History." Ph.D. dissertation, University of Michigan,
         1958.   431p.   UM 58-7749.   *DAI* 19/6 (December 1958): 1394.

         "The purpose of this study is to reconstruct the catalogues
of Philadelphia publishers of engraved music between 1800 and 1820,
and to relate their music to the cultural environment they served."
An appendix includes a list of 1,200 publications.   Publishers
examined include George E. Blake, George Willig, John Aitken, and
Allyn Bacon.

1402.   Lippencott, Margaret E.   "Dearborn's Musical 'Scheme.'"   *New-
         York Historical Society Quarterly Bulletin* 25 (1941): 134-
         42.

         Benjamin Dearborn's book was published in 1785 using music
fonts.

1403.   Myers, Gordon.   "Music in the *Massachusetts Magazine*."   *Music
         Journal* 28/9A (November 1970): 26-27, 42-43.

         The *Massachusetts Magazine* was begun by Isaiah Thomas in
January 1789 and was published until 1796.   Myers discusses the
music that was published, including works by Hans Gram, William
Selby, Samuel Holyoke, Horatio Garnett, Elias Mann, and others.
Facsimile.

1404.   Osterhout, Paul R.   "Andrew Wright: Northampton Music
         Printer."   *American Music* 1/4 (Winter 1983): 5-26.

         Discusses music printing in New England from 1698-1805.
Includes a list of "Andrew Wright's Musical Imprints" from 1797-
1812.   Cites Evans (see entry 45) and Shaw (see entry 73) numbers.

1405.   Priest, Daniel B.   *American Sheet Music with Prices: A Guide
         to Collecting Sheet Music from 1775 to 1975*.   Des Moines,
         Iowa: Wallace-Homestead, 1978.   82p.

         Includes a brief history of American sheet music with only
scanty data on music before 1820.   Illustrations of sheet music

covers date from a later period and have, for the most part, been previously shown in other sources.

1406. Shipton, Clifford K. *Isaiah Thomas, Printer, Patriot and Philanthropist, 1749-1831.* Rochester, N.Y.: Hart, 1948. xii, 94p.

1407. Sommer, Frank H. "German Language Books, Periodicals, and Manuscripts." In *Arts of the Pennsylvania Germans.* Ed. by Scott T. Swank. New York: W.W. Norton, 1983, pp. 265-304.

Primarily a historical view with examples of printing and manuscripts in Pennsylvania in the eighteenth century. The author discusses various collections of music from the Ephrata Cloister. `Included is a facsimile of the title page of John Dotterer's "Noten Buchlein" handwritten in Lehigh County in 1800. The author also discusses briefly Moravian music at Bethlehem, with a facsimile of "Harmonische Melodeyen Büchlein," Bucks County, 1813.

1408. Stapleton, Ammon. "Early German Musical Publications in Pennsylvania." *Pennsylvania-German* 7 (1906): 174-76.

1409. Strunk, Oliver. "Early Music Publishing in the United States." *Papers of the Bibliographical Society of America* 31 (1937): 176-79.

Dance

The following bibliographies are noteworthy:

1410. Forbes, Fred R., Jr. *Dance: An Annotated Bibliography, 1965-1982.* New York: Garland Publishing, 1986. xii, 261p.

1411. Keller, Kate Van Winkle. "A Bibliography of Eighteenth Century American Social Dance." *Country Dance and Song* 18 (June 1988): 9-22.

Includes a list of books, pamphlets, broadsides, and other sources before 1801 that contain specific dance figures. Includes brief imprint data, sources of information, names of dancing masters, and an excellent bibliography of 18th-century American social dance, with library locations and other sources.

1412.   Shipton, Clifford K.   "American Dance Bibliography to 1820." *Proceedings of the American Antiquarian Society* 59/2 (1949): 217-20.

1413.   Aldrich, Elizabeth.   "A Rare American Dance Manual: Saltator's *A Treatise on Dancing* Boston, 1802."   In *Proceedings of the Ninth Annual Conference Society of Dance History Scholars.*   Riverside: University of California for Dance History Scholars, 1986, pp. 228-41.

Saltator was an early dancing master active in Boston.   In his work, he provides descriptions of the steps necessary to perform cotillions and country dances from that period.

1414.   Barzel, Ann.   "European Dance Teachers in the United States." *Dance Index* 3 (1944): 56-100.

Discusses dance teachers from the 1700s on.

1415.   Bond, Chrystelle T.   "A Chronicle of Dance in Baltimore 1780-1814." *Dance Perspectives* 66 (Summer 1976): 1-49.

A chronology that lists numerous dancing masters and is based on notices from newspapers.   Facsimiles.

1416.   DeLaban, Juana.   "The Dance on the New York Stage from 1750 to 1821."   Ph.D. dissertation, Yale University, 1947.

1417.   Emery, Lynne F.   *Black Dance from 1619 to Today.*   2nd ed. Princeton, N.J.: Princeton Book Co., 1988.   xii, 397p.

1418.   Gardner, John.   "Contradances and Cotillions: Dancing in
              Eighteenth-Century Delaware."   *Delaware History* 22/1
              (Spring-Summer 1986): 39-47.

1419.   Keller, Kate Van Winkle and Ralph Sweet.   *A Choice Selection
              of American Country Dances of the Revolutionary Era, 1775-
              1795.*   New York: Country Dance and Song Society, 1976.
              52p.

1420.   Marks, Joseph E., III.   *America Learns to Dance: A Historical
              Study of Dance Education in America before 1900.*   New York:
              Exposition Press, 1957.   Reprint, New York: Dance Horizons,
              1976.   133p.

        Discusses the Puritan attitude towards dancing as compared
to dancing in the South.

1421.   Mayo, Margot.   "Dancing in New York City, 1687-1887."   *New
              York Folklore Quarterly* 10 (1954): 85-94.

1422.   Mayo, Margot.   "Directory of New York Dancing Masters."   *New
              York Folklore Quarterly* 10 (1954): 189-93.

1423.   Moore, Lillian.   "Ballet Music in Washington's Time."   *Etude*
              74/7 (September 1956): 17, 47, 51.

        Includes Boston, Charleston, and Philadelphia.   Individuals
discussed include Pierre Landrin Duport, Alexander Reinagle, and
Rayner Taylor.

1424.   Moore, Lillian.   "The Duport Mystery."   *Dance Perspectives* 7
              (1960): 1-103.

        A thorough study of a major dancing master and
choreographer of social and theatrical dance active 1790-1834.

1425.   Moore, Lillian.   "John Durang, the First American Dancer."
              Dance Index 1 (1942): 120-39.

John Durang (c. 1804) was active in New York during the post-Revolutionary period.

1426.   Morrison, James E. *Twenty Four Early American Country
        Dances, Cotillions & Reels for the Year 1976.* New York:
        Country Dance Society, 1976. 72p.

        An excellent collection of dances from the colonial period.

1427.   Morrison, James E. "Two Centuries of Dance in Albemarle
        [Virginia]." *Magazine of Albemarle County History* 42
        (1984): 23-39.

1428.   Valenchik, Cathy. "Dancing Their Way Through a War: The
        Effect of the American War for Independence on Colonial
        Ball." In *Proceedings of the Ninth Annual Conference
        Society of Dance History Scholars.* Riverside: University
        of California for Dance History Scholars, 1986, pp. 242-54.

        Includes a number of references to dance and concerts in
early sources, such as travel journals and diaries, for the period
after 1769.

1429.   Van Cleef, Joy. "Rural Felicity: Social Dance in 18th-
        Century Connecticut." *Dance Perspectives* 65 (Spring 1976):
        1-45.

        An excellent introduction to the subject. Includes a list
of "Dance Titles in New England Manuscripts." Illustrations.

1430.   Winter, Marian Hannah. "American Theatrical Dancing from
        1750 to 1800." *Musical Quarterly* 24/1 (January 1938): 58-
        73.

        An excellent article for its valuable information and
sources provided. Includes dancing and ballad operas and other
theatrical entertainments, and performers in most major cities.

1431. Wynne, Shirley. "From Ballet to Ballroom: Dance in the
        Revolutionary Era." *Dance Scope* 10/1 (Fall-Winter 1975-
        76): 65-73.

      A brief introduction with references to dance manuals of
the period, specific dances, and Theobald Hackett, dancing master.

Theater

For a concise introduction to opera in colonial America, refer to
Susan L. Porter's "Ballad Opera" in *The New Grove Dictionary of
American Music*, vol. 1, pp. 119-20 (see entry 30).

The following reference works are recommended:

1432. Bailey, Claudia Jean. *A Guide to Reference and Bibliography
        for Theatre Research.* Columbus: Ohio State University
        Libraries, 1983. 2nd ed. xi, 149p.

      Includes "a basic list of both general and specialized
sources of reference and bibliographical information." Divided into
2 principal parts: General Reference and Theatre and Drama.
Includes a number of theater sources that pertain to early opera in
America. Author-title index.

1433. Bergquist, G. William. *Three Centuries of English and
        American Plays, a Checklist. England: 1500-1800, United
        States: 1714-1830.* New York: Hafner, 1963. xii, 281p.

      Includes ballad operas performed in colonial America and an
illustration of the title page of Andrew Barton's *The
Disappointment: or, The Force of Credulity* (1796).

1434. Mattfeld, Julius. *A Handbook of American Operatic Premieres,
        1731-1962.* Detroit Studies in Music Bibliography, 5.
        Detroit: Information Coordinators, Inc., 1963. 142p.

      Listed by title, with a composer's index.

1435.   Adler, Dick.   "The Man Who Knew Mozart."   *American Heritage*
        37 (1986): 50-55.

        Discusses Lorenzo Da Ponte, Mozart's librettist, who came
to America in 1805 and introduced Italian opera here by establishing
the Italian Opera House in New York.

1436.   Albrecht, Otto E.   "Opera in Philadelphia, 1800-1830."
        Journal of the American Musicological Society 32/3 (Fall
        1979): 499-515.

        Discusses an assortment of operas and a number of
musicians, including John Bray, Anthony Philip Heinrich, Alexander
Reinagle, and Rayner Taylor.   Includes a list of operas performed in
Philadelphia, 1800-30.

1437.   Anderson, Gillian B.   "'The Temple of Minerva' and Francis
        Hopkinson: A Reappraisal of America's First Poet-Composer."
        Proceedings of the American Philosophical Society 120
        (1976): 166-77.

1438.   Armstrong, W.G.   *A Record of the Opera in Philadelphia.*
        Philadelphia: Porter & Coates, 1884.   Reprint, New York:
        AMS Press, 1976.   274p.

        Although principally a chronological list of operas
performed in Philadelphia for the period 1827-83, there is
information on Benjamin Franklin and early musicians, such as Thomas
Willig, Franklin Peale, and Benjamin Carr.

1439.   Ashbrook, William S., Jr.   "Glimpses of Opera in Boston."
        Opera News 12/21 (March 8, 1948): 9-12, 26-27, 30.

        Discusses key ballad operas performed, beginning with *Love
in a Village* (July 1769).

1440.   Bieber, Albert A.   *American Plays, Poetry and Songsters.*
        New York: Cooper Square, 1963.   103p.

Includes a list of "American verse printed in broadside form" and a list of songsters owned by Bieber. The author's personal comments in the annotations are interesting. No index.

1441.   Bonawitz, Dorothy M. "The History of the Boston Stage from the Beginning to 1810." Ph.D. dissertation, University of Pennsylvania, 1937.

1442.   Bordman, Gerald. *American Musical Theatre: A Chronicle.* New York: Oxford University Press, 1978. viii, 749p.

Includes a brief chapter on theater to 1866, with mention of early productions in Philadelphia and New York, the companies, and composers, including Benjamin Carr, Francis Hopkinson, Peter Markoe, Rayner Taylor, and James Hewitt.

1443.   Brooks, William. "Good Musical Paste: Getting the Acts Together in the Eighteenth Century." In *Musical Theatre in America: Papers and Proceedings of the Conference on the Musical Theatre in America.* Ed. by Glenn Loney. Contributions in Drama and Theatre Studies, 8. Westport, Conn.: Greenwood Press, 1984, pp. 37-58.

Focuses on the nature and function of musical interludes that occurred between the acts of dramatic productions in colonial America. Includes programs for theatrical productions in Boston and Philadelphia.

1444.   Brown, T. Allston. *A History of the New York Stage.* New York: Dodd, Mead, 1903. Reprint, New York: Benjamin Blom, 1964. 3 vols.

Includes a chronological account of performances undertaken at each New York theater, including, for example, information and programs for ballad operas that took place at Lewis Hallam's Nassau Street Theatre, David Douglass' theaters, and the John Street Theater are cited.

1445.   Cline, Julia. "Opera in America, 1735-1850." *Poet Lore* 41 (1930): 239-50.

1446.   Cogdill, John Lindsay. "An Analytical Study of the Development of the American Colonial Theatre." Ph.D. dissertation, University of Denver, 1955. 241p.

1447.   Craven, H.T. "Philadelphia's Operatic History." *Opera News* 12/3 (November 3, 1947): 9-11.

Discusses ballad operas, beginning with Colley Cibber's *Flora, or Hob in the Well* on May 7, 1754.

1448.   Curtis, Mary Julia. "The Early Charleston Stage: 1703-1798." Ph.D. dissertation, Indiana University, 1968. 484p. UM 68-13699. *DAI* 29/4 (October 1968): 1312-13-A.

Discusses the sites and includes descriptions of various playhouses. Also discusses Henry Holt, dancing master, and the Hallam and Douglass companies. Based on primary sources.

1449.   Dircks, Phyllis T. "London's Stepchild Finds a Home." In *Musical Theatre in America: Papers and Proceedings of the Conference on the Musical Theatre in America.* Ed. by Glenn Loney. Contributions in Drama and Theatre Studies, 8. Westport, Conn.: Greenwood Press, 1984, pp. 23-35.

Discusses the beginnings of the burletta in colonial America, with the production of *Midas* in 1769 in Philadelphia.

1450.   Durham, Weldon B. *American Theatre Companies, 1749-1887.* Westport, Conn.: Greenwood Press, 1986. 598p.

A significant work that includes a profile of some 81 theaters, with a chronology of theater companies. Index of personal names and play titles.

1451.   Flusser, Beth. "An 18th-Century Treasure Hunt: A Search for Our Musical Heritage." *Music Clubs Magazine* 53/1 (Autumn 1973): 11, 45.

Mentions some early American landmark works and asks that old music not be discarded.

1452. Glazer, Irvin R. *Philadelphia Theatres, A-Z: A
       Comprehensive, Descriptive Record of 813 Theatres
       Constructed Since 1724.* Westport, Conn.: Greenwood Press,
       1986. 277p.

       Recommended as a useful, quick source for information on
theaters prior to 1820.

1453. Gombert, Karl E. "The First Opera in America, or Who's on
       First." *Music Journal* 39/3 (May-June 1981): 15-17.

       Discusses *Flora, or Hob in the Well*, Andrew Barton's *The
Disappointment: or, The Force of Credulity* (1767), Benjamin Carr's
The Archers; or, The Mountaineers of Switzerland (1796), and other
works.

1454. Green, Elvena Marion. "Theatre and Other Entertainments in
       Savannah, Georgia, from 1810 to 1865." Ph.D. dissertation,
       University of Iowa, 1971. 608p. UM 72-8255. *DAI* 32/9
       (March 1972): 5391-A.

       A chronological study with an index of plays and
playwrights. Provides some information on the lack of adequate
playhouse facilities before 1818 and the effect of the War of 1812
on theatrical productions.

1455. Groth, Howard. "Ballad Opera in America." *Opera Journal* 9/4
       (1976): 3-10.

1456. Henderson, Mary C. "The Theatre and the City: A Study of the
       Evolution of the Theatrical District in the Urbanization of
       New York City." Ph.D. dissertation, New York University,
       1972. 315p. UM 73-11711. *DAI* 33/11 (May 1973): 6499-6500-
       A.

       Includes information on a few 18th-century theaters.

1457. Hitchcock, H. Wiley. "An Early American Melodrama: The
       Indian Princess of J.N. Barker and John Bray." *Notes* 12/3
       (June 1955): 375-88

Written in 1808, it was the first American play produced in London. Hitchcock discusses its musical elements and significance.

1458.   Hoover, Cynthia Adams. "Music in Eighteenth-Century American Theater." *American Music* 2/4 (Winter 1984): 6-18.

Discusses the Thomas Keane and Walter Murray Company and Louis Hallam's Company. Illustrations of American theaters.

1459.   Ireland, Joseph N. *Records of the New York Stage from 1750 to 1860.* New York: T.H. Morrell, 1866. Reprint, New York: Benjamin Blom, 1966; New York: B. Franklin, 1968. 2 vols.

Includes programs and information for 18th-century ballad opera productions in New York.

1460.   Johnson, H. Earle. *Operas on American Subjects.* New York: Coleman-Ross, 1964. 125p.

1461.   King, Clyde Richard. "A History of the Theater in Texas, 1722-1900." Ph.D. dissertation, Baylor University, 1963.

1462.   Krehbiel, Henry Edward. *Chapters of Opera; Being Historical and Critical Observations and Records Concerning the Lyric Drama in New York from Its Earliest Days Down to the Present Time.* 1908. 435p. 3rd ed. New York: Holt, 1911.

A substantial work that includes an introductory chapter on ballad opera in New York, including illustrations of early playhouses.

1463.   Krummel, Donald W. "The Displaced Prima Donna: Mrs. Oldmixon in America." *Musical Times* 108/1487 (January 1967): 25, 27-28.

Mrs. Oldmixon's debut in America occurred on May 14, 1793 in Philadelphia. She performed there until 1805, and also visited Baltimore, Boston, Charleston, and New York.

1464.   Kussrow, Van Carl, Jr.   "On with the Show: A Study of Public
          Arguments in Favor of Theatre in America during the
          Eighteenth Century. . . ."   Ph.D. dissertation, Indiana
          University, 1959.   405p.   UM 60-829.   *DAI* 20/10 (April
          1960): 4217.

          Based on "prologues and epilogues to stage performances,
books, essays, pamphlets, letters-to-the-editor, verses, editorials,
petitions, memorials, playbills and other theatrical advertisements,
speeches, and the like."

1465.   LaFargue, André.   "Past Glories of Opera in New Orleans,
          1718-1859."   *Opera News* 10/3 (1945): 10-12; 10/4 (1945):
          10-13.

1466.   Lahee, Henry C.   *Grand Opera in America.*   Boston: L.C. Page,
          1902.   Reprint, New York: AMS Press, 1973.   348p.

          Includes an account of ballad opera in early America.

1467.   Langworthy, Helen.   "The Theatre in the Frontier Cities of
          Lexington, Kentucky and Cincinnati, Ohio 1797-1835."   Ph.D.
          dissertation, State University of Iowa, 1952.   347p.   UM
          4079.   *DAI* 12/5 (May 1952): 636.

          Compares 45 productions undertaken in Lexington and
Cincinnati with similar productions in Philadelphia, Boston, and New
York.   At least 683 performances of various works are recorded in
the two towns during the period studied.   Based on primary
documents.

1468.   Lawrence, Vera Brodsky.   "Mr. Hewitt Lays It on the Line."
          19th-Century Music 5/1 (Summer 1981): 3-15.

          Concerns a number of unpaid rehearsals scheduled for the
production of *Cinderella* in March 1808.   James Hewitt, conductor of
the orchestra, was threatened with dismissal.

1469.   Layng, Judith.   "America's First Comic Opera."   *Opera Journal*
          9/3 (1976): 3-7.

Brief introduction to Andrew Barton's *The Disappointment: or, The Force of Credulity* (1767).

1470.   Le Gardeur, René J.   *The First New Orleans Theatre, 1792-1803*.   New Orleans: Leeward Books, 1963.   viii, 58p.

Discusses some of the early comic operas produced there. The bibliography is recommended.

1471.   Loeb, Henry B.   "The Opera in New Orleans: A Historical Sketch from the Earliest Days through the Season 1914-15."   *Publications of the Louisiana Historical Society* 9 (1916): 29-41.

1472.   McKay, David.   *"The Fashionable Lady*: The First Opera by an American."   *Musical Quarterly* 65/3 (July 1979): 360-67.

This work by James Ralph (1695-1762) was written in 1730.

1473.   McKay, David.   "Opera in Colonial Boston."   *American Music* 3/2 (Summer 1985): 133-42.

The first opera presented in Boston was *The Beggar's Opera* on September 29, 1769.   Discussed are theatrical productions to the early 1790s.

1474.   McNamara, Brooks.   *The American Playhouse in the Eighteenth Century*.   Cambridge: Harvard University Press, 1969. xviii, 174p.

A brief introduction to principal theaters.   Illustrations and an index.

1475.   Mates, Julian.   *The American Musical Stage before 1800*.   New Brunswick, N.J.: Rutgers University Press, 1962.   xi, 331p.

This survey is based on a selection of primary and secondary sources and focuses on theaters and audiences, orchestras, companies, repertory, librettists and composers, and performance and criticism.   Index.

1476.   Meserve, Walter J.   *An Emerging Entertainment; the Drama of the American People to 1828.*   Bloomington: Indiana University Press, 1977.   x, 342p.

   An excellent work that surveys the development of theater in America.   Provides information on early ballad operas and includes a list of dissertations for the period studied.

1477.   Michael, Mary Ruth.   "A History of the Professional Theatre in Boston from the Beginning to 1816."   Ph.D. dissertation, Radcliffe University, 1942.

1478.   Molnar, John W.   *Songs from the Williamsburg Theatre: A Selection of Fifty Songs Performed on the Stage in Williamsburg in the Eighteenth Century.*   Williamsburg: Colonial Williamsburg Foundation, 1972.   xix, 227p.

   The songs are taken from English ballad operas and plays. The author includes an essay on the history of ballad opera in Williamsburg, the components of a typical production, and critical notes on the works included.   Index.

1479.   Morse, William N.   "Contributions to the History of the New England Stage in the Eighteenth Century, with Special Reference to Boston and Portsmouth."   Ph.D. dissertation, Harvard University, 1936.   347p.

1480.   Moss, Harold Gene.   "Ballad-Opera Songs: A Record of the Ideas Set to Music, 1728-1733."   Ph.D. dissertation, University of Michigan, 1970.   1,613p.   UM 71-23921.   *DAI* 32/3 (September 1971): 1483-A.

   An analysis and history of 2,000 songs set to tunes and includes some 3,000 lyric poems.   A number of these ballad operas were performed subsequently in the colonies.

1481.   Muldrow, Blanche.   "The American Theatre as Seen by British
          Travelers, 1790-1860; a Survey of Theatre Production,
          Comment, and Opinion."   Ph.D. dissertation, Cornell
          University, 1948.

1482.   Obenshain, Kathryn.   "Opera in America."   *American Music
          Teacher* 26/2 (November-December 1976): 22-24.

          A brief survey, mentioning some of the landmark operas,
from Andrew Barton's *The Disappointment: or, The Force of Credulity*
(1767) on.

1483.   Odell, George C.D.   *Annals of the New York Stage.*   New York:
          Columbia University Press, 1927.   15 vols.

          A significant, comprehensive work for New York productions,
including opera and other musical entertainments.   Volumes 1-2 focus
on the beginning of theatrical production to 1821.   Recommended also
is an *Index to the Portraits in Odell's Annals of the New York Stage*
(Princeton, N.J.: American Society for Theatre Research, 1963).

1484.   Oliver, Peter.   "The Boston Theatre, 1800."   *Publications of
          the Colonial Society of Massachusetts* 34 (1943): 554-70.

1485.   Peeler, Clare.   "End of Eighteenth Century Sees French Opera
          Here."   *Musical America* 29/21 (1919): 24-25.

1486.   Peeler, Clare.   "Opera in English Thrived in U.S. 150 Years
          Ago."   *Musical America* 29/20 (1919): 17, 19.

1487.   Pollock, Thomas Clark.   *The Philadelphia Theatre in the
          Eighteenth Century, Together with the Day Book of the Same
          Period.*   New York: Greenwood Press, 1968.   xviii, 445p.

          Originally a Ph.D. dissertation (University of
Pennsylvania, 1930).

1488.   Porter, Susan L.   "Eighteenth-Century Opera—What's in a
          Name?"   *Sonneck Society Newsletter* 6/2 (1980): 17-18.

1489.   Porter, Susan L.   "English-American Interaction in American
        Musical Theater at the Turn of the Nineteenth Century."
        American Music 4/1 (Spring 1986): 6-19.

        Includes a survey of the significant operas and musical
productions at that time; compares New York, Boston, Philadelphia,
and Charleston.   Of note is a list of "The ten works performed most
often in five American theatrical centers. . . ," including towns
cited above and Baltimore from 1790 to 1810.

1490.   Porter, Susan Loraine.   "Performance Practice in American
        Opera at the Turn of the Nineteenth Century as Seen in
        Children in the Wood, a Representative Musical
        Entertainment."   Ph.D. dissertation, University of Colorado
        at Boulder, 1977.   498p.   UM 77-24272.   *DAI* 38/5 (November
        1977): 2405-A.

        Includes a background study and a list of musical
entertainments performed in America in 1790-1810, lists of English
and American companies, librettists and actors, and the score of the
work studied.

1491.   Rabson, Carolyn.   *"Disappointment* Revisited: Unweaving the
        Tangled Web: Part I."   *American Music* 1/1 (Spring 1983):
        12-35.

        Overview of the production history of the first American
opera *The Disappointment: or, The Force of Credulity* (1767).   (See
also part 2, entry 1492.)

1492.   Rabson, Carolyn.   *"Disappointment* Revisited: Unweaving the
        Tangled Web: Part II."   *American Music* 2/1 (Spring 1984):
        1-28.

        Discusses the reconstruction of the music of this American
ballad opera.   Includes musical examples.   (See also part 1, entry
1491.)

1493.   Rankin, Hugh F.   *The Theatre in Colonial America.*   Chapel
        Hill: University of North Carolinan Press, 1965.   xiii,
        239p.

An introductory survey of theater for the period studied. Companies discussed include the Murray-Keane Company, Hallam Company, Douglass Company, and New American Company.   Index.

1494.   Ray, Sister Mary Dominic.   "Drums, Wigs & Six Wax Lights. *Musical America* 25 (August 1975): 14-17.

Surveys the beginning of opera in the colonies.   Facsimiles and other illustrations.

1495.   Reardon, William Robert.   "Banned in Boston: A Study of Theatrical Censorship in Boston from 1630 to 1950."   Ph.D. dissertation, Stanford University, 1953.   253p.   UM 5386. *DAI* 13/4 (April 1953): 609.

Includes a legislative history of the banning of theater and a list of performances censored in Boston.

1496.   Ritchey, Robert David.   "A History of the Baltimore Stage in the Eighteenth Century."   Ph.D. dissertation, Louisiana State University and Agricultural and Mechanical College, 1971.   373p.   UM 72-3520.   *DAI* 32/7 (January 1972): 4162-A.

Discusses David Douglass' American Company and Thomas Wall's Maryland Company of Comedians, and includes a daybook of every recorded performance in 18th-century Baltimore.

1497.   Robinson, Alice Jean McDonnell.   "The Developing Ideas of Individual Freedom and National Unity as Reflected in American Plays and the Theatre, 1772-1819."   Ph.D. dissertation, Stanford University, 1965.   471p.   UM 65-12848.   *DAI* 26/7 (January 1966): 4119.

A chronological study of dialogues, plays, masques, and operas.

1498.   Shapiro, Anne Dhu.   "Action Music in American Pantomime and Melodrama, 1730-1913."   *American Music* 2/4 (Winter 1984): 49-72.

Discusses theatrical stage music. Includes a list of
extant pantomime music from the late 1700s. Musical examples.

1499. Sherman, Constance D. "The Theatre in Rhode Island before
       the Revolution." *Rhode Island History* 17/1 (January 1958):
       10-14.

       Mentions an early concert which took place in Providence on
August 10, 1762.

1500. Shockley, Martin S. "A History of the Theatre in Richmond,
       Virginia, 1819-1838." Ph.D. dissertation, University of
       North Carolina, 1938. 610p.

1501. Singleton, Esther. "History of the Opera in New York from
       1750 to 1898." *Musical Courier* [National Edition, Second
       Section] 37/23 (1898).

1502. Smither, Nelle Kroger. "A History of the English Theatre at
       New Orleans, 1806-1842." Ph.D. dissertation, University of
       Pennsylvania, 1942.

1503. Sonneck, Oscar George. "Early American Operas." In
       Miscellaneous Studies in the History of Music. New York:
       Macmillan, 1921. Reprint, New York: Da Capo Press, 1968,
       pp. 16-92.

       This pioneering work with musical examples is still useful
today because of Sonneck's meticulous use of primary sources. The
title refers, in part, to English ballad opera as performed in the
colonies. Numerous composers' names are cited. Originally appeared
in *Sammelbände der internationalen Musikgesellschaft* 6 (1905), pp.
428-95.

1504. Sonneck, Oscar G. *Early Opera in America*. New York: G.
       Schirmer, 1915. Reprint, New York: Benjamin Blom, 1963.
       viii, 230p.

       Despite its early date of publication, this work remains a
standard study, due to Sonneck's careful analysis of contemporary

newspapers.   Divided into 2 principal parts: pre-revolutionary and post-revolutionary opera, with emphasis on New York, Philadelphia, Boston and New England, Baltimore, Charleston and the South.   Index.

1505.   Sonneck, Oscar G.   "Opera in America from 1783 to 1800."   *New Music Review* 7 (1908): 502-06, 554-57, 562-603.

Published later as a revised version in *Early Opera in America* (see entry 1504).

1506.   Sonneck, Oscar G.   "Pre-Revolutionary Opera in America."   *New Music Review* 6 (1907): 438-44, 500-06, 562-69.

Later incorporated into Sonneck's *Early Opera in America* (see entry 1504).

1507.   Stine, Richard D.   "The Philadelphia Theatre, 1682-1829: Its Growth as a Cultural Institution."   Ph.D. dissertation, University of Pennsylvania, 1952.   193p.

1508.   Virga, Patricia H.   "The American Opera to 1790."   Ph.D. dissertation, Rutgers University, 1981.   641p.   UM 81-15233. *DAI* 42/1 (July 1981): 17-A.

Includes an edition of music and text of all American operas printed to 1790: *The Disappointment* (1767) by Andrew Barton; *The Better Sort* (1789) and *The Reconciliation* (1790) by Peter Markoe; and *The Blockheads* (1782), *May Day in Town* (1787), and *Darby's Return* (1789) by William Dunlap.   Published under the same title (Ann Arbor, Mich.: UMI Research Press, 1982).

1509.   Walsh, Lorna G.   "Early Concerts and Ballad Opera."   *Opera Magazine* 2/12 (1915): 22-24, 26.

1510.   Walsh, Lorna G.   "In the Days of Ballad Opera."   *Etude* 63/11 (November 1945): 620, 650, 660.

Discusses some of the early operas performed in America, beginning with Charleston, S.C.

1511.   Willis, Eola. *The Charleston Stage in the XVIII Century.*
        Columbia, S.C.: The State Co., 1924.   xv, 483p.

        Although dated, this work is an excellent chronological
survey of operas, plays, and other events, with primary sources
noted. Many of the events consisted of or included music. For
example, cited are performances of music by Maria Storer in 1785,
pp. 92-94. Refer to the index under the heading "Music."

1512.   Winesanker, Michael. "American Comic Opera: Yesterday and
        Today." *American Music Teacher* 9/4 (1960): 8, 23-27.

1513.   Wolcott, John Rutherford. "English Influences on American
        Staging Practice: A Case Study of the Chestnut Street
        Theatre, Philadelphia, 1794-1820." Ph.D. dissertation,
        Ohio State University, 1967. 504p. UM 68-3091. *DAI* 28/12
        (June 1968): 5184-A.

        Alexander Reinagle and Thomas Wignell opened the theater.
Discusses physical aspects of the theater and is based, in part, on
a scrapbook that belonged to Henry Warren, a scene designer at that
theater.

1514.   Wolz, Larry Robert. "Opera in Cincinnati: The Years before
        the Zoo, 1801-1920." Ph.D. dissertation, University of
        Cincinnati, 1983. 259p. UM 83-23251. *DAI* 44/6 (December
        1983): 1624-A.

        Based primarily on contemporary newspapers, and includes an
appendix of operatic works performed before 1840.

1515.   Yellin, Victor Fell. "The Indian Princess; or, 'La belle
        sauvage.'" *World of Opera* 1/6 (1979): 29-34.

        An introduction to this work, which was premiered on April
6, 1808 at the Chestnut Street Theatre in Philadelphia. Discusses
the problems regarding the creation of an authentic performance.

1516.   Yellin, Victor. "Opera's American History." *Music Journal*
        19/3 (March 1961): 60-61, 68-70.

A survey that mentions some of the early theatrical productions that included music and early French opera in New Orleans.

1517.   Yellin, Victor Fell.   "Rayner Taylor's Music for *The AEthiop*: Part 1, Performance History."   *American Music* 4/3 (Fall 1986): 249-67.

The work was first performed in 1814 in Philadelphia. Includes a list of the musicians.

1518.   Yellin, Victor Fell.   "Rayner Taylor's Music for *The AEthiop*: Part 2, The Keyboard Score (*The Ethiop*) and Its Orchestral Restoration."   *American Music* 5/1 (Spring 1987): 20-47.

A continuation of part 1 (see entry 1517).   "My orchestral restoration is based upon the complete keyboard score. . . , now in the possession of the Eda Kuhn Loeb Music Library of Harvard University."   Musical examples.

1519.   Zimmerman, Elena Irish.   "American Opera Librettos, 1767-1825: The Manifestation and Result of the Imitative Principle in an American Literary Form."   Ph.D. dissertation, University of Tennessee, 1972.   294p.   UM 72-21369.   *DAI* 33/2 (August 1972): 737-A.

Discusses 21 operas, including *The Disappointment*, *Tammany*, *Slaves in Algiers*, *La Foret Noire*, *Americana*, *The Indian Princess*, and *The Forest Rose*, among others.

Organology

For a concise introduction to musical instruments in colonial America, refer to Laurence Libin's "Instruments" in *The New Grove Dictionary of American Music*, vol. 2, pp. 480-83 (see entry 30).

1520.   Albright, Frank P.   "The Restoration of a Tannenberg Organ." *Moravian Music Foundation Bulletin* 9/1 (Fall 1964): 1-2, 4.

On the restoration of a Tannenberg organ built in 1797-98 in Salem, N.C. Includes historical background.

1521. Althouse, Ella Krauss. "Krauss Family Organ Builders." *Tracker* 21/1 (Fall 1976): 3.

Includes excerpts from the diary of John Krauss for 1796-99, regarding organs he installed.

1522. "America Has Old Organs, Too. . . ." *High Fidelity* 10/8 (1960): 38-39.

1523. Armstrong, William H. *Organs for America: The Life and Work of David Tannenberg*. Philadelphia: University of Pennsylvania Press, 1967. xvi, 154p.

Tannenberg, a Moravian immigrant from Central Europe, constructed some 50 organs in the United States. Includes a biography and a chronology, based on primary sources, of information concerning his organs. Photographs.

1524. Arnold, Janice M. "American Pianos: Revolution and Triumph." *Clavier* 26/6 (July-August 1987): 16-22.

A discussion of some early American piano manufacturers. Mentions the "first American-built piano on record" by Johann Behrent (1775), the New York firm of Dodds and Claus (1792), and others. Illustrations.

1525. Arnold, Robert A. "The Krauss Organ and Church of the Most Blessed Sacrament." *Historical Review of Berks County* 33 (1968): 98-101.

On an organ built during the late eighteenth century in Bally, Pa.

1526. Ayars, Christine M. "Earliest Beginnings of Organ History in New England Traced." *Diapason* 27/9 (1936): 20; 27/10 (1936): 20; 27/11 (1936): 27; 27/12 (1936): 27.

1527.   Bailey, Jay.   "Historical Origin and Stylistic Developments
        of the Five-String Banjo." *Journal of American Folklore*
        85/335 (January-March 1972): 58-65.

        From the 18th century on.

1528.   Belsheim, George N.   "The Pipe Organ Comes to America."
        Journal of Church Music 25/4 (April 1983): 18-19.

        Brief article on early organs in the 17th-century Spanish
missions in the New Mexico area, and Protestant organs in various
churches in the 18th-century middle colonies.

1529.   Benton, Rita.   "The Early Piano in the United States."   In
        Music Libraries and Instruments.   London: Hinrichsen, 1961,
        pp. 179-88.

        An excellent introduction to pianos in America, beginning
with a public notice of a piano in the *Massachusetts Gazette* (March
7, 1771).   The author mentions the principal piano makers in various
cities and their notices in newspapers.

1530.   Biancolli, Louis.   "T. Jefferson, Fiddler."   *Life* 22/14
        (April 7, 1947): 13, 16, 19-20.

        Includes biographical information and discusses the history
of Jefferson's personal violin and its whereabouts after Jefferson
died.   Photo.

1531.   Bigg, Edward G.P.   "Franklin and the Armonica."   *Daedalus* 86
        (1957): 231-41.

1532.   Biggs, E. Power.   "The Story of Benjamin Franklin and the
        Armonica."   *Music Clubs Magazine* 35/5 (1956): 4-5, 22.

1533.   Blanchard, Homer D. and Eliot I. Wirling.   "That New 'Oldest'
        Organ."   *American Organist* 32 (1949): 443-44.

        On an organ built by John Snetzler in 1762 at the
Congregational Church in South Dennis, Mass.

1534.   Bleyle, Carl Otto.   "Georg Andreas Sorge's Influence on David
        Tannenberg and Organ Building in America during the
        Eighteenth Century."   374p.   UM 70-1779.   Ph.D.
        dissertation, University of Minnesota, 1969.   *DAI* 30/8
        (February 1970): 3489-90-A.

        Includes translations of two of Sorge's treatises, and an
examination of three of Tannenberg's extant organs.

1535.   Boeringer, James.   "Wurttemberg Organs in America."   *Tracker*
        29/2 (1985): 19-21.

        Discusses early organs in St. Michael's Lutheran Church in
Philadelphia, and elsewhere.

1536.   Brayley, Arthur W.   "The First Organ in America."   *New
        England Magazine* 27 (1902): 212-19.

1537.   Bruce, W.J.   "A Chapter on Church Organs."   *American
        Historical Record* 3 (1874): 161-70.

        Discusses organs in America during the 18th and early 19th
centuries.

1538.   Brunner, Raymond J.   "A Conrad Doll Chamber Organ."   *Tracker*
        25/2 (Winter 1981): 16-19.

        The organ was built between 1805 and 1810, and is one of
two extant Doll organs.   Includes biographical information on Doll.

1539.   Cameron, Peter T.   "A History of the Organs of the Collegiate
        Church of New York City, 1727-1861."   *Tracker* 25/1 (Fall
        1980): 82-85.

        Church records discussing organs and organists, including
Peter Erben, Adam Geib, and a Mr. Gilfers.

1540.   Clarke, W. Horatio.   "Early Organ Building in Boston."
        Musician 1 (1896): 90.

1541.   Clemens, Gurney W.   "The Dieffenbach Organ." *Historical Review of Berks County* 11/1 (1945): 18-21.

1542.   Crehore, Charles L. *The Benjamin Crehore Piano: An Account in the Form of Notes.* Boston, 1926.

1543.   Dean, Talmage Whitman.   "The Organ in Eighteenth Century English Colonial America." Ph.D. dissertation, University of Southern California, 1960. 276p. UM 60-5474. *DAI* 21/6 (December 1960): 1583.

Discusses organs in New England, the German-American tradition, and is based on published histories, newspapers, and selected documents. Organ builders include Johann Klemm, Gustavus Hesselius, and Christopher Witt. Mentions the organ that belonged to Johannes Kelpius.

1544.   "Details of the Brattle Organ." *Tracker* 13/4 (Summer 1969): 9-11.

A reprint of an article originally titled "The First Organ in America," printed in *New England Magazine*, New Series, 27 (September 1902-February 1903). Concerns an organ imported by Thomas Brattle in 1708 or 1709 in Boston.

1545.   Dieffenbach, Ray J. "The Will of Johan Conrad Dieffenbach." *Tracker* 21/1 (Fall 1976): 14.

The will of this organ builder is dated July 22, 1737 and is translated here.

1546.   Dieffenbach, Victor C. *The Dieffenbach Organ Builders.* Elizabethtown, Pa.: privately printed, 1967. 17p.

History of the Dieffenbach family, with information on principal organs built in the United States.

1547.   Donaldson, Bryna. "Ben Franklin's Glass Harmonica." *Music Journal* 26/3 (March 1968): 117-18.

An overview as to how Franklin invented the armonica.

1548.   Donaldson, Bryna. "Benjamin Franklin's Armonica." *Daughters of the American Revolution Magazine* 103 (1969): 30-31, 40.

1549.   Eader, Thomas S. "The Baltimore Organ Builders." *Tracker* 2/3 (April 1958): 2-5; 2/4 (July 1958): 3-5; 3/1 (October 1958): 3-4; 3/3 (April 1959): 4-5.

Discusses a Tannenberg organ of 1798, a Thomas Hall organ built in 1818 for the First Unitarian Church, and others.

1550.   Eader, Thomas S. "Baltimore Organs and Organ Building." *Maryland Historical Magazine* 65/3 (Fall 1970): 263-82.

Focuses on organs beginning with the first installed in St. Paul's Church in 1750. Organ builders and musicians discussed include Benjamin Carr, John Geib, Thomas Hall, James Stewart, and David Tannenberg.

1551.   Eader, Thomas S. "The David Dieffenbach Organ." *Tracker* 19/2 (Winter 1975): 10.

On an 1820s organ located in the home of Curtis Dieffenbach in Bethel, Pa.

1552.   Eader, Thomas S. "David Tannenberg's Last Organ." *Tracker* 4/3 (April 1960): 3-4.

Tannenberg's organ was installed in Christ Lutheran Church in York, Pa., in May 1804.

1553.   Eader, Thomas S. "The 1808 Christian Dieffenbach Organ." *Tracker* 15/3 (Spring 1971): 3-4.

The organ was dedicated on October 16, 1808 in Zion Lutheran and Reformed Congregation, Orwigsburg, Pa.

1554.   Eader, Thomas S.   "The 1816 Christian Dieffenbach Organ in Altalaha Lutheran Church, Rehrersburg, Pennsylvania." *Tracker* 19/2 (Winter 1975): 3-5.

Includes a complete examination of the organ in view of a restoration.

1555.   Eader, Thomas S.   "The 1776 Dieffenbach Organ." *Tracker* 15/3 (Spring 1971): 5.

Originally installed in Epplers Church, near Reading, Pa.

1556.   "Early History of the Organ in America." *Organ* 1 (1892): 174-75.

1557.   Edmonds, John H.   "Some Organs and Organists in Colonial Boston." *Diapason* 14/9 (1923): 4, 29.

1558.   Eliason, Robert E.   *Keyed Bugles in the United State*s. Washington, D.C.: Smithsonian Institution Press, 1972. 44p.

From 1810 to the Civil War.

1559.   Eliason, Robert E.   "The Lititz Instrument Collection." *Moravian Music Foundation Bulletin* 25/2 (Fall-Winter 1980): 11-12.

Describes Moravian musical instruments in the collection at Lititz, Pa.   Includes string and brass instruments, with dates noted.

1560.   Eliason, Robert E.   "The Meachams, Musical Instrument Makers of Hartford and Albany." *Journal of the American Musical Instrument Society* 5-6 (1979-80): 54-73.

John and Horace Meacham were active in the early 1800s as makers of flutes, oboes, and bassoons.   Includes a list of extant instruments.

1561.   Eliason, Robert E.   "Oboes, Bassoons, and Bass Clarinets Made
        by Hartford Connecticut, Makers before 1815." *Galpin
        Society Journal* 30 (May 1977): 43-51.

        Discusses George Catlin, Uzal Miner, Gottlieb Wolhaupter,
instrument maker and importer of instruments in New York around
1761, and Jacob Anthony (1736-1804), instrument maker in
Philadelphia.   Illustrations.

1562.   Ellinwood, Leonard W.   "Snetzler's American Organs."
        American Organist 35 (1952): 297-98.

1563.   Ervin, Horace.   "Notes on Franklin's Armonica and the Music
        Mozart Wrote for It."   *Franklin Institute Journal* 262
        (1956): 329-48.

1564.   "Evolution of American Church Music."   *American Organist* 17/8
        (August 1934): 358-61.

        A chronicle on the organs and choirs of St. George's Church
in New York.   Its first organ was purchased in December 1817.

1565.   Fesperman, John T.   "Music and Organs at 'The Old North':
        Then and Now." *Organ Institute Quarterly* 10/3 (1963): 15-
        28.

        Discusses the organs in Christ Church, Boston's oldest
church building, beginning with the William Claggett organ (1736)
and the Thomas Johnston organ (1752-59), and other later organs.
Based on church records and other primary sources.

1566.   Fesperman, John T.   "Three Snetzler Organs in the United
        States." *Organ Yearbook* 2 (1971): 23-32.

        The organs were built by John Snetzler in the 18th century,
and are in Yale University, Congregational Church, South Dennis,
Mass., and the Smithsonian Institution.   Illustrations.

1567.   "The First American Pianoforte Made in Philadelphia."
        American Art Journal 55 (1890): 13.

Discusses Charles Albrecht, piano maker.

1568.   Fisher, Cleveland.   "The Port Royal Confusion—Among Other
            Things." *Tracker* 12/1 (Fall 1967): 1-2, 7-9.

        Concerns an organ first used in Mount Church, near Port
Royal, Va., and purchased in 1810 by Christ Church, Alexandria, Va.

1569.   Fix, Carolyn E.   "The Dieffenbach Saga." *Tracker* 19/2
            (Winter 1975): 6-10.

        Discusses the Dieffenbach organ builders and is based on
published and unpublished accounts by Victor C. and Ray J.
Dieffenbach, descendants.

1570.   Freeman, Andrew.   "John Snetzler and His Organs." *Organ: A
            Quarterly Review for Its Makers, Its Players, and Its
            Lovers* 14 (1934): 24-42, 92-101, 163-71.

1571.   Frischmann, Charles.   "Organs and Organ Music in Colonial
            America." *Journal of Church Music* 17/10 (December 1975):
            2-4.

        Mentions some early organs and lists composers.

1572.   Giroux, Paul H.   "The History of the Flute and Its Music in
            the United States." *Journal of Research in Music Education*
            1/1 (Spring 1953): 68-73.

        Discusses the physical nature of the flute that was likely
used in colonial America, music written for it, and a notice for a
flute for sale in Boston in 1716. Based on the author's master's
thesis with the same title (University of Washington, 1952).

1573.   Groce, Nancy Jane.   "Musical Instrument Making in New York
            City during the Eighteenth and Nineteenth Centuries."
            Ph.D. dissertation, University of Michigan, 1982. 2 vols.,
            561p. UM 82-24957. *DAI* 43/6 (December 1982): 1740-A.

Includes a "Biographical-Dictionary," with information on over 700 craftsmen for the period 1690-1890, and a history of the music instrument business in New York.

1574.   Hanstein, George. "John Jacob Dieffenbach, Wheelwright and Organ Builder." *American-German Review* 11/4 (1945): 4-6, 22.

1575.   Harriman, Helen. "Gleanings from Boston Newspapers." *Tracker* 12/1 (Fall 1967): 3.

        Quotes taken from Boston newspapers concerning organs in 1716, 1753, 1763, and 1769.

1576.   Holmes, Charles N. "America's Oldest Organ." *Musical Courier* 72/11 (1916): 5-6.

        On the Brattle organ.

1577.   Holmes, Charles N. "The Oldest Organ in the United States." *Granite Monthly* 52 (1920): 293-95; 60 (1928): 502-03.

1578.   Jordan, John W. "Early Colonial Organ-Builders of Pennsylvania." *Pennsylvania Magazine of History and Biography* 22/2 (1898): 231-33.

        Mentions early organ builders, including Gustavus Hesselius and David Tannenberg. Includes a brief list of Tannenberg's organs, 1761-1804.

1579.   Kasling, Kim R. "A Priceless Musical Heritage." *American Music Teacher* 23/5 (1973): 36-40; 23/6 (1973): 10-12.

1580.   Kaufman, Charles H. "Musical-Instrument Makers in New Jersey, 1796-1860." *Journal of the American Musical Instrument Society* 2 (1976): 5-33.

Discusses James Sylvanus McLean, piano maker, whose known activity was ca. 1797. The author includes a table of musical instrument makers.

1581.   Keller, Kate Van Winkle. "Musical Clocks of Early America
            and Their Music." *Music & Automata* 2/6 (October 1985): 84-
            96; 2/7 (April 1986): 141-54; 2/8 (October 1986): 202-20.

This is an expanded version of an article that was published in the *Bulletin of the National Association of Watch and Clock Collectors* 24/3 (June 1982), pp. 252-316. A thorough and excellent introduction to musical clocks. Keller includes lists of musical clocks, clockmakers, importers, and repairers of musical clocks. Includes an extensive discussion of the musical tunes discovered, including transcriptions, their sources and background. Musical examples and bibliography.

1582.   Kienzle, Rich. "The Guitar in American Life: From the Voyage
            of the Mayflower to the Sinking of the Maine." *Guitar
            Player* 14/10 (1980): 22-27.

1583.   King, A. Hyatt. "The Musical Glasses and Glass Harmonica."
            Proceedings of the Royal Music Association 72 (April 1946):
            97-120.

A history of musical glasses, Benjamin Franklin's invention called the armonica, and performances on the musical glasses in the colonies, including Philadelphia and Charleston.

1584.   Knox, Julie LeC. "Indiana's First Piano." *Indiana History
            Bulletin* 25 (1948): 169-70.

The piano was built by Muzio Clementi of London and was in use in Indiana in 1817.

1585.   Labaree, Leonard W., ed. *The Papers of Benjamin Franklin.*
            24 vols. New Haven, Conn.: Yale University Press, 1966,
            vol. 10, pp. 116-30.

Includes a reprint of a letter from Benjamin Franklin to Giambatista Beccaria regarding the armonica, Franklin's variation of

the music glasses.   Footnotes contain references to additional
relevant literature.

1586.   Lahee, Henry C.   "Organs and Organ Building in New England."
         New England Magazine 17 (1897): 485-505.

1587.   Laubenstein, Sarah.   "An Organ in 16th-Century Florida?"
         American Guild of Organists Quarterly 12 (1967): 66-67, 78,
         90.

1588.   Laubenstein, Sarah.   "Two Early American Organ Builders."
         Music: The A.G.O./R.C.C.O. Magazine 9/12 (1975): 39-40.

1589.   Laufman, Alan.   "A Walking Tour of Charleston Churches."
         Tracker 29/1 (1985): 20-30.

         An excellent introduction to organs and church music in
Charleston.   Includes photographs of several 18th-century organs.

1590.   Libin, Laurence.   *American Musical Instruments in the
         Metropolitan Museum of Art.*   Foreword by Philippe de
         Montebello.   New York: Metropolitan Museum of Art and W.W.
         Norton, 1985.   224p.

         Beautiful examples of instruments, a number of which were
built before 1820.   Arranged by types of instruments.   Index.

1591.   Libin, Laurence.   "New Facts and Speculations on John Clemm."
         Tracker 31/2 (1987): 19-23.

         A chronology on the life of John Clemm or Johann Gottlob
Klemm (b. 1690), an American who built an organ in Trinity Church in
New York.   Based on vestry records.

1592.   Loest, Roland.   "American Pianos: Evolution and Decline."
         Clavier 26/6 (July-August 1987): 34-39.

Although focusing mostly on the 19th century, the author
mentions a few 18th-century examples of piano manufacturers in
America.   Illustrations.

1593.   Loewen, Esko.   "An 18th Century German Organ in Kansas."
Tracker 21/2 (Winter 1977): 3-6.

The organ is located in the Kauffman Museum at Bethel
College, North Newton, Kansas.

1594.   Lutz, Charles.   "Krauss Organs in Pennsylvania." *American
Organist* 52/1 (1969): 12-13, 15.

1595.   McCorkle, Donald M.   "Musical Instruments of the Moravians in
North Carolina." *American-German Review* 21/3 (February-
March 1955): 12-17.

1596.   McCorkle, Donald M.   "Prelude to a History of American
Moravian Organs." *American Guild of Organists Quarterly* 3
(October 1958): 142-48.

1597.   McCracken, Eugene M.   "Pennsylvania, the Keystone State."
Tracker 4/2 (January 1960): 1, 3-4.

Brief survey of early organ builders, including Philip
Feyring and David Tannenberg.

1598.   McFarland, James.   "The Organs in Trinity Church, Lancaster,
Pennsylvania." *Tracker* 23/1 (Fall 1978): 3-8.

A history beginning with information on an organ installed
by George Kraft in 1744 in Trinity Lutheran Church.

1599.   McGeary, Thomas.   "David Tannenberg and the Salem 1800
Organ." *Moravian Music Journal* 31/2 (Fall 1986): 18-23.

Brief biography, a description of the organ for the Salem,
N.C. community, and a translation of Tannenberg's instructions on
how to tune the instrument.   Facsimiles.

1600. McManis, Charles W. "David Tannenberg and the Old Salem
        Restoration." *American Organist* 48/5 (1965): 15-20.

1601. McManis, Charles W. "Restoration of Tannenberg Organ at Old
        Salem." *Diapason* 57/4 (1965): 36-37.

1602. McManis, Charles W. "The Tannenberg." *Music Ministry* 6/10
        (1965): 2-4.

1603. McManis, Charles W. and Frank P. Albright. "Tannenberg
        Restoration: Presenting Two Interesting Views." *Tracker*
        9/2 (Winter 1965): 1-2, 7-8.

        Concerns a Tannenberg organ built in 1797-98 in Salem, N.C.

1604. Mangler, Joyce Ellen. "The Deblois Concert Hall Organ—1763-
        1851." *Tracker* 3/1 (October 1958): 1, 8.

        Discusses a Thomas Johnston (1708-1767) organ in Boston.

1605. Mangler, Joyce Ellen. "First 'Dissenting' Church Organ."
        Choral & Organ Guide 9/10 (1957): 12, 14.

        Focuses on a 1770 organ in the First Congregational Church
in Providence, R.I.

1606. Mangler, Joyce Ellen. "Some Letters from Mr. John Geib of
        New York." *Tracker* 2/2 (January 1958): 1-3.

        Letters written in 1802 by John Geib, organ builder, to
David Vinton.

1607. Mann, Walter Edward. "Piano Making in Philadelphia before
        1825." Ph.D. dissertation, University of Iowa, 1977.
        236p. UM 77-28484. *DAI* 38/7 (January 1978): 3795-A.

        Discusses piano manufacturers in Philadelphia from 1775 on,
including John Behrent, James Juhan, Charles Trute, John Sellers,
John Harper, Charles Albrecht, Charles Taws, and others.

1608.   Maurer, Maurer.   "Colonial Organs and Organists Are Research
        Subject." *Diapason* 48/4 (1957): 24-25.

1609.   "The Musical Instrument Trade in New York City." *Musical and
        Dramatic Courier* 2 (1881): 129, 153, 170, 192, 229-30, 260-
        61, 278, 293, 310, 357, 405-06, 437; 3 (1881): 9, 57-58,
        169-70, 281, 291, 293; 4 (1882): 232.

        Focuses on the 18th and 19th centuries.

1610.   Noack, Fritz.   "The Doll Organ at Peach Church."   *Tracker*
        20/1 (Fall 1975): 7-10.

        Conrad Doll, maker of an organ in 1807 in Peach Church near
Camp Hill, Pa., was organist of the German Reformed Church School in
Lancaster, Pa., in 1806.

1611.   Nye, Eugene M.   "The Work of John Snetzler in America."
        *Organ: A Quarterly Review for Its Makers, Its Players, and
        Its Lovers* 50 (1971): 97-105.

1612.   Ochse, Orpha.   *The History of the Organ in the United States.*
        Bloomington: Indiana University Press, 1975.   xv, 494p.

        A principal work that discusses organs and organ builders
beginning with the Spanish missions and British colonies for the
period 1524-1760.   For the years 1760-1810, the author examines
organ builders in Pennsylvania, including Johann Philip Bachmann,
Philip Feyring, David Tannenberg, and others, and in New England,
New York and the South.   Includes an excellent bibliography of 524
items.   Photos and index.

1613.   Ogasapian, John.   "American Organ Research: An
        Interdisciplinary Approach."   *Tracker* 28/1 (1984): 12-14.

        A call for more area studies, monographs on the lives of
organ builders, and an interdisciplinary approach to the study of
American organ history.   See also Ogasapian's article, "American
Organ Research in American Universities," in *Tracker* 28/4 (1984), p.
15.

1614.   Ogasapian, John.   "New Data on John Geib."   *Tracker* 23/4
          (Summer 1979): 12-14.

          Biographical information on the organ builder John Geib
(1744-1818) in New York.

1615.   Ogasapian, John Ken.   "Organ Building in New York City: 1700
          to 1900."   Ph.D. dissertation, Boston University, 1977.
          484p.   UM 77-11412.   *DAI* 37/12 (June 1977): 7397-A.

          Published: Braintree, Mass.: The Organ Literature
Foundation, 1977.   Discusses organs built by John Geib, Thomas Hall,
Henry Erben, Richard Ferris, Levi U. Stuart, George Jardine, and
others.

1616.   Oliver, Henry K.   "An Account of the First Organs in
          America."   *Organist's Quarterly Journal and Review* 2/1
          (1875): 4-6.

1617.   "Organ-Building in New England."   *Tracker* 12/4 (Summer
          1968): 17-20; 13/1 (Fall 1968): 6-8, 14-15, 18.

          A reprint of an article originally published in *New-England
Magazine* 6 (March 1834), pp. 207-10.   A historical study from the
1700s on.   Barbara Owen examines this work in her article,
"Eighteenth-Century Organs and Organ-Building in New England," in
Music in Colonial Massachusetts, 1630-1820 (see entry 533).

1618.   Owen, Barbara and Donald R.M. Paterson.   "American
          Organists."   *Tracker* 11/1 (Fall 1966): 9-15; 11/2 (Winter
          1967): 12-15; 11/3 (Spring 1967): 9-13.

          Reprint of chapter 10 of *The Organ and Its Masters* (Boston:
L.C. Page, 1902) by Henry C. Lahee, with additions and corrections
by the authors.   Includes organs, organ builders, and concerts from
the 1700s on.

1619.   Owen, Barbara.   "Early Organs and Organ Building in
          Newburyport."   *Essex Institute Historical Collections* 121/3
          (July 1985): 172-95.

Discusses organs before 1820 at St. Paul's Church, Battle Square Society Church, and First Religious Society in Newburyport, Mass. Organ builders include Thomas Johnston (1708-1767) and Josiah Leavitt (1744-1804).

1620.   Owen, Barbara. "New Revised Builders' List." *Tracker* 9/2 (Winter 1965): 9-12; 9/3 (Spring 1965): 13-16.

A list of organ builders and dates of activity from the 1700s on.

1621.   Owen, Barbara. "The Organ in Colonial America." *Journal of Church Music* 18/4 (April 1976): 2-4, 48.

Brief introduction, mentioning organs in New York, Philadelphia, Charleston, and other cities. Organ builders include Philip Feyring, Thomas Johnston, Johann G. Klemm, David Tannenberg, and others.

1622.   Owen, Barbara. *The Organ in New England: An Account of Its Use and Manufacture to the End of the Nineteenth Century.* Raleigh, N.C.: Sunbury Press, 1979. xx, 629p.

Discusses the importation of organs from England during the colonial period, the first New England builders of organs, including William and Ebenezer Goodrich, Thomas Johnston, Josiah Leavitt, and Henry Pratt, and builders from the early 19th century. A number of excellent plates serve to illustrate the author's discussion.
Index.

1623.   Owen, Barbara. "Organs at Harvard." *Tracker* 12/2 (Winter 1968): 4-5, 14; 12/3 (Spring 1968): 7.

One organ was built by William Gray of London in 1805.

1624.   Owen, Barbara. "Some Early American Organ Oddities." *American Organist* 44/1 (January 1961): 16-18.

Discusses Joseph Leavitt (b. 1744), organ builder in Boston, and William M. Goodrich (1777-1833), organ builder. Illustrations.

1625. Owen, Barbara. "Tracing an English Chamber Organ." *Tracker*
       22/2 (Winter 1978): 1, 3-6.

       On an 1805 organ built by William Gray and located in
Harvard University.

1626. Pinel, Stephen. "A Comparator of American Organ
       Manufacturing." *Tracker* 30/4 (1986): 20-33.

       Based on federal and state censuses of 1810-80. An
excellent introduction to the value of census data for the study of
American music. This article includes an excerpt concerning organs
and organbuilders in early America taken from the 1860 compendium,
Manufactures in the United States (Washington, D.C.: Government
Printing Office, 1865).

1627. Pressley, Ernest Wayne. "Musical Wind Instruments in the
       Moravian Musical Archives, Salem, North Carolina: A
       Descriptive Catalogue." D.M.A. dissertation, University of
       Kentucky, 1975. 178p. UM 76-16594. *DAI* 37/1 (July 1976):
       28-A.

       Includes 4 chapters on the musical practices of the
Moravian Church and the Collegium Musicum Salem as begun by Johann
Friedrich Peter. The catalog includes a description of each
instrument, including its pitch, dimensions, and place of
manufacture.

1628. Pressley, Nancy Gamble. "Winterthur Museum's Early American
       Keyboard and Music Collections: An Example of Museum
       Resources for Music in Higher Education." Ph.D.
       dissertation, Southern Illinois University at Carbondale,
       1982. 121p. UM 82-29304. *DAI* 43/7 (January 1983): 2151-
       A.

       Instruments include pianos made in Boston (1808),
Philadelphia, Washington, D.C. (Charles Taws, 1791), New York (John
Geib and Son, 1804-14 and John Geib, Jr, 1818). The author
establishes a correlation between the instruments and music
published at that time. Composers include Benjamin Carr, James
Hewitt, Alexander Reinagle, Rayner Taylor, Francis Hopkinson, James
Bremner, and others.

1629.   Radzinsky, Charles A.   "Organ Builders of New York, 1800 to 1909."   *New Music Review* 9 (1910): 165-68.

1630.   Radzinsky, Charles A.   "Organ Building and Organ Builders of New York City."   *Tracker* 15/3 (Spring 1971): 11-12.

        A reprint from a book titled *Dictionary of Organs and Organists*.   Ed. by Frederick W. Thornsby (Bournemouth, Eng.: H. Logan, 1912).   Mentions John Geib.

1631.   Radzinsky, Charles A.   "St. Paul's Chapel, New York: Its Organs from 1802 to 1904."   *Tracker* 21/2 (Winter 1977): 18-19.

        Discusses a George Pike England organ imported from London in 1802.

1632.   Reich, Robert J.   "An Historical Organ at Schuylerville, N.Y."   *Tracker* 5/2 (1961): 3-4, 8.

        The organ was installed in 1756 in King's Chapel, Boston.

1633.   Reich, Robert J.   "The Organ at the First Religious Society, Newburyport."   *Tracker* 2/1 (October 1957): 1-4.

        Discusses, in part, the first organ built in 1794 by Josiah Leavitt at the First Religious Society in Newburyport, Mass.

1634.   Robinson, Albert F.   "Historic American Organ Builders."   *Music: The A.G.O./R.C.C.O. Magazine* 10/1 (1976): 34-37; 10/2 (1976): 36-38; 10/3 (1976): 48-51; 10/4 (1976): 40-43; 10/5 (1976): 42-45; 10/6 (1976): 38-40; 10/7 (1976): 34-37.

1635.   Robinson, Albert F.   "The Organ Historical Society: A Commentary by One of Its Founders."   *Journal of Church Music* 24/4 (April 1982): 2-6.

        Includes a photo of a John Snetzler organ built in 1762 and now located in the Congregational Church in Dennis, Mass.

1636. Robinson, Albert F. "Tracking Down the Oliver Holden Organ."
       Tracker 26/3 (Spring 1982): 8-10.

       Includes biographical information on Oliver Holden (1765-
1844) and an organ built in 1809 and owned by him.

1637. Sachs, Curt. "American Contributions to the Development of
       Musical Instruments." *Musical America* 59/14 (1939): 14.

1638. Salter, Sumner. "An Echo of the Past: Early Organs in
       America." *Organ: A Quarterly Review for Its Makers, Its
       Players, and Its Lovers* 7 (1928): 251-52; 8 (1928): 55-58.

1639. Salter, Sumner. "Long and Interesting Career for America's
       Second Oldest Organ." *Diapason* 28/11 (1937): 28.

       The organ was located in the Trinity Church, Portsmouth,
R.I. in 1733. Article reprinted in *Tracker* 24/1 (1979), pp. 13-15.

1640. Salter, Sumner. "Organs of Early Day Built for Historic
       Churches of Boston." *Diapason* 28/12 (1937): 28.

       Reprinted in *Tracker* 24/2 (1980), p. 18.

1641. Saxton, Stanley E. "The Schuylerville Organ of 1756. . .
       Again?" *Tracker* 11/3 (Spring 1967): 3.

       An organ in Schuylerville, N.Y. was restored in 1963.

1642. Scholes, Percy A. "The Organ in Church, Home, and Tavern in
       Puritan Days." *New Music Review* 33 (1934): 37-39, 47.

1643. Selch, Frederick R. "Early American Violins and Their
       Makers." *Journal of the Violin Society of America* 6/1
       (Spring 1980): 33-42.

       Discusses American violin makers of the 18th and 19th
centuries.

1644.   Selch, Frederick R.   "Yankee Bass Viol Makers." *Journal of the Violin Society of America* 2/2 (1976): 26-37.

1645.   Shields, T. Edgar.   "Two Eighteenth-Century Organ Builders." *American Organist* 27 (1944): 129-30.

On David Tannenberg and Johann Gottlob Klemm.

1646.   Smith, Maria Pratt.   "Organ Building History: Something About the Organs Built by Henry Pratt of Winchester Who Built His First Organ There in 1779." *American Organist* 16/10 (October 1933): 514.

Henry Pratt (1771-1849) of Winchester, N.H. was an organ builder active from the 1790s on.

1647.   "Snetzler Restored at Smithsonian." *Tracker* 14/3 (1970): 13, 19.

1648.   "Some Curious and Interesting Experiments in American Piano Construction." *American Art Journal* 59 (1892): 99, 101, 103.

Mentions Benjamin Franklin and Francis Hopkinson.

1649.   Speller, John L.   "A Double Tannenberg Legacy: Restoration of the 1787 and 1793 Organs in Lititz, Pennsylvania." *Tracker* 31/3 (1987): 24-31.

Includes a history with photographs.

1650.   Speller, John L.   "The Pennsylvania Dutch School of Organbuilders." *Tracker* 31/2 (1987): 13-18.

Reprinted from *Musical Opinion* 108/11 (November 1985). An introduction to organs and organbuilders in Pennsylvania. Includes photos of a 1787 Tannenberg organ, a 1793 Tannenberg organ, a Philip Feyring organ case, and an 1800 Dieffenbach organ.

1651. Spillane, Daniel. "A Curiosity in American Music Trade
         Literature." *American Art Journal* 59 (1892): 309, 311.

         Discusses an article in *Columbian Magazine* (May 1787) that
was written by Francis Hopkinson concerning his innovation for
quilling a harpsichord.

1652. Spillane, Daniel. *History of the American Pianoforte: Its
         Technical Development and the Trade.* New York: D.
         Spillane, 1890. Reprint, New York: Da Capo Press, 1969.
         369p.

         Lists patents from 1796-1890.

1653. Stoddard, Hope E. "Early Colonists and the Bars-Vile."
         Music Educators Journal 67/8 (April 1981): 50-51.

         Discusses musical instruments, including the "Bars-Vile" or
bass viol, in New England and of the Wissahickon Mystics and
Moravians from 1664 on. Illustrations.

1654. Storer, H.J. "Old Boston Organs." *Church Music Review* 3
         (1904): 518-19.

1655. Storer, H.J. "Organists in Early Boston." *New Music Review*
         4 (1904): 23-24.

1656. Taylor, Barbara and Raymond Taylor. "The Colonial Musical
         Instrument Maker." *Early American Life* 4/6 (1973): 38-41.

1657. Tilton, Edwin A. "Notable Organs, IV: The Brattle Organ."
         Organ 1 (1892): 173-74.

1658. Tufts, Nancy Poore. "Bells of Colonial America and of the
         Early Republic." *Journal of Church Music* 18/1 (January
         1976): 2-5.

         This brief introduction mentions some of the early churches
having bells. Sources not cited.

1659.   Vaughan, Donald.   "The Brattle Organ: First Organ in the
        United States." *Clavier* 14/4 (1975): 32-33.

1660.   Waldo, Frank.   "The First American Violin Maker." *Musician*
        10 (1905): 192-93.

        Discusses Benjamin Crehore.

1661.   "Washington's Violin." *American Art Journal* 34 (1881): 481-
        82.

        On a violin George Washington might have owned.

1662.   Watkins, C. Malcolm.   "American Pianos of the Federal Period
        in the United States National Museum." *Antiques* 59 (1951):
        58-61.

1663.   Watson, John.   "Claviers for Salem: Historic Keyboard
        Instruments in the Salem Moravian Community." *Moravian
        Music Journal* 31/1 (Spring 1986): 9-12.

        Discusses 5 square pianos, 3 organs, and 2 clavichords
dating from the 18th century on. Includes photographs, one of a
square piano made by John Kearsing & Son in New York, ca. 1810.

1664.   Williams, George W.   "The Snetzler Organ at St. Michael's
        Church, Charleston." *Organ: A Quarterly Review for Its
        Makers, Its Players, and Its Lovers* 33 (1954): 134-36.

1665.   Wirling, Eliot I.   "Pipe Organs of New England." *Old-Time
        New England* 45 (1954): 37-48.

1666.   Wolf, Edward C.   "The Organs at St. Michael's and Zion
        Lutheran Churches, Philadelphia." *Tracker* 6/3 (April
        1962): 6-8.

        A description of the organs dedicated in the 1790s.

1667. Wolf, Edward C. "The Schmahl and Krauss Organs in Old St. Michael's, Philadelphia." *Tracker* 17/4 (Summer 1973): 8-11.

The Johann Schmahl organ was installed in 1750, the Andrew Krauss organ in 1815.

1668. Wolf, Edward C. "The Tannenberg Organ at Old Zion Church Philadelphia." *Journal of Church Music* 3/4 (April 1961): 2-5.

The organ, built by David Tannenberg, was completed in 1790. The author describes the physical characteristics of the organ.

VII.   BIOGRAPHIES

Indexes

1669.   *Bio-Bibliographical Index of Musicians in the United States
          of America Since Colonial Times.*   2nd ed.   Washington,
          D.C.: Pan American Union, 1956.   Reprint, New York: Da Capo
          Press, 1971; New York: AMS Press, 1972; St. Clair Shores,
          Mich.: Scholarly Press, 1972.   xxiii, 439p.

        An index to works that contain biographies, some of which
are not likely to be found in other sources.   Arranged
alphabetically by name of individual.   Includes an appendix of
biographies.

1670.   *Biography and Genealogy Master Index.*   2nd ed. by Miranda C.
          Herbert and Barbara McNeil.   Detroit: Gale, 1980.   8 vols.

        An index to over 3 million biographies and sketches found
in some 350 biographical dictionaries.   Readers can expect to find
numerous entries for early American musicians.   A supplement (5
vols.) for 1981-85 adds another 2 million entries.   Indexes are not
cumulative.

1671.   *Biography Index, a Cumulative Index to Biographical Material
          in Books and Magazines.*   Vol. 1- .   New York: H.W. Wilson,
          1947- .

        This index to books and periodicals includes a few music
journals.   However, the *Music Index* (see entry 147) is the better
choice.

Collective Biographies

1672.   *The American Biographical Archive: A Single-Alphabet
        Cumulation of 367 Original Biographical Reference Works
        Covering 300,000 Individuals from the Earliest Period of
        North American History through the Early Twentieth Century.*
        Ed. by Laureen Baillie and Gerry Easter.   New York: K.G.
        Saur, 1986.   Microfiche; 11 x 15 cm.   With guide (20p.).

        A significant tool.   "Individuals of every class, religious
affiliation, ethnic group, profession and state are included."
Musicians are well represented.

1673.   *Baker's Biographical Dictionary of Musicians.*   7th ed.   New
        York: Schirmer, 1984.   xlii, 2,577p.

        A standard comprehensive work, with brief biographies of
early American musicians.

1674.   Butterworth, Neil.   *A Dictionary of American Composers.*   New
        York: Garland Publishing, 1984.   xiv, 523p.

        Includes brief biographies and information on works by 35
musicians active in America before 1820.

1675.   Cansler, Jeannine Ann.   "An Annotated Listing of Organists
        Flourishing in Five American Cities between 1700 and 1850."
        D.M.A. dissertation, University of Oregon, 1984.   223p.   UM
        85-01979.   *DAI* 45/12 (June 1985): 3474-A.

        Includes 265 organists, with an appendix of 154 additional
organists.   Another appendix includes a list of organ builders.   The
cities are Charleston, Boston, Philadelphia, Bethlehem, Pa., and
Salem, N.C.

1676.   Claghorn, Charles Eugene.   *Biographical Dictionary of
        American Music.*   West Nyack, New York: Parker Publishing
        Company, 1973.   491p.

        Serves as a ready-reference tool.   Contains over 5,200
entries.   "You will find biographical information on persons active

in American music life during the Colonial period, the Revolution, and during the 1790s in Boston, New York City, Philadelphia, and Charleston, South Carolina." Brief entries, a number of which, including Joel Harmon, Jr., John Alexander Granade, Joseph Herrick, and Florant Meline, are not entered separately in *The New Grove Dictionary of American Music* (see entry 30).

1677. *Dictionary of American Biography.* Published under the auspices of the American Council of Learned Societies. New York: Scribner, 1928- . 20 vols., with 7-volume supplement.

Includes articles on Americans considered to be significant in their fields. The first 20 volumes include persons who died before 1927. There is also a *Concise Dictionary of American Biography* that is an abridged version of the larger work and includes all entries from the 20 volumes plus two supplements. Readers can expect to find brief biographies on William Billings, Benjamin Carr, Josiah Flagg, James Hewitt, Thomas Johnston, James Lyon, John Frederick Peter, Daniel Read, Isaiah Thomas, and others. A handy list of composers represented in the work is found in Richard Jackson's *United States Music* (see entry 103).

1678. Ewen, David. *American Composers: A Biographical Dictionary.* New York: G.P. Putnam's Sons, 1982. 793p.

Out of some 300 biographies, only a few are devoted to early American composers. These include William Billings, Anthony Philip Heinrich, James Hewitt, Francis Hopkinson, and Alexander Reinagle.

1679. Frim, Rose. "A Concise Chronological List of American-Born Composers and Music Workers." *Etude* 40/3 (March 1922): 214; 40/4 (April 1922): 237-38.

Includes a list of names, dates, and cities. Where the information was obtained is not known.

1680. Greene, David Mason. *Greene's Biographical Encyclopedia of Composers.* New York: Doubleday, 1985. xl, 1,348p.

A popular biographical dictionary having entries that include composers whose works are available on recordings. Includes most major early American composers. Entries are arranged chronologically, so readers must refer first to the list of composers to determine entry number.

1681.   Hood, George. "Sketches of American Musical Biography and History." *Musical Herald* 3/6 (June 1882): 149; 3/9 (September 1882): 229.

Brief biographies of Daniel Bayley, James Lyon, Asahel Benham, Hans Gram, and Elias Mann.

1682.   Metcalf, Frank Johnson. *American Writers and Compilers of Sacred Music*. New York: Russell & Russell, 1967. 373p.

Includes 91 biographies of mostly New England composers of the 18th and 19th centuries. Sources are not provided. However, Metcalf provides information not necessarily found in other sources. Facsimiles and index.

1683.   "Musical Authors and Publications of the United States." *Musical Magazine* 1/3 (July 1835): 85-91.

A number of character sketches of various tunebook compilers, including James Lyon, William Billings, Andrew Law, G.K. Jackson, Justin Morgan, William Little, William Smith, Daniel Read, Amos Bull, Samuel Holyoke, Jacob Kimball, Jr., William Tuckey, and others, and candid comments regarding their work. The article was possibly written by Thomas Hastings, the magazine's editor. Reprinted in *American Periodicals, 1800-1850*, reel 840 (see entry 131).

1684.   *The National Cyclopedia of American Biography*. 63 vols. With supplementary index (1984).

Includes biographies of William Billings, Johann Conrad Beissel, Andrew Law, Daniel Read, and others. Readers should note that there are also a number of entries under "Music" in the subject index.

1685.   "New England Singing Masters." *Musical Review* 1/28 (2 March
         1839): 387-88.

         Principally a discussion and comparison of William
Billings, Oliver Holden, and Elias Mann, the latter who taught "the
choir attached to the Berry-street Church" in Boston. Discusses
performance practice, and the use of a clarinet in Mann's singing
school. Interesting due to its candid commentary.

1686.   Parker, John Rowe. *A Musical Biography*. Boston: Stone &
         Fovell, 1825. Reprint, Detroit: Information Coordinators,
         1975. viii, 250p.

         Although Parker's main focus is on European composers, he
does include brief biographies of George K. Jackson and Rayner
Taylor.

1687.   Patterson, Relford. "Three American "Primitives": A Study of
         the Musical Style of Hans Gram, Oliver Holden, and Samuel
         Holyoke." Ph.D. dissertation, Washington University, 1963.
         283p. UM 64-2329. *DAI* 25/3 (September 1964): 1957.

         The three individuals were co-compilers of *The
Massachusetts Compiler* (1795).

1688.   Rose, Kenneth. "Early American Votaries of the Violin, 1763-
         1800." *Violins and Violinists* 11 (1950): 4-8, 58-61.

         Sketches of various violinists.

1689.   Simpson, Clinton. "Some Early American Guitarists." *Guitar
         Review* 23 (June 1959): 16.

         Brief information on Henry Capron, Robert Carter of Nomini
Hall, Va., Benjamin Franklin, John Gualdo, Francis Hopkinson, and
other lesser-known guitarists.

1690.   *Who's Who in American Music: Classical*. 2nd ed. Ed. by
         Jacques Cattell Press. New York: R.R. Bowker, 1985. xiii,
         783p.

Includes 9,038 entries representing a broad spectrum of current musical activity by scholars, teachers, and composers in American music. Includes biographies of American music studies scholars. Geographic index and professional classifications index.

1691.   Wiggin, Frances Turgeon. *Maine Composers and Their Music: A Biographical Dictionary*. N.p.: Maine Federation of Music Clubs, 1959. xvii, 121p.

Includes entries for Supply Belcher, Nathaniel Deering, Ezekiel Goodale, Henry Little, James Lyon, Abraham Maxim, Japeth Washburn, and others. Composer index. See also Wiggin's supplement (Portland: Maine Historical Society, 1976).

Individual Biographies

Andrew Adgate
(1762-1793)

1692.   Cummings, Harmon Dean. "Andrew Adgate: Philadelphia Psalmodist and Music Educator." Ph.D. dissertation, Eastman School of Music, 1975. 382p. UM 75-26155. *DAI* 36/5 (November 1975): 2476-A.

A study of the life and publications of Adgate. Discusses his singing schools, in particular his Uranian Academy, and his relationship with Andrew Law. Included is a checklist of Adgate's publications with library locations noted.

John Antes
(1740-1811)

1693.   Boeringer, James. "John Antes." *Journal of Church Music* 26/7 (September 1984): 16-17.

Brief biography of this American-born Moravian musician who later left America.

1694. Claypool, Richard D. "Mr. John Antes: Instrumentmaker."
      Moravian Music Foundation Bulletin 23/2 (Fall-Winter 1978):
      10-13.

   Discusses the life of Antes, with information on his
endeavors as an instrumentmaker. Includes a photograph of a viola
he made in 1764.

1695. Hamilton, J. Taylor. "Experiences of the First American
      Missionary in Egypt." *Transactions of the Moravian
      Historical Society* 12 (1938): 26-39.

1696. Kroeger, Karl. "John Antes at Fulneck." *Moravian Music
      Journal* 30/1 (Spring 1985): 12-18.

   Includes biographical information, especially his tenure as
president of the College of Overseers, a post he held in England
from 1787-1801. Also discusses musical compositions of Antes.

1697. McCorkle, Donald M. "John Antes, 'American Dilettante.'"
      Musical Quarterly 42/4 (October 1956): 486-99.

   A significant article for the study of Antes. The author
includes concise biographical information, a description and list of
his works, and a photograph of a violin built by Antes in Bethlehem,
Pa., in 1759. Reprinted as Moravian Music Foundation Publications,
no. 2 (Winston-Salem: Moravian Music Foundation, 1956).

1698. "Sketches of Moravian Composers: A Footnote for John Antes."
      Moravian Music Foundation Bulletin 3/1 (Winter 1959): 3.

   A brief biography.

1699. Stolba, K. Marie. "Evidence of Quartets by John Antes,
      American-Born Moravian Composer." *Journal of the American
      Musicological Society* 33/3 (Fall 1980): 565-74.

   Correspondence from John Antes to Benjamin Franklin during
1779-80 is used as evidence to support the claim that Antes was the
first native-born American to write chamber music. The author
corrects dates cited by McCorkle in his article, "John Antes,

'American Dilettante'" (see entry 1697), regarding Antes' ordination
and departure for Egypt.

1700.   Stolba, K. Marie.   "From John Antes to Benjamin Franklin: A
        Musical Connection."   *Moravian Music Foundation Bulletin*
        25/2 (Fall-Winter 1980): 5-9, 18-19.

        Concerns a recently discovered letter dated July 10, 1779,
its contents, and what it reveals about their relationship, and
Antes' set of quartets.   Includes a facsimile of the letter.

1701.   Stolba, K. Marie.   "A Newly Discovered Letter from John Antes
        to Benjamin Franklin."   *Moravian Music Foundation Bulletin*
        25/1 (Spring-Summer 1980): 9.

        The letter is dated July 10, 1779.   A brief description of
its contents.

Thomas Appleton
(1785-1872)

1702.   Clarke, W. Horatio.   "Thomas Appleton, an Early New England
        Organ-Builder."   *Organ: A Monthly Journal Devoted to the
        King of Instruments* 1 (1892): 29-30.

        Thomas Appleton worked with William Goodrich, instrument
maker, in 1805, and was later part owner of the Franklin Musical
Warehouse in Boston.

Alpheus Babcock
(1785-1842)

1703.   Grafing, Keith Gerhart.   "Alpheus Babcock, American
        Pianoforte Maker (1785-1842): His Life, Instruments, and
        Patents."   D.M.A. dissertation, University of Missouri-
        Kansas City, 1972.   132p.   UM 73-19723.   *DAI* 34/3
        (September 1973): 1312-13-A.

Discusses his life and activities in Milton and Boston, Mass., and Philadelphia.   Examines 15 extant Babcock pianos.

<u>Thomas Bacon</u>
(c. 1700-1768)

1704.   Deibert, William E.   "Thomas Bacon, Colonial Clergyman."
Maryland Historical Magazine 73/1 (Spring 1978): 79-86.

Bacon was rector of All Saints Parish in Frederick, Md., in 1762, a honorary member of the Tuesday Club of Annapolis, and a composer of the earliest extant chamber music in America.

<u>Johann Christian Bechler</u>
(1784-1857)

1705.   Allen, Walser H.   "John Christian Bechler."   *Moravian Music Journal* 28/2 (Summer 1983): 40-43.

A biography of Bechler, who was active in Nazareth and Lititz, Pa., and Salem, N.C. during the early 1800s.   He played the piano, organ, and various string instruments.   Portraits.

1706.   Boeringer, James.   "Johann Christian Bechler."   *Journal of Church Music* 25/6 (June 1983): 7, 13.

Brief biography of this Moravian musician, who arrived in Nazareth, Pa. in 1806.

<u>Johann Conrad Beissel</u>
(1691-1786)

1707.   Briner, Andres.   "Wahrheit und Dichtung um J.C. Beissel; Studie um sine Gestalt in Thomas Mann's 'Dr. Faustus.'"
Schweizerische Musikzeitung 98/10 (October 1958): 365-69.

Beissel came to America in 1720 and in 1732 founded the Ephrata Cloister, a semimonastic community where a number of significant hymn collections were compiled. Discusses Beissel's compositions.

1708.   Bunners, C. "The Birth of Freedom Out of Bondage: Thomas Mann and the German-American Poet-Composer Johann Conrad Beissel." *Hymn* 36/3 (1985): 7-10.

1709.   Kilian, Otto. "Konrad Beisel [*sic*] (1691-1786): Founder of the Ephrata Cloister in Pennsylvania." *Bach* 7/3 (July 1976): 25-28; 7/4 (October 1976): 31-36; 8/1 (January 1977): 23-24.

Article originally published in *Eberbacher Geschichtsblatt* (July 1957), and translated here by Wiltrud Cornish. A biography but sources are not noted.

1710.   Klein, Walter Conrad. *Johann Conrad Beissel, Mystic and Martinet*. Philadelphia: University of Pennsylvania Press, 1942. Reprint, Philadelphia: Porcupine Press, 1972. ix, 218p.

<u>Supply Belcher</u>
(1751-1836)

1711.   Owen, Earl McLain, Jr. "The Life and Music of Supply Belcher (1751-1836), 'Handel of Maine.'" D.M.A. dissertation, Southern Baptist Theological Seminary, 1969. 2 vols., 385p. UM 69-4446. *DAI* 29/9 (March 1969): 3172-73-A.

Belcher was a New England composer and tunebook compiler. The author discusses Belcher's life, works, and includes a discussion of performance practice of that time, and a supplement of all of his works. For extensive commentary on this work, see Sterling E. Murray's article in *Current Musicology* 12 (1971), pp. 102-08.

Daniel Belknap
(1771-1815)

1712.   Hood, George.   "Sketches of American Biography and History:
Daniel Belknap." *Musical Herald* 3/11 (November 1882): 286.

This New England composer, tunebook compiler, and singing
teacher composed some 86 works.   A brief biography with information
on his tunebooks.

William Billings
(1746-1800)

1713.   "An Account of Two Americans of Extraordinary Genius in
Poetry and Music." *Columbian Magazine or Monthly
Miscellany* 2 (April 1788): 211-213.

One of the earliest sources for information on Billings.
The other composer is Francis Hopkinson.   The article is discussed
in McKay, *William Billings of Boston* (see entry 1733).

1714.   Anderson, Gillian B.   "Eighteenth-Century Evaluations of
William Billings: A Reappraisal." *Quarterly Journal of the
Library of Congress* 35/1 (January 1978): 48-58.

Includes biographical background.   Discusses the "lack of
sympathy" for early American music and attitudes expressed by
various writers, and how Billings has been unjustly evaluated as a
composer.   Recommended reading.

1715.   Andrews, P. and S. Rodd.   "Pioneers of American Music."
Keyboard Classics 4/4 (1984): 6-7.

1716.   Barbour, J. Murray.   *The Church Music of William Billings.*
East Lansing: Michigan State University Press, 1960.
Reprint, New York: Da Capo Press, 1972.   xvi, 167p.

Each chapter focuses on a theoretical aspect of Billings'
sacred music, including texts, rhythm and meter, melody,

counterpoint and harmony, modality and tonality, and texture and form.   A series of appendixes include indexes of the music and text of Billings' psalm tunes and anthems.   Musical examples and general index.   Chapter 1 is also published by Barbour under the title "The Texts of Billings' Church Music" in *Criticism, a Quarterly for Literature and the Arts* 1/1 (Winter 1959), pp. 49-61.

1717.   "Billings's Psalmody."   *Dwight's Journal of Music* 3/1 (April 9, 1853): 2.

Includes short biography, information on his tunebook collections, and comments regarding their musical qualities.

1718.   Chase, Gilbert.   "Billings of Boston."   *Music: The A.G.O./R.C.C.O. Magazine* 9/9 (1975): 30-31.

1719.   Daniel, Oliver.   "America's First Troubadour."   *Music Clubs Magazine* 32/3 (January 1953): 8, 28.

Brief introduction to Billings and mentions some recent editions of his music.

1720.   Daniels, Rose Dwiggins.   "William Billings: Teacher, Innovator, Patriot."   *Music Educators Journal* 74/9 (May 1988): 22-25.

A brief biography mentioning aspects of his musical innovations and musical patriotism.   Includes facsimiles from his tunebooks.

1721.   Ellsworth, Ray.   "William Billings and Early American Music: Rush On Ye Sons of Harmony!"   *Sing Out* 10/4 (1960-61): 24-26.

1722.   Ferris, William R., Jr.   "William Billings: The Musical Tanner.   *Keystone Folklore Quarterly* 12/4 (Winter 1967): 261-78.

Discusses three periods in the development of Billings' musical style, critical reactions to Billings' music by other writers, the composer's publications, and includes information on singing schools.

1723.   Funk, Joseph. "Billings a Pioneer." *Southern Musical Advocate and Singer's Friend* 1/7 (January 1860): 105.

Funk provides a brief biography and comments that Billings "wrote his first tunes with chalk, on the wall of his building, while tending the mill to grind bark."

1724.   Gamet, Vera. "'Billings Best.'" *Etude* 57 (1939): 777-78, 816.

1725.   Garrett, Allen McCain. "The Works of William Billings." Ph.D. dissertation, University of North Carolina, 1952. 177p.

1726.   Goldberg, Isaac. "The First American Musician." *American Mercury* 14/53 (May 1928): 67-75.

Includes a brief biography, with a number of notions not necessarily supported by sources, and information on his tunebooks. Musical examples.

1727.   Hall, Roger L. "William Billings of Boston." *Journal of Church Music* 25/5 (May 1983): 2-4.

1728.   Hitchcock, H. Wiley. "William Billings and the Yankee Tunesmiths." *HiFi/Stereo Review* 16/2 (1966): 55-65.

1729.   Johnson, Carl. "From Tanner to Tunesmith." *Music Ministry* 4/11 (1963): 13-14, 36.

1730.   Lindstrom, Carl E. "William Billings and His Times." *Musical Quarterly* 25/4 (October 1939): 479-97.

A short biography and description of the composer's tunebooks as a point of departure for further discussion of other

New England composers, including Josiah Flagg, William Selby, and other lesser-known musicians.

1731.   Lingg, Ann M.   "The Musical Tanner."   *Opera News* 34/16 (14 February 1970): 27-28.

Brief information on the composer's musical background.

1732.   McKay, David P.   "William Billings and the Colonial Music 'Patent.'"   *Old-Time New England* 63 (1973): 100-07.

Pertains to Billings' attempt to secure copyright protection.

1733.   McKay, David P., and Richard Crawford.   *William Billings of Boston: Eighteenth-Century Composer*.   Princeton: Princeton University Press, 1975.   xii, 303p.

The principal biography of Billings that not only includes a chronology study of his life and tunebooks, but also places Billings in the cultural tradition of that time through a consideration of sacred music in New England during the 18th century, Billings as an "American artist," and the reputation of the composers and his music.   Two appendixes discuss problems of copyright and Billings in the 18th century, and performance practice.   Facsimiles, list of Billings' tunebooks, and index.

1734.   Morin, Raymond.   "William Billings: Pioneer in American Music."   *New England Quarterly* 14/1 (March 1941): 25-33.

A brief biography with mention of his tunebooks.   Based on secondary sources.

1735.   Nathan, Hans.   *William Billings: Data and Documents*.   Detroit: Information Coordinators, 1976.   69p.

Includes a biography and a bibliography of tunebooks, single compositions and small collections, manuscript literary contributions, and posthumous publications.   See also the author's article "William Billings: A Bibliography," in *Notes* 29/4 (June 1973), pp. 658-69.

1736. Upton, George P. "The First American Composer." In *Musical Pastels*. Chicago: A.C. McClurg, 1902, pp. 59-71.

A brief biography, with information on the composer's tunebooks.

1737. "William Billings." *Musical Herald* 3/7 (July 1882): 172-73.

A brief survey of Billings' life and works. The author (unsigned) states that, "In regard to his [Billings] talents and influence, we think justice has never been done them."

1738. "William Billings." *Musical Reporter* 1 (July 1841): 297-304; (August 1841): 350-53.

Contains considerable information on Billings, including candid comments regarding his popularity at that time. Includes a list of Billings' tunebooks, and information on the origin of the tune "Jargon." Reprinted in *American Periodicals, 1800-1850*, reel 840 (see entry 131).

1739. Young, J.I. "The Pioneer of American Church Music." *Potter's American Monthly* 7 (1876): 255-56.

<u>Henry Blake</u>
(1755-1833)

1740. Cifaldi, Susan. "Henry Blake, A New Hampshire Fifer in the Revolutionary War." *Sonneck Society Bulletin* 14/3 (Fall 1988): 115-16.

Henry Blake was a fifer in the New Hampshire regiment. The author includes biographical information and an account of Blake's tour of duty based on his diary. Included are the names of 19 tunes Blake played at the time of the Revolutionary War.

William Brown
(fl. 1783-88)

1741.   Engel, Carl.   "Introducing Mr. Braun."   *Musical Quarterly*
          30/1 (January 1944): 63-83.

          Discusses the life of William Brown of Philadelphia and the
author's endeavor to publish the composer's *Three Rondos for the
Piano Forte or Harpsichord* (1787).   Included is a facsimile of
"Rondo III."

Benjamin Carr
(1768-1831)

1742.   Davis, Helen E.   "The Carrs, a Musical Family."   *Pennsylvania
          Genealogical Magazine* 24 (1965): 57-68.

1743.   Lehman, Carroll James.   "Benjamin Carr: His Contribution to
          Early American Solo Vocal Literature."   D.M.A.
          dissertation, University of Iowa, 1975.   181p.   UM 75-
          23060.   *DAI* 36/4 (October 1975): 1892-A.

          Discusses Carr's musical activities, including his music
store business, as editor of music journals, church musician, and
his writings.   Included is an analysis of 60 solo vocal works, a
list of these works with library locations, transcriptions of
letters from Carr to John Rowe Parker, and copies of 8 songs.

1744.   Redway, Virginia Larkin.   "The Carrs, American Music
          Publishers."   *Musical Quarterly* 18/1 (January 1932): 150-
          77.

          Musical members of the Carr family included Joseph, Thomas,
and Benjamin.   Benjamin Carr is the more significant musician and is
the principal subject of this article.   Included is biographical
information on his life as a music publisher in Philadelphia and New
York and composer.   Included is a list with library locations of
Benjamin's compositions, including his arrangements of other
composers' works.   Musical examples.

1745.   Smith, Ronnie L.   "The Church Music of Benjamin Carr (1768-
        1831)."   Ph.D. dissertation, Southwestern Baptist
        Theological Seminary, 1969.   305p.

1746.   Sprenkle, Charles A.   "The Life and Works of Benjamin Carr
        (1768-1831)."   D.M.A. dissertation, Peabody Conservatory of
        Music, 1970.   2 vols., 493p.

        Includes the following 5 chapters: "A Biographical Sketch";
"Keyboard Works"; "Analysis of the 'Duett for Two Harpsichords'";
"Secular Vocal Works"; "Sacred Works."   Included is an inventory of
compositions and arrangements by Carr and programs, advertisements,
and pamphlets.

1747.   Wilhite, Charles S.   "An Early American Organist."   *Clavier*
        12/2 (February 1973): 25-31.

        Brief background with a performance edition of Carr's
"Voluntary" for keyboard.

Amzi Chapin (1768-1835)
and
Lucius Chapin (1760-1842)

1748.   Eddy, Mary O.   "Three Early Hymn Writers."   *Southern Folklore
        Quarterly* 10 (1946): 177-82.

        Includes a discussion of Amzi Chapin.

1749.   Hamm, Charles.   "The Chapins and Sacred Music in the South
        and West."   *Journal of Research in Music Education* 8/2
        (Fall 1960): 91-98.

        The first significant article that focuses on the Chapins.
Includes biographical information, information on sources, the
likely relationship of Andrew Law with Lucius Chapin, and Chapin
works in (Robert) *Patterson's Church Music* (Cincinnati, 1813).

1750.   Scholten, James W.   "Amzi Chapin: Frontier Singing Master and
        Folk Hymn Composer." *Journal of Research in Music
        Education* 23/2 (Summer 1975): 109-119.

        Amzi Chapin lived in a number of places, including
Hartford, Conn. and North Carolina.   Cites tunes attributed to him.

1751.   Scholten, James William.   "The Chapins: A Study of Men and
        Sacred Music West of the Alleghenies, 1795-1842."   Ed.D.
        dissertation, University of Michigan, 1972.   167p.   UM 72-
        28984.   *DAI* 33/5 (November 1972): 2416-17-A.

        Discusses these singing teachers based, in part, on the
Blinn Papers in the Cincinnati Historical Society and other primary
sources, and an examination of 196 tunebooks.   Also reviews previous
research.

1752.   Scholten, James W.   "Lucius Chapin: A New England Singing
        Master on the Frontier." *Contributions to Music Education*
        4 (Winter 1976): 64-76.

        Based on the author's dissertation (see entry 1751).   A
good introductory biography of Chapin and based on correspondence
from the early 19th century.

<u>Philip Anthony Corri</u>
(1784?-1832)

1753.   Metcalf, Frank J.   "Philip Anthony Corri and Arthur Clifton."
        Journal of the Presbyterian Historical Society 11/7 (April
        1923): 268-72.

        A biographical account.   Clifton's real name was Philip
Anthony Corri.   Discusses Corri's position as organist at the First
Presbyterian Church in Baltimore in 1819.

Ananias Davisson
(1780-1857)

1754. Harley, Augusta Brett. "Ananias Davisson: Southern Tune-Book Compiler (1780-1857)." Ph.D. dissertation, University of Michigan, 1972. viii, 312p. UM 72-29077. *DAI* 33/5 (November 1972): 2411-A.

This composer and tunebook compiler was active in Harrisonburg, Va. Includes the following 4 chapters: "Ananias Davisson: Who He Was and Where He Lived"; "Davisson's Tune-Books"; "Music Claimed by Davisson"; "Conclusion." Of note are the appendixes which include, for example, "transcriptions of 24 tunes set by Davisson" and some 47 settings attributed to Davisson.

Jacob Eckhard
(1757-1833)

1755. Williams, George W. "Jacob Eckhard and His Choirmaster's Book." *Journal of the American Musicological Society* 7/1 (Spring 1954): 41-47.

Jacob Eckhard came to the colonies in 1776 and was an organist at St. Michael's Church in Charleston, S.C. This study consists of a biography and a description of the tunes in the organist's manuscript collection. Photo.

Lewis Edson, Sr. (1748-1820)
and
Lewis Edson, Jr. (1771-1845)

1756. Lowens, Irving. "The Musical Edsons of Shady: Early American Tunesmiths." Bulletin of the New York Public Library 65/4 (April 1961): 236-48.

Includes biographical information on both Edsons and on popular fuging tunes found in the elder Edson's *The Social Harmonist*, 2nd edition (New York, 1801). Lowens also discusses his discovery of a musical notebook kept by Edson, Jr. Musical examples.   Reprinted in Lowens, *Music and Musicians in Early America* (see entry 371).

<u>Benjamin Franklin</u>
(1706-1790)

The following general bibliography of writings on Franklin includes a number of entries on music:

1757.   Buxbaum, Melvin H.   *Benjamin Franklin, 1721-1906: A Reference Guide*.   Boston: G.K. Hall, 1983.   xxiii, 334p.

Includes entries for literature on the musical side of Franklin for the following years: 1767, 1790, 1812, 1852, 1855, 1857, 1876, 1885, 1890, and 1900.

1758.   Freedman, Roma Sachs.   "The Musical Ben Franklin."   *Music Journal* 28/9 (October 1970): 40, 43.

An introduction to the musical side of Franklin, discussing his musical instruments, including musical glasses and a harp. Sources are not provided for quoted material.

1759.   Heller, George N.   "'To Sweeten Their Senses': Music, Education, and Benjamin Franklin."   *Music Educators Journal* 73/5 (January 1987): 22-26.

Introduction to Franklin's musical endeavors, including his invention of the armonica and his two songs.

1760.   La Laurencie, Lionel de.   "Benjamin Franklin and the Claveciniste Brillon de Jouy."   *Musical Quarterly* 9/2 (April 1923): 245-59.

Regarding Franklin's stay in Paris, 1777-85, and his visits with Mme. Brillon de Jouy, amateur musician who played the harpsichord.

1761.   Myers, Gordon.   "Benjamin Franklin and Other Early American
        Music Critics."   *NATS Bulletin* 38/1 (September-October
        1981): 12-15.

        Concerns performance practice and is based on primary
sources.   The "other" critics are Oliver Brownson, Jonathan
Huntington, Jacob Kimball, Cotton Mather, Thomas Symmes, John Tufts,
and Thomas Walter.   Illustrations.

1762.   Schiller, Andrew.   "Franklin as Music Critic."   *New England
        Quarterly* 31/4 (December 1958): 505-14.

        Discusses Franklin's aesthetic views regarding music and
proposes 4 principles upon which those views are based.

1763.   Sonneck, Oscar George.   "Benjamin Franklin's Musical Side."
        In *Suum Cuique: Essays in Music*.   New York: G. Schirmer,
        1916.   Reprint, Freeport, N.Y.: Books for Libraries Press,
        1969, pp. 59-84.

        An excellent article with sources provided.   Discusses
Franklin's armonica, and other examples of musical glasses in the
colonies, Franklin's attendance at concerts, and his other interests
in music.   Musical examples.   (See also entry 400.)

1764.   Sonneck, Oscar George.   "Benjamin Franklin's Relation to
        Music."   *Music: A Monthly Magazine* 19 (1900): 1-14.

1765.   Stolba, K. Marie.   "Benjamin Franklin and Music."   *American
        Music Teacher* 26/2 (November-December 1976): 8-11.

        Discusses his musical glasses and letters he wrote.

1766.   Stolba, K. Marie.   "Music in the Life of Benjamin Franklin."
        Daughters of the American Revolution Magazine 106/1
        (January 1972): 4-7.

        A discussion of Franklin as a performer, music critic, and
composer.

<u>Jacob French</u>
(1754-1817)

1767.   Genuchi, Marvin Charles.   "The Life and Music of Jacob French (1754-1817), Colonial American Composer."   Ph.D. dissertation, State University of Iowa, 1964.   2 vols., 307p.   UM 64-7918.   *DAI* 25/2 (August 1964): 1247-48.

French was a tunebook compiler, singing teacher, and composer active in Massachusetts and Connecticut.   Volume 1 includes musical background, a biography, a study of his music, and performace practice in French's writings.   Volume 2 consists of musical examples.   For extensive commentary on this work, see Charles H. Kaufman's article in *Current Musicology* 10 (1970), pp. 111-16.

1768.   Jones, Dankel.   "A Reappraisal of Jacob French, American Psalmodist."   *Sonneck Society Bulletin* 13/3 (Fall 1987): 87-90.

Examines previous writings on French and offers some new interpretations as to French's development as a composer.

<u>Johann Friedrich Frueauff</u>
(1762-1839)

1769.   Claypool, Richard D.   "A Personal Journal Kept by Johann Friedrich Frueauff."   *Moravian Music Journal* 26/4 (Winter 1981): 76-81.

A biography of Frueauff, who taught in Nazareth, Pa., in 1788, and later was in Bethlehem and Lititz, Pa.   He wrote at least one musical composition.   The journal includes information on concerts and the distribution of music during 1788-99.

<u>Joseph Funk</u>
(1777-1862)

1770.   Wayland, John W.   "Joseph Funk, Father of Song in Northern
        Virginia." *Pennsylvania-German* 12 (1911): 580-94.

        Funk was a tunebook compiler whose earliest work was titled
Choral-Music (Harrisonburg, 1816).   The article includes a number of
letters written by Funk and herein transcribed.   A reprint of the
article is found in *Sheet Music Exchange* 4/5 (October 1986), pp. 25-
44.

<u>Johann Gottfried Gebhard</u>
(b. 1755)

1771.   Spice, Gordon Philip.   "Johann Gottfried Gebhard: Moravian
        Musician."   Ph.D. dissertation, University of North
        Carolina at Chapel Hill, 1975.   220p.   UM 75-29078.   *DAI*
        36/6 (December 1975): 3206-A.

        Discusses works by Gebhard held in Moravian repositories in
Bethlehem, Pa. and Winston-Salem, N.C.

<u>Johann Christian Geisler</u>
(1729-1815)

1772.   Poole, Franklin Parker.   "The Moravian Musical Heritage:
        Johann Christian Geisler's Music in America."   Ph.D.
        dissertation, George Peabody College for Teachers, 1971.
        vi, 352p.

        Includes 8 chapters.   A biographical study of Geisler and a
stylistic analysis of his anthems.   Also discusses Christian
Gottfried Geisler and Johannes Herbst.   Of note are the 6 appendixes
which include a list of Geisler's anthems and a selection of anthems
transcribed by the author, Geisler's diary, and a "facsimile copy of
the dedication ode for the Gnadenberg chapel."

<u>William M. Goodrich</u>
(1777-1833)

1773.   "Biographical Memoir of William M. Goodrich, Organ-Builder."
        Tracker 12/1 (Fall 1967): 13-18; 12/2 (Winter 1968): 6-8,
        15-16.

        A reprint from *New-England Magazine* (January 1834).
Goodrich began constructing church organs in Boston in 1805.   The
article discusses his life and the organs he built.   See also
Barbara J. Owen's "The Goodriches and Thomas Appleton" in *Tracker*
4/1 (October 1959).

<u>Hans Gram</u>
(1754-1804)

1774.   King, Rolf.   "The Significance of Hans Gram for Early
        American Musical Development."   *American-German Review* 12/3
        (1946): 17-22.

        Gram arrived in Massachusetts in 1785, and was a
contributor of music to the *Massachusetts Magazine*.

<u>Gottlieb Graupner</u>
(1767-1836)

1775.   King, Rolf.   "Gottlieb Graupner, Musical Pioneer."   *American-
        German Review* 11/1 (1944): 19-22.

        Graupner was an oboist in Hanover and later emigrated to
America where he was active as a composer, performer, and printer in
Charleston, Boston and elsewhere.

<u>Bernhard Adam Grube</u>
(1715-1808)

1776.   Hamilton, J.T., trans.   "Autobiography of Bernhard Adam
        Grube." *Transactions of the Moravian Historical Society* 11
        (1936): 199-207.

1777.   Hartzell, Lawrence W.   "Musical Moravian Missionaries: Part
        II: Bernhard Adam Grube." *Moravian Music Journal* 30/1
        (Spring 1985): 18-19.

        A brief biography of Grube, who came from Germany to
Pachgatgoch, N.Y. in 1750.   He played the zither and spinet for
services, and sang as well.

1778.   Jordan, John W.   "Biographical Sketch of Rev. Bernhard Adam
        Grube." *Pennsylvania Magazine of History and Biography*
        25/1 (1901): 14-19.

        A biography, with an illustration of Grube and a facsimile
of the title page of his manuscript "Dellawaerisches Gesang-
Büchlein."

<u>Peter Albrecht Von Hagen</u> (1755-1803)
and
<u>Peter Albrecht Von Hagen, Jr.</u> (ca. 1779-1837)

1779.   Johnson, H. Earle.   "The Musical Von Hagens." *New England
        Quarterly* 16 (March 1943): 110-17.

        The Hagen family were musicians active in Charleston, New
York, and Boston.   Hagen, Sr. was a composer and importer of musical
instruments.   Hagen, Jr. was a violinist and composer.   Johnson also
discusses other musical members of the family.

1780.   "A Unique Letter." *Dwight's Journal of Music* 18/2 (13
        October 1860): 232.

Concerns a letter from P.A. Hagen, "Organist of the Trinity Church, Boston," to the church expressing that the organ is in need of repair and that Hagen's salary should be increased. Includes biographical information on Hagen and information on members of the church choir.

<u>Thomas Hastings</u>
(1784-1872)

1781.   Bristol, Lee H., Jr. "Thomas Hastings, 1784-1872." *Hymn* 10/4 (1959): 105-10.

1782.   Dooley, James Edward. "Thomas Hastings: American Church Musician." Ph.D. dissertation, Florida State University, 1963. 278p. UM 64-3594. *DAI* 24/11 (May 1964): 4725-26.

Discusses the life of this music teacher, choir director, lecturer, and author and editor of some 50 publications, including his *Musica Sacra* (1815) and *The Musical Reader* (1817).

1783.   Scanlon, Mary B. "Thomas Hastings." *Musical Quarterly* 32/2 (April 1946): 265-77.

Thomas Hastings published his *Utica Collection* (1816) and *The Musical Reader* (1817) and went on to become a composer of popular reknown.

1784.   Teal, Mary D. "Letters of Thomas Hastings." *Notes* 34/2 (December 1977): 303-18.

The letters were written during the period 1817-52 and are held in the Burton Historical Collection, Detroit Public Library.

<u>Anthony Philip Heinrich</u>
(1781-1861)

1785.   Barron, David Milton. "The Early Vocal Works of Anthony
        Philip Heinrich." Ph.D. dissertation, University of
        Illinois at Urbana-Champaign, 1972. 465p. UM 72-19793.
        DAI 33/1 (June 1972): 344-A.

        Discusses the vocal works that were published between 1819
and 1826. One appendix includes a list of poets, biographical
information on them, and first lines to texts. Other appendixes
include a list of publishers and an annotated catalog of Heinrich's
vocal works.

1786.   Bruce, Frank Neely. "The Piano Pieces of Anthony Philip
        Heinrich Contained in *The Dawning of Music in Kentucky* and
        The Western Minstrel." D.Mus.A. dissertation, University
        of Illinois at Urbana-Champaign, 1971. 426p. UM 72-6875.
        DAI 32/10 (April 1972): 5822-A.

        Discusses his musical compositions and includes 14 edited
works from *The Dawning of Music in Kentucky* and *The Western
Minstrel*.

1787.   Chmaj, B.E. "Father Heinrich as Kindred Spirit; or, How the
        Log-House Composer Became the Beethoven of America."
        American Studies 24/2 (Fall 1983): 35-37.

1788.   Filbeck, Loren Harold. "The Choral Works of Anthony Philip
        Heinrich." D.M.A. dissertation, University of Illinois at
        Urbana-Champaign, 1975. 625p. UM 75-24301. *DAI* 36/9
        (March 1976): 5625-A.

        Includes biographical information and a study of the choral
works divided into 4 categories: hymns, small secular works, larger
sacred and quasi-sacred pieces, and oratorios and cantatas.

1789.   Lowens, Irving. "The Triumph of Anthony Philip Heinrich."
        Musicology 2/1 (Spring 1948): 365-73.

Discusses the reception of Heinrich's music in New York and Boston.   Reprinted in Lowens, *Music and Musicians in Early America* (see entry 371).

1790.   Maust, Wilbur Richard.   "The Symphonies of Anthony Philip Heinrich Based on American Themes."   Ph.D. dissertation, Indiana University, 1973.   374p.   UM 73-19743.   *DAI* 34/3 (September 1973): 1315-A.

Includes a survey of the composer's life, his historical importance to American music, and an analysis of American themes in his symphonies.

1791.   Mussik, F.A.   *Skizzen aus dem Leben des sich in Amerika befindenden deutschen Tondichters Anton Philipp Heinrich.* Prag: G. Haase Söhne, 1843.   51p.

A brief biography of the composer and description of some of his major works, based, in part, on excerpts from contemporary newspaper commentary.

1792.   Upton, William Treat.   *Anthony Philip Heinrich: A Nineteenth-Century Composer in America.*   New York: Columbia University Press, 1939.   Reprint, New York: AMS Press, 1967.   xiv, 337p.

The principal biography of Heinrich with a discussion of his early years in Philadelphia and Kentucky.   Includes facsimiles, musical examples, a list of compositions, and index.

<u>Justus Henry Christian Helmuth</u>
(1745-1825)

1793.   Wolf, Edward C.   "Justus Henry Christian Helmuth—Hymnodist."   *German-American Studies* 5 (1972): 117-47.

Helmuth immigrated to Philadelphia.

<u>Johannes Herbst</u>
(1735-1812)

1794.   Boeringer, James. "Johann Herbst." *Journal of Church Music*
25/7 (September 1983): 16-17.

Brief biography of this Moravian musician active in Lititz,
Pa., and Salem, N.C.   Article is based on Joan Falconer's
dissertation (see entry 1795).   Facsimile.

1795.   Falconer, Joan Ormsby.   "Bishop Johannes Herbst (1735-1812):
An American Moravian Musician, Collector and Composer."
Ph.D. dissertation, Columbia University, 1969.   564p.   UM
72-15571.   *DAI* 32/11 (May 1972): 6475-A.

A study of the manuscripts compiled by Herbst, and an
analysis of his musical style.   Musical works reprinted here include
33 "geistliche Lieder" and 21 anthems.

<u>James Hewitt</u>
(1770-1827)

1796.   "Homage to an Early American Composer, Contemporary of
Beethoven." *Music Clubs Magazine* 49/5 (Summer 1970): 8,
21.

A brief survey of the life and musical activities of
Hewitt.

1797.   Howard, John Tasker.   "The Hewitt Family in American Music."
Musical Quarterly 17/1 (January 1931): 25-39.

Discusses James Hewitt, his life and works, and later
members of the family.   Includes Hewitt's arrangement of "The Star
Spangled Banner."   Illustrations.

1798.   Lawrence, Vera Brodsky.   "Mr. Hewitt Lays It on the Line."
Nineteenth Century Music 5/1 (1981): 3-15.

1799.   Wagner, John W.   "James Hewitt: His Life and Works."   Ph.D.
          dissertation, Indiana University, 1969.   620p.   UM 69-
          17775.   *DAI* 30/5 (November 1969): 2068-A.

          Discusses the many aspects of Hewitt's life in New York,
Boston, and other places for the period 1792-1825.   Appendixes list
his addresses, concert appearances, publication endeavors, works,
with a supplement of complete works and treatises.   Included is
information on Hewitt's musical descendants.

1800.   Wagner, John W.   "James Hewitt, 1770-1827."   *Musical
          Quarterly* 58/2 (April 1972): 259-76.

          Based on the author's dissertation (see entry 1799).
Includes a facsimile of the first page of Hewitt's arrangement of
"The Star Spangled Banner."

Michael Hillegas
(1728-1804)

1801.   Egle, William Henry.   "Michael Hillegas."   *Pennsylvania
          Magazine of History and Biography* 11/4 (January 1888): 406-
          09.

          Hillegas was a fiddle player and owner of a music store in
Philadelphia.   A brief biography of his non-musical endeavors, and
is based, in part, on a letter written by Hillegas in 1781.

John Hodgkinson
(1765-1805)

1802.   Porter, Susan L.   "John Hodgkinson in England: The Early Life
          of an American Actor-Singer."   *American Music* 6/3 (Fall
          1988): 264-80.

          John Hodgkinson came to America in 1792 and was successful
as an actor, singer and manager of the Old American Company.   Porter
examines Hodgkinson's life and career while in England and details

concerning Hodgkinson's decision to emigrate. Refer to Porter's notes for additional studies on Hodgkinson.

<u>Oliver Holden</u>
(1765-1844)

1803. Brown, Abram E. "Oliver Holden, the Composer of
'Coronation.'" *New England Magazine* 16 (1897): 708-19.

1804. McCormick, David W. "Oliver Holden, Composer and
Anthologist." S.M.D. dissertation, Union Theological
Seminary, 1963. 501p. UM 63-7551. *DAI* 24/5 (November
1963): 2072.

A study of his life and his residence in Massachusetts, his
relationship with Samuel Holyoke and Hans Gram, his publications,
and includes a stylistic analysis of his compositions.

1805. McCormick, David W. "Oliver Holden, 1765-1844." *Hymn* 14/3
(July 1963): 69-77, 79.

Discusses his early life, his business career, and as a
public servant, and his musical activities. Includes a list of his
tunebooks and a facsimile of the composer's "Coronation."

1806. "Oliver Holden: The First Baptist Composer in America."
Quarterly Review: A Survey of Southern Baptist Progress
(October-December 1980).

<u>Samuel Holyoke</u>
(1762-1820)

1807. Hood, George. "Sketches of American Musical Biography and
History: Samuel Holyoke, A.M." *Musical Herald* 3/12
(December 1882): 318.

Holyoke was a composer, tunebook compiler, and singing master in Massachusetts. A brief biography worth reviewing, with information on his publications.

1808.   Willhide, James Laurence. "Samuel Holyoke: American Music Educator." Ph.D. dissertation, University of Southern California, 1954. 421p.

Includes an examination of his tunebooks.

1809.   Wright, Richardson. "Our Singing Craft." *Transactions of the American Lodge of Research* 5/1 (18 December 1947-31 May 1949): 39-51.

Discusses Samuel Holyoke's masonic career. He wrote masonic music, selected and composed for the installation of the Merrymack Lodge, Haverhill, Massachusetts, c. 1800.

<u>Francis Hopkinson</u>
(1737-1791)

1810.   Albrecht, Otto. "Francis Hopkinson, Musician, Poet, and Patriot, 1737-1937." *University of Pennsylvania Library Chronicle* 6/1 (March 1938): 3-15.

See entry 223.

1811.   Cumming, Robert. "Francis Hopkinson, America's First Composer." *Daughters of the American Revolution Magazine* 101 (1967): 124-25, 205.

Reprinted in *Music Journal* 25/3 (1967), and in *Music Clubs Magazine* 46/4 (April 1967).

1812.   Ewen, David. "Francis Hopkinson, Inspired Song Composer of Early America." *Musical Courier* 109/6 (1934): 6, 19.

1813. Hastings, George E. *The Life and Works of Francis Hopkinson.*
       New York: Russell & Russell, 1968. xi, 516p.

       A revised doctoral study (Harvard University, 1918).
Includes a list of works.

1814. Hildeburn, Charles R. "Francis Hopkinson." *Pennsylvania
       Magazine of History and Biography* 2/3 (1878): 314-24.

       An early biography, with no mention of his musical
activities.

1815. Keefer, Lubov. "Hopkinson and the First American Art-Song:
       Taste and Models of a Colonial Composer." *Musical America*
       62/16 (1942): 8, 31.

1816. Kinscella, Hazel G. "Francis Hopkinson's Reactions to the
       Three Choirs Festival in England." *Musical America* 73/15
       (1953): 5, 27.

1817. Mahan, Katherine Hines. "Hopkinson and Reinagle: Patriot-
       Musicians of Washington's Time." *Music Educators Journal*
       62/8 (April 1976): 40-50.

       A discussion of the composers' lives and musical
contributions. Includes a facsimile of "General Washington's
March," a performance edition of "The Trav'ler Benighted" by
Hopkinson, a facsimile of "America, Commerce and Freedom," and a
performance edition of "The Tars of Columbia" by Reinagle.

1818. Marble, Annie R. "Francis Hopkinson: Man of Affairs and
       Letters." *New England Magazine* 27 (1902): 289-302.

1819. [Milligan, Harold V.] "Francis Hopkinson." *American
       Organist* 2 (1919): 279-81.

1820. Sonneck, Oscar George. "The First American Composer:
       Hopkinson or Lyon?" *Musical America* 37/7 (1923): 9, 40.

1821.   Sonneck, Oscar George.   "Francis Hopkinson (1737-1791); the
        First American Composer." *Sammelbände der internationalen
        Musikgesellschaft* 5 (1903): 119-54.

1822.   Sonneck, Oscar George.   *Francis Hopkinson, the First American
        Poet-Composer (1737-1791) and James Lyon, Patriot,
        Preacher, Psalmodist (1735-1794): Two Studies in Early
        American Music.* Washington, D.C.: H.L. McQueen, 1905.
        Reprint, with a new introduction by Richard A. Crawford
        (xiiip.), New York: Da Capo Press, 1967.   ix, 213p.

        Despite its date of publication, Sonneck's work is
scholarly and still useful today.   Discusses Hopkinson's musical
life, including his concerts, musical education, musical life in
Philadelphia, and includes a chronology of publications and musical
events from 1728 to 1759.   The second half of this book is devoted
to James Lyon, and a history and analysis of his *Urania* (1761).
Includes an appendix of works by Hopkinson and Lyon.   Index.

1823.   Sonneck, Oscar G.   "Francis Hopkinson: Some Corrections and
        Additions." *American Organist* 2 (1919): 337-39.

1824.   Stolba, K. Marie.   "Francis Hopkinson: Amateur de Musique."
        American Music Teacher 26/5 (April-May 1977): 18-22.

        A brief biography and a list of music that Hopkinson
apparently owned.

1825.   Stolba, K. Marie.   "Music in the Life of Francis Hopkinson."
        Daughters of the American Revolution Magazine 109/7
        (August-September 1975): 772-77.

        Biographical survey, including information on his poetry
and compositions.   Based, in part, on Hopkinson's correspondence.

1826.   Wilkinson, Norman B.   "Francis Hopkinson: Humor Propagandist
        of the American Revolution." *Historian* 4 (1941): 5-33.

<u>Charles Edward Horn</u>
(1786-1849)

1827.   Montague, Richard Addison.   "Charles Edward Horn: His Life
            and Works (1786-1849)."   Ed.D. dissertation, Florida State
            University, 1959.   212p.   UM 59-6921.   *DAI* 20/8 (February
            1960): 3325.

Discusses his contributions to American music, and his
participation in musical societies in New York, Philadelphia, and
Boston.   Included are 15 examples of his works.

<u>George K. Jackson</u>
(1757-1822)

1828.   Johnson, H. Earle.   "George K. Jackson, Doctor of Music
            (1745-1822)."   *Musical Quarterly* 29/1 (January 1943): 113-
            21.

Jackson immigrated to America in 1796 where he resided in
Elizabethtown, N.J. and New York.   This short biography includes
information on his musical endeavors as organist and teacher.

1829.   Oliver, H.K.   "An Early Boston Musician."   *Musical Herald* 3/8
            (August 1882): 204-05.

Uncomplimentary commentary regarding John Sullivan Dwight's
positive assessment of George K. Jackson as a musician.

<u>Thomas Jefferson</u>
(1743-1826)

*For additional articles and theses on Jefferson and music not
included in the list below, refer to the following guides:*

1830.   Huddleston, Eugene L.   *Thomas Jefferson: A Reference Guide.*
            Boston: G.K. Hall, 1982.   xxiii, 374p.

1831.   Shuffelton, Frank. *Thomas Jefferson: A Comprehensive
          Annotated Bibliography of Writings about Him (1826-1980).*
          New York: Garland Publishing, 1983. xix, 486p.

1832.   Allan, Alfred K. "The Music Lover of Monticello." *Music
          Journal* 13/7 (September 1955): 39, 58.

          Brief biography. Sources are not provided.

1833.   Berman, Eleanor D. *Thomas Jefferson among the Arts.* New
          York: Philosophical Library, 1947. xviii, 305p.

          Although the author devotes separate chapters to
Jefferson's interest in the various arts, including painting and
sculpture, she chooses to interweave the subject of music throughout
the body of the work.

1834.   Bullock, Helen Duprey. "Mr. Jefferson—Musician." *Etude*
          61/10 (October 1943): 633-34, 688.

          Consists of biographical information on Jefferson and his
musical interests. Includes a facsimile of a letter from Jefferson
to John Hawkins, June 17, 1802, stating that Jefferson's piano was
on route to Philadelphia.

1835.   Cripe, Helen. "Music: Thomas Jefferson's 'Delightful
          Recreation.'" *Antiques* 102 (July 1972): 124-28.

          Discusses Jefferson's love for instruments and songs.

1836.   Cripe, Helen. *Thomas Jefferson and Music.* Charlottesville:
          University of Virginia Press, 1974. viii, 157p.

          Based on her Ph.D. dissertation (University of Notre Dame,
1972). Discusses American secular music of the time, Jefferson's
musical activities, his violins, the music collection at Monticello
and the musical education of his daughters and granddaughters. See
a review by James R. Heintze in *Musical Quarterly* 61/1 (January
1975), pp. 151-53.

1837.   Fuller, Albert. "Thomas Jefferson and Music." *High Fidelity/Musical America* 26/7 (July 1976): 51.

Brief statement as to Jefferson's musical abilities and interests.

1838.   Garbett, Arthur S. "Thomas Jefferson's Life-Long Love of Music." *Etude* 59/8 (August 1941): 510, 568.

Biographical information, including information pertaining to a piano he ordered. Although based on letters, sources are not provided.

1839.   Gauss, Charles E. "Thomas Jefferson's Musical Interest." *Etude* 51 (June 1933): 367-68, 419.

Describes Jefferson's interest in the metronome, harpsichord, and the harmonica. Includes a list of books on music in his library in 1815.

1840.   Gelders, Ruth Beall. "The World of Music for Thomas Jefferson and Other Presidents." *Daughters of the American Revolution Magazine* 105 (April 1971): 403-07, 475.

Addresses Jefferson's association with the violin, music in his family, and songwriting.

1841.   Kuper, Theodore F. "Thomas Jefferson, Lover of Music." *Tempo* 1 (1934): 18.

1842.   Padover, Saul K. "Thomas Jefferson: Philosopher, Statesman—And Musician." *Stereo Review* 21/5 (1968): 82-86.

1843.   Pierce, E.H. "Thomas Jefferson and His Violin." *Etude* 47/9 (September 1929): 684-85.

Mentions some of the music he likely played and his practicing and playing habits.

1844. Shepperson, Archibald B. "Thomas Jefferson Visits England
         and Buys a Harpsichord." In *Humanistic Studies in Honor of
         John Calvin Metcalf*. New York: Columbia University Press,
         1941, pp. 80-106.

        An excellent article, including transcribed letters and a
number of additional primary sources regarding Jefferson's purchase
in 1786.

1845. Stolba, K. Marie. "Music in the Life of Thomas Jefferson."
         Daughters of the American Revolution Magazine 108 (March
         1974): 196-202.

        Discusses the correspondence between Jefferson and Thomas
Adams, Giovanni Fabbroni, and Francis Hopkinson, and includes
information on Jefferson's instruments, and a list of his books on
music. Reprinted in *American Music Teacher* 25/5 (April-May 1976),
pp. 6-8, 12.

<u>Stephen Jenks</u>
(1772-1856)

1846. Steel, David Warren. "Stephen Jenks (1772-1856): American
         Composer and Tunebook Compiler." Ph.D. dissertation,
         University of Michigan, 1982. 487p. UM 83-04604. *DAI*
         43/10 (April 1983): 3151-A.

        Jenks wrote some 125 compositions found in 10 tunebooks
compiled in 1799-1818. The author discusses his life and works and
his association with Amos Doolittle, engraver, and Herbert Mann,
printer.

<u>Thomas Johnston</u>
(c. 1708-1767)

1847. Hitchings, Sinclair. "Thomas Johnston." In *Boston Prints
         and Printmakers 1670-1775; a Conference Held by the
         Colonial Society of Massachusetts, 1 and 2 April 1971*. Ed.

by W.M. Whitehill and S. Hitchings. Boston: Colonial
Society of Massachusetts, 1973, pp. 83-132.

Johnston was an organ builder and printer of tunebooks who
lived in Boston.

<u>Jacob Kimball, Jr.</u>
(1761-1826)

1848.   "Jacob Kimball." *Historical Collections of the Topsfield
Historical Society* 12 (1907): 96H.

1849.   Wilcox, Glenn C.   "Jacob Kimball, a Pioneer American
Musician." *Essex Institute Historical Collections* 94
(1958): 356-78.

Kimball was a composer and tunebook compiler active in
Massachusetts.

1850.   Wilcox, Glenn C.   "Jacob Kimball, Jr. (1761-1826): His Life
and Works." Ph.D. dissertation, University of Southern
California, 1957.   273p.

<u>John Krauss</u>
(1770-1819)

1851.   Schultz, Selina G.   "John Krauss (1770-1819)."
Schwenckfeldiana 1/5 (1945): 21-33.

<u>Andrew Law</u>
(1749-1821)

1852.   Crawford, Richard A.   *Andrew Law, American Psalmodist.*
Evanston: Northwestern University Press, 1968. Reprint,
New York: Da Capo Press, 1981. xix, 424p.

A chronological discussion of Law's various tunebooks and theoretical aspects including musical style and notations. Included is a useful "index of composers to whom Law attributed tunes" and other composers identified by Crawford. Index lists many individuals and topics representative of the period studied. Based on the author's dissertation "Andrew Law (1749-1821): The Career of an American Musician" (Ph.D. dissertation, University of Michigan, 1965. UM 66-5054. *DAI* 26/10: 6086-87).

1853.   Higginson, J. Vincent.   "Andrew Law, American Psalmodist."
         Hymn 20/2 (April 1969): 53-57, 63-64.

         Brief article discussing Law's early life and publications, his "activities outside New England," and information on his shape-note notation.

1854.   Lowens, Irving.   "Copyright and Andrew Law."   *Papers of the Bibliographical Society of America* 53 (1959): 150-59.

1855.   Mangler, Joyce E.   "Andrew Law, Class of 1775: The Contributions of a Musical Reformer."   *Books at Brown* 18 (1957): 61-77.

<u>Abraham Luckenbach</u>
(d. 1854)

1856.   Hartzell, Lawrence W.   "Musical Moravian Missionaries: Part IV: Abraham Luckenbach."   *Moravian Music Journal* 31/1 (Spring 1986): 13-14.

         Discusses the life of Luckenbach, who was living in Nazareth, Pa., in 1798 and in Goshen, Ohio in 1807.

James Lyon
(1735-1794)

*   Sonneck, Oscar George. *Francis Hopkinson, the First American
        Poet-Composer (1737-1791) and James Lyon, Patriot,
        Preacher, Psalmodist (1735-1794).* Cited above as item
        1822. (See also entry 1820.)

Alexander Malcolm
(1685-1763)

1857. Heintze, James R. "Alexander Malcolm: Musician, Clergyman,
        and Schoolmaster." *Maryland Historical Magazine* 73/3
        (September 1978): 226-35.

        Malcolm lived in Marblehead, Mass. and later in Annapolis,
Md. where he was musically active as a member of the Tuesday Club,
and as rector of St. Anne's Church.

1858. Lloyd, Malcolm, Jr. "Alexander Malcolm, Writer on
        Mathematics and Music." *Scottish Notes & Queries*, Third
        Series, 6 (December 1928): 234-36.

1859. Maurer, Maurer. "Alexander Malcolm in America." *Music and
        Letters* 33/3 (July 1952): 226-31.

        Discusses his tenure at St. Michael's Church in Marblehead,
Mass., and in Annapolis, Md. Malcolm is best remembered for his *A
Treatise of Musick* (Edinburgh, 1721).

1860. Stone, Reppard. "An Evaluative Study of Alexander Malcolm's
        Treatise of Music: Speculative, Practical and Historical."
        Ph.D. dissertation, Catholic University of America, 1974.
        104p. UM 74-14948. *DAI* 35/1 (July 1974): 504-05-A.

        Although the major portion of this work focuses on
Malcolm's treatise written in Scotland, chapter 2 is a discussion of
Malcolm's life as a musician and his tenure in Maryland.

David Moritz Michael
(1751-1827)

1861.   Boeringer, James.   "David Moritz Michael."   *Journal of Church Music* 26/3 (March 1984): 7.

Very brief biography of Michael a Moravian musician who lived in Bethlehem, Pa.   Reprinted in *Moravian Music Journal* 29/2 (Summer 1984), pp. 47-48.

1862.   Roberts, Dale Alexander.   "The Sacred Vocal Music of David Moritz Michael: An American Moravian Composer."   D.M.A. dissertation, University of Kentucky, 1978.   508p.   UM 79-18113.   *DAI* 40/2 (August 1979): 532-33-A.

Consists of a biography of Michael, an analysis of his works, and a general discussion of music in Bethlehem and Nazareth, Pa., and Salem, N.C.   An appendix includes the full scores for all of Michael's anthems and "Psalm 103."

John Christopher Moller
(1755-1803)

1863.   Stetzel, Ronald Delbert.   "John Christopher Moller (1755-1803) and His Role in Early American Music."   Ph.D. dissertation, State University of Iowa, 1965.   2 vols., 581p.   UM 65-6712.   *DAI* 26/3 (September 1965): 1689.

Moller was an organist, composer, and music publisher active in Philadelphia and New York in the 1790s.   Volume 1 consists of a biography and description of his works.   Volume 2 includes a thematic index to his works and selections of various compositions.

<u>Justin Morgan</u>
(1747-1798)

1864.   Bandel, Betty. *Sing the Lord's Song in a Strange Land: The
Life of Justin Morgan.*   Rutherford, N.J.: Fairleigh
Dickinson University, 1981.   263p.

This composer and singing master was active in New England.
Discusses the composer's life and his 9 known musical compositions.
An appendix includes an analysis of the texts used in his "Judgment
Anthem."

<u>Asahel Nettleton</u>
(1783-1844)

1865.   Birney, George H., Jr.   "The Life and Letters of Asahel
Nettleton, 1783-1844."   Ph.D. dissertation, Hartford
Theological Seminary, 1943.

Nettleton was a New England evangelist and hymnbook
compiler, and is best remembered for his *Village Hymns for Social
Worship* (Hartford, 1824).

1866.   Tyler, Bennet.   *Memoir of the Life and Character of Rev.
Asahel Nettleton.*   Hartford, Conn.: Robins & Smith, 1844.
xi, 372p.

Reprinted in *American Culture Series*, reel 257.5 (see entry
31).

<u>Charles Theodore Pachelbel</u>
(c. 1690-1750)

1867.   Redway, Virginia Larkin.   "Charles Theodore Pachelbell,
Musical Emigrant." *Journal of the American Musicological
Society* 5/1 (Spring 1952): 32-36.

This article was the first extended work on Pachelbel, an organist who arrived in the colonies from Germany in 1730.

1868.   Welsh, Wilmer H.   "Mr. Patchable of Charleston." *Diapason* 71/12 (December 1980): 12-14.

An introduction to Charles Pachelbel worth reviewing. The author proposes that Pachelbel was musically more active than the few surviving records on him indicate.

<u>James Parker</u>
(1714-1770)

1869.   Redway, Virginia L.   "James Parker and the 'Dutch Church.'" *Musical Quarterly* 24/4 October 1938): 481-500.

Parker owned a printing firm in New York. Includes biographical information and Parker's relationship with Benjamin Franklin and John Holt, and Parker's publication of a number of Dutch books, including the *Psalms of David* (1767).

<u>John Rowe Parker</u>
(1777-1844)

1870.   Cuthbert, John A.   "John Rowe Parker and *A Musical Biography*." *American Music* 1/2 (Summer 1983): 39-52.

Parker was a Boston music dealer and editor of *The Euterpeiad*. The author includes information on Parker, a description, contents and sources of Parker's publication, *A Musical Biography* (see entry 1686). Of additional interest is Parker's association with Benjamin Carr as reflected in correspondence between the two cited herein.

1871.   Haskins, John C.   "John Rowe Parker and *The Euterpeiad*." *Notes* 8/3 (June 1951): 447-56.

The first issue of *The Euterpeiad* was published on April 1, 1820.   The author discusses its publication history.

1872.   Johnson, H. Earle.   "The John Rowe Parker Letters." *Musical Quarterly* 62/1 (January 1976): 72-86.

A look at the life of Parker based on correspondence of some 400 letters to Parker during 1802 and 1840.   Some notable personalities include Benjamin Carr and Anthony Philip Heinrich. Included is a facsimile of a title page from Parker's *Catalogue of Music and Musical Instruments* (Boston, 1820).

Peter Pelham, Jr.
(1721-1805)

1873.   Colket, Meredith B., Jr.   "The Pelhams of England and New England: Peter Pelham of Boston, Massachusetts." *American Genealogist* 20/2 (October 1943): 65-76.

Provides detailed biographical information on Peter Pelham, Jr., who was organist in 1755-1802 at Bruton Parish Church in Williamsburg.

1874.   Maurer, Maurer.   "The Gaoler Played the Organ." *Etude* 68/5 (May 1950): 18-19.

A brief biography of Pelham, an organist at Bruton Parish Church in Williamsburg, ca. 1760.

1875.   Maurer, Maurer.   "Peter Pelham: Organist-Jailer." *Tyler's Quarterly Historical and Genealogical Magazine* 28/1 (July 1946): 6-13.

A principal source for Pelham.   Discusses his period in Charleston and Williamsburg.   Also discusses Cuthbert Ogle, another Williamsburg musician.

Victor Pelissier
(c. 1740-c. 1820)

1876. Saloman, Ora F. "Victor Pelissier, Composer in Federal New
York and Philadelphia." *Pennsylvania Magazine of History
and Biography* 102/1 (January 1978): 93-102.

Discusses Pelissier's immigration from Paris and his
subsequent career in the United States, 1792-1817.

Johann Friedrich Peter
(1746-1813)

1877. Boeringer, James. "Johann Friedrich Peter." *Journal of
Church Music* 26/10 (December 1984): 10-12.

Brief biography of this 18th-century Moravian active in
colonial America.   Facsimile.

1878. McCorkle, Donald M.   "Johann Friedrich Peter in North
Carolina: Some New Material for an Incomplete Biography."
Journal of the American Musicological Society 7/1 (Spring
1954): 89.

The author corrects errors in some previously printed
literature on Peter.

1879. Nolte, Ewald V.   "The Chronology of Johann Friedrich Peter."
Moravian Music Foundation Bulletin 12/1 (1967): 4.

1880. Nolte, Ewald V.   "The Paradox of the Peter Quintets."
Moravian Music Foundation Bulletin 12/1 (Fall 1967): 2-3.

Includes biographical information and information on his
six quintets written in 1789.

1881. Rau, Albert G. "Johann Frederick Peter." *Musical Quarterly*
23/3 (July 1937): 306-13.

An introduction to Peter, with an emphasis on his compositions.   Sources are not cited.

1882.   Schnell, William Emmett.   "The Choral Music of Johann
          Friedrich Peter, 1746-1813."   D.Mus.A. dissertation,
          University of Illinois at Urbana-Champaign, 1973.   427p.
          UM 74-5688.   *DAI* 34/9 (March 1974): 6029-30-A.

          Includes biographical information and a discussion of 76
extant choral works.   Includes a catalog of Peter's choral works
held in 9 Moravian repositories.

1883.   "Sketches of Moravian Composers: Johann Friedrich Peter."
          Moravian Music Foundation Bulletin 2/2 (Spring-Summer
          1958): 3.

          A brief biography of Peter.

<u>Abraham Prescott</u>
(1789-1858)

1884.   Wall, Edward.   "Abraham Prescott: Bass Viol Maker of
          Deerfield and Concord."   *Historical New Hampshire* 42/2
          (1987): 101-23.

          Prescott began building bass viols in 1819.   His company
was in existence until 1917.   Based on primary sources.

<u>Johann Christopher Pyrlaeus</u>
(b. 1713)

1885.   Hartzell, Lawrence W.   "Musical Moravian Missionaries: Part
          I: Johann Christopher Pyrlaeus."   *Moravian Music Journal*
          29/4 (Winter 1984): 91-92.

          Pyrlaeus came from Leipzig to Bethlehem, Pa. in 1741, where
he established America's first Collegium Musicum on December 13,
1744.

Daniel Read
(1757-1836)

1886.   Bushnell, Vinson C.   "Daniel Read of New Haven (1757-1836):
The Man and His Musical Activities."   Ph.D. dissertation,
Harvard University, 1978.

Read, who was a composer and tunebook compiler, wrote over
80 works.

1887.   Hood, George.   "Sketches of American Musical Biography and
History: Daniel Read."   *Musical Herald* 3/10 (October 1882):
260.

A brief biography with some interesting comments on Read as
a person.   Includes information on his publications.

1888.   Lowens, Irving.   "Daniel Read's World: The Letters of an
Early American Composer."   *Notes* 9/2 (March 1952): 233-48.

Biographical information on Read, based on some 1,000
letter-drafts written by Read and left to the New Haven Colony
Historical Society in 1855.   Reprinted in Lowens, *Music and
Musicians in Early America* (see entry 371).

1889.   Owen, Barbara J.   "A Brief Glimpse of Daniel Read."   *Choral &
Organ Guide* 9/6 (1956): 20, 22.

Alexander Reinagle
(c. 1756-1809)

1890.   Drummond, Robert R.   "Alexander Reinagle and His Connection
with the Musical Life of Philadelphia."   *German-American
Annals* 5 (1907): 294-306.

1891.   Krauss, Anne McClenny.   "Alexander Reinagle, His Family
Background and Early Professional Career."   *American Music*
4/4 (Winter 1986): 425-56.

Includes programs, musical examples, and discusses his compositions and residency in New York and Philadelphia.

1892. Krauss, Anne McClenny. "More Music by Reinagle." *Clavier* 15/5 (May-June 1976): 17-24.

Includes some biographical background with information on Reinagle's collections, *Twenty-Four Short and Easy Pieces* and *A Selection of Most Favorite Scots Tunes.* Includes musical examples, and a performance edition of "Lee Rigg" from the latter collection.

1893. McClenny, Anne. "Alexander Reinagle." *American Music Teacher* 19/1 (September-October 1969): 38, 50.

A brief biography based, in part, on notices from newspapers.

*   Mahan, Katherine Hines. "Hopkinson and Reinagle: Patriot-Musicians of Washington's Time." Cited above as entry 1817.

1894. Sonneck, Oscar G. "Zwei Briefe C. Ph. Em. Bach's an Alexander Reinagle." *Sammelbände der internationalen Musikgesellschaft* (1906): 112-14.

1895. Strauss, John F. "Alexander Reinagle: Pianist—Composer—Impresario in Federalist America." *Clavier* 15/5 (May-June 1976): 14-16, 25-27.

Brief survey with information on a concert program of June 12, 1787 arranged by Reinagle and attended apparently by George Washington. Includes a study edition of the final movement of Reinagle's Sonata in F Major.

Peter Ricksecker
(1791-1873)

1896.   Hartzell, Lawrence W.   "Musical Moravian Missionaries: Part
        V: Peter Ricksecker." *Moravian Music Journal* 32/1 (Spring
        1987): 14-15.

        A brief biography of Ricksecker, who was a teacher at
Nazareth Hall in Nazareth, Pa. in 1811-21.   He played the violin,
organ, and sang, and later composed songs in "three-part keyboard
settings with the melody in the top voice."

Silas Robinson
(fl. 1815)

1897.   Howe, Warren P.   "An Original Bandsman: The Story of Silas
        Robinson." *Military Collector & Historian* 39/1 (1987): 21-
        26.

        Robinson was from Vermont and served in the U.S. Military
Academy Band in 1813 as a drum major and field musician.

Johann Jakob Schmick
(1714-1778)

1898.   Hartzell, Lawrence W.   "Musical Moravian Missionaries: Part
        III: Johann Jakob Schmick." *Moravian Music Journal* 30/2
        (Fall 1985): 36-37.

        A brief biography of Schmick, a Lutheran pastor in Livonia,
Russia, who came as a missionary to America in 1751, and in 1753 was
in Meniolagomeka, Pa.   Schmick played several instruments, sang, and
taught music.

Gottlieb Schober
(1756-1838)

1899. Surratt, Jerry L. *Gottlieb Schober of Salem.* Macon,
       Georgia: Mercer University Press, 1983. viii, 243p.

       Schober was a Moravian organist and music director in
Salem, N.C.

William Selby
(c. 1738-1798)

1900. McKay, David. "William Selby, Musical Émigré in Colonial
       Boston." *Musical Quarterly* 57/4 (October 1971): 609-27.

       A detailed biography of Selby as performer and composer,
including a chronology of his musical career (1771-98) and checklist
of extant musical compositions.

Oliver Shaw
(1779-1848)

1901. Degen, Bruce N. "Oliver Shaw: His Music and Contribution to
       American Society." D.M.A. dissertation, University of
       Rochester, 1971. 230p.

       Shaw was a composer, teacher, singer, and publisher active
in New England.

1902. Denison, Frederic, Albert A. Stanley and Edward K. Glezen,
       ed. *Memorial of Oliver Shaw.* Providence, R.I.: J.A. and
       R.A. Reid, 1884. 46p.

       Includes a catalog of Shaw's published works, pp. 35-46.

1903. Thompson, J. William. "Oliver Shaw, 1779-1848: Forgotten
       Master." *Hymn* 11/3 (July 1960): 83-90.

Discusses Shaw's educational background, his teaching and composing career, and his publications.

1904.   Thrasher, Herbert C.   "Oliver Shaw."   *Books at Brown* 8/4
         (1945-46): 1-4.

1905.   Williams, Thomas.   *A Discourse on the Life and Death of
         Oliver Shaw.*   Boston: Charles C.P. Moody, 1851.   39p.

Includes concise information on the Shaw family, the musical career of Oliver Shaw, with information on a psalmody club, including its members during the early 1800s.   Reprinted in *American Culture Series* (see entry 31).

<u>Joseph Stone</u>
(1758-1837)

1906.   Criger, Wanda Jean.   "Joseph Stone (1758-1837), an Early
         American Tunesmith."   D.M.A. dissertation, University of
         Oregon, 1987.   229p.   UM 88-08676.   *DAI* 49/4 (October
         1988): 652-A.

Includes a biography and an examination of 68 hymns by Stone, including those in *The Columbian Harmony* (co-compiled with Abraham Wood in 1793).

<u>Timothy Swan</u>
(1758-1842)

1907.   "Biographical Sketch of Timothy Swan."   *Musical Review and
         Choral Advocate* 3/5 (May 1852): 67-68.

A brief biography, with information on his tunebooks and his work "China."

1908.   Hood, George. "Sketches of American Musical Biography and
         History: Timothy Swan." *Musical Herald* 3/10 (October
         1882): 255.

         A brief biography with information on his publications.
States that his tune "'China' places him among those long to be
cherished by the lovers of American music at that time. . . ."

1909.   Murray, Sterling E. "Timothy Swan and Yankee Psalmody."
         Musical Quarterly 61/3 (July 1975): 433-63.

         Swan was a New England hatter and also a teacher of singing
schools. This biography provides detailed information on the
composer and his works, a number of other musicians and
personalities, including Alexander Ely, Simeon Jocelin, and John
Rhea, and information on the Swan Papers in the American Antiquarian
Society.

1910.   Webb, Guy Bedford. "Timothy Swan: Yankee Tunesmith." D.M.A.
         dissertation, University of Illinois at Urbana-Champaign,
         1972. 210p. UM 73-17467. *DAI* 34/2 (August 1973): 816-17-
         A.

         A biography of Swan and description of his works. Three
appendixes include a catalog of manuscripts and correspondence in
the American Antiquarian Society, an index of 27 tunebooks having
tunes by Swan, and a performance edition of the set pieces and
anthems.

David Tannenberg
(1728-1804)

1911.   Beck, Abraham R. "David Tannenberg." *Pennsylvania-German*
         10 (1909): 339-41.

         Tannenberg was a significant Moravian organ builder active
during the 1700s.

1912.   Beck, Paul E.   "David Tannenberg, Organ Builder."   *Papers Read before the Lancaster County Historical Society* 30 (January 1926): 3-11.

1913.   Diffenderffer, F.R.   "Some Historical Mistakes Corrected."   *Papers Read before the Lancaster County Historical Society* 21 (1917): 143-44.

On David Tannenberg.

1914.   Hensel, W.U.   "A Famous Organ Builder."   *Papers Read before the Lancaster County Historical Society* 11 (1907): 351-54.

<u>Rayner Taylor</u>
(1747-1825)

1915.   Cuthbert, John A.   "Raynor Taylor and Anglo-American Musical Life."   Ph.D. dissertation, West Virginia University, 1980. 521p.   UM 81-10619.   *DAI* 41/12 (June 1981): 4879-A.

Discusses his career and his significance as a musician. Includes a list of compositions and arrangements, and a bibliography of biographical sources.

1916.   Doran, Carol Ann.   "The Influence of Raynor Taylor and Benjamin Carr on the Church Music in Philadelphia at the Beginning of the Nineteenth Century."   Ph.D. dissertation, Eastman School of Music, 1970.   2 vols.

Includes vocal music by both composers.

1917.   Yellin, Victor Fell.   "Rayner Taylor."   *American Music* 1/3 (Fall 1983): 48-71.

Discusses Taylor's early years in England and later in Philadelphia.

<u>William Tuckey</u>
(1708-1781)

1918.   Aaron, Amy.   "William Tuckey, a Choirmaster in Colonial New
York."   *Musical Quarterly* 64/1 (January 1978): 79-97.

Tuckey's position was at Trinity Church during the 1750s.
The author presents a detailed account, including information on
Tuckey's compositions and a list of his works found in tunebooks of
the period.

<u>John Tufts</u>
(1689-1750)

1919.   Butler, John H.   "John Tufts: Aurora Unaware."   *Music
Educators Journal* 55/5 (January 1969): 44-46, 105-06.

A biography, with information on his *An Introduction to the
Singing of Psalm-Tunes* (Boston 1721).

1920.   Hood, George.   "Sketches of American Musical Biography and
History: Rev. John Tufts."   *Musical Herald* 3/3 (March
1882): 65.

A brief biography that rightfully names Tufts as a "pioneer
in church music" in America.

<u>Thomas Walter</u>
(1696-1725)

1921.   Hood, George.   "Sketches of American Musical Biography and
History: Rev. Thomas Walter."   *Musical Herald* 3/5 (May
1882): 116-17.

A brief biography, with information on Walter's tunebook,
The Grounds and Rules of Musick Explained (Boston 1721), and various
sermons.

Jedidiah Weiss

1922.   Boeringer, James.   "Jedidiah Weiss and His Musical Family."
Moravian Music Journal 28/1 (Spring 1983): 8-12.

Discusses various members of this musical Moravian family,
active during the early 1800s.

Truman S. Wetmore
(1774-1861)

1923.   Steel, David Warren.   "Truman S. Wetmore of Winchester and
His 'Republican Harmony.'" *Connecticut Historical Society
Bulletin* 45/3 (July 1980): 75-89.

Includes biographical information on Wetmore, his
manuscript tunebook "Republican Harmony" in the Newberry Library,
Chicago, and a list of printings of his tunes, "America" and
"Florida" for the years 1798-1810.

Peter Wolle
(1792-1871)

1924.   Allen, Walser H.   "Three Musical Moravians Named Wolle."
Moravian Music Foundation Bulletin 18/2 (Fall-Winter 1973):
2-7.

Principally a biography of Peter Wolle, who was a teacher
in Salem, N.C. and who wrote the anthem, "For Me, O Lord My God."

Abraham Wood
(1752-1804)

1925.   Held, Jerrold.   "Abraham Wood: An Early American Composer."
American Choral Review 7/1 (1964): 1, 14-16; 7/2 (1964): 8-
10.

Wood was a composer and tunebook compiler active in Massachusetts. A brief biography with musical examples.

<u>John Wyeth</u>
(1770-1858)

1926. Ellison, Ross W. "John Wyeth: Early American Tunebook
           Publisher." *American Music Teacher* 25/1 (September-October
           1975): 22-24.

Wyeth was a publisher active in Harrisburg, Pa. in the early 1800s. Provides biographical information on Wyeth and his various publications.

VIII. CRITICAL AND FACSIMILE EDITIONS OF MUSIC

The two and only monumental scholarly editions of early American
music, *Earlier American Music* and *Recent Researches in American
Music*, are included below. For an annotated list of facsimile
reprints of American music to 1865, as well as critical editions not
included below, refer to *American Music before 1865* (see entry 82).
See also entries 705, 748, 892, 1229, 1258, 1786, 1795, 1799, 1862-
63.

1927. *The American Musical Magazine. Vol. 1.* New Haven: Amos
       Doolittle and Daniel Read, 1786. Reprint, Scarsdale, N.Y.:
       Annemarie Schnase, 1961. 50p.

       Contents include sacred and secular choral music (two,
three, and four parts) and songs for solo voice with instrumental
accompaniment. Composers include William Billings, Daniel Read, and
others.

1928. *The American Musical Miscellany: A Collection of the Newest
       and Most Approved Songs, Set to Music.* Northampton, Mass.:
       Andrew Wright, 1798. Reprint, Earlier American Music, 9,
       with new intro. by H. Wiley Hitchcock, New York: Da Capo
       Press, 1972. 300p.

       Includes over 100 songs. The compiler is unknown.

1929. *Anthology of Early American Keyboard Music, 1787-1830.*
       Recent Researches in American Music, 1-2. Ed. by J. Bunker
       Clark. Madison, Wis.: A-R Editions, 1977. 2 vols.

       Includes 36 works. A preface includes information on the
music, composers, sources, forms, performance practice, and critical
notes on the works. Editorial additions in [brackets].

1930. Barton, Andrew. *The Disappointment: or, The Force of Credulity* (New York, 1767). Recent Researches in American Music, 3-4. Ed. by Jerald C. Graue and Judith Layng. Madison, Wis.: A-R Editions, 1976. xvi, 169p. With keyboard-vocal score (58p.)

This work was written to be produced at the Southwark Theatre in Philadelphia on April 20, 1767. However, the production never took place. Preface includes information on the play, the problem of authorship, musical reconstruction, performance practice, the additional instrumental music appended to this score, critical notes, and sources for the airs.

1931. Belcher, Supply. *The Harmony of Maine*. Boston: Isaiah Thomas & Ebenezer T. Andrews, 1794. Reprint, Earlier American Music, 6, with new intro. by H. Wiley Hitchcock, New York: Da Capo Press, 1972. 104p.

Contains 57 plain and fuging tunes and 6 anthems and set pieces.

1932. Billings, William. *Complete Works*. American Musicological Society & The Colonial Society of Massachusetts, Boston, 1977- . Vol. 1- . Edited by Karl Kroeger.

Vol. 1. *The New England Psalm-Singer* (1770). lxviii, 383p. Includes an extensive introduction, including information on music in Boston, 1750-70, Billings' musical style, editorial policy, and the tunebook. Facsimiles.

Vol. 2. *The Singing Master's Assistant* (1778) and *Music in Miniature* (1779). xv, 361p. Includes a number of lists and extensive commentary on the tunebooks.

Vol. 3. *The Psalm-Singer's Amusement* (1781), *The Suffolk Harmony* (1786), and independent publications. Three appendixes include recently discovered works and arrangements.

Vol. 4. *The Continental Harmony* (1794). Forthcoming.

1933. Billings, William. *The Continental Harmony*. Boston: Isaiah Thomas and Ebenezer T. Andrews, 1794. Reprint, ed. by Hans

Nathan, Cambridge: Belknap Press of Harvard University Press, 1961. xix, 201p.

Includes 50 works by Billings.

1934. Billings, William. *The Psalm-Singer's Amusement.* Boston: the author, 1781. Reprint, Earlier American Music, 20, with new intro. by H. Wiley Hitchcock, New York: Da Capo Press, 1974. 104p.

1935. Bray, John. *The Indian Princess: or La Belle Sauvage.* Philadelphia: T & G Palmer, 1808. Text by James Nelson Barker. Reprint, Earlier American Music, 11, with new intro. by H. Wiley Hitchcock, New York: Da Capo Press, 1972. 74; 42p.

Contains libretto and score. First performed at the Chestnut Street Theatre in Philadelphia on April 6, 1808.

1936. Carr, Benjamin. *The Federal Overture.* Philadelphia, New York: B. Carr; Baltimore: J. Carr, 1794. Reprint, Philadelphia: Musical Americana, 1957. 18; 7p.

Reprinted under the title *Benjamin Carr's Federal Overture.* For piano (2 hands).

1937. Carr, Benjamin. *Musical Journal for the Pianoforte.* Philadelphia: Carr & Schetky, 1800-04. 5 vols. Reprint, Wilmington, Del.: Scholarly Resources, 1972. 2 vols.

American composers include Benjamin Carr, James Hewitt, G.C. Schetky, Alexander Reinagle, Rayner Taylor, and others.

1938. Carr, Benjamin. *Musical Miscellany in Occasional Numbers.* Baltimore, Philadelphia, 1812-25. Reprint, Earlier American Music, 21, with new intro. by Eve R. Meyer, New York: Da Capo Press, 1982. 324p.

Contains 86 instrumental and vocal works. Americans include Joseph Taws, William Darley, and others.

1939. Carr, Benjamin. *Selected Secular and Sacred Songs*. Recent
       Researches in American Music, 15. Ed. by Eve R. Meyer.
       Madison, Wis.: A-R Editions, 1986. xxiii, 86p.

       Includes 23 works. Preface includes information on the
composer, the music, performance practice, editorial methods, the
sources consulted, and critical notes on the works. Facsimiles.

1940. *The Core Repertory of Early American Psalmody*. Recent
       Researches in American Music, 11-12. Ed. by Richard A.
       Crawford. Madison, Wis.: A-R Editions, 1984. lxxxiii,
       164p.

       Includes "101 sacred pieces most often printed in America
between 1698 and 1819." An extensive preface includes information
on "Three Stages of American Tunebook Publishing: 1698-1810," how
the core repertory was chosen, the music, performance practice,
editorial policy, and critical commentary on the works. Three
appendixes include: "Core Repertory Compositions: Historical
Commentary"; "Collections Containing Core Repertory Compositions";
and "Tables." Facsimile.

1941. Davisson, Ananias. *Kentucky Harmony*. Lexington, Ky., 1816.
       Reprint, with new intro. by Irving Lowens, Minneapolis:
       Augsburg Publishing House, 1976. 160p.

       Includes folk hymns, anthems, psalm-tunes for 2-4 voices.
Extensive preface.

1942. [Eckhard, Jacob]. *Jacob Eckhard's Choirmaster's Book of
       1809*. Reprint, with a new intro. and notes by George W.
       Williams, Columbia: University of South Carolina Press,
       1971. xvi, 124p.

       Includes psalm-tunes, hymns, and anthems for 1-3 voices of
German, English, and American origin. The music consists of
melodies with figured bass; some with text.

1943. Heinrich, Anthony Philip. *The Dawning of Music in Kentucky*
       and *The Western Minstrel*. Philadelphia: Bacon & Hart,
       1820. Reprint, Earlier American Music, 10, with new intro.

by H. Wiley Hitchcock. New York: Da Capo Press, 1972.
269; 39p.

Includes vocal (solo and choral) and instrumental works for
piano, violin, and chamber ensemble.

1944. Hewitt, James. *Selected Compositions.* Recent Researches in
American Music, 7. Ed. by John W. Wagner. Madison, Wis.:
A-R Editions, 1980. xix, 106p.

Includes 31 vocal and keyboard works. Preface includes
information on Hewitt, the music, performance practice, the sources,
and critical notes on the works. Facsimiles.

1945. Hopkinson, Francis. *Francis Hopkinson's Lessons: A Facsimile
Edition of Hopkinson's Personal Keyboard Book. An
Anthology of Keyboard Compositions & Arrangements Copied in
Hopkinson's Own Hand.* Reprint, with notes by Davd P.
McKay, Washington, D.C.: Wagner, 1979. vii, 178p.

Manuscript was compiled ca. 1764. Contains works by
European composers.

1946. Hopkinson, Francis. *Seven Songs for the Harpsichord or Forte
Piano.* Philadelphia: T. Dobson, I. Aitken, 1788. Reprint,
with notes by Harry Dichter, Philadelphia: Musical
Americana, 1954, 1959. 15p.

This work actually includes 8 songs for voice with
instrumental bass accompaniment.

1947. Ingalls, Jeremiah. *The Christian Harmony or Songster's
Companion.* Exeter, N.H.: Henry Ranlet, 1805. Reprint,
Earlier American Music, 22, with new intro. by David
Klocko, New York: Da Capo Press, 1981. xii, 200p.

Includes 137 works.

1948. Lyon, James. *Urania.* Philadelphia, 1761. Reprint, with new
preface and sources by Richard Crawford, New York: Da Capo
Press, 1974. 198p.

Includes sacred choral music by British and American composers compiled by Lyon.

1949.   Mason, Lowell. *The Boston Handel and Haydn Society Collection of Church Music*. Boston: Richardson and Lord, 1822. Reprint, Earlier American Music, 15, with new intro. by H. Wiley Hitchcock, New York: Da Capo Press, 1973. 320p.

Includes sacred choral music by mostly European composers.

1950.   *The Music of the Bay Psalm Book (The Psalms, Hymns and Spiritual Songs, of the Old & New Testament)*. 9th ed. Boston: B. Green and F. Allen, 1698. Transcription and foreword by Richard G. Appel. Brooklyn: Institute for Studies in American Music, 1975.

The *Bay Psalm Book* was originally published in 1640 in Cambridge, Mass., under the title *The Whole Book of Psalms*.

1951.   *Nineteenth-Century American Piano Music*. Comp. by John Gillespie. New York: Dover Publications, 1978. xxi, 323p.

Facsimiles of sheet music representing some 27 American composers. Pre-1820 works include: "Fantasia on the Air 'Gramachree'" by Benjamin Carr; "United States Grand Waltz" by Charles Grobe; "La Buona Mattina" by Anthony Philip Heinrich; "Mark My Alford: A Favorite Air with Variations" by James Hewitt. Biographies of composers are included.

1952.   O'Keeffe, John and William Shield. *The Poor Soldier* (Philadelphia: T. Seddon and W. Spotswood, 1783). Recent Researches in American Music, 6. Ed. by William Brasmer and William Osborne. Madison, Wis.: A-R Editions, 1978. xiii, 82p.

This work was premiered in America on December 2, 1785 in New York. Preface includes information on the libretto and stage history, the music and its sources, the revised libretto and score, and textual and musical sources. Facsimiles.

1953. Pelissier, Victor. *Pelissier's Columbian Melodies: Music for
       the New York and Philadelphia Theatres* (Philadelphia: G.
       Willig). Recent Researches in American Music, 13-14. Ed.
       by Karl Kroeger. Madison, Wis.: A-R Editions, 1984.
       xxviii, 178p.

       Pelissier was a composer for New York and Philadelphia
theaters from the mid-1790s to approximately 1813. Preface includes
information on the American musical theater at the turn of the 19th
century, the life, career, and works of Pelissier, editorial
methods, and critical commentary on the works. Includes 48 works
consisting of theater music, and vocal and instrumental music.
Facsimiles.

1954. *Popular Songs of Nineteenth-Century America.* Comp. by
       Richard Jackson. New York: Dover Publications, 1976. xiv,
       290p.

       Facsimiles of original sheet music of some 64 songs.
Includes 1 pre-1820 work: "Adeste Fideles" (1803) by John Francis
Wade.

1955. Reinagle, Alexander. *The Philadelphia Sonatas.* Recent
       Researches in American Music, 5. Ed. by Robert Hopkins.
       Madison, Wis.: A-R Editions, 1978. xiv, 84p.

       Transcription of these sonatas is based on the original
manuscript in the Library of Congress. The works were written by
Reinagle between 1786-94. Preface includes information on the
composer, the music, notes on performance, the edition, and critical
notes. Editorial additions in [brackets]. Facsimile. See also
entry 715.

1956. Riley, Edward. *Riley's Flute Melodies.* New York: Riley,
       1814-20. 2 vols. Reprint, Earlier American Music, 18,
       with new intro. by H. Wiley Hitchcock, New York: Da Capo
       Press, 1973. 100p.

       Includes some 700 airs, dances and marches of European and
American origin. Music consists of melodies only, with some
suggestions for other instruments.

1957. *Series of Old American Songs Reproduced in Facsimile from Original or Early Editions in the Harris Collection of American Poetry and Plays, Brown University.* With brief annotations by S. Foster Damon. Providence, R.I.: Brown University Library, 1936. 216p.

Facsimile editions of 50 ballads and minstrel songs from 1759-1858. No index of composers.

1958. Wyeth, John. *Repository of Sacred Music.* Harrisburg, Pa.: John Wyeth, 1820; 5th ed. Reprint, with new intro. by Irving Lowens, New York: Da Capo Press, 1974. xviii, 131p.

Includes sacred choral music in shape-note notation.

1959. Wyeth, John. *Repository of Sacred Music: Part Second.* Harrisburg, Pa.: John Wyeth, 1820; 2nd ed. Reprint, with new intro. by Irving Lowens, New York: Da Capo Press, 1964. xvi, 132p.

Includes sacred choral music in shape-note notation.

AUTHOR-TITLE INDEX

Citations are by entry number, or to the notes following a specific entry (indicated by "n" following the number), or to the introductory notes preceding a section (indicated by "p" following the number). This index also includes names of editors, compilers, and translators. Titles of articles and dissertations are not included.

Aaron, Amy   1918
Aboudara, Elizabeth S.   313
Academic American Encyclopedia   1
Account of the Bay Psalm Book   878
Acculturation in the Americas: Proceedings and Selected Papers of the XXIXth International Congress of Americanists   1092
Additions and Corrections to History and Bibliography of American Newspapers, 1690-1820   155n
Address on Music, Delivered before the Singing-Society of the Second Baptist Church in Boston, 7th April, 1814   998
Address on Music, Delivered to the First Baptist Singing Society, Boston, Thursday Evening, May 15, 1806   869
Address on Music, Delivered to the Salisbury and Amesbury Singing Societies, Convened at Salisbury, April 3, 1812   841
Adkins, Cecil   288
Adler, Dick   1435
Adler, Guido   301
Afro-American Religious Music: A Bibliography and a Catalogue of Gospel Music   101
Agreeable Situations: Society, Commerce, and Art in Southern Maine, 1780-1830   577
Agrippa, Brother   1138
Alamoth: An Address Delivered to the Singing Schools in the First and Second Societies in Groton   901
Albrecht, Otto E.   223, 1436, 1810
Albright, Frank P.   1520, 1603
Alden, John   178
Alderfer, E. Gordon   1124

Aldrich, Elizabeth   1413
Allan, Alfred K.   1832
Allen, Nathan H.   413
Allen, Walser H.   1705, 1924
Allen, William Francis   1062
Allis, Marguerite   414
Allwardt, Anton Paul   415
Althouse, Ella Krauss   1521
America and French Culture 1759-1848   1153
America: History and Life   38n, 129, 223p
*America Learns to Dance: A Historical Study of Dance Education in
    America before 1900*   1420
*American Bibliography: A Chronological Dictionary of All Books,
    Pamphlets, and Periodical Publications Printed in the United
    States of America from the Genesis of Printing in 1639 Down to and
    Including the Year 1820*   43n, 44n, 45, 73n, 97n, 99n, 371n, 1319n
American Bibliography: A Preliminary Checklist, 1801 to 1819   73,
    106n
*American Biographical Archive: A Single-Alphabet Cumulation of 367
    Original Biographical Reference Works Covering 300,000 Individuals
    from the Earliest Period of North American History through the
    Early Twentieth Century*   1672
American Civilisation: An Introduction   304
American Composer Speaks: A Historical Anthology, 1770-1965   322
American Composers: A Biographical Dictionary   1678
American Composers and American Music   109
American Counties   413p
American Culture Series   31, 988n, 1866n, 1905n
*American Diaries: An Annotated Bibliography of American Diaries
    Written Prior to the Year 1861*   271n, 272
*American Diaries: An Annotated Bibliography of Published American
    Diaries and Journals*   269, 272n
*American Diaries in Manuscript, 1580-1954: A Descriptive
    Bibliography*   273
American Doctoral Dissertations   289
American Historical Review   145n
American History and Encyclopedia of Music   28
American Hymns Old and New   1020
American Labor Songs of the Nineteenth Century   767
American Music (journal)   37n
American Music: A Panorama   366
*American Music before 1865 in Print and on Records: A Biblio-
    Discography*   82, 280n, 837p, 1927p
*American Music, From Plymouth Rock to Tin Pan Alley: A Lecture on
    American Music*   318
American Music, 1698-1800: An Annotated Bibliography   97, 1319n

American Music Studies: A Classified Bibliography of Master's Theses
293, 299n
American Musical Directory, 1861   255p
American Musical Instruments in the Metropolitan Museum of Art   1590
American Musical Stage before 1800   1475
American Musical Theatre: A Chronicle   1442
*American Oratorios and Cantatas: A Catalog of Works Written in the
United States from Colonial Times to 1985*   93
*American Patriotic Songs: Yankee Doodle to The Conquered Banner with
Emphasis on the Star-Spangled Banner*   224
American Periodical Series, 18th Century   130
American Periodical Series, 1850-1900, Civil War and Reconstruction
131n
American Periodicals, 1800-1850   131, 810n, 946n, 981n, 1683n, 1738n
*American Periodicals, 1741-1900: An Index to the Microfilm
Collections*   130n
American Playhouse in the Eighteenth Century   1474
American Plays, Poetry and Songsters   1440
American Popular Culture: A Historical Bibliography   132
*American Popular Music and Its Business: The First Four Hundred
Years*   391
*American Psalmody or Titles of Books Containing Tunes Printed in
America from 1721 to 1820*   75n, 111
*American Sheet Music Illustration: Reflections of the Nineteenth
Century*   234
*American Sheet Music with Prices: A Guide to Collecting Sheet Music
from 1775 to 1975*   1405
American Studies: A Guide to Information Sources   61
*American Studies and American Musicology: A Point of View and a Case
in Point*   859
American Theatre Companies, 1749-1887   1450
*American Theatrical Arts: A Guide to Manuscripts and Special
Collections in the United States and Canada*   177
American Women Composers before 1870   407
American Writers and Compilers of Sacred Music   877n, 1682
America's Music: From the Pilgrims to the Present   323
America's Musical Heritage   321
Ammer, Christine   15, 314
And So to Bed: A Bibliography of Diaries Published in English   271
And the Band Played On: 1776-1976   228
*And They All Sang Hallelujah: Plain-Folk Camp-Meeting Religion,
1800-1845*   1018
Anderson, Edward P.   416
Anderson, Garland   315, 676
Anderson, Gillian B.   154, 154p, 254p, 611, 753, 754, 1437, 1714
Anderson, John   837, 838

Anderson, Simon Vance   269p, 316, 677
Anderson, Thomas Jerome   1206
Andrew Law, American Psalmodist   1852
Andrews, Edward D.   1334
Andrews, Frank D.   255
Andrews, P.   1715
Andrus, Helen Josephine   417
Annals of Music in America   410
*Annals of Music in Philadelphia and History of the Musical Fund
   Society from Its Organization in 1820 to the Year 1858*   521
Annals of the New York Stage   1483
Annotated Bibliography of Woodwind Instruction Books, 1600-1830   79
Annotated Bibliography on the Amish   1177
Anthem in England and America   639
Anthem in New England before 1800   615
Anthology of Early American Keyboard Music, 1787-1830   1929
Anthony Philip Heinrich: A Nineteenth-Century Composer in America
   1792
Antrim, Doron K.   640, 641
Apel, Willi   24n
Appel, Richard G.   839, 1950
Arksey, Laura   269, 272n
Armstrong, Janice Gray   231
Armstrong, W.G.   1438
Armstrong, William H.   1523
Arndt, Karl J.R.   1155, 1156
Arnold, Denis   25
Arnold, Janice M.   1524
Arnold, Robert A.   1525
Arrington, Golden Elwyn   317
Art and Music in the South   530
*Art of Music: A Comprehensive Library of Information for Music
   Lovers and Musicians*   343
Art of Music: American Paintings and Musical Instruments, 1770-1910
   226
Art-Song in America: A Study in the Development of American Music
   831
Art-Song in the United States, 1801-1976   85
*Articles in American Studies, 1954-1968: A Cumulation of the Annual
   Bibliographies from American Quarterly*   133
Articles of the Handel Society   418
Arts & Crafts in New England, 1704-1775   462
Arts and Crafts in New York, 1726-1776   485n
*Arts and Crafts in New York, 1777-1799: Advertisements and News
   Items from New York City Newspapers*   485
Arts and Crafts in New York, 1800-1804   485n

Arts & Crafts in Philadelphia, Maryland, and South Carolina   548
Arts and Humanities Citation Index   134
Arts in America: A Bibliography   32
Arts of the Pennsylvania Germans   1407
*As the Black School Sings: Black Music Collections at Black
  Universities and Colleges, with a Union List of Book Holdings*   176
Ascher-Nash, Franzi   419
Ashbrook, William S., Jr.   1439
Asti, Martha Secrest   1207
Atkins, Charles L.   840
Atlas of American History   300
Aurand, A. Monroe, Jr.   1125
Ausbund, Das ist: Etliche schöne Christliche Lieder   1180
Austin, Raymond   1208
*Author-Title Index to Joseph Sabin's Dictionary of Books Relating to
  America*   71n
Ayars, Christine Merrick   420, 1526

Babcock, Mary K.D.   421
Bacon, Jean C.   141n
Baer, Elizabeth   422
Bagdon, Robert Joseph   423
Bailey, Claudia Jean   1432
Bailey, Jay   1527
Baillie, Laureen   1672
Baker, Nancy   287n
Baker's Biographical Dictionary of Musicians   1673
Bakkegard, B.M.   1348
Bakken, Howard Norman   678
Balch, William   841
Baldridge, Terry L.   1197
*Ballad of America: The History of the United States in Song and
  Story*   817
Baltimore Directory, for 1799   259
Baltimore Town and Fell's Point Directory   266
Baltimore's Music: The Haven of the American Composer   504
Bandel, Betty   1864
Barbour, J. Murray   842, 843, 1181, 1716
Barck, Dorothy C.   424
Barksdale, A. Beverly   247
Barnes, Edwin N.C.   318
Barnes-Ostrander, M.E.   425
Baron, John H.   426
Barron, David Milton   1785
Bartlett, Hazel   47n
Bartlett, Homer N.   755

Barton, Andrew   1930
Barzel, Ann   1414
Basic Concepts in Music Education   849
Basic Music Library: Essential Scores and Books   33
Basler, Roy P.   50
Bassett, T.D. Seymour   34, 53
Basso, Alberto   7
Bastin, Bruce   1063
Bay Psalm Book: A Facsimile Reprint of the First Edition of 1640
   888
Baynham, Edward Gladstone   427
Bean, Helen J.   756
Beck, Abraham R.   1911
Beck, Herbert H.   1209
Beck, Paul E.   1912
Beck, Roger Lawrence   428
Becker, Laura L.   844
Becker, Warren   348
Beers, Henry Putney   35, 1346
Behrend, Jeanne   757
Behrens, Edith   1210
Bell, Marion V.   141n
Bellows, George Kent   429
Belsheim, George N.   1528
Bender, Harold S.   1182, 1183
Benes, Peter   430
Benjamin Crehore Piano: An Account in the Form of Notes   1542
Benjamin Franklin, 1721-1906: A Reference Guide   1757
Bennett, Lawrence   832
Benson, Louis F.   845
Benson, Norman Arthur   431, 1349
Benton, Rita   1529
Bergquist, G. William   1433
Berman, Eleanor D.   1833
Bethlehem Bach Choir: An Historical and Interpretive Sketch   1313
Betsky, Celia   226
Beveridge, Lowell P.   432
Bialosky, Marshall   319
Biancolli, Louis   1530
Bibliographic Index: A Cumulative Bibliography of Bibliographies
   135
Bibliographical Handbook of American Music   107, 178p
*Bibliographies in American History, 1942-1978: Guide to Materials
   for Research*   35
Bibliography of American County Histories   413p
Bibliography of American Directories through 1860   257n, 265

Bibliography of American Hymnals   1007, 1009n
Bibliography of American Presbyterianism during the Colonial Period   1319
Bibliography of Black Music   89
Bibliography of Early Secular American Music: Eighteenth Century   119
Bibliography of German Culture in America to 1940   68
Bibliography of Mennonite Hymnals and Songbooks, 1742-1972   1178
Bibliography of Nineteenth-Century American Piano Music   95
Bibliography of North American Folklore and Folksong   54
Bibliography of Religion in the South   60
Bibliography of Songsters Printed in America before 1821   128
Bibliotheca Americana: Dictionary of Books Relating to America from Its Discovery to the Present Time   71
Bieber, Albert A.   1440
Bigg, Edward G.P.   1531
Bigger, William George   433
Biggs, E. Power   1532
Billings to Joplin: Popular Music in 19th Century America: An Exhibition March-May 1980   227
Binder, Abraham W.   1166
Bio-Bibliographical Index of Musicians in the United States of America Since Colonial Times   1669
Biographical Dictionary of American Music   1676
Biography and Genealogy Master Index   1670
Biography Index, a Cumulative Index to Biographical Material in Books and Magazines   1671
Birge, Edward Bailey   846
Birney, Allan D.   1211
Birney, George H., Jr.   1865
Black, Mary   232
Black American Music: Past and Present   1089
Black Dance from 1619 to Today   1417
Black Music in America: A History through Its People   359
Black Music in the United States: An Annotated Bibliography of Selected Reference and Research Materials   94
Black Song: The Forge and the Flame: The Story of How the Afro-American Spiritual Was Hammered Out   1078
Blakely, Lloyd G.   1126
Blanchard, Homer D.   1533
Blanck, Jacob   758
Bleyle, Carl Otto   1534
Bloom, Sol   648
Blume, Friedrich   21, 612
Bly, Leon Joseph   679

Boeringer, James   179, 180, 1212, 1213, 1350, 1535, 1693, 1706, 1794, 1861, 1877, 1922
Bollman, James R.   248n
Bonawitz, Dorothy M.   1441
Bond, Chrystelle T.   1415
Books in Print: An Author—Title—Series Index to the "Publishers' Trade List Annual"   36
Books on Music: A Classified List   81
Bordman, Gerald   1442
Bornemann, Robert   1376
Borroff, Edith   302, 320
Boston Directory   256
Boston Prints and Printmakers 1670-1775; a Conference Held by the Colonial Society of Massachusetts, 1 and 2 April 1971   1847
Bowen, Jean   225
Bowes, Frederick P.   434
Bradley, Carol June   168, 796, 920, 1395
Braff, Phyllis   533n
Branstine, Wesley R.   1214
Brant, Cyr de   759
Brasmer, William   1952
Braun, Frank X.   852
Brayley, Arthur W.   1536
Breed, David R.   1016
Breslaw, Elaine G.   435, 436, 550
Brethren Encyclopedia   2
Brethren Hymn Books and Hymnals, 1720-1884   1106
Breton, Arthur J.   181
Brewster, Paul G.   1157
Brief Discourse Concerning Regular Singing   847
Brigham, Clarence S.   155
Briner, Andres   1707
Bristol, Lee H., Jr.   1781
Bristol, Roger P.   45n
Britt, Judith S.   642, 643
Britton, Allen P.   83, 84, 837p, 848, 849, 850, 851, 917n
Brobston, Stanley Heard   1017
Brockman, William S.   37
Brooks, Henry M.   437
Brooks, Tilford Uthratese   1064
Brooks, William   1443
Broucek, Jack W.   438
Brown, Abram E.   1803
Brown, H. Glenn   1382
Brown, Maude O.   1382
Brown, Robert Benaway   852

Brown, T. Allston   1444
Browne, C.A.   760
Bruce, Dickson Davies, Jr.   1018
Bruce, Frank Neely   1786
Bruce, W.J.   1537
Brumbaugh, Martin Grove   1127
Brunkow, Robert deV.   38
Brunner, Raymond J.   1538
Bryant, Carolyn   228
Buch der Deutschen in Amerika   303
Buckley, Peter G.   231n
Buechner, Alan Clark   853
Buijtenen, Mari P. van   1266
Bullock, Helen Duprey   1834
Bultmann, Phyllis W.   1019
Bunners, C.   1708
Burk, Cassie   321
Burkhart, Charles   1184, 1185
Burkitt, Lemuel   1093
Burnham, Collins G.   439
Burr, Nelson R.   39
Bushnell, Vinson C.   1886
Butler, John H.   1919
Butterfield, Lee S.   182
Butterworth, Neil   1674
Buxbaum, Melvin H.   1757
Byrnside, Ron   440

*Calendar of American Poetry in the Colonial Newspapers and Magazines
   through 1765*   154p, 159
Cameron, Kenneth Walter   270
Cameron, Peter T.   1539
Campbell, Frank C.   229
Campbell, Jane   441
Camus, Raoul F.   114, 232, 533n, 680, 681, 682, 683, 684
Cansler, Jeannine Ann   1675
Cantors at the Crossroads   1181
Cappers, Paul Kenwood   613
Carden, Joy   442
Carey, John Thomas   1383
Carl Haverlin Collection/BMI Archives   249n
Carlson, Charles Howard   1128
Carlson, Joyce Mangler   443
Carman, Judith E.   85
Carpenter, Edmund J.   854
Carpenter, Kenneth William   685, 686

Carpitella, Diego   20n
Carroll, George   687
Carroll, Kenneth L.   1324
Carroll, Lucy Ellen   444
Carroll, Thomas   688
Carruth, Gorton   409
Carson, Jane   274
Caswell, Austin B.   380n
Catalog of Broadsides in the Rare Book Division   254
Catalog of Copyright Entries   64n
Catalog of the Johannes Herbst Collection   198
Catalog of the Lititz Congregation Collection   219
Catalog of the Salem Congregation Music   190
Catalogue of Early Books on Music (before 1800)   47
Catalogue of Music by American Moravians, 1742-1842   213
Catalogue of the Annapolis Circulating Library   55p, 184
Catalogue of the Exhibition   230
Catching the Tune: Music and William Sidney Mount   231
Celebrations: Studies in Festivity and Ritual   1343
Century of Music in Poughkeepsie, 1802-1911   417
Champlin, John D.   445
Chancellor, Paul G.   446, 1129, 1215
*Chapters of Opera; Being Historical and Critical Observations and
    Records Concerning the Lyric Drama in New York from Its Earliest
    Days Down to the Present Time*   1462
Charleston Stage in the XVIII Century   1511
Chase, Gilbert   4n, 20n, 322, 323, 324, 1718
Chauncey, Nathaniel   855
*Check List of American Eighteenth Century Newspapers in the Library
    of Congress*   156
Checklist of American Music Periodicals, 1850-1900   151n, 152
Checklist of Four-Shape Shape-Note Tunebooks   120, 938n
Checklist of Keyboard Instruments at the Smithsonian Institution
    183
Checklist of New London, Connecticut, Imprints, 1709-1800   57
Cheek, Curtis Leo   856, 857
Chmaj, B.E.   1787
*Choice Selection of American Country Dances of the Revolutionary
    Era, 1775-1795*   1419
Christ-Janaer, Albert   1020
Christenson, Donald E.   1335
Christian Hymnody   1037
*Chronicon Ephratense: A History of the Community of Seventh Day
    Baptists at Ephrata*   1138
Chronological Tables of American Newspapers, 1690-1820   158
Church Music: An International Bibliography   121

Church Music and Musical Life in Pennsylvania in the Eighteenth Century   447
Church Music in America   626, 1026n
Church Music in Farmington in the Olden Time.   An Historical Address Delivered at the Annual Meeting of the Village Library Company of Farmington, Conn.   482
Church Music of William Billings   1716
Cifaldi, Susan   1740
Cipolla, Frank J.   232
City Directories of the United States in Microform   255n, 256n, 257, 258n, 259n, 262n, 266n, 267n
Claghorn, Charles Eugene   1676
Clark, G.   226
Clark, J. Bunker   86, 689, 690, 691, 692, 1397, 1929
Clark, Keith C.   1008
Clark, Stephen   178p, 184
Clark, Thomas D.   275, 279n
Clarke, Garry E.   325
Clarke, W. Horatio   1540, 1702
Claypool, Richard D.   185, 186, 187, 1216, 1694, 1769
Cleef, Joy van   533n
Clemens, Gurney W.   1541
Cleveland, Pat   448
Cline, Julia   1445
Cogdill, John Lindsay   1446
Cole, Garold L.   276
Cole, Ronald Fred   449
Coleberd, Robert E., Jr.   450
Colket, Meredith B., Jr.   1873
Collection of Millenial Hymns, Adapted to the Present Order of the Church   1336
College Music Society Proceedings: The National and Regional Meetings, 1983-84   930
"Collegium Musicum Salem": Its Music, Musicians and Importance   1278
Colliers's Encyclopedia   1p
Colonial American Jew, 1492-1776   1167
Colonial Anglicanism in New England: A Guide   270
Colwell, Richard J.   290
Comberiati, Carmelo P.   1052
Companion to the Hymnal: A Handbook of the 1964 Methodist Hymnal   1198
Complete Catalogue of Sheet Music and Musical Works, 1870   255p
Complete Encyclopedia of Music   3
Complete Works [of William Billings]   1932
Comprehensive Dissertation Index, 1861-1972   291
Compton, Benjamin Richard   693

Computer Catalog of Nineteenth-Century American-Imprint Sheet Music for the University of Virginia   188
Concise Dictionary of American Biography   1677n
Concise History of the Kehukee Baptist Association, from Its Original Rise Down to 1803   1093
Condit, Lester   87
Connecticut: A Bibliography of Its History   65
Connecticut's Music in the Revolutionary Era   604
Conservatory of Music, University of Missouri-Kansas City Presents Treasures from the Collection of the Institute for Studies in American Music   233
Contributions to the Art of Music in America by the Music Industries of Boston: 1640 to 1936   420
Cook, Harold E.   1337
Cooke, Nym   430n
Coover, James   169, 223p, 796, 920, 1395
Copeland, Robert M.   1106
Copyright Record Books of the District Courts, 1790-1870   268
Core Repertory of Early American Psalmody   1940
Courlander, Harold   1065
Covey, Cyclone   451, 614, 858
Cox, Edward Godfrey   277, 278n
Craig, Tracey Linton   166
Crain, Charles Robert   452
Craven, H.T.   1447
Crawford, Richard   25n, 88, 189, 326, 327, 328, 498n, 533n, 837p, 859, 860, 861, 862, 1021, 1217, 1384, 1733, 1822, 1852, 1940, 1948
Crehore, Charles L.   1542
Crews, Emma Katherine   453, 454
Criger, Wanda Jean   1906
Cripe, Helen   1835, 1836
Cross, Virginia Ann   1022
Crossman, Frederic S.   1012
Crouch, Margaret L.   1351
Crouch, Milton   129p
Cudworth, Charles   1352
Cultural History of the American Revolution   310
Culture of Early Charleston   434
Cumming, Robert   1811
Cummings, Harmon Dean   1692
Cumnock, Frances   190, 191, 1218, 1219
Cumulative Book Index: A World List of Books in the English Language   40
Current Thought in Musicology   488
Curtis, Mary Julia   1448
Curtis, Prudence B.   694

Cushing, Helen Grant   140
Cuthbert, John A.   1870, 1915

Da Silva, Owen Francis   1353
Damon, S. Foster   1957
Dana, Daniel   455
Dance: An Annotated Bibliography, 1965-1982   1410
Danforth, John   979
Danforth, Samuel   979
Daniel, Oliver   456, 457, 1719
Daniel, Ralph T.   615, 616, 734n, 863
Daniels, Rose Dwiggins   1720
Danner, Peter   695
Darby, W. Dermot   343
Darcy, Capt. Thomas F., Jr.   762
Darling, James S.   458
David, Hans T.   213, 459, 1130, 1131, 1220, 1221, 1222
Davidson, James Robert   6
Davidson, Mary Wallace   172, 178p
Davis, Elizabeth A.   280
Davis, Harold   763
Davis, Helen E.   1742
Davis, Josephine K.R.   329, 864
Davis, Ronald L.   330
Davis-Millis, Nina   170
Davison, Marjorie Risk   460
Davison, Nancy R.   234
Davison, Sister Mary Veronica   149
Dawning of American Keyboard Music   690
*Day of Solemn Thanksgiving: Moravian Music for the Fourth of July,
    1783, in Salem, North Carolina*   1229
De Jong, Mary Gosselink   837p, 865
De Lerma, Dominique René   89
De Venney, David P.   90
Dean, Talmage Whitman   1543
Degen, Bruce N.   1901
Deibert, William E.   1704
DeLaban, Juana   1416
Delaplaine, Edward W.   764
Delli, Bertrun   32
Demarest, Alison   1385
Denison, Frederic   1902
*Descriptive Checklist of Book Catalogues Separately Printed in
    America 1693-1800*   1381
Despard, Mabel H.   331
Dichter, Harry   91, 92, 403n, 696, 1386, 1946

Dickinson, Alis   288

Dictionnaire de la Musique   14n

Dictionary of American Biography   1677

Dictionary of American Composers   1674

Dictionary of American History   4

Dictionary of American Hymnology: First-Line Index   1007n, 1009

Dictionary of Hymnology: Origin and History of Christian Hymns and Hymnwriters of All Ages and Nations   5

Dictionary of Music and Musicians   22n

Dictionary of Organs and Organists   1630n

Dictionary of Protestant Church Music   6

Dieffenbach, Ray J.   1545, 1546

Dieffenbach Organ Builders   1546

Diehl, Katherine   1010

Diffenderffer, F.R.   1913

Dinneen, William   192, 461

Dircks, Phyllis T.   1449

Directory and Strangers' Guide for the Year 1816   258

Directory for the City of Hartford for the Year 1799   255

Directory of Archives and Manuscript Repositories in the United States   165

Directory of Historical Societies and Agencies in the United States and Canada   166

Directory of International Music Education Dissertations in Progress   290

Directory of Music Collections in the Greater New York Area   170

Directory of Music Libraries and Collections in New England   171

Directory of State and Local History Periodicals   129p

Disappointment: or, The Force of Credulity   1930

Discourse, at a Public Meeting of the Singers, in the North Parish in Wrentham, 13th May, 1817   996

Discourse on Music, Addressed to the Essex Musical Association, at their Annual Meeting at Boxford, Sept. 12, 1803   455

Discourse on Psalmody: Delivered at Newburgh, before the Presbytery of Hudson, September, 1801   881

Discourse on Psalmody: In Which It Is Clearly Shewn that It Is the Duty of Christians to Take the Spiritual Songs from the Gospel of Christ   914

Discourse on Sacred Music, Delivered before the Essex Musical Association at Their Anniversary Meeting, Boxford, Sept. 19, 1804   607

Discourse on the Divine Ordinance of Singing Psalms. . .   837

Discourse on the Life and Death of Oliver Shaw   1905

Dissertation Abstracts International   288n, 291n, 292

Dizionario Enciclopedico Italiano   1p

Dizionario Enciclopedico Universale Della Musica e dei Musicisti   7

Doctoral Dissertations Accepted by American Universities 289n
Doctoral Dissertations in American Music: A Classified Bibliography 297
Doctoral Dissertations in Musicology 288
Doll, Eugene E. 1123, 1132
Dolmetsch, Christopher L. 1386
Donakowski, Conrad L. 332
Donaldson, Bryna 1547, 1548
Dooley, James Edward 1782
Doran, Carol Ann 1916
Dorenkamp, J.H. 866
Doughty, Gavin Lloyd 1320
Douglas, Charles W. 1145
Dow, George F. 462
Downey, James C. 1023
Dox, Thurston J. 93
Drewry, Cecelia Hodges 4n
Drummond, Robert Paul 1094
Drummond, Robert Rutherford 463, 464, 465, 1890
Dubbs, Joseph Henry 1024, 1133
Duckles, Vincent H. 41
Duffy, John 42
Duncan, Barbara 1387
Duncan, Curtis Daniel 1095
Durham, Weldon B. 1450
Duty of God's Professing People in Glorifying Their Heavenly Father, Preached at a Singing-Lecture in Hartford East Society, June 28, 1727 1002
Duty of Singing 970
Dwight, John S. 466, 467, 468, 542
Dwight, Josiah 867
Dyen, Doris J. 175

Eader, Thomas S. 1549, 1550, 1551, 1552, 1553, 1554, 1555
Eames, Wilberforce 71, 868
Earle, Alice Morse 617
Early American Choral Music: An Annotated Guide 90
Early American Imprints: A Collection of Works Printed in America between 1669 and 1800 56
Early American Imprints, 1639-1800 43, 74n, 99n, 184n, 260n, 837n, 838n, 855n, 873n, 934n, 936n, 945n, 967n, 974n, 982n, 987n, 990n, 1002n
Early American Imprints, Second Series: Shaw-Shoemaker Bibliography, 1801-1819 44, 455n, 498n, 515n, 607n, 841n, 869n, 881n, 914n, 993n, 996n, 998n
Early American Music: Music in America from 1620 to 1920 348

Early American Periodicals Index to 1850   136
Early American Sheet Music: Its Lure and Its Lore, 1768-1889   91
Early Concert-Life in America (1731-1800)   397
Early German Music in Philadelphia   463
Early New England Psalmody   520
Early Opera in America   1504
Early Pennsylvania Arts and Crafts   582
Early Vermont Broadsides   42
Easter, Gerry   1672
Eastman, Allan J.   333
Eaton, Quaintance   382
Eberlein, Harold Donaldson   334, 469
Eddy, Mary O.   1748
Edmonds, John H.   1557
Edmunds, John   618
Edwards, Arthur C.   335
Edwards, George Thornton   470
Egle, William Henry   1801
18th-Century American Secular Music Manuscripts: An Inventory   172,
   173n, 181n
Ekwueme, Lazarus E.N.   1066
Eliason, Robert E.   1558, 1559, 1560, 1561
Ellington, Charles Linwood   1025
Ellinwood, Leonard   619, 620, 621, 1007, 1009, 1026, 1199, 1562
Ellis, Ferdinand   869
Ellison, Ross W.   697, 698, 1926
Ellsworth, Ray   1721
Elson, Arthur   336, 471
Elson, Louis C.   27, 337, 338, 339, 340, 341, 472
Emerging Entertainment; the Drama of the American People to 1828
   1476
Emery, Lynne F.   1417
Emery, Samuel Hopkins   979
Enciclopedia della Musica   8
Encyclopedia Americana   1p
Encyclopedia of American Facts and Dates   409
Encyclopedia of American History   9
Encyclopedia of American Music   10
Encyclopedia of Black America   11
Encyclopédie de la Musique et Dictionnaire du Conservatoire   12
Encyclopédie des Musiques Sacrées   13
Engel, Carl   301n, 1134, 1741
Engel, Lehman   765
Engelke, Hans   870
England, Martha W.   1200
Engler, Martha C.   473, 1027

Enigma of the Bay Psalm Book   889
Ephrata Cloister: An Annotated Bibliography   1123
Ephrata Cloister: An Introduction   1132
Ephrata Commune: An Early American Counterculture   1124
Epstein, Dena J.   176n, 255p, 474, 1067, 1068, 1069, 1070, 1388
Erb, Peter C.   1135
Ervin, Horace   1563
Erwin, Paul Francis   699
Eskew, Harry B.   871, 872, 1028, 1029, 1096
*Essay on Music Pronounced before the Middlesex Musical Society,
   Sept. 9, A.D. 1807*   498
*Essay Preached by Several Ministers of the Gospel for the
   Satisfaction of Their Pious and Consciencious Brethren, as to
   Sundry Questions and Cases of Conscience, Concerning the Singing
   of Psalms*   979
*Essay to Silence the Outcry That Has Been Made in Some Places
   Against Regular Singing*   867
Essays Honoring Lawrence C. Wroth   774
Essays in Musicology: A Birthday Offering for Willi Apel   1369
Essays on American Music   325
Etherington, Charles L.   622
Evans, Charles   43n, 45, 73n, 74n, 84n, 97n, 99n, 371n, 1121n, 1319n
Ewen, David   342, 1678, 1812
Exhibit of Music and Materials on Music Early and Rare   235
*Expediency and Proper Application of Sacred Music: A Discourse,
   Preached at Heath, Feb. 21, 1816, as a Musical Lecture*   993

Fain, Samuel Samson   700
Falconer, Joan Ormsby   198n, 1223, 1795
Farish, Hunter Dickinson   475
Farnsworth, H.   873
Farwell, Arthur   343
Faulcon, Clarence   476
Fauley, Leonore Lynne   1071
Faust, Patricia   344
Fay, Peter J.   67
Fennell, Frederick   345
Ferguson, Allan J.   701, 702
Ferris, Sharon Paugh   62
Ferris, William R., Jr.   1722
Fesperman, John T.   236, 1565, 1566
Filbeck, Loren Harold   1788
Filby, P. William   193, 237, 413p
Fillmore, John C.   346
Findley, Rowe   1224
Finney, Theodore M.   194, 874, 875

First New Orleans Theatre, 1792-1803   1470
First Performances in America to 1900: Works with Orchestra   718
Fisher, Cleveland   1568
Fisher, James L.   876
Fisher, Miles Mark   1072
Fisher, Nevin W.   1105
Fisher, William Arms   477, 644, 645, 877, 1389
Fitz, Adeline F.   347
Fitzpatrick, John C.   683n, 703
Fix, Carolyn E.   1569
*Flashes of Merriment: A Century of Humorous Songs in America, 1805-
    1905*   792
Fleck, Hattie C.   478
Fleming, Shirley   1225
Flexner, Beatrice Hudson   479
Fling, Robert Michael   33
Flood, W.H. Grattan   766
Floyd, Samuel A., Jr.   94
Flusser, Beth   1451
Folk Music in America: A Reference Guide   112
Foltz, Roger E.   930
Foner, Philip S.   767
Foote, Henry Wilder   480, 623, 878, 879, 1375
Forbes, Fred R., Jr.   1410
Ford, Worthington C.   195
Forthcoming Books   36n
Four Centuries of Music: An Exhibit   238
Fouts, Gordon E.   880
Francis Hopkinson, Musician, Poet and Patriot: 1737-1937   223
*Francis Hopkinson, the First American Poet-Composer (1737-1791) and
    James Lyon, Patriot, Preacher, Psalmodist (1735-1794): Two Studies
    in Early American Music*   1822
*Francis Hopkinson's Lessons: A Facsimile Edition of Hopkinson's
    Personal Keyboard Book.   An Anthology of Keyboard Compositions &
    Arrangements Copied in Hopkinson's Own Hand*   1945
Frank, Mortimer   624
Freedman, Roma Sachs   1758
Freedom's Voice in Poetry and Song   154p, 753
Freeman, Andrew   1570
Freeman, Jonathan   881
Freidel, Frank   51, 274p
Fries, Adelaide L.   1226
Frim, Rose   1679
Frischmann, Charles   1571
*From Jehovah to Jazz: Music in America from Psalmody to the Present
    Day*   364

Frost, Ruth G.   1227
Fuging Tunes in the Eighteenth Century   977
Fuld, James J.   172, 173n, 181n, 196, 794
Fuller, Albert   1837
Funeral Chorals of the Unitas Fratrum or Moravian Church   1226
Funk, Joseph   1723
Funke, Anneliese M.   1123
Furcha, Edward J.   1325

Gable, Martin D., Jr.   1146
Gaeddart, William K.   85
Gaines, William H., Jr.   481
Gamet, Vera   1724
Garbett, Arthur S.   1838
Gardner, John   1418
Garfield, Ann M.   62
Garrett, Allen M.   882, 1725
Garrison, Webb B.   496n
Gates, J. Terry   883, 1390
Gaul, Harvey   556n
Gauss, Charles E.   1839
Gawalt, Gerald W.   208
Gay, Julius   482
Gee, Harry   704
Geiger, Maynard   1354
Geil, Jean   175, 197
Geisler, John H.   1228
Gelders, Ruth Beall   1840
Genuchi, Marvin Charles   1767
George Washington as a Friend and Patron of Music   669
Gephart, Ronald M.   46
*German-American Relations and German Culture in America: A Subject
   Bibliography, 1941-1980*   68n
German-Americana: A Bibliography   77
German Pietists of Provincial Pennsylvania, 1694-1708   1379
*German Sectarians of Pennsylvania, 1708-1800: A Critical and
   Legendary History of the Ephrata Cloister and the Dunkers*   1141
Gerson, Robert A.   483, 484
Getz, Russell P.   1136
Gibbs, Giles   705
Gilbert, Donald K.   706
*Giles Gibbs, Jr., His Book for the Fife, Ellington, Connecticut,
   1777*   705
Gillespie, Anna   95
Gillespie, John   95, 1951
Giroux, Paul H.   1572

Glazer, Irvin R.   1452
Gleason, Harold   348, 375
Glezen, Edward K.   1902
Glory, Hallelujah! The Story of the Campmeeting Spiritual   1044
Göllner, Theodor   1355
Goepp, Philip H.   349
Goldberg, Isaac   1726
Golden Age of Colonial Culture   312
Gombert, Karl E.   1453
Gombosi, Marilyn   198, 1229, 1230
Goodell, Abner C.   625
Gottesman, Rita S.   485
Gottlieb Schober of Salem   1899
Gottschall, Robert J.   1326
Gould, Nathaniel Duren   626, 1026n
Grafing, Keith Gerhart   1703
Grand Opera in America   1466
Grashel, John W.   884
Graue, Jerald C.   1930
Gray, Leon Wilbur   768
Great Song Thesaurus   789
Green, Abel   411
Green, Elvena Marion   1454
Greene, David Mason   1680
Greene's Biographical Encyclopedia of Composers   1680
Gregory, Julia   47
Grenander, M.E.   707, 708
Grider, Rufus A.   1216n, 1231, 1316n
Griffin, Francis   1232
Grimes, Calvin Bernard   1391
Groce, Nancy Jane   1573
Grosse Lexikon der Musik   14
Groth, Howard   1455
Grounds and Rules of Musick Explained   987
Grout, Donald J.   301p
Grove's Dictionary of Music and Musicians   22n
Grubb, Marion   1233
Grubbs, John W.   488
Gryc, Stephen M.   885
Guide for Dating Early Published Music: A Manual of Bibliographical Practices   268p, 1400
Guide to American Trade Catalogs, 1744-1900   263
Guide to Major Manuscript Collections Accessioned and Processed by the Library of the Western Reserve Historical Society since 1970   212n
Guide to Musical America   351

Guide to Newspaper Indexes in New England   157
Guide to Reference and Bibliography for Theatre Research   1432
Guide to Reference Books   48, 49n
Guide to Reference Materials   49
Guide to Research in Music Education   116
Guide to Shaker Manuscripts in the Library of the Western Reserve Historical Society: With an Inventory of Its Shaker Photographs   1329
Guide to Special Collections in the OCLC Database   178p
Guide to the Hymns and Tunes of American Methodism   1203
Guide to the Lester S. Levy Collection of Sheet Music   199
Guide to the Manuscript Collection of the South Carolinian Library   220
Guide to the Manuscript Collections of the New Jersey Historical Society   218
Guide to the Manuscript Collections of the New-York Historical Society   181
Guide to the Manuscripts and Archives of the Western Reserve Historical Society   212
Guide to the Study of the United States of America; Representative Books Reflecting the Development of American Life and Thought   50
Guide to the Study of United States Imprints   76, 105n
Guitar and Vihuela: An Annotated Bibliography   110
Gunn, Glenn D.   350
Gusikoff, Lynne   351

Haberlen, John   986
Hackett, Karleton   352
Hadland, F.A.   353
Hahn, Henry   1356
Hahn, Ruth S.   1158
Hall, A. Oakley   486
Hall, Harry H.   496n, 1234, 1235, 1236, 1237, 1238, 1239, 1240
Hall, James William, Jr.   886
Hall, Roger L.   487, 770, 1339, 1727
Hallelujah, Amen! The Story of the Handel and Haydn Society of Boston   500
Halpin, Joseph   1357
Hamblen, David   709
Hamburger, Roberta   72
Hamilton, Alexander   278
Hamilton, J. Taylor   1695, 1776
Hamilton, Kenneth G.   1241
Hamm, Charles   354, 488, 887, 1749
Hammond, Paul Garnet   627
Handbook for Research in American History   154p, 178p, 274p, 413p

Handbook of American Music and Musicians, Containing Biographies of American Musicians and Histories of the Principal Musical Institutions, Firms and Societies 29
Handbook of American Operatic Premieres, 1731-1962 1434
Handbook of American Sheet Music 92
Handbuch der Musikgeschichte 301
Hanstein, George 1574
Haraszti, Zoltan 888, 889
Hare, Maud Cuney 1073
Hark, J. Max 1138
Harley, Augusta Brett 1754
Harmonious Craft: American Musical Instruments 239
Harper Dictionary of Music 15
Harper's Encyclopaedia of United States History 16
Harriman, Helen 1575
Harrington, Alice M. 355
Harris, Ernest E. 96
Hart, Charles Henry 771, 822n
Hartzell, Lawrence W. 356, 357, 358, 1242, 1243, 1358, 1777, 1856, 1885, 1896, 1898
Harvard Dictionary of Music 24n
Harvard Guide to American History 51, 274p
Haskell, John D., Jr. 52, 53
Haskins, James 359
Haskins, John C. 1871
Hastings, George E. 1813
Hastings, Thomas 1683n
Haussman, William A. 1030
Haverlin, Carl 646
Havlice, Patricia P. 271
Haydn in America 727
Haydn Studies; Proceedings of the International Haydn Conference, Washington, D.C., 1975 1276
Haywood, Charles 54
Hazen, Margaret Hindle 710, 772
Heard, Priscilia S. 97, 1319n
Heath, Trudy 130n
Hehr, Milton Gerald 418n, 491, 492
Heinrici, Max 303
Heintze, James R. 22n, 200, 281, 282, 293, 299n, 1836n, 1857
Held, Jerrold 1925
Heller, George N. 1759
Hellyer, Roger 1244
Henderson, Mary C. 1456
Hennig, Julia A. 711
Hennig, Cohen 133

Henry, Hugh T.   447n, 773, 1109, 1110
Henry, Nelson B.   849
Henry, Thomas L.   1137
Hensel, W.U.   1914
Herbert, James W.   712
Herbert, Miranda C.   1670
Hermann, Myrl Duncan   713
Hess, Albert G.   1377, 1378
Hessler, M. Hunt   231n
Higgins, Ardis O.   1359
Higginson, J. Vincent   1111, 1112, 1113, 1360, 1853
Hildebrand, David K.   287n
Hildeburn, Charles R.   55, 1814
Hill, Double E.   1201
Hill, Richard S.   774
Hill, Thomas C.   775
Hindley, Geoffrey   18
Hindman, John Joseph   493
Hines, James Robert   494
Hinke, William J.   447n, 1321
Hinks, Donald R.   1106
Hinson, Maurice   714
Hinton, Sam   1031
*Historical Account of the Ephrata Cloister and the Seventh Day
  Baptist Society*   1125
*Historical Notes on Music in Bethlehem, Pennsylvania, from 1741 to
  1871*   1216n, 1231, 1316n
History: A Catalog of Selected Doctoral Dissertations   292n
History and Bibliography of American Newspapers, 1690-1820   155
History and Use of Hymns and Hymn-Tunes   1016
*History of a Church (Dunker) with Comments Featuring the First
  Church of the Brethren of Philadelphia, Pa., 1813-1943*   1107
History of American Catholic Hymnals: Survey and Background   1112
History of American Church Music   620
History of American Music   338
History of Brethren Hymnbooks   1105
History of Military Music in America   683n, 751
History of Music and Musical Style   311
History of Music Education in the United States   899
History of Music in American Life   330
History of Music in New England   3n, 437n, 495
History of Popular Music in America   403
History of Public School Music in the United States   846
History of Song   807
*History of the American Pianoforte: Its Technical Development and
  the Trade*   1652

History of the Choir and Music of Trinity Church, New York from Its Organization, to the Year 1897 633
History of the German Baptist Brethrens in Europe and America 1127
History of the Handel and Haydn Society of Boston, Massachusetts: 1815-1890 542
History of the New York Stage 1444
History of the Organ in the United States 1612
History of the Star-Spangled Banner from 1814 to the Present 828
History of Western Music 301p
History Sings: Backgrounds of American Music 367
Hitchcock, H. Wiley 30, 98, 189, 304n, 313p, 360, 892, 1457, 1728, 1928, 1931, 1934, 1935, 1943, 1949, 1956
Hitchings, Sinclair 533n, 1847
Hixon, Donald 97n, 99, 105n, 1319n
Hoglund, A. William 294
Hohmann, Rupert Karl 1186
Holder, Edward M. 1245
Holibaugh, Ralph W. 1392
Holl, Herbert 776
Hollander, A.N.J. den 304
Hollister, Florence Hartman 361
Holmes, Charles N. 1576, 1577
Honegger, Marc 14
Hood, George 3n, 437n, 495, 1681, 1712, 1807, 1887, 1908, 1920, 1921
Hoogerwerf, Frank W. 496
Hooper, William L. 1097
Hoople, Donald Graham 1246
Hoornstra, Jean 130n
Hoover, Cynthia Adams 183, 254p, 533n, 647, 1458
Hopkins, Robert 715, 1955
Horn, David 100
Horn, Dorothy 890, 891, 1032
Horton, Charles Allison 716
Hostetler, John A. 1177
Housewright, Wiley L. 717
Howard, Edward G. 237
Howard, John Tasker 318n, 362, 403n, 648, 778, 805, 1797
Howe, M.A. DeWolfe 1247
Howe, Mabel Almy 1393
Howe, Roland L. 1107
Howe, Warren P. 1897
Hoxie, Frances Alida 497
Hubbard, John 498
Hubbard, Cortlandt Van Dyke 334, 469
Hubbard, W.L. 28

Huddleston, Eugene L.   1830
Hudson, Arthur Palmer   1248
Huebener, Mary A.   1249
Huggins, Harold C.   649
Hughes, Charles W.   1020
Hulan, Richard Huffman   1033, 1034
Humanistic Studies in Honor of John Calvin Metcalf   1844
Humanities: A Selective Guide to Information Sources   70
Humanities Index   137
Hundred Years of Music in America   376
Hunnicutt, Judy   1035
Hymn Tune Names: Their Sources and Significance   1011
Hymnbook Collections of North America   1015
Hymnodie der Mennoniten in Nordamerika (1742-1860): Eine Studie zur Verpflanzung, Bewahrung und Umformung europäischer Kirchenliedtradition   1189
Hymnody in the American Indian Missions   1360
Hymns and Tunes, an Index   1010

Immigrants and Their Children in the United States: A Bibliography of Doctoral Dissertations, 1885-1982   294
IMS Report, Berkely, 1977   1372
Incunabula and Americana, 1450-1800: A Key to Bibliographic Study   75
Index of Obituaries in Boston Newspapers, 1704-1800   283
Index of the Recorded Anthology of American Music   280n
Index to Personal Names in the National Union Catalog of Manuscript Collections, 1959-1984   167n
Index to Religious Periodical Literature   143n
Index to the New World Recorded Anthology of American Music: A User's Guide to the Initial One Hundred Records   280
Index to Theses Accepted for Higher Degrees by the Universities of Great Britain and Ireland   295n
Index to Theses with Abstracts Accepted for Higher Degrees by the Universities of Great Britain and Ireland   295n
Information on Music: A Handbook of Reference Sources in European Languages   62
Ingram, Jeannine   1250, 1251, 1252, 1253, 1254, 1255
Ingram, John Van Ness   156
Inserra, Lorraine   892
International Cyclopedia of Music and Musicians   17
Introduction to the Singing of Psalm-Tunes   982
Ireland, Joseph N.   1459
Irwin, Joyce   893
Isaiah Thomas, Printer, Patriot and Philanthropist, 1749-1831   1406
Issues of the Press in Pennsylvania, 1685-1784   55

Italian-American History   1165
Itinerancy in New England and New York   430
Itinerarium Being a Narrative of a Journey. . . 1744   278

Jabbour, Alan   17n
Jablonski, Edward   10, 380n
Jackson, George Pullen   894, 1036, 1187, 1394
Jackson, Irene V.   101, 1074, 1084
Jackson, Kenneth T.   300
Jackson, Richard   102, 240, 1677n, 1954
Jacob Eckhard's Choirmaster's Book of 1809   1942
Jarboe, Betty   284
Jefferys, C.P.B.   499
Jenkins, John H.   56
Jerde, Curtis D.   1075
Joan of Arc, Sister M.   1361
*Johann Conrad Beissel and the Ephrata Community: Mystical and
    Historical Texts*   1135
Johann Conrad Beissel, Mystic and Martinet   1710
Johannes Herbst Collection   201
Johansen, John H.   1256, 1257
John, Robert W.   202
Johnson, Carl   1729
Johnson, H. Earle   150, 500, 501, 502, 650, 718, 1395, 1460, 1779,
    1828, 1872
Johnson, Hazel A.   57
Jones, Dankel   1768
Jones, F.O.   29
Jones, Howard Mumford   1153
Jones, Matt B.   895, 896
Jones, Stuart E.   719
Jordan, John W.   1578, 1778
Jost, Walter James   1188
*Journal and Letters of Philip Vickers Fithian, 1773-1774: A
    Plantation Tutor of the Old Dominion*   475
Joyce, William Leonard   1384
Joyful Sound: Christian Hymnody   1046
Judson Concordance to Hymns   1012
Jueckstock, John Douglas   1258
Julian, John   5

Kadelbach, Ada   1189, 1190
Kaminkow, Marion J.   78, 413p
Kane, Joseph Nathan   413p
Kapoor, Lakshmi   170
Karpel, Bernard   32

Kasling, Kim R. 1579
Kass, Philip 241
Katz, Bernard 1076
Kaufman, Charles H. 503, 1580, 1767n
Kaufman, Lee Jack 897
Kaufmann, Helen L. 364
Kaufmann, Helen Stewart 898
Kearns, William 545, 906
Keast, Laury S. 780
Keast, Naomi Atkins 365
Keck, George Russell 203
Keefer, Lubov 504, 1815
Keene, James A. 505, 899
Keets, Alfred 781
Kegerreis, Richard I. 900
Keim, Betty 1347
Keith, Edmond D. 1037
Keller, Kate Van Winkle 115, 173, 430n, 533n, 604, 1411, 1419, 1581
Keller, Michael A. 41
Kendall, Raymond 1154
Kenney, Alice P. 1120
Kepple, Robert J. 58
Keyed Bugles in the United States 1558
Kidson, Frank 782, 783
Kiehner, Anton F. 506
Kienzle, Rich 1582
Kilian, Otto 1709
Kimball, Frank W. 784
King, A. Hyatt 1583
King, Clyde Richard 1461
King, Percy 1114
King, Rolf 1774, 1775
Kingman, Daniel 366
Kinkeldey, Otto 720
Kinne, Aaron 901
Kinscella, Hazel Gertrude 367, 507, 1816
Kirk, Elise K. 651, 652
Kirkham, E. Kay 285
Klamkin, Marian 785
Klassen, A.J. 1179
Klauss, Walter 1375p
Klein, Ursula 21n
Klein, Walter Conrad 1710
Klocko, David Grover 902, 1947
Kmen, Henry A. 508
Knerr, R.M. 675

Knox, Julie LeC.   1584
Kochan, James L.   721
Kohn, Karl   368
Kolb, Margaret Leinbach   1259
Kolman, Barry H.   722
Konig, Linda   1260
Kortz, Edwin W.   1261
Kouwenhoven, John A.   786, 903
Kramer, Marilyn M.   204
Krauss, Anne McClenny   724, 1891, 1892
Krehbiel, Henry Edward   628, 1462
Kriebel, Howard Wiegner   1327
Kring, Hilda Adam   1159
Kroeger, Karl   725, 787, 904, 905, 906, 907, 908, 909, 910, 911,
    1038, 1262, 1263, 1264, 1265, 1266, 1267, 1268, 1269, 1270, 1271,
    1272, 1396, 1696, 1932, 1953
Krohn, Ernst C.   104, 509, 726, 912, 1397
Krueger, Karl   369
Krummel, Donald W.   82p, 105, 106, 107, 175, 178p, 268p, 1381p,
    1384, 1392, 1398, 1399, 1400, 1401, 1463
Kuper, Theodore F.   1841
Kussrow, Van Carl, Jr.   1464

Labaree, Leonard W.   1585
LaFargue, André   1465
Lahee, Henry Charles   410, 510, 1466, 1586
Laine, Juliette   1362
La Laurencie, Lionel de   1760
Lambert, Barbara   286p, 511, 533
Lamech, Brother   1138
*Land Marks of American Music History: An Exhibit in Honor of Oscar
    George Sonneck, 1873-1928*   242
Landon, Esther Abrams   913
Lang, Paul Henry   305
Langworthy, Helen   1467
Lansing, Richard H.   512
Larousse Encyclopedia of Music   18
Larsen, Jens Peter   1276
LaRue, Jan P.   1273
Lathem, Edward Connery   158
Latta, James   914
Laubenstein, Sarah   1587, 1588
Laufman, Alan   1589
Lawrence, Vera Brodsky   653, 788, 1468, 1798
Lawson, Charles Truman   1274
Lax, Roger   789

Layng, Judith   1469, 1930
Leaman, Jerome   1275
Lechford, Thomas   513
Lee, William   915
Le Gardeur, René J.   1470
Lehman, Carroll James   1743
LeMassena, C.E.   790
Lemay, J.A. Leo   154p, 159, 791
Levine, Lawrence W.   1077
Levy, Lester S.   199, 205, 792, 793, 794
Lewis, Thomas P.   59
Libin, Laurence   178p, 231n, 1520p, 1590, 1591
Library Literature   138, 223p
Lichtenwanger, William   174, 447n, 573n, 795, 796, 797
Life and Works of Francis Hopkinson   1813
Lindsay, Bryan Eugene   798
Lindsley, Charles Edward   108, 206, 837p, 916
Lindstrom, Carl E.   1730
Lingg, Ann M.   1731
Link, Eugene P.   917
Lippencott, Margaret E.   799, 1402
Lippincott, Horace Mather   514
Lippy, Charles H.   60
List of Editions of the Bay Psalm Book or New England Version of the Psalms   868
Literature of American Music in Books and Folk Music Collections: A Fully Annotated Bibliography   100
Livermore, Solomon Kidder   515
Lloyd, Malcolm, Jr.   1858
Lockwood, Elizabeth   1007
Loeb, Henry B.   1471
Loessel, Earl Oliver   918
Loest, Roland   1592
Loewen, Esko   1593
Loney, Glenn   1443, 1449
Lorenz, Ellen Jane   629, 919
Loring, Florence B.   370
Lossing, Benson J.   800
Lovell, John, Jr.   1078
Low, W. Augustus   11
Lowens, Irving   21n, 84, 109, 127, 127p, 128, 129p, 207, 242n, 371, 372, 516, 517, 533n, 630, 654, 727, 801, 802, 917n, 920, 921, 922, 923, 924, 925, 926, 927, 928, 929, 982n, 1276, 1277, 1756, 1789, 1854, 1888, 1941, 1958, 1959
Lucas, Clarence   373
Luening, Otto   374

Lutkin, Peter Christian   631
Lutz, Charles   1594

Mack, Elmer L.   1285
Mackie, Shirley   655
McBride, Lucia   392
McCausland, Susan A. Arnold   518
McClellan, Major Edwin North   728
McClenny, Anne   1893
McCorkle, Donald M.   8n, 1278, 1279, 1280, 1281, 1282, 1283, 1284, 1595, 1596, 1697, 1699n, 1878
McCormick, David W.   1804, 1805
McCracken, Eugene M.   1597
McCrum, Blanche P.   50
McCue, George   380
McCutchan, Robert Guy   1011
McCutcheon, Meredith Alice   110
McDaniel, Stanley Robert   519
McDormand, Thomas B.   1012
MacDougall, Hamilton C.   520
McFarland, James   1598
McGeary, Thomas   1599
McGill, Anna Blanche   1363
McGraw, Hugh   930
McKay, David P.   931, 1472, 1473, 1713n, 1732, 1733, 1900, 1945
McKenzie, Wallace   632
McKim, Lucy   1062
McManis, Charles W.   1600, 1601, 1602, 1603
McNamara, Brooks   1474
McNeil, Anna W.   803
McNeil, Barbara   1670
McRae, Lynn T.   188
Madeira, Louis C.   521
Magazine Index   139
Mahan, Katherine Hines   522, 1817
Mahar, William J.   523
Main, Gloria L.   286
Maine: A Bibliography of Its History   52
Maine Composers and Their Music: A Biographical Dictionary   1691
Mangler, Joyce Ellen   461, 524, 729, 1604, 1605, 1606, 1855
Mann, Walter Edward   1607
Manns, Charles G.   977
Manufactures in the United States   1626
Manuscript Collections of the Maryland Historical Society   211
Manuscript Sources in the Library of Congress for Research on the American Revolution   208

Marble, Annie R. 1818
Marcell, David W. 61
Marco, Guy A. 62
Marcus, Jacob R. 1167
Marini, Stephen A. 1039
Marks, Harold K. 525
Marks, Joseph E., III 1420
Marraro, Howard R. 1164
Marrocco, W. Thomas 335, 375, 730, 932, 933
Martin, Betty Jean 1139
Martin, Raymond Jones 1322
Maryland Inventories and Accounts 287
Massenkeil, Günther 14
Master's Abstracts International 296, 298n
Master's Theses in the Arts and Social Sciences in the United States and Canada 296n, 298
Mates, Julian 1475
Mattfeld, Julius 411, 1434
Matthews, William 271n, 272, 273
Mathews, William Smythe Babcock 376
Maultsby, Portia Katrenia 1079, 1080, 1081, 1082, 1083, 1084
Maurer, Joseph A. 1286, 1287, 1288, 1289, 1290
Maurer, Maurer 377, 656, 657, 658, 1608, 1859, 1874, 1875
Maust, Wilbur Richard 1790
Mayo, Margot 1421, 1422
Mead, Rita H. 297
Media, Jay 1291, 1292
Meeting House Hill, 1630-1783 999
Meierhoffer, Virginia 321
Mellen, John 934
Mellers, Wilfrid 378
Mellin, Ted 1293
Memoir of the Life and Character of Rev. Asahel Nettleton 1866
Memorial History of the City of New-York 445
Memorial of Oliver Shaw 1902
Mennonite Bibliography: 1631-1961 1179
Mennonite Encyclopedia 19
Meserve, Walter J. 1476
Messenger, Ruth Ellis 1013
Messiter, A.H. 633
Metcalf, Frank J. 75n, 111, 527, 877n, 935, 1041, 1682, 1753
Metcalfe, Ralph H., Jr. 1085
Metz, Charles Jonathan, II 731
Meyer, Eve R. 659, 1938, 1939
Michael, Mary Ruth 1477
Microbook Library of American Civilization 63

Microprint Edition of Early American Newspapers, 1704-1820   160
Mifflin, Benjamin   279
Military Music of the American Revolution   682
Miller, Geoffrey   273n
Miller, Terry E.   112
Milligan, Harold V.   379, 528, 529, 1819
Mills, Samuel J.   936
Milner, Anita Cheek   161
Ministry of Taunton, with Incidental Notices of Other Professions   979
Miscellaneous Studies in the History of Music   399, 822n, 1503
Mission Music of California: A Collection of Old California Mission Hymns and Masses   1353
Missouri Music   509
Mitchell, Nathan   1115
Molen van Ee, Patricia   208
Molnar, John Edgar   71n
Molnar, John W.   530, 660, 1478
Montague, Richard Addison   1827
Montani, Nicola A.   1116
Montebello, Philippe de   1590
Mooney, James E.   74
Moore, John Hammond   162, 1086
Moore, John W.   3
Moore, Lillian   1423, 1424, 1425
Moravian Contribution to American Music   1281
More than Dancing: Essays on Afro-American Music and Musicians   1074, 1084
Morehen, John   732
Morgan, Catharine   1202
Morin, Raymond   1734
Morris, Adah V.   140
Morris, Richard B.   9
Morris, Robert C.   218
Morrison, James E.   1426, 1427
Morse, William N.   1479
Moss, Harold Gene   1480
Mott, Margaret M.   113
Motte, Abraham   258
Mugridge, Donald H.   50
Muldrow, Blanche   1481
Muller, Joseph   805
Mullin, John   259
Murray, Sterling E.   661, 662, 937, 1711n, 1909
Murrell, Irvin Henry, Jr.   1098

Muse for the Masses: Ritual and Music in an Age of the Democratic Revolution, 1770-1870 332
Music, David W. 938, 939, 940, 1042, 1099, 1100
Music: A Guide to the Reference Literature 37
Music and Dance in the New England States, Including Maine, New Hampshire, Vermont, Massachusetts, Rhode Island & Connecticut 574
Music and Education in Vermont, 1700-1900 505
Music and Musicians in Early America 129p, 371, 517n, 921n, 922n, 925n, 926n, 927n, 982n, 1756n, 1789n, 1888n
Music and Musicians of Maine 470
Music and Musicians of Pennsylvania 556
Music and Musket: Bands and Bandsmen of the American Civil War 737
Music Article Guide 146
Music at Harvard: A Historical Review of Men and Events 575
Music at the White House: A History of the American Spirit 652
Music Collections in American Libraries: A Chronology 168
Music Comes to America 342
Music Directory of Early New York City 261
Music Education: A Guide to Information Sources 96
Music for Patriots, Politicians, and Presidents: Harmonies and Discords of the First Hundred Years 653
Music from the Middle Ages through the Twentieth Century: Essays in Honor of Gwynn McPeek 1052
Music in a New Found Land: Themes and Developments in the History of American Music 378
Music in America (Farwell/Darby) 343
Music in America (Ritter) 387
Music in America (Rublowsky) 389
Music in America: An Anthology from the Landing of the Pilgrims to the Close of the Civil War, 1620-1865 335n, 375
Music in American Life 368
Music in American Society, 1776-1976: From Puritan Hymn to Synthesizer 380
Music in Boston: Readings from the First Three Centuries 532
Music in Charleston from 1732 to 1919 570
Music in Colonial America: An Exhibition Opened at the John Carter Brown Library, November 14, 1975 243
Music in Colonial Massachusetts, 1630-1820 127p, 254p, 286p, 533, 1617n
Music in Early America: A Bibliography of Music in Evans 97n, 99, 105n
Music in Europe and the United States: A History 302
Music in Georgia 496
Music in Harvard Libraries: A Catalogue of Early Printed Music and Books on Music in the Houghton Library and the Eda Kuhn Loeb Music Library 222

Music in Lexington before 1840   442
Music in New Hampshire: 1623-1800   543
Music in New Jersey, 1655-1860: A Study of Musical Activity and Musicians in New Jersey from Its First Settlement to the Civil War   503
Music in New Orleans: The Formative Years, 1791-1841   508
Music in New York during the American Revolution: An Inventory of Musical References in Rivington's New York Gazette   154
Music in Philadelphia   483
Music in the Church   631
Music in the New World   354
Music in the United States   335
Music in the United States: A Historical Introduction   360
Music in Western Civilization   305
Music Index: A Subject-Author Guide to Current Music Periodical Literature   123n, 129n, 134n, 137n, 142n, 145n, 147, 148n, 1671n
Music Libraries and Instruments   1529
Music Materials and the Public Library   374
Music Men: An Illustrated History of Brass Bands in America, 1800-1920   710
Music of Black Americans: A History   401, 1069n
Music of George Washington's Time   648
Music of Henry Ainsworth's Psalter   892
Music of the Bay Psalm Book   1950
Music of the Ephrata Cloister   1142
Music of the Old South: Colony to Confederacy   583
Music of the Pilgrims: A Description of the Psalm-Book Brought to Plymouth in 1620   635
Music of the United States: Its Sources and History   331
Music of the World: A History   307
Music Publishers in New York City before 1850   1393
Music Publishing in St. Louis   1397
Music Reference and Research Materials: An Annotated Bibliography   41
Music That Washington Knew, with an Historical Sketch   645
Musica   20
Musical Biography   1686, 1870n
Musical Heritage of the United States: The Unknown Portion   369
Musical Instrument Collections: Catalogues and Cognate Literature   169, 223p
Musical Instruments and Their Portrayal in Art   244
Musical Interludes in Boston, 1795-1830   502
Musical Life in the Pennsylvania Settlements of the Unitas Fratrum   1222
Musical Taste as a Religious Question in Nineteenth-Century America   1148

Musical Theatre in America: Papers and Proceedings of the Conference on the Musical Theatre in America   1443, 1449
Musical U.S.A.   382
Musik in Geschichte und Gegenwart; allgemeine Enzyklopädie der Musik   21
Mussik, F.A.   1791
Myers, Gordon   85n, 806, 942, 1403, 1761
Myers, Richmond E.   1294

Nathan, Hans   21n, 807, 905n, 943, 1735, 1933
National Cyclopedia of American Biography   1684
National Index of American Imprints through 1800: The Short-Title Evans   43n, 74, 97n
National Inventory of Documentary Sources in the United States   178p
National Music of America and Its Sources   339
National Tune Index: Early American Wind and Ceremonial Music, 1636-1836   114
National Tune Index: 18th-Century Secular Music   115, 173n
National Union Catalog: Music and Phonorecords   64n
National Union Catalog: Music, Books on Music, and Sound Recordings   64
National Union Catalog of Manuscript Collections   178p, 167
Nature and Importance of the Duty of Singing Praise to God, Considered   936
Nef, Karl   306
Negro Folk Music, U.S.A.   1065
Negro Musicians and Their Music   1073
Negro Slave Songs in the United States   1072
Nelson, Larry L.   733
Nemmers, Erwin E.   1117, 1118
Nettl, Paul   383, 734
New Grove: A Bibliography of Reviews and Other Writings   22n
New Grove Dictionary of American Music   1p, 10n, 22n, 30, 82p, 127p, 129p, 178p, 313p, 413p, 498n, 837p, 1375p, 1381p, 1410p, 1432p, 1520p, 1676n
New Grove Dictionary of Music and Musicians   22, 30n
New Grove Dictionary of Musical Instruments   23
New Hampshire: A Bibliography of Its History   53
New Harvard Dictionary of Music   24
New Oxford Companion to Music   25
New Sabin: Books Described Again on the Basis of Examination of Originals, and Fully Indexed by Title, Subject, Joint Authors, and Institutions and Agencies   71n
New Trade Directory, for Philadelphia, Anno 1800   260
New World Records   354n
Newspaper Indexes: A Location and Subject Guide for Researchers   161

Newspapers in Microform: United States, 1948-1983   163
Nichols, H.   226
Nicolisi, Robert J.   384
Nin-Culmell, Joaquin   238
Ninde, Edward S.   1043
19th Century American Music Periodicals on Microfilm   151, 152n
Nineteenth-Century American Piano Music   1951
Nineteenth Century Readers' Guide to Periodical Literature   140
Nitz, Donald A.   455n, 498n, 515n, 534, 944, 993n, 994n, 996n
Noack, Fritz   1610
Noble, Oliver   945
Nolte, Ewald V.   1295, 1296, 1879, 1880
North, Louise J.   245
Norton, M.D. Herter   726n, 735
Norton, Pauline Elizabeth Hosack   736, 1410p
Notes on Music in Old Boston   477
Nothing More Agreeable: Music in George Washington's Family   643
Noyes, Samuel Bradley   578n
Nutter, Charles S.   535
Nye, Eugene M.   1611

Obenshain, Kathryn   1482
Obituaries: A Guide to Sources   284
Ochs, Michael   246
Ochse, Orpha   1612
O'Connell, L.   536
Odell, George C.D.   1483
Ogasapian, John   1613, 1614, 1615
Ohio Composers and Musical Authors   539
Ohio Moravian Music   1242
Old Sheet Music: A Pictorial History   785
*Old Stoughton Musical Society: An Historical and Informative Record
  of the Oldest Choral Society in America*   578
Olden-Time Music: A Compilation from Newspapers and Books   437
Oliver, Henry K.   1616, 1829
Oliver, Peter   1484
Olsen, Dale A.   663
Olson, Ivan Walter, Jr.   537, 538
Olson, Kenneth E.   737
*On the Practice of Music: A Discourse Pronounced at Pepperell,
  Massachusetts, May 17th, 1809, before the Middlesex Musical
  Society*   515
*One Hundred and Fifty Years of Music Publishing in the United
  States: An Historical Sketch with Special Reference to the Pioneer
  Publisher, Oliver Ditson Company, Inc., 1783-1933*   1389
Oom Pah Pah: The Great American Band   232

Operas on American Subjects   1460
Oration on Music   873
Organ in New England: An Account of Its Use and Manufacture to the End of the Nineteenth Century   1622
Organs for America: The Life and Work of David Tannenberg   1523
Organs in Early America   236
Osborne, William   1952
Osburn, Mary H.   539
Oscar Sonneck and American Music   573n
Osman, Stephen E.   738
Osterhout, Paul Ragatz   540, 947, 1404
Ota, Diane O.   1p
Ottenberg, June C.   1297
Our American Music (Howard)   318n, 362
Our American Music: A Comprehensive History   362n
Outline of the History of Music   306
Owen, Barbara   255p, 533n, 739, 740, 812, 1617n, 1618, 1619, 1620, 1621, 1622, 1623, 1624, 1625, 1773n, 1889
Owen, Earl McLain, Jr.   1711
Oxford Companion to Music   25n
Oyler, Edna B.   541

Padover, Saul K.   1842
Pahlen, Kurt   307
Paperbound Books in Print   36n
Papers from the Third Conference on German-Americana in the Eastern United States, November 6-7, 1982   419, 1144
Papers of Andrew Law in the William L. Clements Library   189
Papers of Benjamin Franklin   1585
Parker, John Rowe   1686, 1870n
Parker, Rodger D.   252
Parks, Roger   65, 66
Parsons, Henry S.   156
Paterson, Donald R.M.   1618
Patten, Lawton M.   786
Patterson, Daniel W.   1340, 1341, 1342, 1343
Patterson, Relford   1687
Peabody, Herbert C.   634
Pease, Elaine K.   204
Pedley, Avril J.M.   211
Peeler, Clare   1485, 1486
Peeples, Georgia Kay   741
Pennsylvania 1776   523
Performing Arts, 1876-1981: Books   67
Periodical Literature on American Music, 1620-1920: A Classified Bibliography with Annotations   123, 129p

Perkins, Charles C.   542
Perrin, Phil Daniel   948, 949
Peyse, Herbert F.   382n
Peyser, Herbert F.   385
Pfatteicher, Helen   1013
Pfohl, Bernard J.   1298
Pfohl, Mrs. J. Kenneth   386
Phelps, Roger P.   116, 742
Philadelphia   514
Philadelphia Sonatas   1955
*Philadelphia Theatre in the Eighteenth Century, Together with the
  Day Book of the Same Period*   1487
*Philadelphia Theatres, A-Z: A Comprehensive, Descriptive Record of
  813 Theatres Constructed Since 1724*   1452
Phillips, Claude Anderson   321
Pichierri, Louis   543
*Picture the Songs: Lithographs from the Sheet Music of Nineteenth-
  Century America*   793
Pierce, Edwin Hall   950, 1843
Pike, Kermit J.   212, 1329
Pike, Martha V.   231n
Pinel, Stephen   1626
Ping-Robbins, Nancy R.   544, 545, 1087
Pisk, Paul A.   311
Plain Dealing or News from New England   513
Pochmann, Henry A.   68
Poladian, Sirvart   951
Pollock, Thomas Clark   1487
Poole, Franklin Parker   1772
Poole's Index: Date and Volume Key   141n
Poole's Index to Periodical Literature   141
*Popular Secular Music in America through 1800: A Preliminary
  Checklist of Manuscripts in North American Collections*   173
Popular Songs of Nineteenth-Century America   1954
Porte, Jacques   13
Porter, Ellen Jane L.   1015, 1044, 1045
Porter, Susan L.   1432p, 1488, 1489, 1490, 1802
Post, Jennifer C.   112n
Potter, Warren H.   813
Powell, Martha C.   69
Pratt, Waldo S.   546, 635
Pressley, Ernest Wayne   1627
Pressley, Nancy Gamble   1628
Price, Robert Bates   547
Pries, Nancy   269
Priest, Daniel B.   1405

Prime, Alfred C.   548
Printed Note: 500 Years of Music Printing and Engraving   247
Printing and Society in America   1384
Private Schools of Colonial Boston   586n
Private Side of American History   1077
Pro/Am Guide to U.S. Books about Music: Annotated Subject Guide to Current and Backlist Titles   59
Proceedings of the Ninth Annual Conference Society of Dance History Scholars   1413, 1428
Protestant Church Music: A History   612
Protestant Church Music in America: A Short Survey of Men and Movements from 1564 to the Present   636
Protestant Worship Music: Its History and Practice   622
Prucha, Francis P.   154p, 178p, 274p, 413p
Pruett, James W.   117
Psalms and Hymns of Protestantism from the Sixteenth to the Nineteenth Century: An Introduction to the History of Protestant Hymnody as Illustrated by an Exhibition in the Library of Drew University, in June, 1936   245
Puissegur, Jo Ann Theresa   814
Puritans and Music in England and New England   563
Putney, Martha S.   1088

Rabson, Carolyn   115, 1491, 1492
Raddin, George G., Jr.   549
Radzinsky, Charles A.   1629, 1630, 1631
Ralston, Jack L.   233, 242
Randall, David A.   224
Randel, Don Michael   24
Rankin, Hugh F.   1493
Rasmussen, Jane E.   1147, 1148
Rau, Albert F.   213, 1299, 1881
Raum, Hans   129p
Ray, Sister Mary Dominic   1494
Readers' Guide to Periodical Literature   137n, 139n, 142
Readings in Black American Music   402
Reardon, William Robert   1495
Reasonableness of Regular Singing   974
Recent American Hymnody   623
Recent Studies in Music: A Catalog of Doctoral Dissertations   292n
Record of the Opera in Philadelphia   1438
Records in the Copyright Office Deposited by the United States District Courts Covering the Period 1790-1870   268n
Records of the New York Stage from 1750 to 1860   1459
Records of the Tuesday Club of Annapolis, 1745-56   550
Redway, Virginia Larkin   261, 551, 664, 1744, 1867, 1869

Reed, Marcia   269
Reeves, William   545, 906
Reference Guide to the Literature of Travel   277, 278n
Reference Works for Theological Research: An Annotated Selective Bibliographical Guide   58
Regular and Skilful Music in the Worship of God, . . . Shewn in a Sermon Preached at the North Meeting-House, Newbury-Port, at the Desire of the Church and Congregation, February 8th, 1774   945
Regular Singing Defended and Proved to be the Only True Way of Singing the Songs of the Lord   855
Reich, Robert J.   1632, 1633
Reider, Joseph   447n
Reines, Philip   552
Reisser, Marsha J.   94
Religion and Society in North America: An Annotated Bibliography   38
Religion in American Life   39, 621
Religion Index One: Periodicals   143, 144n
Religion Productive of Music: A Discourse Delivered at Marlborough, March 24th, 1773 at a Singing Lecture   934
Religious and Theological Abstracts   144
Rensch-Erbes, R.   665
Report of Proceedings: Ph.D. in Music Symposium   545, 906
Report of the Eighth Congress, New York, 1961   851
Report on "The Star-Spangled Banner"; "Hail Columbia"; "America"; "Yankee Doodle"   823
Research Guide to Musicology   117
Resh, Rita M.   85
Resources of American Music History: A Directory of Source Materials from Colonial Times to World War II   167n, 168n, 170n, 173n, 175, 176n, 177n, 178p, 181n, 211n, 212n, 254p
Ressler, Martin E.   1178, 1191, 1192
Revolutionary America, 1763-1789: A Bibliography   46
Reynolds, Jeff   1300
Reynolds, William J.   1046, 1101
Rhode Island: A Bibliography of Its History   66
Rhode Island Music and Musicians, 1733-1850   524
Rice, Albert R.   215
Richard S. Hill: Tributes from Friends   796, 920, 1395
Richards, Henry M.M.   1140
Richmond, Mary L.   1330, 1333n
Ridgway, Thomas   447n
Riedel, Johannes   387, 495, 952, 1181
Rieder, Kathryn S.   554
Rierson, Charles Frederick, Jr.   1301

RILM Abstracts: Répertoire International de la Littérature Musicale/International Repertory of Music Literature 123n, 145n, 148, 223p
Ring the Banjar!: The Banjo in America from Folklore to Factory 248
Ritchey, Robert David 1496
Ritter, Frédéric Louis 387
Roach, Hildred 1089
Roberts, Dale Alexander 1862
Roberts, Martin 268n
Robinson, Albert F. 815, 1634, 1635, 1636
Robinson, Alice Jean McDonnell 1497
Robinson's Philadelphia Register and City Directory, for 1799 262
Rodd, S. 1715
Rogal, Samuel J. 1014, 1047, 1203
Rogers, A. Robert 70
Rogers, Delmer D. 555
Rogers, James A. 1048
Rogers, Samuel Kirby 953
Rohrer, Gertrude Martin 556
Romaine, Lawrence B. 263, 264
Root, Deane L. 175
Roots of American Culture 388
Rose, Kenneth 216, 666, 667, 1688
Rosenberry, M. Claude 557
Rosenstiel, Léonie 308
Rosewall, Richard Byron 954
Rothrock, Donna K. 1302
Rourke, Constance 388
Rouse, Father Warren 1364
Roy, G. James, Jr. 249
Rublowsky, John 389
Runner, David Clark 558
Ruth, John Landis 1049
Rutman, Darrett B. 513

Sabbath in Puritan New England 617
Sabin, Joseph 71
Sabin, Robert 17n
Sablosky, Irving 390
Sachs, Curt 1637
Sachse, Julius F. 1141, 1142, 1379
Sadie, Stanley 22, 23, 30
Saerchinger, Cesar 559
Salisbury, Stephen 816
Saloman, Ora F. 1876
Salter, Sumner 1638, 1639, 1640

Saltzman, Herbert   1108
Sanders, Robert L.   955
Sandford, Gordon   560
Sanjek, Russell   391
Satcher, Herbert B.   447n, 1149
Savelle, Max   309
Sax, Margaret F.   227
Saxton, Stanley E.   1641
Sayre, John L.   72
Scanlon, Mary B.   1783
Schaffner, Anne   743
Schalk, Carl   1169
Schiavo, Giovanni Ermenegildo   1165
Schieber, Philip   178p
Schiller, Andrew   1762
Schirmer History of Music   308
Schnell, William Emmett   1882
Scholes, Percy A.   25n, 561, 562, 563, 564, 565, 566, 1642
Scholten, James William   1751, 1752
Schonberg, Harold C.   668
Schrader, Arthur F.   127p, 217, 254p, 533n
Schreiber, William I.   1193
Schultz, Arthur R.   68
Schultz, Selina G.   1851
Schwartz, Charles   956
Schwartz, G.F.   567
Schwarze, W.N.   130
*Schwenkfelder Hymnology and the Sources of the First Schwenkfelder
   Hymnbook Printed in America*   1328
Schwenkfelders in Pennsylvania: A Historical Sketch   1327
Scott, John Anthony   817
Sears, Donald   568
Secular Music in America, 1801-1825: A Bibliography   106n, 126, 394n
Secular Music in Colonial Annapolis: The Tuesday Club, 1745-56   587
Seeds of Liberty   309
Seidensticker, Oswald   1380
Seilhamer, Larry   1143
Seip, Oswell J.   569
Seipt, Allen A.   1328
Selch, Frederick R.   226, 1643, 1644
Selden, Margery Stomne   744
Selected Bibliography of Church Music and Music Reference Materials
   69
Selective Bibliography for the Study of Hymns, 1980   1008
Selected Compositions [of James Hewitt]   1944
Sellers, John R.   208

Series of Old American Songs Reproduced in Facsimile from Original or Early Editions in the Harris Collection of American Poetry and Plays, Brown University   1957
Sermon Preached at a Singing Lecture: in Braintree May 21st, MDCCLXXXVIII   990
Sermon: Preached at an Exhibition of Sacred Musick, in Lincoln, on the Nineteenth of April, 1792   967
Serwer, Howard   1276, 1304, 1305
'76 to '76: A Study of Two Centuries of Sacred Music in America   629
Seybolt, Robert F.   586n
Shaker Collection, 1723-1952   1331
Shaker Collection of the Western Reserve Historical Society: A Reel List to the Manuscripts and a Short Title List of the Printed Materials Contained in the Microform Collection   1331
Shaker Literature: A Bibliography   1330, 1333n
Shaker Manuscript Hymnals from South Union, Kentucky   1332
Shaker Music: Inspirational Hymns and Melodies Illustrative of the Resurrection Life and Testimony of the Shakers   1338
Shaker Music: Original Inspirational Hymns and Songs Illustrative of the Resurrection Life and Testimony of the Shakers   1338n
Shapiro, Anne Dhu   1498
Shapiro, Elliott   91
Shapiro, Michael Edward   226
Shaver, Lillie T.   1365
Shaw, Ralph R.   73, 106n
Shedlock, John S.   818
Sheehy, Eugene P.   48, 49n
Shelton, Frances   392
Shepard, Nelson McD.   393
Shepperson, Archibald B.   1844
Sherman, Constance D.   1499
Sherman, Elna   957
Shields, T. Edgar   1645
Shippen, Rebecca Lloyd   819
Shipton, Clifford K.   43n, 74, 97n, 451n, 1406, 1412
Shockley, Martin S.   1500
Shoemaker, Richard H.   73, 106n
Short Bibliography for the Study of Hymns   1013
Short Titles of Books Relating to or Illustrating the History and Practice of Psalmody in the United States, 1620-1820   111n, 125
Shuffelton, Frank   1831
Silver, Rollo G.   958
Silverman, Kenneth   310
Silvey, Herbert M.   296n, 298
Simkins, Francis B.   530
Simmons, David   745

Simons, Elizabeth P.   570
Simpson, Clinton   1689
Sims, John Norman   1050
Sinful Tunes and Spirituals: Black Folk Music to the Civil War   1069
Sing the Lord's Song in a Strange Land: The Life of Justin Morgan   1864
Singer, David   1102
Singleton, Esther   12n, 571, 572, 1501
Skard, Sigmund   304
Skemer, Don C.   218
Skizzen aus dem Leben des sich in Amerika befindenden deutschen Tondichters Anton Philipp Heinrich   1791
Slave Songs of the United States   1062
Slavens, Thomas P.   117
Slonimsky, Nicholas   14n
Sluder, Claude K.   960
Smith, Alice T.   820
Smith, Carleton Sprague   126, 254p, 394, 533n, 961, 1020, 1121
Smith, Carlton York   1170
Smith, Frederick   789
Smith, Gregg   395
Smith, Harold Vaughan   1344
Smith, Lucy   396
Smith, Maria Pratt   1646
Smith, Paul H.   208
Smith, Ronnie L.   1745
Smith, Timothy Alan   962, 1051
Smither, Nelle Kroger   1502
Snyder, Robert P.   1306
Snyder, Suzanne   299
Social Implications of Early Negro Music in the United States   1076
Sohlmans Musiklexikon   26
Sollinger, Charles Edmond   963
Sommer, Frank H.   1407
Song in America from Early Times to about 1850   836
Songs from the Williamsburg Theatre: A Selection of Fifty Songs Performed on the Stage in Williamsburg in the Eighteenth Century   1478
Sonneck, Oscar George   47, 118, 119, 397, 398, 399, 400, 447n, 570n, 573, 669, 670, 746, 821, 822, 823, 824, 1503, 1504, 1505, 1506, 1763, 1764, 1820, 1821, 1822, 1823, 1894
South Carolina Newspapers   162
Southern, Eileen   401, 402, 1069n, 1090
Southern Humanities Conference: Winston-Salem, 1977   1250
Souvenir of Romanticism in America; or, An Elegant Exposition of Taste and Fashion from 1812 to 1865   250

Spaeth, Sigmund   403, 574
Spalding, Dan C.   747
Spalding, Walter Raymond   575
Spaner, Richard   576
*Spanish and Mexican Records of the American Southwest: A
   Bibliographical Guide to Archive and Manuscript Sources*   1346
Spear, Dorothea N.   257n, 265
Spear, Lee S.   1160
Spell, Lota M.   404, 964, 1366
Speller, John L.   1649, 1650
Spencer, Jon Michael   176
Spice, Gordon Philip   1771
Spiess, Lincoln B.   1367, 1368, 1369
Spillane, Daniel   1651, 1652
Sprague, Laura F.   577
Sprenkle, Charles A.   1746
Springer, Nelson P.   1179
Standish, Lemuel W.   578
Stanislaw, Richard J.   120, 938n, 965, 966
Stanley, Albert A.   1902
Stapleton, Ammon   1408
Star Spangled Banner: Words and Music Issued Between 1714-1864   805
*Star-Spangled Books: Books, Sheet Music, Newspapers, Manuscripts,
   and Persons Associated with "The Star-Spangled Banner"*   237
Stearns, Charles   967
Steel, David Warren   579, 936n, 970n, 1002n, 1052, 1846, 1923
Steel, Mathew C.   1052
Steelman, Robert F.   186, 219, 1307, 1308, 1309
Steers, Katherine V.   827
Stefani, Marie T.   1331
Steimle, A.   1171
Steinberg, Judith T.   968
Stetzel, Ronald Delbert   1863
Stevens, Denis   807
Stevens, Harry R.   580, 581
Stevenson, Arthur Linwood   1053
Stevenson, Robert   13, 636, 671, 1054, 1055, 1056, 1091, 1204, 1370
Stillwell, Margaret Bingham   75
Stine, Richard D.   1507
Stoddard, Hope E.   1653
Stokes, Allen H., Jr.   220
Stolba, K. Marie   1699, 1700, 1701, 1765, 1766, 1824, 1825, 1845
Stone, Reppard   1860
Storer, H.J.   1654, 1655
Story of Southern Hymnology   1053
Story of the American Hymn   1043

Stoudt, John J. 582, 1310
Stoughton, Marion Wilberforce 1057
Stoutamire, Albert T. 583, 584
Strauss, Barbara 1311
Strauss, John Felix 748, 1895
Strickling, George F. 969
Strong, Joseph 970
Stroud, William Paul 971
Strunk, Oliver 1409
Stuart, Angela 637
Stutsman, Grace M. 585
Sudlow, Paul 295n, 405
Summers, William 1371, 1372
Sunderman, Lloyd Frederick 586, 972, 973
Surratt, Jerry L. 1899
Survey of American Church Records 285
Survey of Musical Instrument Collections in the United States and Canada 174
Sutton, Brett 1103
Suum Cuique: Essays in Music 118n, 400, 670n, 1763
Svejda, George J. 828
Swan, John C. 532
Swank, Scott T. 1407
Sweet, Ralph 1419
Sweet Psalmist of Israel, a Sermon Preach'd at the Lecture Held in Boston, by the Society for Promoting Regular & Good Singing 988
Sweet Songs for Gentle Americans: The Parlor Song in America, 1790-1860 830
Sweetman, Mrs. Laurence D. 406
Symmes, Thomas 974, 975

Talley, John Barry 587
Tallmadge, William 976
Tanselle, George Thomas 76, 105n
Tappert, Theodore G. 1172
Taricani, Jo Ann 588
Tawa, Nicholas E. 589, 590, 672, 673, 829, 830
Tax, Sol 1092
Taylor, Barbara 1656
Taylor, Phyllis J. 638
Taylor, Raymond 1656
Teal, Mary Evelyn Durden 591, 1784
Temperley, Nicholas 977, 978
Terri, Salli 1345
Thacher, Peter 979
Theatre in Colonial America 1493

Thieme, Darius L.   17n
Thomas, Henry L.   1137
Thomas, Ruth Colby   251
Thomas Jefferson: A Comprehensive Annotated Bibliography of Writings about Him (1826-1980)   1831
Thomas Jefferson: A Reference Guide   1830
Thomas Jefferson among the Arts   1833
Thomas Jefferson and Music   1836
Thomason, Jean Healan   1332
Thompson, James William   592, 593, 1903
Thompson, Lawrence Sidney   71n
Thompson, William   266
Thorndike, S. Lothrop   980
Thornsby, Frederick W.   1630n
Thrasher, Herbert Chandler   594, 1904
Three Centuries of American Hymnody   623
Three Centuries of English and American Plays, a Checklist. England: 1500-1800, United States: 1714-1830   1433
Tick, Judith   407, 408
Tilton, Edwin A.   1657
Timetables of American History   409n, 412
Tischler, Hans   1369
Tolzmann, Don Heinrich   77
Tools for Theological Research   72
Travelers in Tidewater Virginia, 1700-1800: A Bibliography   274
Travels in America, from the Voyages of Discovery to the Present: An Annotated Bibliography of Travel Articles in Periodicals, 1955-1980   276
Travels in the Old South: A Bibliography   275, 279n
Trinterud, Leonard J.   1319
Tufts, John   982
Tufts, Nancy Poore   1658
Turner, Maxine Thompson   983
Turner, Victor   1343
Twenty Four Early American Country Dances, Cotillions & Reels for the Year 1976   1426
Two Centuries of Nazareth, 1740-1940   595
Two Hundred and Fifty Years of Music in Providence, Rhode Island, 1636-1886: Rhode Island Composers Native and Adopted   594
Tyler, Bennet   1866

Ulrich, Homer   311
Umble, John S.   1194
Unitas Fratrum: Herrnhuter Studien   1266
United States Local Histories in the Library of Congress: A Bibliography   78, 413p

United States Music: Sources of Bibliography and Collective Biography   103, 1677n
United States Newspaper Program National Union List   164
University Musical Encyclopedia   27
University of Iowa Theses in American Music   299
Unsung: A History of Women in American Music   314
Upton, William Treat   119, 221, 674, 831, 1736, 1792
Urdang, Laurence   412
Urkowitz, Steven   832
U.S. Bicentennial Music I   102
Use and Design of Sacred Music, in a Discourse Preached March 19, 1811, as a Musical Lecture in Greenfield   994
Utile Dulci or, a Coco-Serious Dialogue, Concerning Regular Singing: Calculated for a Particular Town, (Where It Was Publickly Had, on Friday Oct. 12, 1722)   975

Vail, George   447n
Valenchik, Cathy   1428
Van Burkalow, Anastasia   1205
Van Camp, Leonard   833, 984, 985, 986
Van Cleef, Joy   1429
Variety Music Cavalcade, 1620-1961: A Chronology of Vocal and Instrumental Music Popular in the United States   411
Vaughan, Donald   1659
Vermont: A Bibliography of Its History   34
Viehmeyer, L. Allen   1144
Vindiciae Cantus Dominici; or, A Vindication of the Doctrine Taught in a Discourse on the Divine Ordinance of Singing Psalms   838
Vinton, J.   26n
Virga, Patricia H.   1508
Voedisch, Virginia G.   178p
Voight, Louis   1015
Von Ende, Richard Chaffey   121

Wagner, John W.   122, 496n, 596, 597, 1799, 1800, 1944
Wakeling, Arthur   598
Waldo, Frank   1660
Walford, A.J.   49
Walker, James L.   266
Wall, Edward   1884
Walsh, Lorna G.   1509, 1510
Walter, Thomas   987, 988
Walters, Raymond   1312, 1313, 1314
Waltner, Rachel   19n
Warburton, Thomas   749
Ware, Charles Pickard   1062

Warkentin, Larry   1373
Warner, Thomas E.   79, 123, 129p, 599
Warrington, James   111n, 124, 125
Washington Directory   267
Washington, Eugenia   834
Waterman, Richard Alan   1092
Watkins, C. Malcolm   1662
Watson, Dorothy D.   675
Watson, John   1663
Wayland, John W.   1770
Weadon, David A.   1058
Weaver, James M.   239
Weaver, Philip D.   750
Webb, Guy Bedford   1910
Webb, Robert Lloyd   248
Webster, James   1276
Webster, Philip J.   600
Weegar, Carlton E.   1122
Weichlein, William   151n, 152
Weidman, Wanda   1315
Weinlick, John R.   1316
Weiss, Joanne Grayeski   989
Weiss, Lewis H.   1216n
Weissman, George   232
Weld, Ezra   990
Weller, Philip T.   1119
*Wellsprings of a Nation; America before 1801: A Bicentennial
    Exhibition from the Collections of the American Antiquarian
    Society at the Worcester Art Museum, April 19-June 5, 1977*   252
Welsh, Wilmer H.   1868
Wentworth, E.   991
Wertenbaker, Thomas J.   312
West, Edward N.   1150, 1151
Westermeyer, Paul   1059
*Western Americana, 1550-1900: Frontier History of the Trans-
    Mississippi West*   80
Western Americana: Guide and Index to the Microfilm Edition   80
Western Reserve Historical Society Shaker Collection   1333
Wetzel, Richard D.   992, 1156, 1161, 1162, 1163
Whipple, George M.   601
White, William Carter   683n, 751
White Spirituals in the Southern Uplands   1036
Whitehill, W.M.   1847
Whitinger, Julius Edward   1374
Who's Who in American Music: Classical   1690
Wicks, Sammie Ann   1104

Wienandt, Elwyn A.   1n, 639
Wiggin, Frances Turgeon   1691
Wiggins, Maureen McF.   458
Wilcox, Glenn C.   1849, 1850
Wilhite, Charles S.   1747
Wilhoit, Melvin Ross   1060
Wilkinson, Norman B.   1826
Willard, Samuel   993, 994
Willhide, James Laurence   1808
William Billings: Data and Documents   1735
William Billings of Boston: Eighteenth-Century Composer   1713n
Williams, Albert S.   995
Williams, George W.   602, 603, 1664, 1755, 1942
Williams, Henry L.   1317
Williams, Thomas   996, 1905
Willis, Eola   1511
Willman, Frederick R.   997
Wilson, James Grant   445
Wilson, Ruth Mack   604, 1152
Winans, Robert B.   1381
Winchell, James Manning   998
Winesanker, Michael   81, 1512
Winslow, Ola Elizabeth   835, 999, 1000
Winter, Marian Hannah   1430
Wirling, Eliot I.   1533, 1665
Wister, Frances A.   605
Wörner, Karl H.   21n
Wohlgemuth, Paul William   1195
Wolcott, John Rutherford   1513
Wolf, Edward C.   606, 1001, 1061, 1168, 1173, 1174, 1175, 1666,
   1667, 1668, 1793
Wolf, Eugene K.   1318
Wolf, Jean K.   1318
Wolfe, Richard J.   106n, 126, 394n
Wolverton, Byron Adams   752
Wolz, Larry Robert   1514
Wood, David A.   222
Woodall, William L.   1003
Woodbridge, Timothy   1002
Woods, Leonard   607
Woodward, Henry   608
Worner, William F.   1176, 1323
Worst, John William   1004
Wright, Becky A.   178p
Wright, Edith A.   1005
Wright, Richardson   1809

Writings on American History: A Subject Bibliography of Articles 145
Wunderlich, Charles Edward 153
Wynne, Shirley 1431

Yankee Lyre: Musical Instruments by American Makers: An Exhibition of Instruments by 19th-Century American Makers with Supplementary Exhibits of Graphics, Books, and Furniture 253
Ye Olde New-England Psalm-Tunes: 1620-1820 877
Yellin, Victor F. 7n, 20n, 609, 1515, 1516, 1517, 1518, 1917
Yerbury, Grace H. 610, 836
Yoder, Paul Marvin 1196
York, Terry W. 1006
Young, J.I. 1739
Young, William C. 177

Zimmerman, Elena Irish 1519

SUBJECT INDEX

Accomplished Singer   532, 896
Adams, Abigail   650
Adams, John   400, 650, 652, 673
Adams, John Quincy   649, 665
Adams, Thomas   668, 1845
Adams, Zabdiel   560
"Adams & Washington A New Patriotic Song"   224
Address on Music, Delivered before the Singing-Society of the Second Baptist Church in Boston, 7th April, 1814   998
Address on Music, Delivered to the First Baptist Singing Society, Boston, Thursday Evening, May 15, 1806   869
Address on Music, Delivered to the Salisbury and Amesbury Singing Societies, Convened at Salisbury, April 3, 1812   841
"Adeste Fideles"   1954
Adgate, Andrew   932, 992, 1692
Aethiop   1517-18
Afro-American music   4, 11-12, 17, 20, 39, 60, 89, 94, 101, 112, 147, 176, 243, 313, 331-32, 351, 354, 359, 361, 368, 390-91, 401-02, 438, 508, 547, 621, 636, 767, 1036, 1062-92, 1095, 1417
Ainsworth, Henry   520, 635, 892
Ainsworth psalter   866, 877, 892, 961, 1020, 1037
Aitken, John   1109, 1111, 1113, 1115-16, 1118, 1401
Alamoth: An Address Delivered to the Singing Schools in the First and Second Societies in Groton   901
Albert, John   258
"Albion"   955
Albrecht, Charles   183, 1567, 1607
Albright, George   259
All Saints Parish (Frederick, Md.)   1704
Allen, Mr.   255
Allgemein nützliche Choral-Music   871
almanacs   653
Altalaha Lutheran Church (Rehrersburg, Pa.)   1554
"America" (Smith)   230
"America" (Wetmore)   1923
"America, Commerce and Freedom"   1817
"America Independent: An Oratorical Entertainment"   754

American Harmonist   992
American Harmony (Bayley)   923
American Harmony (Shumway)   929
American Harmony: or, Royal Melody Compleat   235, 923
"American Hero"   765
American Musical Magazine   130, 1927
American Musical Miscellany   235, 1928
"American Roast Beef, a Song, Composed for the 4th March, 1801"   254
"American Star"   765
Americana   1519
Amesbury Singing Society (Massachusetts)   841
Amherst Handelian Society   900
Amish   19, 77.   *See also* Mennonites
Amphion or the Chorister's Delight   920
Anabaptists   19
Anderson, John   181, 837-38
Antes, John   7, 17, 116, 210, 219, 320, 379, 558, 743, 1215, 1228,
    1230, 1260, 1279, 1693-701
"Anthem Designed for Thanksgiving Day"   247
"Anthem for Easter"   787
anthems   6, 24, 90, 198, 613, 615-16, 632, 639, 787, 863, 909, 1065,
    1174, 1207, 1211, 1716, 1772, 1795, 1862, 1864, 1910, 1924, 1931,
    1941-42
Anthems, Hymns, Etc. Usually Sung at the Catholick Church in Boston
    1118
Anthony, Jacob   1561
Apollonian Society (Pittsburgh)   427
Appleton, Thomas   1702
Appo, William   1090
Archers   252, 1453
archives.   *See* libraries, archives, and museums
Arden, Francis   224
arias   198
armonica   23, 174, 239, 669, 1531-32, 1547-48, 1563, 1583, 1585,
    1758-60, 1763, 1765.   *See also* musical glasses
Arnold, Adam   1061
Arrow Against Profane and Promiscuous Dancing   31
Art of Singing   252, 311, 894
atlases   300
Ausbund, Das ist   1180, 1182, 1187-88, 1193

Babcock, Alpheus   1703
Bach family   209, 770, 1312, 1894
Bachmann, Johann Philip   1612
Bacon, Allyn   1401
Bacon, Thomas   270, 435-36, 587, 1704

Balch, William   841
Ball, Thomas   379
ballad opera.   *See* opera
balladry   211, 217, 817, 1957
balls.   *See* dance
Baltimore Collection of Sacred Music   876
Band of the Independent Volunteers   733
bands   228, 232, 316, 428, 648, 677, 680-88, 699, 701-03, 709-10,
    719, 728, 733, 737, 745, 751, 1088, 1234, 1897
  —uniforms of musicians   687, 721, 738, 750
Bankson, John   499
banjo   239, 248, 1527
Baptists   269, 1093-104, 1343
Barker, J.N.   1457, 1515, 1519, 1935
Barrett, Ezra   880
Barton, Andrew   1433, 1453, 1469, 1482, 1491-92, 1508, 1519, 1930
bassoon   741, 1560-61
Bassoon Preceptor   741
Bates, Issachar   1340
Battle of New Orleans (Etienne)   711
Battle of New Orleans (Ricksecker) 711
Battle of Trenton   711
Battle Square Society Church (Newburyport, Mass.)   1619
Battles of Lake Champlain and Plattsburg   711
Battle of the Memorable 8th of January 1815   711
Bay Psalm Book   20, 26, 229, 240, 245, 247, 252, 365, 371, 470, 520,
    532, 617, 622, 839, 854, 866, 868, 877-79, 883, 888-89, 922, 930,
    961, 969, 983, 995, 1037, 1043, 1395, 1950
Bayley, Daniel   616, 921, 923, 1681
Beach, John   684
Beauties of Psalmody   876
Beccaria, Giambatista   1585
Bechler, Johann Christian   213, 219, 558, 1228, 1705-06
Beethoven, Ludwig van   718, 720
Beethoven Society (Portland, Me.)   720
Beggar's Opera   1473
Behrent, Johann   1524, 1607
Beissel, Johann Conrad   2, 303, 419, 459, 484, 1124, 1125-26, 1129,
    1133, 1135, 1138-39, 1141-43, 1684, 1707-10
Belcher, Supply   325, 457, 470, 568, 859, 1691, 1711, 1931
Belknap, Daniel   1712
Bell, Andrew   880
Bellamy Band Music Book   228, 732
bells   1658
Beneficent Congregational Church (Providence)   461
Benham, Asahel   233, 1681

Bent, William   183
Benzien, C.L.   1254
Benzien, Wilhem Ludwig   1278
Bethlehem Bach Choir   1312-13
Better Sort   1508
Bicentennial   228, 249, 252, 380, 395, 1035
Bickerstaff's Genuine Boston Almanack; or Federal Calendar   233
Billings, Nathaniel   917
Billings, William   1, 3, 15, 17-18, 20-21, 27-29, 47, 227, 229-30,
    235, 247, 251-52, 304, 310, 319, 322, 325, 333, 341, 351, 363,
    374, 376, 378-80, 388, 391, 437, 457, 468, 472, 477, 479, 482,
    488, 532, 611, 629, 631-32, 639, 754, 756, 765, 787, 806, 813,
    840, 842-43, 858-59, 861-62, 865, 874, 882, 884-85, 905-08, 910,
    943, 950, 958, 984, 986, 1026, 1038, 1677-78, 1683-85, 1713-39,
    1927, 1932-34
Bingham, Lemuel   1386
biographies and lists of musicians, collective   1-3, 7-18, 20-22,
    27-30, 376, 505, 539, 542, 556, 575, 579, 586, 591, 594, 604,
    620, 694, 716, 814, 877, 968, 1035, 1053, 1098, 1165, 1231, 1383-
    84, 1503, 1573, 1620, 1626, 1672-91, 1852, 1951
biographies, individual   1692-926
Blake, George E.   215, 741, 1399, 1401
Blake, Henry   1740
Blickensderfer, Jacob   1242
Blockheads   1508
Boccherini, Luigi   1273
Böhner, Johann   1236
Bohler, Peter   1235
Booth, Nathaniel   273
Boston Gazette   608
Boston Handel and Haydn Society Collection of Church Music   1949
Boston Magazine   130
Bowne, Eliza S.   1269
Boyd, Robert   939
Boyer, John   266
brass ensembles   1208, 1214, 1226, 1233, 1235-39, 1243, 1275, 1281,
    1289, 1292, 1294, 1298, 1300, 1308
Brattle, Thomas   567, 1544, 1576-77, 1657, 1659
Bray, John   224, 1436, 1457, 1515, 1519, 1935
Bremner, James   95, 658, 671, 752, 831, 1628
Brethren   2, 1105-08
Brief Discourse Concerning Regular Singing   847
Brigade Band (Boston)   709
Brigade Band (Salem, Mass.)   688, 709
broadsides   42-44, 56, 80, 176, 217, 224, 254, 533, 653, 754, 817,
    824, 835, 1330, 1333, 1395, 1411, 1440, 1957

Brown, Bartholomew   230
Brown, Morris, Jr.   1090
Brown, Sally   243
Brown, William   95, 714, 724, 752, 1741
Brownson, Oliver   604, 1761
Bruton Parish Church (Williamsburg)   1873-75
Bryne, Ellen Maria   192
Buckingham, Joseph Tinker   589-90, 1395
bugles   702, 1558
Bull, Amos   984, 1683
"Buona Mattina"   1951
Burckhardt, Christian   1274
Burkitt, Elder   1093
burletta   1449
Burney, Charles   184
Byhan, Gottlieb   1274
Byles, Mather   1043

Cadet Band (Salem, Mass.)   688
Callister, Henry   436
campmeetings   6, 368, 401, 496, 547, 621, 965, 1017-18, 1022, 1034, 1036, 1044-46, 1050, 1072, 1076
cantatas   1263, 1307, 1788
Capron, Henry   1689
Carden, Allen B.   233, 912, 955, 1397
Carew, Eunice   192
Carr, Benjamin   79, 95, 110, 221, 224, 252, 371, 444, 484, 521, 556, 624, 659, 662, 689, 692, 696, 711, 713, 752, 831, 836, 1152, 1175, 1438, 1442, 1453, 1550, 1628, 1677, 1742-47, 1870, 1872, 1916, 1936-39, 1951
Carr, Joseph   193, 259, 1118, 1744
Carr, Thomas   193, 1118, 1744
Carter, Robert   458, 475, 481, 647, 657, 673, 1689
Cartier, Jacques   599
Carusi, G.   267
Carusi, Lewis   267
Carusi, Nathaniel   267
Carusi, Samuel   267
Catalog of a Small Collection of Books   263
Catalog of Music and Musical Instruments   263, 1872
Catalogue of the Annapolis Circulating Library   184
Catholics   426, 447, 622, 1109-19. *See also* Spanish mission music
Catlin, George   255, 1561
Central Musical Society (Concord, N.H.)   900
chamber music. *See* ensembles and music
Chapin, Amzi and Lucius   1748-52

Chauncey, Nathaniel   855
"Chester"   765, 1026
Chestnut Street Theatre (Philadelphia)   1513, 1515, 1935
Cheverus, John   1118
Children in the Wood   1490
"China"   1907-08
Choice Collection of Hymns and Spiritual Songs   1042
*Choral-Buch fuer die Erbauliche Lieder-Sammlung der deutschen
    Evangelisch-Lutherischen Gemeinden in Nord Amerika*   1173
Choral-Harmonie   204
Choral-Music   1770
Christ Church (Alexandria, Va.)   1568
Christ Church (Boston)   421, 1565
Christ Lutheran Church (York, Pa.)   1552
Christian Harmonist   1099
Christian Harmony: Or, Songster's Companion   902, 948, 1947
Christian Psalmody in Four Part, etc.   230
"Christmas Hymn Composed for the Hon. Royall Tyler, Chief Justice of
    the State of Vermont, and Sung at Clarement, N.H. 1793"   42
chronologies   2, 9, 16, 22, 117, 390, 409-12, 1415, 1450, 1822
Church Music in Farmington in the Olden Time   482
Church of the Brethren (Philadelphia)   1107
Churchman's Choral Companion to His Prayer Book   1152
Cibber, Colley   1447
Cinderella   1468
city directories   255-67
City Historical Society (Philadelphia)   441
Claggett, William   1565
clarinet   704, 1561, 1685
Clark, Stephen   184
Clarke, Jeremiah   1055
Clauder, Henry   1274
clavichord   752
Clementi, Muzio   1584
Clifton, Arthur.   *See* Corri, Philip Anthony
Cole, John   27, 193, 230, 876, 898, 928, 1152
Collection of Hymns for Social Worship   1042
Collection of Psalms and Hymns   440, 1042, 1199-200, 1202, 1204-05
Collection of the Best Psalm Tunes   1042
Collegiate Church (New York)   1539
Columbian Anacreontic Society (New York)   424
Columbian and European Harmony   230
Columbian Band   1234
Columbian Harmonist   863
Columbian Harmony   1906
Compilation of Genuine Church Music   1191

Compilation of the Litanies and Vespers, Hymns and Anthems   1109, 1113, 1115, 1118
concerts   12, 110, 154, 310, 329, 334, 343, 354, 360-61, 382, 390, 397-98, 423, 431, 437-38, 442, 449, 454, 463, 469, 471, 477, 481, 491-94, 497, 502-03, 508-09, 530, 543, 551, 555, 559, 570, 580, 583-84, 588, 608, 610, 650, 654, 663-64, 669, 695, 1090, 1311, 1499, 1509, 1618, 1895
   —lists   22, 493, 593, 596, 608, 968, 1428
Congregational Church (South Dennis, Mass.)   1533, 1566, 1635
Continental Harmony   235, 252, 322, 874, 905, 943, 1932-33
Cook, Joseph B.   1053
Cooper, Samuel   611, 754
Cooper, William   247
copyright and music   268, 391, 502, 958, 1400, 1732-33, 1854
"Coronation"   403, 846, 1805
correspondence.   *See* diaries and letters
Corri, Philip Anthony   752, 1753
Cotton, John   47, 432, 893
country dances.   *See* dance
Coupee, Francis   1386
Crane's Band of Music   677
Crehore, Benjamin   1542, 1660
Cross, Benjamin   444, 689
Cuesta, Arroyo de la   1353
Cushing, Joshua   751
Custis (Eleanor Parke) Collection   425
Custis, Nelly   643, 651, 669, 672-73
Custis, Patsy   672
Cutts, Eunice   577

Dana, Daniel   455
dance   31, 115, 154, 227, 231, 255, 259, 261, 267, 274-75, 360, 397, 430-31, 438, 447, 454, 475, 492, 508, 514, 524, 531, 533, 540, 574, 584, 587, 645, 648, 736, 1067-68, 1071, 1087, 1410-31, 1448, 1956
Danforth, John   979
Danforth, Samuel   979
Daniel, Robert T.   1053
Da Ponte, Lorenzo   1435
Darby's Return   1508
Dare, Elkanah Kelsey   832
Darley, William   1938
Davies, Samuel   1037, 1043, 1322
Davis, Richard   218
Davisson, Ananias   856, 939, 965, 1029, 1051, 1754, 1941
Dawning of Music in Kentucky   322, 1786, 1943

"Dead March and Monody"   624
Dearborn, Benjamin   543, 932, 1402
Dearborn, S.H.   427
"Death of Commodore O.H. Perry"   224
Declary, Peter   427
Deering, Nathaniel   1691
Delights of Harmony   933
"Dellawaerisches Gesang-Büchlein"   1778
Dencke, Jeremiah   214, 219, 558, 1230, 1258, 1268, 1297
D'hattentot, Lewis   256
diaries and letters   80, 167, 208, 269-73, 431, 475, 491, 565, 573,
    677, 819, 832, 1159, 1179, 1235, 1246, 1269, 1274, 1380, 1428,
    1585, 1699-701, 1743, 1769, 1770, 1772, 1784, 1801, 1825, 1834,
    1838, 1844-45, 1865, 1870, 1872, 1888, 1894.   *See also* travel
    accounts
Dieffenbach, Christian   1553-54
Dieffenbach, Curtis   1551
Dieffenbach, David   1551
Dieffenbach, John J.   582, 1541, 1574
Dieffenbach family   1545, 1546, 1555, 1569, 1650
Dielman, Louis H.   221
Disappointment: or, The Force of Credulity   1433, 1453, 1469, 1482,
    1491-92, 1508, 1519, 1930
discographies   10, 37, 62, 82, 175, 280-82, 335, 369, 378, 817
*Discourse, at a Public Meeting of the Singers, in the North Parish
    in Wrentham, 13th May, 1817*   996
*Discourse on Music, Addressed to the Essex Musical Association, at
    Their Annual Meeting at Boxford, Sept. 12, 1803*   455
*Discourse on Psalmody: Delivered at Newburgh, before the Presbytery
    of Hudson, September, 1801*   881
*Discourse on Psalmody: In Which It Is Clearly Shewn That It Is the
    Duty of Christians to Take the Principal Subjects and Occasions
    of Their Psalms, Hymns, and Spiritual Songs from the Gospel of
    Christ*   914
Discourse on the Divine Ordinance of Singing Psalms   837
dissertations.   *See* theses and dissertations
Ditson, Oliver   1389
"Divertimenti, or Familiar Lessons for the Piano Forte"   233
Divine Songs   247
Doll, Conrad   852, 1538, 1610
Doll, Joseph   204, 1061
Doolittle, Amos   1846, 1927
Dorsey, William   1053
Dotterer, John   1407
Douglass, David   1448, 1493, 1496
drums and drumming   244, 706, 709, 747, 1897

Dubois, William   732
Dunlap, William   1508
Dupee, John   283
Duport, Pierre Landrin   1423-24
Durán, Fray   1354
Durán, Narciso   1353, 1357
Durang, John   1425
Dutch and music   1020, 1120-22, 1869
*Duty of God's Professing People in Glorifying Their Heavenly Father,
    Preached at a Singing-Lecture in Hartford East Society, June 28,
    1727*   1002
Duty of Singing   970
Dwight, Josiah   867
Dwight, Timothy   1037
Dyer, Samuel   876, 1267

Eastern Shore Triumvirate (Maryland)   436
Easy Instructor   87, 247, 924, 935, 953, 992
Ecclesiae Harmonia   992
Eckhard, George B.   258
Eckhard, Jacob   258, 602, 1755, 1942
Eckhard, Jacob, Jr.   258, 752
"Eden"   611
Edson, Lewis, Sr. and Jr.   27, 371, 629, 1756
Eisenbrandt, C.H.   244
"Elegiac Verse to the Memory of James Lawrence"   224
Ellis, Ferdinand   869
Ely, Alexander   1909
engraving and engravers. *See* printing and publishing
ensembles and music   647, 693, 707-08, 713, 717, 742-43, 749, 1232,
    1278, 1699-700, 1704, 1880, 1943. *See also* brass ensembles
Enstone, Edward   752
Ephrata Cloister 2, 8, 39, 68, 75, 77, 303, 375, 419, 447, 459, 557,
    582, 1123-44, 1407, 1707. *See also* Beissel, Johann Conrad
Episcopalian Harmony   1152
Episcopalians and music   447, 1074, 1145-52
Epplers Church (near Reading, Pa.)   1555
Erbauliche Lieder-Sammlung   1173
Erben, Henry   1615
Erben, Peter   1539
*Essay on Music Pronounced before the Middlesex Musical Society,
    Sept. 9, A.D. 1807*   498, 532
*Essay Preached by Several Ministers of the Gospel for the
    Satisfaction of Their Pious and Consciencious Brethren, as to
    Sundry Questions and Cases of Conscience, Concerning the Singing
    of Psalms*   979

Essay to Silence the Outcry That Has Been Made in Some Places Against Regular Singing   867
Essex Musical Association (Massachusetts)   455, 491-92, 607
Essex South Musical Society (Salem)   491
Etienne, Denis-Germain   711
Etts, Robert   259
Euterpeiad   150, 532, 1870-71
Evens, William   427
exhibition catalogs and literature   129, 138, 148, 169, 223-53
Expediency and Proper Application of Sacred Music: A Discourse, Preached at Heath, Feb. 21, 1816, as a Musical Lecture   993
explorers and music   547, 599, 612, 636
Eyerly, Theodora S.   1270

Fabbroni, Giovanni   1845
Falckner, Justus   447
"Fantasia on the Air 'Gramachree'"   1951
Farnsworth, H.   873
Fashionable Lady   1472
"Federal Constitution and Liberty for Ever"   252
Federal Harmony   233
Federal Overture   1936
Ferris, Richard   1615
Feyring, Philip   1597, 1612, 1621, 1650
fife and drum music   316, 523, 677, 701.   *See also* bands
fifers and music   181, 705, 751, 1740
Fifers Companion   751
First Baptist Church (Boston)   1100
First Baptist Church (Providence)   461
First Baptist Singing Society (Boston)   869
First Congregational Church (Providence)   461, 1605
First Congregational Church (Williamstown, Mass.)   244
First Parish Church (Portland)   449
First Presbyterian Church (Baltimore)   1753
First Religious Society (Newburyport, Mass.)   1619, 1633
First Unitarian Church (Baltimore)   1549
First Verse of Every Psalm of David   1152
Fithian, Philip Vickers   475, 657
Flagg, Josiah   247, 283, 329, 616, 813, 863, 1042, 1677, 1730
Flora, or Hob in the Well   1447, 1453
"Florida" (Wetmore)   1923
flute   244, 1560, 1572
folk music   17, 22, 54, 100, 112, 129, 147, 306, 338, 354, 547, 1089
Font, Pedro   1353
"For Me, O Lord My God"   1924
For the Gentlemen   723

Forest Rose   1519
Foret Noire   1519
Foucard, Joseph W.   258
Fourth of July   711
Franklin, Benjamin   14, 17, 174, 320, 368, 381, 390, 400, 446-47, 484, 521, 588, 669, 683, 707-08, 713, 730, 777, 1438, 1531-32, 1547-48, 1563, 1583, 1585, 1648, 1689, 1699-701, 1757-66, 1869
Franklin Musical Warehouse (Boston)   1702
Franks, David   1167
Freeman, Jonathan   881
French
  —explorers, music of   547
  —mission music   39, 321
  —music and culture   1153-54
French, Jacob   247, 1767-68
"Friendship"   1005
Frobel, John J.   200, 643
Frueauff, Johann Friedrich   1769
fuging tunes   1, 6, 24, 371, 498, 865, 909, 927, 950, 965, 977, 990, 994, 1931
funeral practices and music   611
Funk, Joseph   448, 871, 1105, 1191, 1770
Furman, Richard   1053

Gambold, Anna Rosina Kliest   1274
Gansevoort Collection   425
Gansevoort, Maria   425
Gansevoort, Peter   425
Garnett, Horatio   1403
Gauline, John B.   221
Gay, Julius   482
Gebhard, Johann Gottfried   1771
Gehot, Jean   713
Geib, Adam   1539
Geib, John (Sr. and Jr.)   183, 1550, 1606, 1614-15, 1628
Geisler, Christian Gottfried   1772
Geisler, Johann Christian   1772
Geistliche Ton-Kunst   1061
Geistreicher Lieder   247
"General Washington's March"   1817
Genet, Edmond Charles   425
gentlemen amateurs   390. *See also* names of individuals
Gerhart, Isaac   204
German-Americans and music   39, 54-55, 68, 77, 100, 204, 303, 305, 308, 333, 358, 383, 419, 433, 447, 463-65, 523, 537, 557, 569, 612, 623, 636, 849, 954, 1020, 1024, 1030, 1059-60, 1408

German Reformed Church School (Lancaster, Pa.)   1610
Gerrish, Samuel   1390
Gesäng der einsamen und verlassenen Turtel-Taube   1142
Gibbs, Giles   604, 705
Gilet, Wheeler   876
Gilfers, Mr.   1539
Gilfert, Charles   258, 752
Gillingham, George   262
glass harmonica.   *See* armonica
Goodale, Ezekiel   723, 741, 1691
Goodrich, Eben   183, 1622
Goodrich, William   1622, 1624, 1702, 1773
Gram, Hans   256, 1403, 1681, 1687, 1774, 1804
Granade, John Alexander   1676
Graupner, Gottlieb   29, 79, 233, 341-42, 467-68, 473, 502, 655, 704,
    720, 735, 752, 831, 1395, 1775
Gray, William   1623, 1625
Green, Jonas   283, 587
Greenleaf, Jonathan   256
Gregor, Christian   1207, 1267
Griffiths, John   430
Grobe, Charles   1951
Grounds and Rules of Music Explained   247, 526, 883, 895, 987, 1921
Grube, Bernhard Adam   1776-78
Grube, Rev. Bernard 558
Grunsweig, Frederick   603
Gualdo, Giovanni   655, 658, 713, 1689
guitar   577, 695, 1582
   —music   110
guitarists   1689

Hackett, Theobald   514, 1431
Hagen, Francis Florentine   213
Hagen, Peter Albrecht von, Sr. and Jr.   224, 379, 502, 1779-80
"Hail Columbia"   224, 769, 771, 808, 821-23
Hall, Thomas   1549-50, 1615
Hallam, Lewis   1444, 1448, 1458
Hamilton, Alexander   278, 435, 550
Hampton, Oliver C.   1344
Handel and Haydn Society (Boston)   150, 314, 466, 473, 489-90, 500,
    542, 553, 593, 600, 944, 1949
Handel Society (Dartmouth)   900
Handel Society (Salem, Mass.)   418, 491
Handel, George Frideric   661, 664, 678, 770, 841, 863, 1212, 1304-05
Hans Gram Musical Society (Maine)   470
"Hark! from the Tombs, &c., and Beneath the Honors, &c"   233

Harmon, Joel   376, 859, 1676
Harmonia Sacra (Buckingham)   589
harmonica   1839
"Harmonische Melodeyen Büchlein"   1407
Harmonists   1155-63
Harmony of Maine   1931
harp   729, 1758
Harper, John   183, 1607
harpsichord   1651, 1760, 1839, 1844
   —music   86, 752, 1741, 1746
Hartford East Society   1002
Hartley, George Harland   603
Harvard University   575
Hastings, Thomas   29, 498, 991, 1021, 1037, 1683, 1781-84
Haverlin, Carl   249
Hawkins, John   184, 1834
Hawkins, Micah   425
Haydn, Joseph   718, 726-27, 735, 788, 1273, 1276, 1313
Haydn Society (Cincinnati)   581
Hazard, Isaac   1090
Heinrich, Anthony Philip   17, 95, 250, 320, 322, 442, 692, 752, 776,
   1436, 1678, 1785-92, 1872, 1943, 1951
Helmuth, Justus Henry Christian   1173-74, 1793
Hemmenway, James   1090
Herbst, Johannes   7, 198, 201, 210, 213, 219, 558, 1207, 1223, 1268,
   1270, 1772, 1794-95
Herrick, Joseph   723, 741, 1676
Hesselius, Gustavus   1543, 1578
Hewitt, James   17, 122, 221, 241, 319, 371, 597, 692, 711, 714, 752,
   778, 831, 1442, 1468, 1628, 1677-78, 1796-800, 1937, 1944, 1951
Hill, Uri K.   662
Hillegas, Michael   588, 647, 1801
historical societies   166, 175
   —Cincinnati Historical Society   1751
   —Historical Society of Pennsylvania   247
   —Maryland Historical Society   193, 211, 221, 237
   —Massachusetts Historical Society   240, 247
   —New Haven Colony Historical Society   1888
   —New Jersey Historical Society   218
   —New-York Historical Society   181, 225, 232
   —Topsfield Historical Society   1848
   —Western Reserve Historical Society   212, 1329, 1333, 1337
Hodgkinson, John   255, 1802
Hoff, Frederick   603
Holbrook, Samuel   915

Holden, Oliver   17, 29, 238, 379, 403, 477, 629, 662, 846, 863, 907, 984, 1037, 1043, 1636, 1685, 1687, 1803-06
Holt, Henry   1448
Holt, John   1869
Holyoke, Samuel   17, 29, 233, 492, 543, 684, 723, 732, 741, 1031, 1099, 1403, 1683, 1687, 1804, 1807-09
Hommann, Charles   187, 713
Hopkins, John   235, 238, 245, 617, 1020
Hopkinson, Francis   17-18, 178, 223, 247, 251, 322, 333-34, 341, 363, 368, 379, 381, 390, 403, 406, 444, 446-47, 484, 556, 645-46, 668, 671, 746, 752, 754, 806-07, 831, 932, 1121, 1437, 1442, 1628, 1648, 1651, 1678, 1689, 1713, 1810-26, 1845, 1945-46
Hopkinson, Joseph   771
Horn, Charles Edward   1827
horns   702
Hubbard, John   498, 532, 543, 900
Huntington, Jonathan   1761
Hupfield, Henry   259
Hutton, John   1264
Hymn and Prayer Book   1169
hymnbooks   2, 176, 208, 245, 483, 527, 627, 629, 891, 918, 1007-16, 1022, 1040-42, 1045, 1058, 1090, 1093, 1095, 1097-98, 1102, 1105-06, 1109-16, 1118, 1168, 1178, 1184, 1188, 1195-96, 1198-200, 1203, 1290, 1302, 1317, 1321, 1332, 1375
hymnody   1, 5-6, 22, 24, 27, 39, 60, 63, 67, 69, 72, 90, 100, 112, 123, 129, 167, 309, 368, 380, 390, 401, 447, 621, 623, 862, 872, 879, 926, 960, 1007-61, 1086, 1095-98, 1101, 1103, 1139, 1144-46, 1168-70, 1174, 1177, 1183, 1190-94, 1197, 1202, 1205, 1241, 1256-57, 1262, 1302, 1320, 1322, 1325-28, 1336-39, 1360, 1374, 1707, 1788, 1906
Hymns and Sacred Poems   1042
Hymns and Spiritual Songs   245, 1042, 1097

Ibaniz, Florencio   1353
immigration and American music   1, 383
Independant Congregational Church (Charleston)   602
Indian Princess   1457, 1515, 1519, 1935
Ingalls, Jeremiah   27, 29, 326, 629, 902, 948, 1031, 1947
Instrumental Assistant   723, 741
Instrumental Director   723, 741
Instrumental Preceptor (Herrick)   723, 741
Instrumental Preceptor (Whiteley)   723, 741
instruments   12, 30, 52, 123, 183, 211, 226, 231, 287, 309, 310, 321, 376, 379, 423, 437, 449, 462, 470-72, 475, 480, 484-85, 494, 509, 518, 521, 530, 533, 536, 540, 543, 557, 582, 588, 593, 620-

21, 638, 647-48, 669, 671, 681, 693, 963, 1067-70, 1175, 1222, 1227, 1266, 1281, 1290, 1343, 1368, 1520-668, 1637
—collections 23, 30, 169, 174, 175, 179-80, 230, 239, 241, 248, 251, 253, 1559, 1627-28
—dealers 445, 524, 548, 1561, 1573
—dictionaries 23
—iconography 226, 244
—makers 255, 263-64, 283, 420, 427, 437, 445, 503, 523, 533, 582, 591, 1213, 1524, 1529, 1561, 1573, 1578, 1580, 1588, 1607, 1609, 1620, 1626, 1634, 1643, 1648, 1656, 1884. *See also* names of individuals
—tutors and manuals 79, 114, 215, 241, 682, 706, 722-23, 741, 747 *See also* individual instruments
Introduction to the Art of Playing the Bassoon 741
Introduction to the Singing of Psalm-Tunes 247, 875, 883, 925, 932, 950-51, 982, 1919
Italian musicians 712, 1164-65
itinerancy and music 430-31
Ives, Mr. 255

Jackson, George K. 497, 662, 752, 1152, 1683, 1686, 1828-29
Jardine, George 1615
"Jargon" 885, 1738
Jefferson, Martha 668
Jefferson, Thomas 14, 320, 368, 381, 390, 400, 641, 652, 668, 673, 743, 749, 1530, 1830-45
Jenks, Stephen 27, 29, 376, 933, 1846
Jews and music 39, 438, 447, 1166-67
Jocelin, Simeon 1909
John Beach's Selection of Airs, Marches, Etc. 684
John Street Theater (New York) 1444
Johnson, Alexander 938
Johnson, Francis 232, 1090
Johnston, Thomas 533, 1565, 1604, 1619, 1621-22, 1677, 1847
Jones, Darius E. 1090
Jones, W.W. 741
"Judgment Anthem" 1864
Juhan, James 1607

Keane, Thomas 1458, 1493
Kearsing, John 1663
Kehukee Baptist Association (N.C.) 1093
Keller, Heinrich 1242
Kelpius, Johannes 303, 419, 447, 483-84, 557, 1376-77, 1379-80, 1543
Kentucky Harmony 856, 939, 1029, 1051, 1941

Ketcham, John   960
Key, Francis Scott   764, 786, 796, 819, 824.   *See also* "Star-
    Spangled Banner"
keyboard, music for   676, 689-92, 714, 724, 726, 731, 752, 1746-47,
    1929, 1945, 1955
Kimball, Jacob, Jr.   27, 29, 252, 378, 457, 492, 1683, 1761, 1848-50
King's Chapel (Boston)   1632
King's Church (Providence)   461
Kinne, Aaron   901
Kleine Davidische Psalterspiel   1105
Klemm, Johann G.   241, 1543, 1591, 1621, 1645
Knapp, William   616
Kraft, George   1598
Krauss, Andrew   1667
Krauss, John   1521, 1851
Krauss family   1525, 1594
Kunze, J.C.   1169

Labat, Jane   258
"Lamenting Voice of the Hidden Love"   447, 1377-79
Lancaster, Joseph   880
Lancon, Joseph   255
Lane, Isaac   967
Langdon, W.   221
Larken, Edmund   423
Laroque, Philip   711
Lasuen, Fermin de   1353
Latta, James   914
Law, Andrew   3, 13, 29, 65, 130, 189, 235, 238, 243, 252, 310-11,
    371, 391, 488, 765, 832, 862, 884, 894, 920-21, 928, 932, 992,
    1021, 1683-84, 1692, 1749, 1852-55
Leavitt, Josiah   1619, 1622, 1624, 1633
Le Barre, Trille   283
Lechford, Thomas   513
Lee, Ann   1335
Lee, John   915
Lee, Samuel   432
Leichter Unterricht in der vocal Musik   204
Levy, Nathan   1167
libraries, archives, and museums, collections in   22, 30, 165-253,
    177
  —American Antiquarian Society   217, 252, 1909-10
  —Baltimore Museum of Art   244, 250
  —Bethel College   1593
  —BMI/Haverlin Archives   249
  —Boston Public Library   104, 247

—Brown University   192, 243, 1957
—Claremont College   206
—Daughters of the American Revolution Museum   251
—Detroit Public Library   1784
—Drew University   245
—Fort Ontario State Historic Site (Oswego, N.Y.)   702
—Franklin and Marshall College   204
—George Washington Masonic Museum (Alexandria, Va.)   200
—Goshen College   880
—Hamilton College   226
—Hartford Seminary Foundation   247, 371
—Harvard University   222, 246-47, 1518
—Horticultural Hall (Boston)   230
—Indiana University   224
—Johns Hopkins University   199, 205
—Lenox Library (New York)   104
—Library of Congress   208, 235, 254, 425, 732, 748, 1955
—Lititz Museum   179-80, 558
—Massachusetts Institute of Technology   248
—Moravian Archives and Museum (Bethlehem)   182, 185, 213, 727, 1212, 1304-05
—Moravian Archives (Winston-Salem)   116, 186, 190-91, 198, 201-02, 209, 214-15, 558, 727, 1207, 1219, 1251, 1255, 1273, 1277, 1279, 1301, 1627
—Moravian Museum (Lititz, Pa.)   1559
—New York Institute Museum   577
—New York Public Library   229, 240
—Newberry Library (Chicago)   104, 235, 247, 1054-55, 1923
—Oxford University   197
—Peabody Conservatory of Music   250
—Pierpont Morgan Library   247
—Pittsburgh Theological Seminary, Clifford E. Barbour Library 194, 875
—Radcliffe College   246
—Renwick Gallery (Washington, D.C.)   239
—Rutgers University   177
—Smithsonian Institution   183, 228, 236, 1566, 1662
—State University of Iowa   235
—Toledo Museum of Art   247
—Trinity College   227
—University Illinois   235
—University of Kansas   684
—University of Michigan, William L. Clements Library   189, 234, 247
—University of Missouri-Kansas City   233, 242
—University of Pennsylvania   178, 223

—University of Rochester   235
—University of South Carolina   220
—University of Virginia   188, 727
—Washington University   203
—Western Kentucky University   1332
—Williams College   238
—Worcester Art Museum   252
—Yale University   253, 1566
   See also historical societies
Lieder die bey der Evangelisch Lutherischen Synodal-Versammlung   204
lining-out   942, 976, 1006.   *See also* psalmody—performance practice
Linley, Francis   689
*Litanies, Vespers, Chants, Hymns and Anthems as Used in the Catholic
   Churches of Philadelphia and Throughout the United States*   1116
Literary and Musical Magazine   1391
Little, Henry   1691
Little, William   247, 351, 371, 894, 921, 924, 928, 932, 935, 953,
   992, 1683
Livermore, Solomon Kidder   515
Loud, Thomas, Jr.   689
Loughey, Dennis   427
Love in a Village   1439
Luckenbach, Abraham   1242, 1856
Lutherans and music   447, 503, 1168-76
Lyon, James   251, 351, 363, 470, 639, 1005, 1042, 1677, 1681, 1683,
   1691, 1820, 1822, 1948

McDonald & Bonner   258
MacGill, Robert   263
McLean, James Sylvanus   1580
Madan, Martin   13
Madison, James   652
Magnalia Christi Americana   532
Malcolm, Alexander   270, 283, 435, 587, 1857-60
Mallet, Francis   256
Mann, Elias   29, 233, 907, 1403, 1681, 1685
Mann, Herbert   1846
manuscript collections   167, 172-73, 189, 192, 193, 196, 198, 201,
   208-12, 218, 220, 229, 240, 1144, 1337, 1346
marches   224, 679, 725, 736, 746
Margil, Fray Antonio   547
"Mark My Alford: A Favorite Air with Variations"   1951
Markoe, Peter   1442, 1508
Martial Music   723
Martin, John   939
Maryland Company of Comedians   1496

Maryland Gazette   283
Maryland Selection of Sacred Music   876
Masi, Francesco   711
Mason, Lowell   305, 489, 498, 1949
Masonic March   725
masonic music   447, 725, 732, 1809
Massachusetts Band of Boston   688
Massachusetts Compiler   863, 1687
Massachusetts Harmony   230
Massachusetts Magazine   150, 1403, 1774
Massachusetts Musical Society   542
Massachusetts Spy   746
Massi, Vincent   267
Mather, Cotton   432, 532, 893, 896, 931, 1761
Mather, Increase   31
Maxim, Abraham   568, 1691
May Day in Town   1508
Meacham, Horace   1560
Meacham, John   1560
"Medley Overture"   241
Meigner, Leopold   713
Meineke, Christopher   752
Meline, Florant   1676
Mellen, John   934
Mennonites   19, 77, 303, 447, 557, 978, 1105, 1177-96
Mercer, Jesse   1053
Merrimack Collection of Instrumental and Martial Musick   723, 741
Methodists   1044, 1090, 1197-205
metronome   668, 1839
Meyer manuscript   940
Michael, David Moritz   116, 213, 1211, 1238, 1244, 1246, 1263, 1279, 1861-62
Midas   1449
Middlesex Musical Society (Dunstable, Mass.)   498, 515
Mifflin, Benjamin   279
military music   114, 228, 232, 310, 316, 401, 428, 533, 540, 648, 680-83, 685-87, 701-03, 706, 709, 721, 733, 737, 745, 751, 1088, 1740, 1897
Military Sonata   711
Millennial Praises   1339
Mills, Samuel J.   936
Miner, Uzal   1561
Minstrel   230
Missouri Harmony   233, 912, 955, 1397
Mitchell, John   258
Mittelberger, Gottlieb   450, 606

Moller, John Christopher   95, 713-14, 752, 1173, 1175, 1863
Monday, Reubin   939
Monroe, James   653
Monthly Anthologie   150
Moore, Henry   723, 741
Moran, Peter K.   95, 752
Moravian Salem Band   710
Moravians   1-2, 8, 21, 39, 46, 63, 68, 71, 90, 100, 116, 129, 179-
    80, 182, 185-87, 190-91, 198, 201, 210, 213-15, 219, 269, 301,
    303, 309, 319, 351, 369, 375, 378, 392, 419, 438, 444, 447, 459,
    478, 496, 552, 556-58, 595, 639, 661-62, 699, 710, 740, 749, 806-
    07, 1206-318, 1386, 1407, 1595-96, 1627, 1653.   *See also* names of
    individuals
Morgan, Justin   7, 34, 632, 1683, 1864
Morton, Charles   432
Mosely, Gideon   417
Mount, William Sidney   231
Mount Church (near Port Royal, Va.)   1568
Mozart, Wolfgang Amadeus,   718, 734, 1435, 1563
Müller, George Godfrey   213, 558
Müller, Johann Christoph   1156
Mueller, Sussana   192
Murray, Walter   1458
museums.   *See* libraries, archives, and museums
music dealers   261, 267, 454, 463, 477, 492, 502-03, 524, 548, 583,
    591, 1175, 1389-90, 1393, 1702, 1743, 1801
music education   28, 96, 116, 438, 452, 454, 503, 505, 524, 538,
    846, 880, 899, 956, 963-64, 972-73, 997, 1246.   *See also* singing
    schools
Music in Miniature   1932
music instruction
  —advertisements   154
Music Journal for the Piano Forte   696
music periodicals   129-53
  —18th-19th century   30, 149-53, 371, 1391.   *See also* individual
    titles
Musica Sacra   991, 1782
*Musica Spiritualis, or Sacred Music as Performed on Tuesday the 23d
    of April, 1782 at the Stone Chapel, Boston*   534
Musical Biography   1870
musical clocks   548, 1581
musical clubs, societies, and organizations   22, 52, 150, 211, 278,
    314, 333, 338, 343, 418, 423-24, 427, 429, 435-37, 443, 452, 454-
    55, 466-67, 470, 473, 487, 489-92, 498, 500, 504, 515, 518, 521,
    528, 534, 542, 550, 553, 578, 581, 586-87, 591, 593, 600-01, 607,

693, 720, 813, 841, 869, 900-01, 944-45, 970, 988, 996, 998,
1002, 1093, 1167, 1692, 1704, 1827, 1857, 1905
Musical Fund Society (Philadelphia) 521
musical glasses 400, 1583, 1763. *See also* armonica
musical instruments. *See* instruments
Musical Journal for the Pianoforte 1937
Musical Magazine 130
Musical Miscellany in Occasional Numbers 659, 1938
Musical Primer 992
Musical Reader 1782-83
Musical Society (Newburyport) 534
"Musick Club" (Philadelphia) 278
Myers Collection 494

Nashville Female Academy 452
Nassau Street Theatre (New York) 1444
nationalism and American music 317
*Nature and Importance of the Duty of Singing Praise to God,
Considered* 936
Nettleton, Asahel 1865-66
Neu-Eingerichtetes Gesang-Buch 1328
Neu-vermehrt-und vollständiger Gesang-Buch 1321
New American Company 1493
New American Harmony 247
New Brunswick Band 177
New Brunswick Collection of Sacred Music 933
New Collection of Psalm Tunes Adapted to Congregational Worship 921
New England Courant 976
New England Harmony 252
New-England Psalm-Singer 7, 20, 26, 229, 247, 252, 532, 958, 984,
1932
New Instructions for the Piano Forte 215
"New Presidents or Jefferson's March" 483
New Selection of Sacred Music 876, 1267
"New Song on the Repeal of the Stamp-Act" 254
New World Recorded Anthology of American Music 280, 354
"New Yankee Doodle" 224
Newhall, James 859
Newman, Mr. 692
newspapers 154-64, 175, 283, 434, 442, 462, 485, 494, 531, 548,
753, 1575
Nitschmann, Immanuel 185
Noble, Oliver 945
Norfolk Musical Society (Dedham, Mass.) 944, 996
North Meeting-House (Newbury-Port, Mass.) 945
North Presbyterian Church (Hartford) 497

Northampton Collection of Sacred Harmony   233
notation.   *See* shape notes
Noyes, Samuel Bradley   578

Obituaries   283-84
oboe   1560-61
Occum, Samson   1037, 1042
"Odes to be Sung at the Celebration of the Anniversary of American
     Independence, July 4, 1811"   254
Ogle, Cuthbert   656-57, 660, 1875
O'Keeffe, John   1952
Old American Company   1802
Old Stoughton Musical Society.   *See* Stoughton Musical Society
Oldmixon, Mrs.   1463
Olmsted, Timothy   723
*On the Practice of Music: A Discourse Pronounced at Pepperell,
     Massachusetts, May 17th, 1809, before the Middlesex Musical
     Society*   515
opera   12, 27, 29, 115, 129, 177, 309, 314, 343, 354, 360, 380, 382,
     410, 423, 445, 447, 458, 492, 508, 543, 559, 584, 644-45, 1430,
     1432-519, 1930, 1935, 1952
     —librettos   119, 1519
     —lists   22, 674, 1434, 1436, 1490, 1496, 1514
Oration on Music   873
oratorios   93, 1788
orchestras   338, 341, 468, 700, 788, 1475
organ   29, 65, 236, 279, 361, 417, 437, 445, 450, 497, 533, 567,
     582, 594, 606, 619, 638, 739-40, 1174, 1358, 1373, 1520-23, 1525-
     28, 1533-41, 1543-46, 1549-57, 1562, 1564-66, 1568-71, 1574-78,
     1586-89, 1591, 1593-94, 1595-606, 1608, 1610-26, 1629-36, 1638-
     42, 1645-47, 1649-50, 1654-57, 1659, 1663-68, 1773
     —music   86, 689, 694, 752
organists   421, 450, 458, 481, 497, 499, 519, 524, 594, 602-03, 619,
     633, 678, 739, 1272, 1539, 1557, 1675, 1705-06, 1779-80, 1828,
     1863, 1867-68, 1873-75, 1896, 1899
organology.   *See* instruments
Ormsby, John   514, 587
Ott, David   1175
"Our Rights on the Ocean, or Hull, Jones, Decatur & Bainbridge"   224
"Overture to the Harlequin's Invasion"   241

Pachelbel, Charles Theodore   66, 303, 423, 551, 602, 647, 752, 1867-
     68
Palma, John   588
pantomime   1498
parish and other church records   285

Parker, James   1869
Parker, John Rowe   263, 532, 1743, 1870-72
Parker, Joseph   417
patriotic music   12, 102, 119, 224, 243, 246, 310, 338, 351, 533, 666-67, 686, 711, 753, 765, 778-79, 785
Patterson, Robert   1749
Patterson's Church Music   1749
Paulding, James Kirke   275
Peach Church (near Camp Hill, Pa.)   1610
Peale, Franklin   1438
Pelham, Peter, Jr.   274, 329, 458, 481, 657-58, 671, 1873-75
Pelissier, Victor   725, 831, 1876, 1953
Pelissier's Columbian Melodies   1953
Penn, John   334
Pergolesi, Giovanni Battista   1273
Peter, David   1242
Peter, Johann Friedrich   18, 185, 210, 213, 558, 735, 749, 1206, 1211, 1215, 1246, 1253, 1255, 1262, 1278-79, 1282, 1627, 1677, 1877-83
Petersen, Karsten   1274
Philadelphia Harmony   992
Philadelphia Musick Club   1167
Phile, Philip   233, 463
Philharmonic Society of Bethlehem   185, 187
Philo-harmonic Society (Boston)   467
pianoforte   183, 244, 251, 429, 442, 748, 1524, 1542, 1567, 1584, 1592, 1607, 1648, 1652, 1662-63, 1703, 1834, 1838
—music   86, 95, 697-98, 711, 715-16, 748, 1741, 1746, 1786, 1895, 1937, 1943, 1951, 1955
Pike, Thomas   334
Pilsbury, Amos   911
Pious Guide to Prayer and Devotion   1111
Pittsburgh Musical Society   427
Plain Dealing or News from New England   513
playbills   175, 231
Pocket Hymn Book   1042
Polyanthus   150
Poor Soldier   1952
Pratt, Henry   1622, 1646
Presbyterians   1319-23
Prescott, Abraham   1884
"President's March"   229
"President's March and Ca Ira" (Phile)   233
Price, William   533
Priest, Henry   255
Priest, William   275

printing and publishing   29, 55-56, 75, 119, 126, 153, 203-04, 246, 261, 391, 420, 423, 477, 502, 540, 785, 1118, 1123, 1381-409, 1743-44, 1863, 1869, 1926
probate records   286-87
Psallonian Society (Providence)   443
psalm starter (musical instrument)   244
Psalm Tunes   247
psalmody   3, 22, 24, 27-28, 39, 65, 75, 83, 90, 111-112, 120, 123-25, 194, 245-47, 309, 351, 360, 364, 368, 371-72, 375-76, 380, 401, 437, 488, 495, 503, 520, 533, 536, 540, 542, 563, 578-79, 619, 621, 623, 631, 836-1006, 1016, 1037, 1043, 1120-21, 1218, 1320, 1322, 1381, 1728, 1733, 1909, 1940.   *See also* names of individuals
  —performance practice   83, 472, 482, 488, 498, 513, 520, 579, 617, 639, 837-38, 844, 847, 855, 861, 865, 867, 869-70, 877, 881-82, 893, 898, 903-04, 914, 916, 934, 936-37, 942-43, 945, 947, 965-66, 974-75, 978-79, 981, 984-887, 990, 993-94, 998-99, 1002, 1006, 1038, 1051, 1685, 1711, 1733, 1940
Psalms, for the Use of the Reformed Protestant Dutch Church of the City of New York   238
Psalms of David (Hopkinson)   247, 1121, 1869
Psalms of David (Watts)   233
Psalm-Singer's Amusement   235, 1932, 1934
Psalm-Singer's Jewell   235
psalters   5, 13, 100, 111, 235, 238, 245, 386, 437, 520, 586, 617, 623, 856, 866, 957, 1003, 1016, 1020, 1120-21.   *See also* individual titles of psalters
Puritans and music   333, 368, 451, 467, 479, 511, 529, 561, 889
  —attitude towards music   379, 414, 451, 471, 561, 563-66
Pyrlaeus, Johann Christopher   1885

Quakers   1324

Ralph, James   1472
Rapp, George   1155, 1162-63.   *See also* Harmonists
Ravenscroft's psalter   957, 971
Read, Daniel   7, 27, 28, 319, 371, 862-63, 1677, 1683-84, 1886-89, 1927
Reasonableness of Regular Singing   974
Reconciliation   1508
Redfield, Levi   901
Regular and Skilful Music in the Worship of God   945
Regular Singing Defended and Proved to be the Only True Way of Singing the Songs of the Lord   855
"regular singing."   *See* psalmody—performance practice
Reichel, C.G.   1254

Reinagle, Alexander   221, 241, 319, 334, 463, 483, 521, 643, 651, 676, 692, 697-98, 714-16, 724, 726, 732, 735, 748, 752, 831, 1423, 1436, 1513, 1628, 1678, 1817, 1890-95, 1937, 1955
Religion Productive of Music: A Discourse Delivered at Marlborough, March 24th, 1773 at a Singing Lecture   934
Repository of Sacred Music   1052, 1958
Repository of Sacred Music, Part Second   926, 1052, 1959
Republican Harmony   917, 1923
Responsary   984
Reuz, Johannes   191, 1254
Revere, Paul   229, 1385
Revolutionary War and music   10, 12, 46, 102, 208, 251, 310, 316, 363, 370, 483, 567, 604, 648, 654, 677, 680-83, 686, 699, 703, 706, 711, 745, 747, 765, 767, 772, 779, 1026, 1419, 1428, 1431, 1740. *See also* military music
Rhea, Archibald   939
Rhea, John   1909
Rice, John   752
Richmond Enquirer   531
Richmond Street Congregational Church   461
Ricksecker, Abraham   1242
Ricksecker, Peter   213, 711, 1896
Riley, Edward   1956
Riley's Flute Melodies   1956
Rivington's New York Gazette   154
Robert, Eli   497
Robinson, Silas   1897
Rockefeller Foundation   280
Rodgers, Samuel   603
Rosenbaum, Charles   427
Roth, Philip.   *See* Phile, Philip
Rudiments of Music   898
"Rudiments of the Art of Playing On the Piano Forte"   233
Rural Harmony   252

Sacred Dirges, Hymns and Anthems, Commemorative of the Death of General Washington   238
Sacred Harp   1025
sacred music   32, 38-39, 50-51, 58, 60, 65-66, 68-69, 72, 96, 100, 108, 120, 143-44, 243, 246, 295, 304, 332, 334, 338, 354, 360, 368, 387, 401-02, 415, 447, 454, 463, 480, 484, 492, 519, 521, 524, 543, 555, 583-84, 593, 611-39, 658, 1077, 1080-81
Salem Baptist Singing Society   491
Salisbury Singing Society (Massachusetts)   841
Salter, John   655

Sammlung geistlicher Lieder nebst Melodien, von verschiedenen Dichtern und Componisten 852
"Samuel the Priest Gave Up the Ghost" 611, 754
Sancho, Juan 1353
Sargent, L.M. 224
Sarramiac, Arnaud 426
Saur, Christopher 1105
Sauvagan, Phelipe 426
Schaffer, F.C. 79
Scheme for Reducing the Science of Music to a More Simple State 932, 1402
Schetky, George 521, 1937
Schmahl, Johann 1667
Schmick, Johann Jakob 1898
Schober, Gottlieb 1254, 1899
Schubert, Franz 744
Schultz, Christopher 1326
Schwenkfelders 419, 447, 557, 1325-28
Scots and music 438
Second Baptist Church (Boston) 998
Second New York Regiment Band 677
Second Virginia Regiment Band of Musick 687
secular music 12, 20, 22, 27, 30, 334, 339, 360, 368, 373, 396, 401, 414, 446, 463, 477, 480, 484, 503, 533, 543, 555, 587, 593, 640-75, 814
Sedgwick, George C. 1053
Selby, William 329, 577, 655, 689, 752, 813, 831, 1403, 1730, 1900
Select Harmony (Brownson) 604
Select Harmony (Law) 238, 920
Select Number of Plaine Tunes Adapted to Congregational Worship 235, 921
Selection of Most Favorite Scots Tunes 1892
Sellers, John 1607
Sermon Preached at a Singing Lecture: in Braintree May 21st, MDCCLXXXVIII 990
Sermon: Preached at an Exhibition of Sacred Musick, in Lincoln, on the Nineteenth of April, 1792 967
Serra, Junipero 1353
set pieces 909, 933, 1910
Seven Songs for the Harpsichord or Forte Piano 247, 646, 1946
Shakers 53-54, 63, 129, 181, 1329-45
shape notes 22, 120, 227, 380, 448, 856, 872, 887, 890-91, 894, 897, 913, 918, 924, 928, 930, 932, 949, 965-66, 992, 997, 1017, 1025, 1029, 1031, 1036, 1103, 1394, 1853, 1958-59
Shaw, Oliver 66, 79, 224, 443, 594, 723, 752, 1901-05

sheet music   91, 113-115, 126, 188, 196-97, 199, 200, 203, 205, 216, 224, 229, 234, 403, 408, 653, 690, 785, 792-93, 1383, 1387, 1405, 1951
—publishers   91-92
Shield, William   1952
Shumway, Nehemiah   929
"Siege of Tripoli"   224, 711
Simpson, Daniel   709
Simsbury Society (Conn.)   970
Singing Book   229
Singing Master's Assistant   532, 1932
singing schools   112, 123, 227, 301, 310, 314, 325, 360, 368, 374-75, 388, 391, 401, 423, 430, 442, 449, 468, 519, 540, 543, 547, 586, 593, 620-21, 626, 636, 832, 837-1006, 1017, 1036, 1046, 1137, 1692, 1722
singing school tradition.   *See* singing schools
Six Easy Entertainments   658
"Six Duettos"   241
Six Sonatas for the Piano-Forte or Harpsichord   726
Sixteen Anthems   863
Slaves in Algiers   1519
Slaw, Robert   259
Smith, A.   241
Smith, Eliza   220
Smith, John S.   795
Smith, Samuel F.   230
Smith, William   247, 894, 924, 928, 932, 935, 953, 992, 1152, 1683
Snetzler, John   1533, 1562, 1566, 1570, 1611, 1635, 1647, 1664
Social Harmonist   1756
Society for Promoting Regular & Good Singing (Boston)   988
"Song of Liberty"   224
"Song of the Times"   218
songs   27, 68, 85, 113, 115, 129, 132, 167, 181, 211. 218, 227, 354, 403, 475, 492, 587, 621, 645, 648, 666, 673, 768, 776, 780, 789, 793, 804, 806-07, 814, 817, 831, 836, 1022, 1062, 1065, 1070, 1072, 1074, 1076-77, 1087, 1177, 1223, 1268, 1270, 1334, 1395, 1478, 1480, 1743, 1759, 1795, 1927-28, 1939, 1946, 1954, 1957
—humorous   792
—labor   767
—parlor   829-30
—patriotic   12, 208, 214, 224, 229, 233, 237, 246, 254, 310, 533, 644, 753, 755, 758, 761-62, 764-67, 769, 771-75, 778-79, 783-84, 786, 790, 794-97, 799, 803, 805, 808-09, 811, 816, 818-28
—texts   159, 753, 777.   *See also* songsters
Songs of Zion   898

songsters   89, 119, 127-28, 184, 227, 263, 533, 653, 796, 801, 1034, 1440
Sonneck Society   246
Sorge, Georg Andreas   1534
Soto, Hernando de   599
South Carolina Gazette   434
Southwark Theatre (Philadelphia)   1930
Spanish colonies and music   356, 438
Spanish mission music   39, 60, 123, 321, 547, 599, 620, 759, 1118, 1346-74, 1528, 1612
Speissegger, John   258
Spence, Robert   1042
Spicer, Ishmael   876
spinet   1777
spirituals.   *See* Afro-American music
St. Andrew's Church (Charleston)   602
St. Anne's Church (Annapolis)   279, 1857
St. Cecilia Society (Charleston)   423
St. George's Church (New York)   1564
St. John's Church (Portsmouth, N.H.)   567
St. Mary's Church (Charleston)   602
St. Michael's Church (Charleston)   423, 1664, 1755
St. Michael's Church (Marblehead, Mass.)   1859
St. Michael's Church (Philadelphia)   606, 1174-75, 1535, 1666-67
St. Paul's Church (Baltimore)   1550
St. Paul's Church (New York)   1631
St. Paul's Church (Newburyport, Mass.)   1619
St. Peter's Church (Philadelphia)   499
St. Philip's Church (Charleston)   423, 602-03
Stans, Jacob A.   1090
"Star-Spangled Banner"   214, 224, 229, 233, 237, 758, 762, 764, 766, 773-75, 778, 783-84, 786, 790, 794-97, 799, 803, 805, 809, 811, 816, 818-20, 823-26, 828, 1797, 1800
Stearns, Charles   967
Steiner, Melchior   245
Stephenson, Joseph   616
Sternhold, Thomas   235, 238, 245, 617, 1020
Stevens, Jervis Henry   603
Stevens, John   603
Stewart, James   244, 1550
Stone Chapel (Boston)   534
Stone, Henry   1383
Stone, Joseph   1906
Storer, Maria   1511
Story, Deacon   1054-55
Stoughton Musical Society (Massachusetts)   487, 528, 542, 578

string quartets and quintets.   *See* ensembles and music
Strong, Joseph   970
Stuart, Levi U.   1615
Suffolk Harmony   247, 1932
Swan, Timothy   252, 325, 376, 378, 482, 1907–10
Swedish music   447, 1020
"Sweet Lillies of the Valley. . .Composed by Mr. Hook"   56
Sweet Psalmist of Israel, a Sermon Preach'd at the Lecture Held in Boston, by the Society for Promoting Regular & Good Singing   988
Symmes, Thomas   47, 319, 432, 532, 893, 974–75, 1761
Synagogue Beth Elohim (Charleston)   602

Tammany   1519
Taney, Robert B.   819
Tannenberg, David   523, 558, 1174–75, 1230, 1265, 1520, 1523, 1534, 1549–50, 1552, 1578, 1597, 1599–603, 1612, 1621, 1645, 1649–50, 1668, 1911–14
Tansur, William   235, 616, 923
Tapis, Estevan   1353
Tappan, William B.   1043
"Tars of Columbia"   1817
Taws, Charles   251, 334, 1607, 1628
Taws, Joseph   1938
Taylor, Rayner   221, 233, 326, 444, 521, 692, 713, 752, 831, 1152, 1423, 1436, 1442, 1517–18, 1628, 1686, 1915–17, 1937
"Temple of Minerva"   754, 1437
Tennessee Harmony   938
Terril, Israel   1152
Thacher, Peter   979
theater   177, 243, 246–47, 274, 391, 438, 454, 492, 514, 583, 587, 1430, 1432–519, 1953
  —censorship   543, 1495
    See also opera
theses and dissertations   46, 89, 148, 288–99, 1177, 1179, 1476
Thineman, Charles   258
Thomas, Isaiah   195, 217, 863, 909, 953, 1386, 1403, 1406, 1677
Three Rondos for the Piano Forte or Harpsichord   1741
Till, John Christian   213, 1272
"To All Musical Practitioners"   322
"Toast to Washington"   403
Todd, John   47
Tomlinson, Ralph   795
trade directories   255–67
Trajetta, Philippo   713
travel accounts   80, 269, 273–79, 431, 450, 606, 1428, 1481. *See also* diaries and letters

"Trav'ler Benighted"   1817
Treatise of Musick: Speculative, Practical and Historical   1859-60
Treatise on Dancing   1413
Trinity Church (Boston)   1780
Trinity Church (Lancaster, Pa.)   1176, 1598
Trinity Church (New York)   633, 1591, 1918
Trinity Church (Portsmouth, R.I.)   1639
trombone.   *See* brass ensembles
Trumbull, Benjamin   604
trumpets   702
Trute, Charles   1607
Tuckey, William   633, 1683, 1918
Tuesday Club (Annapolis)   211, 435, 504, 550, 587, 1704, 1857
Tuffs, John   247, 319, 371, 432, 480, 520, 849, 875, 883-84, 894,
    925, 932, 942, 950-51, 982, 1319, 1395, 1761, 1919-20
tunebooks   29, 83, 88, 108, 202, 206, 230, 252, 348, 368, 371-72,
    468, 470, 480, 509, 568, 613, 626, 629, 664, 807, 842, 850-51,
    859-60, 862, 864, 870, 872, 886, 916, 919, 926, 928-29, 940-41,
    948-49, 953, 984, 1001, 1004-05, 1029, 1036, 1042, 1044, 1052,
    1061, 1098-99, 1189, 1197, 1267, 1337, 1343, 1384, 1751.   *See*
    also names of compilers and titles of tunebooks
    —facsimile editions, guides to   82
    —library locations   83-84, 88, 108, 111, 120, 235, 247, 917-18,
    924, 1098, 1751
    —lists   54, 68, 82-84, 88, 90, 108, 111, 120, 124-25, 196, 202,
    206, 449, 540, 626, 880, 886, 918, 933, 949, 1168, 1733, 1735,
    1738, 1805, 1910, 1918
    —notation   83, 120
    See also psalmody
Tunes in Three Parts   55
Turtel-Taube, see Gesäng der einsamen und verlassenen Turtel-Taube
    1134, 1142
tutors.   *See* instruments—tutors
Twenty-Four Short and Easy Pieces   1892
Tyler, Edward   427

Union Harmony   984
Unitarians and music   1375
"United States Grand Waltz"   1951
United States Marine Band   685-86, 710, 712, 719, 728
United States Sacred Harmony   911
Unpartheyisches Gesang-Buch   1180
Upper Octorara Presbyterian Church (Lancaster County, Pa.)   1323
Urania   639, 1042, 1822, 1948
Uranian Academy   1692

Use and Design of Sacred Music, in a Discourse Preached March 19,
     1811, as a Musical Lecture in Greenfield 994
Utica Collection 1783
Utile Dulci 532, 975

Valton, Peter 423, 603, 732, 752
Vancourt, Rene 426
Viader, José 1357
Victor, H.B. 658
"View of Modern Psalmody" 230
Village Harmony 233, 953
Village Hymns for Social Worship 1865
Village Library Company (Farmington, Conn.) 482
Vinals, José 1353
Vindiciae Cantus Dominici; or, A Vindication of the Doctrine Taught
     in a Discourse on the Divine Ordinance of Singing Psalms 838
Vinton, David 1606
viol 638, 1644, 1653, 1884
viola 1694
violin 241, 1530, 1643, 1660-61, 1697, 1836, 1840, 1843, 1943
Violin Society of America, 241
violinists 1167, 1688, 1779, 1801, 1896
virginals 714
Virginia Argus 531
Vizcaino, Sebastián 599
Vleck, Jacob van 213, 1228
voluntaries 981
"Voluntary" 1747

Wade, John Francis 1954
Wall, Thomas 1496
Walter, Thomas 29, 47, 230, 247, 319, 432, 477, 480, 520, 526, 849,
     883-84, 893-95, 942, 987-88, 1319, 1761, 1921
War of 1812 and music 224, 244, 667, 711, 733, 765, 1454. *See also*
     military music
Warren, Henry 1513
Washburn, Japeth 1691
Washington, Anne 200, 643, 672
Washington, Bushrod 200, 643, 672
Washington family 731, 804
Washington, George 200, 224, 400, 618, 624, 642-46, 648, 651-52,
     661-62, 669-72, 675, 746, 1661, 1895
Washington, Hariot 672
Washington, Jenny 672
Washington, Martha 672
Washington Guards Band 232

"Washington's March"   224, 746
Watkins, Joshua   229
Watts, Isaac   233, 245, 845, 862, 1026-27, 1043, 1048, 1056, 1095,
    1322
Wayland, John   448
Webster, William C.   1090
Weiser, Frederick S.   1061
Weiss, George   1328
Weiss, Jedidiah   1922
Weld, Ezra   990
Welsh music   447
Wesley, John   438, 440, 1042, 1199-200, 1202, 1204-05
Western Minstrel   1786, 1943
Wetmore, Truman S.   1923
White, Benjamin Franklin   1025
White, Philo   1386
White House   652
Whitefield, George   1042
Whiteley, William   723, 741
Whitman, Samuel   604
Whole Book of Psalmes (Sternhold and Hopkins)   235, 238, 245
Wignell, Thomas   1513
Wilkinson, Brigadier General James   745
Willard, Samuel   993-94
Williams, Aaron   616
Williams, Thomas   996
Willig, George   1399, 1401
Willig, Thomas   1438
Winchell, James Manning   998
Windsor, Ann   603
Winsch, Johnathan   1242
Wissahickon Mystics   419, 444, 447, 557, 1376-80, 1653.   *See also*
    Kelpius, Johannes
Witt, Christopher   1543
Wohlfarth, Jacob   1274
Wolf, W.E.   241
Wolhaupter, Gottlieb   1561
Wolle, Peter   213, 1228, 1924
women and music   314, 407-08
Wood, Abraham   247, 1906, 1925
Woodbridge, Timothy   1002
Woods, Leonard   607
Woodward, Charles   932, 992
Worcester, Samuel   230
Worcester Collection of Sacred Harmony   863, 909, 953

"Words for a Funeral anthem. . .To be Performed at the Funeral of the Reverend Dr. Samuel Cooper, on Friday, Jan. 2, 1784"   56
Works Progress Administration   136
"Wreaths to the Chieftain"   224
Wright, Andrew   1404
Wyeth, John   371, 926, 928, 965, 1031, 1052, 1926, 1958-59

"Yankee Doodle"   224, 228, 744, 760, 763, 781-82, 791, 800, 802, 810, 823, 834
Yarnold, Benjamin   423, 603, 752
Yarnold, William   603
Young, Peter   241

Zeuner, Charles   433, 689
Zion Lutheran and Reformed Congregation Church (Orwigsburg, Pa.)   1553
Zion Lutheran Church (Maryland)   1061
Zion Lutheran Church (Philadelphia)   1174-75, 1666, 1668
zither   1777

ABOUT THE AUTHOR

James R. Heintze, Music Librarian and teacher in the American
Studies Program at The American University, has written numerous
articles and reviews for such journals as *American Music*, *Library
Quarterly*, *Maryland Historical Magazine*, *Musical Quarterly*, *Notes*,
and *Oral History Review*, and has contributed to *The New Grove
Dictionary of Music and Musicians* (1980) and *The New Grove
Dictionary of American Music* (1986). His recent books include
American Music Studies: A Classified Bibliography of Master's Theses
(1984), *Scholars' Guide to Washington, D.C. for Audio Resources*
(1985), *Esther Williamson Ballou: A Bio-Bibliography* (1987), and
*Igor Stravinsky: An International Bibliography of Theses and
Dissertations, 1925-87* (1988). Currently he is editor of
Bibliographies in American Music (College Music Society) and a
reviewer of musical non-print materials for *Choice*.